The Kin

By the same Author

Timeless Flight: The Definitive Biography of the Byrds
Neil Young: The Definitive Story of his Musical Career
Roxy Music: Style with Substance – Roxy's First Ten Years
Van Morrison: Portrait of the Artist

JOHNNY ROGAN

The Kinks

THE SOUND AND THE FURY

ELM TREE BOOKS
London

First published in Great Britain 1984
by Elm Tree Books/Hamish Hamilton Ltd
Garden House 57-59 Long Acre London WC2E 9JZ

British Library Cataloguing in Publication Data

Rogan, Johnny
The Kinks.
1. Kinks
I. Title
784.5'0092'2 ML421.K5

ISBN 0-241-11307-5
ISBN 0-241-11308-3 Pbk

Typeset at The Spartan Press Ltd,
Lymington, Hants
Printed and bound in Great Britain by
Richard Clay (The Chaucer Press) Ltd, Bungay, Suffolk

CONTENTS

ACKNOWLEDGEMENTS

Such a book as this relies on the cooperation of a number of individuals. I would like to thank those who gave up a considerable amount of time in order to provide me with extensive interview material, particularly Larry Page, Andy Pyle, John Gosling, Robert Wace, Sam Curtis, Shel Talmy, John Dalton, Mickey Willett and Nick Trevisick. For additional interview material and Kinks information: Mick Avory, Clem Cattini, Screaming Lord Sutch, Donnie Burke, Jim Rodford, John Turney and Ken Jones. Always there are numerous people who take pleasure in writing letters, submitting xeroxes, exchanging tapes and records, contributing discographical additions and providing gossip and sympathy. Special thanks in this respect are offered to Keith Rodger, Carolyn Mitchell, Doug Hinman, Russell Smith, Peter Seeger, Marianne Collins and Colin Larkin.

A number of institutions and information services were consulted when researching this work. I would particularly like to thank the Bodleian Library, Oxford, the House Of Lords and the Society Of Authors for their assistance. Finally, my gratitude is extended to Lady Margaret Hall for providing idyllic surroundings, superb and inexpensive accommodation and 24 hour library facilities without which this book would have been infinitely poorer.

The author and publishers would like to thank the following for permission to use copyright photographs in this book: p. 2 (bottom) Keystone Press; p. 3 Cyrus Andrews; p. 4 (top and bottom), p. 6 (top and bottom), p. 7 (bottom left) Dezo Hoffmann; p. 5 (top), p. 8 (bottom) Andre Csillag; p. 5 (bottom) Harry Goodwin; p. 7 (bottom right), p. 8 (top) London Features International.

*

Footnote: Since completing this work I have been informed of the existence of two interesting publications dealing with Kinks related activities. *Kinky Mirror* (Postfach 11 09 13, D–6100 Darmstadt 11) and *The Kinks French Konnektion* (Le Mercure, Avenue Denis Semeria, F–06300, Nice) are both worthwhile publications that deserve support. In addition, Doug Hinman is about to launch *The Kinks Archives* (91 E. 3 St.–19, New York 10003) specialising in Kinks vinyl/memorabilia.

INTRODUCTION

It is never easy to deal with the career of a group who have been actively involved in the music business for two decades. Working full time researching their history cost me most of 1982 but it was a fascinating project. I spent many months gathering material until I had a tremendous collection of reviews/interviews from the U.S. and U.K. music and national press. The sheer volume of comments from the Kinks has fashioned our view of their career and the events surrounding their rise to fame. However, the perspectives offered have largely been those of Ray and Dave Davies, unchallenged and unqualified by any of their associates. Such control of the media is not unusual in the rock music world and serves primarily to perpetuate and reinforce a studied image.

The aim of this book is to give a more accurate appraisal of the Kinks story than has previously been offered by the media. Many of the interviewees I approached had never spoken of their experiences with the Kinks outside of a court room and the result is a serious and emphatic attack on the established Kinks myths which are generally accepted without question. It is no wonder that so many people have maintained a diplomatic silence for so long.

While the hard won admissions of former Kinks associates are undoubtedly the most intriguing part of this book one cannot ignore the often excellent music that has kept the group in business since the 60s. Indeed, I would never have attempted such a book unless the quality of the Kinks' recording material merited close attention. Theirs is such a vast body of work that placing it in a critical perspective takes much time and thought. I trust that the amount of space afforded the Kinks' work has proved sufficient to complement the biographical details.

In writing a long book there are always some amusing memories. Readers may be surprised to learn that most of the former Kinks now live in small towns such as Hoddesdon, Berkhamsted and Tring. Tracking them down meant passing many village greens, church steeples and pubs boasting traditional beer. Significantly, all the former Kinks chose to be interviewed in pubs and only once did I come a cropper. Leaving John Gosling I could only get a coach as far as Thame and had to walk fifteen miles along the pitch black motorway to Oxford, laden with a heavy tape recorder. Happy times!

By far the most fascinating part of the saga was the managerial interwrangling that has never been fully revealed before. In spite of numerous solicitations, Larry Page has refused to comment on the Kinks since the 1967 court case and Robert Wace has followed his lead. I am grateful to them both for breaking their long silence in order to provide such a frank assessment of the early years.

Although the Davies brothers are well represented in the text I still regret their minimal involvement in the project since their comments on certain issues are still required reading. After some negotiation with the group's business representative there remained but one problem in securing their full support. For over sixteen years Ray has promised an autobiography telling the behind-the-scenes story of the Kinks and, as a result, biographers' requests have invariably been declined. It was suggested that I might possibly combine my research with his own reminiscences for a definitive volume. The possibility of collaborating with Davies on a writing project involving numerous in-depth interviews was an appealing but restricting proposition. I felt I had more than enough information for a book and, as he would obviously require authorial control, any real objectivity would be absent and dissenting voices silenced. In short, the Davies biography would merely have reinforced the old Kinks mythus. My wariness stemmed mainly from a customary aversion to pop star propaganda in the form of authorised biographies, coupled with the need to represent my own interviewees' feelings and experiences as honestly as possible. The Kinks story is too big to be told from just one point of view and that is the nature of the authorised biography.

Many felt that the true story of the Kinks simply could not be told and, in some respects, they were right. Much information disclosed off the record has obviously not been included in the text and, all things considered, it is probably just as well. By the time libel lawyers have been through the book some of the more controversial material may be lost or severely edited, much to my sadness and regret. What remains may well be the most intriguing series of events I have ever had to unravel in the rock world, but there is no happy ending. Researching the Kinks story was simultaneously fascinating, frustrating and depressing. Without doubt, those last four words also sum up my feelings about the group's twenty-year career.

Johnny Rogan

ONE

Three Steps to Heaven

In researching the Kinks' origins most commentators start with an introduction to the British beat boom of the early 60s followed by an account of the group's sudden emergence in 1964 as a chart-topping act. Such scanty biographical details oversimplify what was undoubtedly a long amateur and semi-professional musical career stretching as far back as the mid-50s. It hardly needs stressing that the key to the Kinks' longevity lies in the complex relationship between the Davies brothers. Yet, in numerous interviews Ray has constantly refused to discuss his childhood and journalists have invariably neglected to pursue the issue. In order to understand and appreciate the group's development, however, it is important to consider those early years and delve into the much overlooked Davies family background.

The Davies's were a working-class family, though the father, a gardener, earned sufficient money for them to live in a house in the sometimes fashionable area of Muswell Hill. Unlike their aspiring working-class neighbours the Davies's firmly believed in strength in numbers, an attitude no doubt instilled by the mother who, according to Dave, was one of twenty-one children! The household was dominated by five sisters, particularly the eldest, Rose. Finally, Mrs Davies produced a couple of sons to challenge this matriarchy. Raymond Douglas Davies was born on 21 June 1944 and his younger brother David Russell, three years later on 3 February 1947. Rose's influence over Ray was strong, particularly during his primary school years when she was a constant source of assurance. In the early 50s Rose married and moved to a nearby house but her contact with the younger brothers remained intact. In fact, Dave admits that Rose's home was frequently used as a temporary sanctuary during the traumas of early childhood:

> Ray and I were always running away to Rose's. Rose never actually sent us home now I come to recall; we always left of our own accord. I think she believed in making us face up to our punishment alone.[1]

It is difficult to determine the effects of such a chaotic household on the personality of the brothers. Without doubt, the open door philosophy practised by the mother ensured that there was little privacy for any member of the family. This may partly explain Ray's childhood introversion and loneliness, which was probably increased by the contrasting bustle of constant household activity. While his elders thrived on the companionship of a large family, Ray had to attend a school for disturbed children for a brief period. Looking back, Ray feels that he learned a great deal from the experience and probably achieved a world view noticeably different from many of his other friends. The effects of all this on the future relationship between the Davies brothers is difficult to determine. According to Dave they led distinctly separate lives during this formative period. Indeed, in commenting on his brother's childhood, Dave betrays a sense of some indeterminable loss:

> He was very quiet, deep and lonely. He never shared anything – least of all his mind. And as a little boy I felt completely left out of his life. Rose was the only one who really understood him. They had a sort of understanding between them that overcame everything, even silence. The only time there was any closeness between Ray and me was when we were in trouble! We would face the storm of Mum's anger together. Ray would smile at me, shrug and say, 'Don't worry – it'll blow over by tomorrow and if it doesn't there is always the next day. He was quite a philosopher really.[1]

Ray's introversion encouraged a somewhat unhealthy independence that often produced flights of fantasy. Frequently, Ray would disappear from school only to be found playing football in the local park, where he imagined he was both teams! It was not easy to monitor Ray's progress which may well have been stifled by the need to fit into a large, sprawling family characterised by disorder. Normal family etiquette was not always recognised by the Davies's and open exchanges of aggressive banter must have proved particularly shocking to the more socially sophisticated visitors. Sam Curtis, one of the Kinks' original road managers, provides an intriguing insight into the Davies's family life:

> It might have been a different situation if Dave had been the elder and not Ray because Ray was *very* embittered. They came from a very sad home in my opinion. I felt uncomfortable sitting down in it . . . The area was very nice, there just happened to be a few slums in it and they were one of them . . .[2]

The unruly behaviour of the brothers in their later career was probably a natural development from their wild, undisciplined childhood.

When the brothers later became famous their record company biographies revealed that they had attended the William Grimshaw Grammar School. Obviously, this was an attempt by their publicist to give the brothers some academic credibility. In reality, the William Grimshaw establishment was an old secondary modern, which in 1967 amalgamated with the rival Tollington Grammar to form Creighton Comprehensive. Both the brothers were 11–plus failures and in the 50s that meant poor schooling with virtually no hope of achieving any academic qualifications. Doomed to a poor education, it was clear that any subsequent success could only be achieved through strong personal motivation. Unfortunately, such qualities were seldom cultivated in 50s secondary moderns and the brothers' school reports provided few clues to their future employment. The same could be said of another pupil in the year below Ray named Roderick Stewart.

It is amusing to imagine Rod Stewart and Ray Davies forming a dynamic school combo, aided by the lead guitar screechings of brother Dave. Realistically, however, such a fantasy line-up was never possible. At this stage Dave Davies was fresh from primary school, a rough kid who, in defiance of his elder brother's aloofness, had settled into the role of black sheep of the family. He was a parody of the disgraced schoolboy – letting off stink bombs, bullying smaller boys and angering neighbours with his unquenchable mischief. Such exploits probably left little time for any thoughts about forming a musical group, at least for the moment. In any case, would he really have wanted to be associated with that third year, Roderick Stewart? Stewart was a self-confessed spoiled brat from an aspiring middle-class Scottish family whose only redeeming feature was his talent as a footballer. A goody goody prefect, and later house captain, Stewart spent most of his time playing with his expensive train set above his parents' newspaper shop in the Archway Road. At that time his musical interests extended only as far as Al Jolson, and he had yet to buy his first rock 'n' roll record. It was a far cry from Dave's turbulent youth as a Fortis Green Road hooligan.

Of the three future mega stars only Ray professed any strong interest in music, but even this tended to be diffuse. Years earlier, his parents had presented him with a ukelele for braving a visit to the dentist after an accident in which he had broken his front teeth. Following this, he took piano lessons, finally graduating to classical Spanish guitar, which would later inspire a deep interest in the blues. His music served as a welcome release from the nervous tension and depression suffered during a tortuous adolescence. Dave recalls his brother experimenting with a bizarre and cacophonous combination of musical chords in an attempt to exorcise the demons within himself. Nowhere was this more morbidly manifested than on a weird piece of tape recorded by Ray and which he steadfastly refuses to allow his brother to play:

> This old instrumental is the most terrifying thing you've ever heard. It's a horrifying, discordant set of shrieks from the guitar. Some of the harmonies that should be picked out with fingers, he played with his thumb. The result is fantastic.[3]

Fortunately, Davies's excursion into the genre of 'music to commit suicide by' was contrasted by a strange passion for musicals such as *Oklahoma!* and *Calamity Jane*. Throughout his early teens Davies continually voiced the praises of such singing stars as Ethel Merman and Doris Day, revealing a musical eclecticism devoid of adolescent prejudice. During the evenings he could also be found hanging around outside his father's favourite pub listening to the half drunken singsongs that gradually increased in volume as the night wore on. It was a myriad of influences that offered no specific route to success, yet somehow Ray's apparent lack of direction was later channelled into a series of classic singles and albums. And when he reached his peak as a songwriter, Davies's favourite themes would be those childhood memories of working-class life, his early schooldays and the problems of achieving individuality in a large family.

It was not until 1958 that young Dave showed any signs of following his brother's musical traces. Inspired by Ray's growing aptitude as a guitarist, Dave decided to take up the instrument and persuaded his parents to part with £40 for a Harmony Meteor electric model. Considering the size of the Davies family it was a surprisingly magnanimous gesture. Initially Dave modelled himself on Eddie Cochran and gradually learned to play by imitating the guitar work on the singles he bought from his local record shop every Saturday afternoon. Characteristically, Dave was impatient to progress and became increasingly upset by the apparent need to learn technique. Bashing away at his favourite three chords, he eventually impressed Ray sufficiently for him to consider the possibility of forming a family duo:

> This was a big step forward. It meant my elder brother was beginning to accept me, and it mattered a lot. We used to play in the lounge of the local pub. I had already started to dream of fame, though I don't think it occurred to Ray that we might one day be professionals.[1]

Clearly, the brothers were influenced by the rock'n'roll craze that had swept Britain during the previous two years. The success of Bill Haley followed by the phenomenal rise of Elvis Presley captured the imagination of thousands of youngsters. Soon, Britain boasted its own rock'n'roll singer in the form of the innocuous Tommy Steele to be followed by Marty Wilde and other members of the Larry Parnes school of pop. The fact that many of these fledgling rock'n'roll stars had sprung to national fame after being discovered in coffee bars propagated the myth that any young kid with image, imagination and rudimentary singing ability would be guaranteed success. Equally importantly, the skiffle boom inaugurated by Lonnie Donegan served to emancipate working-class youth, encouraging kids to buy cheap guitars or homemade instruments in the form of washboards and tea-chest basses. Although the skiffle boom had all but ended by 1958, its spirit of self-sufficiency lived on. Meanwhile, rock'n'roll had entered its second crucial phase with an impressive number of new artists, including Gene Vincent, Buddy Holly and Jerry Lee Lewis, all challenging for Presley's crown. The media coverage afforded rock'n'roll during 1958 was increased when England at last produced a record to rival those of the previously unassailable Americans. The group was Cliff Richard and the Drifters; the song 'Move It'. This was also the year that the great Buddy Holly descended on Britain to be followed by the arrival of Jerry Lee Lewis who immediately hit the headlines when it was learned that he had married his thirteen-year-old cousin. With Elvis stunning his critics by entering the charts at number 1 with 'Jailhouse Rock' and then astonishing his fans by enlisting in the army, it seemed that every major rock'n'roller had become a Fleet Street journalist's dream. Dave noted all this with interest and did not fail to observe that one of the more talented of this latest array of U.S. stars were two brothers who had spent two months at the top of the charts with the plaintive 'All I Have To Do Is Dream'. While Dave dreamed of being an Everly Brothers Mark II, Ray began experimenting with songwriting. His first effort was a country'n'western tune, 'Rocky Mountain', but most of his compositions during the late 50s were schmaltzy love songs, more suited to the likes of Perry Como and Doris Day.

By 1960, Ray had left school and moved into the home of his sister, Rose. For six months he worked in an architect's office, but found the experience unrewarding and so applied to art college. In the meantime, Rose and her husband Arthur fulfilled a long term ambition by emigrating to Australia. For Ray, the loss of the one person capable of understanding him proved disturbing, but a fresh start at Hornsey Art College at least promised new opportunities.

A growing infatuation with the blues was consummated during his first year when Ray found like-minded enthusiasts. Their mutual interest in the music of Leadbelly, Muddy Waters, Slim Harpo and Big Bill Broonzy propelled them into a series of short-lived groups. At first Ray switched to piano and formed a duo with Geoff Prowse that achieved some success on the college circuit. On one fateful night at the college Ray met the celebrated Alexis Korner, the guiding light of multitudinous blues-orientated 60s rock musicians. Ray expressed his desire to form an r'n'b unit in imitation of Big Bill Broonzy with bass and drums. Alexis suggested a visit to the Piccadilly Club, a dive situated opposite the Windmill Theatre in London's Soho. When Ray arrived at the club he was surprised to discover that the music being played was a cross between trad and Chuck Berry style rock, with a loose, funky sound rather than the delicate finger picking he had expected. Hanging out at the club, Ray met Giorgio Gomelsky (later producer of the Yardbirds *et al*) and talked his way into the Dave Hunt Band, a jazz unit that specialised in r'n'b. As well as a guitarist, trombonist and saxophonist, the band boasted a wild pianist who reputedly played 'Honky Tonk Train

Blues' even better than Bob Cosby and the Blue Cats! Davies took some time to adjust to the style of these jazzers and the pianist frequently castigated him for making the wrong changes. Frequent appearances at such well known 60s clubs as the Marquee and the Flamingo gradually built up Davies's confidence and for several months all was well. Apart from their residency at the Piccadilly, the group also played Sundays at the Crawdaddy Club in the Station Hotel, Richmond. Their support act at the time was an embryonic version of the Rolling Stones. In spite of the prestige, good money was not forthcoming and pressures from art college placed Ray under great stress. Often, he would play until 4 a.m., grab a few hours sleep and appear for his studies the following morning in a noticeably wasted state. Eventually, the group split, the Rolling Stones succeeded them and Ray resumed normal college hours. For a brief period he joined Peter Bardens (later Cheynes, Shotgun Express, Them and Camel) in Hamilton King's Blues Messengers but the rigours of student life once again suffocated his musical development.

The pressures of trying to live a double life as a student and rock musician were also taking their toll on Dave Davies. In his final years at school Dave began appearing in social clubs, youth clubs and any other place that would tolerate his makeshift groups. From an early interest in skiffle and folk, Dave was slowly won over by his brother's championing of Sonny Boy Williamson, Big Bill Broonzy and other great blues artists. Refusing to follow his brother into art college, Dave decided to quit school at the earliest opportunity and continue as a semi-professional musician, but after only a few months he was fired from his job at Charing Cross Road's Selmers Music Shop for falling asleep due to post-gig exhaustion. During the same period, Dave became friendly with Peter Quaife, an older school companion of his brother. Like the Davies brothers, Quaife had begun playing guitar in his pre-teen years, though his motives were hardly the result of any musical ambition. His doctor had suggested guitar practice as therapy for a gruesome hand injury sustained when Pete impaled himself on a spike while playing in a corporation rubbish dump. Over the years, he had continued practising, switching to bass guitar in the process. Having recently left college, Pete was finding his career as a nine to five commercial artist for a menswear magazine somewhat unfulfilling. Rather than seeking alternative employment he remained at *The Outfitter*, but invested most of his efforts into forming a pop group with Dave. Ray was already impressed by his younger brother's ideas, but temporarily resisted the temptation of being drawn into the project.

By Michaelmas term 1962, Ray Davies seemed intent on pursuing a career in the arts. He harboured ambitions of succeeding as a theatrical producer or director and assumed that a degree in Fine Art might be his best option. After completing his foundation year at Hornsey, Ray moved to Croydon College of Art and enrolled in a theatre design course. In spite of his aspirations, Ray found it difficult to settle into student life though his relationships with staff were surprisingly cordial. John Turney, a tutor from the period, recalls Davies's progress:

> He was obviously drawn towards theatre, possibly even performance as well . . . I got on fine with him. I can remember him being a very lively, animated person. There was almost *too* much going on. It didn't really impinge on theatre design as such! He had a lively mind. He seemed to get on with the other students, but there was possibly a bit of friction because he was very independent. He was quite a strong person. He went his own way.[4]

In many institutions, Ray would probably have found himself in constant conflict with the college authorities for missing classes due to his extra-curricular activities. Fortunately, Mr Freddie Crookes, the Head of Theatre Design at Croydon College of Art, was perceptive enough to encourage Davies's brash independence and self-assertion and refused to pander towards the rebellious student's paradoxical need for security. According to Ray, Crookes sometimes allowed him to work at home and expended much effort in sorting out his problems.

Ray's college days do not appear to have been the happiest time of his life. His best friend committed suicide and Ray was profoundly upset by the tragedy for some time. Amid his grief, art and music served as a therapeutic release but the excessive pursuit of both activities caused confusion in Ray's mind about his future career development. Crookes listened sympathetically while Ray confessed an envy of his brother's carefree attitude in arrogantly adopting the status of a semi-professional musician by forming his own group. It was obvious that Davies would have been actively involved in the venture were he not already enrolled at art college. Surprisingly, Crookes concluded that the most sensible option might be for Ray to take a sabbatical and recharge his batteries by jamming with his brother's combo. John Turney fully concurred with this advice:

> By then he was already playing gigs so he missed quite a bit of time . . . Basically, one could see that music was his main interest. Freddie Crookes was the sort of man who would tell him that. He wouldn't say: 'You must stay on and do this!' He suggested he stick with the music rather than stay on in a half-hearted way.[4]

Ray was at first astonished by such frank advice until his worldly wise tutor pointed out the probable pitfalls in finding suitable employment after five years of specialised education at an art college. Early in the New Year, Ray joined forces with his brother and Peter Quaife before finally severing his connections with Croydon College of Art. It was no doubt a tortuous decision for the ever indecisive Davies but, as he later admitted, pop music was undoubtedly his salvation.

TWO

The Wayward Wind

The early months of 1963 were a remarkable period in the history of British pop music. In January, the Beatles had topped the *New Musical Express* and *Melody Maker* charts with 'Please Please Me', an achievement that signalled the imminent death of the trad bands, dance crazes and ephemeral fads that had plagued the pop world during the previous two years. Within six months the chart conquering Beatles would be joined by a legion of groups including Gerry and the Pacemakers, Billy J. Kramer and the Dakotas, the Searchers, the Hollies and Freddie and the Dreamers. This twin assault from Liverpool and Manchester momentarily distracted record company A & R men from signing groups from the capital. The long apprenticeship served by the Beatles and their contemporaries in sleazy clubs throughout Germany ensured that they were the undisputed kings of the beat boom. Davies and his cohorts welcomed the Liverpool explosion with open arms but they were also heavily influenced by a similar minor musical revolution that was occurring in London clubs. While national radio was still obsessed with bland solo singers and family entertainers, the more enlightened London clubs were offering some excellent r'n'b music spearheaded by Cyril Davies, Alexis Korner, Graham Bond and John Mayall. Ray Davies was on the fringe of this counter explosion having played with Hamilton King's Blues Messengers and the Dave Hunt Band. The experience he had gained was to have a profound effect on the development of his younger brother's newly formed group.

During early 1963, Ray, Dave and Pete were busy rehearsing and playing occasional gigs at school dances and small clubs, where they impressed their young audiences with instrumental covers of material by such artists as Chet Atkins and Arthur Smith. They went through a series of names beginning with the Ray Davies Quartet and the Pete Quaife Band, top billing being achieved by whoever secured the booking. According to Ray they also played several gigs billed as the Ramrods though this is not corroborated by anyone else connected with the group. By March, the group were still without a permanent drummer, but following a phone call to the Musicians' Union they contacted Mickey Willett, a former member of Tommy Bruce and the Bruisers. Willett was not the world's greatest drummer, but Ray was sufficiently impressed by his musical experience to engage his services. The four-piece underwent strenuous rehearsals in pub rooms and occasionally Mr and Mrs Davies kindly allowed them access to the front room of their home in Fortis Green Road. Dubbing themselves the Bo Weevils and later the Ravens, the quartet played numerous gigs around London including a residency at the Athenaeum in Muswell Hill Broadway. With the Mersey Beat boom underway, the formation of a solid London based r'n'b group seemed a viable proposition, but the Ravens were not without their problems. As a semi-professional group they had limited time in which to rehearse and after four months on the road the set still consisted entirely of cover versions. Ray Davies had yet to develop as a songwriter and his singing was stylistically unorthodox for the period. The group lacked direction and required an astute manager to procure them richer pickings on the live circuit. Their luck changed when they were approached by Robert Wace, a society gentleman who harboured secret ambitions of becoming a pop singer.

Robert Wace was an extremely tall and wealthy gentleman who had declined the opportunity of entering his father's printing business in order to fulfil his show business aspirations. The starstruck would-be singer spent much time hanging out in Denmark Street in the hope of discovering a suitable backing group. Following a tip from musician Terry Kennedy, Wace phoned Mickey Willett who set up a meeting with the Ravens in Muswell Hill. Although the group apparently had no ambitions to turn fully professional they were determined to secure better bookings and listened attentively to Wace's intriguing proposition. A bargain was struck whereby Wace promised to secure lucrative gigs in return for a solo spot in the act. Fortunately for the Ravens, Wace's repertoire consisted of only four cover songs: Trini Lopez's 'If I Had A Hammer', Billy J. Kramer's 'Bad To Me' and a couple of Buddy Holly oldies. Before setting out on the road, Wace and the Ravens cut some demos with engineer Bill Farley at the Regent Sound studio in Denmark Street. According to Willett, however, the results were uninspired.

Wace's extravagant promises of luxurious society gigs, including debutante coming out parties, were by no means exaggerated. The group were paid £40 a night including perks, which generally meant doggy bags all round and draining half-empty bottles of champagne. Although they were less revered than the industrious A Band Of Angels, the Ravens were raucous enough to appeal to this wealthy clientele. Wace recalls the strengths and weaknesses of these seminal deb dates:

> Ray and Dave were singing r'n'b numbers like 'Little Queenie', 'Poison Ivy', 'Route 66' and several Chuck Berry and Bo Diddley numbers. Dave was singing a lot more than he does today. We were always a bit worried

> about Ray's vocal ability in the early days. On record, he didn't have much of a voice compared with Lennon and McCartney or Gerry Marsden. But he did improve his technique a great deal. He realised the limitations of his voice and worked on the strengths. I was doing my four numbers at the end and they were having a good laugh. We were having a great time. I didn't have enough confidence to stay up there for half an hour. It was mainly for a particular social circle. One night, we went outside of the circle and I didn't enjoy it very much.[5]

What Wace neglects to mention is that at this particular traumatic gig he was ignominiously booed off stage. Wace's pride was sufficiently dented to abandon any dreams of stardom but he quickly recovered his spirits when Ray suggested the possibility of his reverting to a full time role as manager. In spite of his inexperience in the music business Wace clearly had enough money and rhetorical skill to encourage Davies to pursue a professional musical career. Realising the need for financial backing, Wace approached a stockbroker friend, Grenville Collins, who proved surprisingly willing to lend his support. A gentleman's agreement was concluded whereby Grenville offered half his lucrative earnings in the City in return for a 50 per cent share of the group's profits. It was an unorthodox deal, typical of men from their background for whom the music business seemed an amusing venture. The Ravens could hardly complain, however, since there was no shortage of prestigious gigs. Indeed, towards the end of 1963, the group played at Jackie Rufus Issacs' 21st birthday extravaganza as well as appearing before a star-studded gathering at a Greek millionaire's party. The toast of English society looked on with amusement and benign condescension at this group of boys who felt more at home playing before a working-class clientele on the North London pub circuit. Meanwhile, Collins and Wace smoothed over the Davies's worst traits with some rudimentary lessons in etiquette. Rather than forcing the group to undergo a long grooming process, the duo taught them by example, and although their efforts were not always rewarded, much was no doubt learned. What Collins and Wace did not realise, however, was that in introducing Ray to this new society they were unconsciously cultivating a class consciousness that would manifest itself in a classic series of satirical vignettes over three years hence.

In spite of their undoubted successes on the deb circuit, the Ravens were not entirely pleased with their management team. Premature hopes of a starring role in a movie based on the Beatles' *A Hard Day's Night* were to remain unrealised. More seriously, Mickey Willett became increasingly concerned about the distribution of income among the Ravens and voiced his objections with some candour:

> The only sore point in the entire business came with the bookings and the money. Ray and Dave looked to me somewhat because I was older and had experience. I had to sort things out with Robert. There was a gig in Lewisham and we were getting about £5 each which in those days wasn't bad. Anyway, we were told that the managers were getting their small cut. Maria (my wife) happened to find a purse in the ladies' toilet that belonged to the girl who ran the place. When Maria opened the purse she found a bill made out to Robert and Grenville for something like £64. I told Ray and Dave about this and they were up in arms . . . That was the start of the rot.[7]

When he approached Wace, Willett was informed that the bill included a variety of other expenses connected with the booking. It was probably an unfortunate misunderstanding, but the confusion bred resentment and suspicion among the Ravens. Willett's fears of exploitation were increased following a memorable appearance at a party thrown by a Greek tycoon. The Ravens had barely completed their pub set when they were ushered to a very large house in Notting Hill where a deb's party was in full swing. Although Willett had to get up for work the following morning he was more than willing to play until 1 a.m. for such a gathering. Having completed their second set of the evening the boys were preparing to leave when Robert Wace intervened with a seemingly generous offer. Willett recalls the ensuing events:

> Robert came over and said that they wanted us to play for another couple of hours. I had a word with the boys but we were dead tired so we packed up and went. The next day when we saw Robert and Grenville again they said, 'You bloody fools! Why didn't you stop and play. You were going to get £100 each from Aristotle Onassis if you'd played a couple of hours longer.' I said, 'That's a bloody difference from what you said last night, Robert.' Robert felt I'd misunderstood and said it was definitely £100 each. But if that had been the case I'd have played until my arms dropped off![7]

Willett's testimony merely underlines the lack of effective communication between himself and Wace who explains how the misunderstanding came about:

> It wasn't Aristotle Onassis's party, it was George Lavanos . . . They played at this party for a friend of mine who was a society swell. He organised this party for George Lavanos who is one of the richest people in the world. His money makes the Onassis family look like paupers! They were all Greeks there and basically they got all excited and kept saying, 'If you play for another fifteen minutes, we'll give you another £20', but it certainly wasn't £100. They did this two or three times

> actually until, as I recall, one of the waiters made a pass at Dave. The waiter was drunk, made a pass and they wouldn't play any more. And that was it.[6]

The personality clash between Willett and the management was clearly causing problems. Wace knew he had treated the group fairly and generously and resented the suspicious nature of the worldly-wise drummer who was always hoping for a better deal. According to Willett, the Davies brothers privately supported him, but were obviously reluctant to argue with their much needed management team. Wace was evidently growing weary of Willett's outspokenness and, backed by Dave, he apparently pressurised Ray into considering a replacement. On one fateful night following a press reception at the *Daily Mail* Willett was informed by Collins and Wace that he was no longer a member of the Ravens. There was no question of long term notice or compensation as Willett realised when he re-read the fourteenth paragraph of the contract he had signed only weeks before: 'This agreement shall be determinable by the personal manager at any time by giving seven days' notice in writing to the performer . . . ' Willett was hurt and confused by being rejected so unceremoniously after nearly eight months as a Raven:

> When I confronted Ray on this he got upset and said 'To be honest Mike, I don't want you to go, but what can I do?' We parted good friends, though I was annoyed at the time. I felt I was being pushed out for being their spokesman . . . Ray and Dave were very gullible in those days. Wace was the villain of the piece as far as I'm concerned. He was instrumental in getting me out. He got at Dave first . . . I said to Robert and Grenville 'I'll take the pair of you on outside now!' I was really fuming about that. I was livid that they'd gone behind my back and persuaded Dave to get at Ray to get me chucked out. We had never had any problems before this.[7]

Although Willett was probably ousted by Collins and Wace, it is questionable whether he would have remained in the group during their subsequent bid for fame. By his own admission, Willett was the outsider, always regarded as a late addition to the group. Living several miles away in Palmers Green, he had little opportunity to see the Muswell Hill boys outside rehearsals and gigs. The visual contrast between the drummer and his fellow Ravens was always uncomfortably noticeable. While they sported long hair, jeans and leather jackets, Willett preferred sharp suits and prided himself on his immaculate grooming. Considerably older than both Ray and Peter, Mike simply did not fit the Ravens' image and his musicianship was not strong enough to compensate for such shortcomings. Willett's view is that his role as mediator between management and group merely precipitated his downfall. There is much truth in this argument, though Collins and Wace would no doubt add that his departure reflected the group's growing desire to succeed as a professional unit.

Although the management continued to provide excellent deb dates, it was proving difficult to secure commercial gigs beyond the Club Norique in the Seven Sisters Road. Wace had also failed to attract the interest of major record companies and although he was considering a publishing agreement with Tony Hiller at Mills Music, his instincts told him to wait for a better deal. For all their social influence, the Collins/Wace duo lacked sufficient knowledge to negotiate the shark-infested waters of the music business. What they needed was an aggressive, uncompromising businessman capable of manipulating the A & R men, promotions people, agents and producers who determined the rise and fall of so many groups during the 60s. Collins and Wace found the perfect master of pop *realpolitik* in Larry Page.

Larry Page was the archetypal working-class hero of British pop music. After leaving school, he secured a job as a packer at E.M.I. Records. Ever inquisitive about the mechanics of the music business, Larry quickly realised that any young kid with looks, image and interesting material had some chance of success in the late 50s pop world. After some consideration, the young factory worker discarded his real name, Davis, and became Larry Page – 'the teenage rage'. Although he failed to set the charts alight, Page secured a number of prestigious support spots, opening for such luminaries as Cliff Richard and the Shadows. He also outraged the elder members of the community by appearing onstage with blue rinsed hair, an act almost unheard of before the 60s. While many of his contemporaries played themselves into oblivion, Page was astute enough to realise that the life of most pop stars was extremely brief. Retiring from the pop scene temporarily to manage a pub in Wales, Page plotted a new career. He ingeniously negotiated the transition from pop singer to businessman achieving considerable success as an impresario on the Mecca circuit. While in Coventry Page managed several acts including the all-female Orchids, Shel Naylor, Little Lenny Davis and pop singer-songwriter, Johnny B. Great. Soon, major entrepreneurs in London were travelling to Coventry and Birmingham to offer Page more lucrative employment. Among them was the renowned music publisher, Eddie Kassner, a man determined to utilise Page's entrepreneural skill for his own benefit. A deal was completed whereby Page was appointed general manager of Kassner Music and allowed to sign up new acts on condition that he passed the publishing over to his partner.

Following his trip to Mills Music, Wace had instructed Grenville Collins to approach Kassner and a meeting was set up with Larry Page. Collins and Wace invited Page to audition the Ravens at a small rehearsal room and his decision on that day was to have far reaching consequences for both parties. What Larry saw were four boys in leather jackets playing a fiery synthesis of r'n'b and Chuck Berry style rock'n'roll. Their equipment was pathetic, the amps constantly issued feedback and the group appeared oblivious to any notions of stage presence. However, Page was clever enough to realise the possibility of moulding this unruly quartet into a headlining beat group. Much to the relief of Collins and Wace, Page agreed to take a 10 per cent interest in the Ravens. Although the group now seemingly had three managers, Robert Wace maintains that Page's power was severely limited:

> Larry Page was recruited because he worked for a music publishing company. I felt that he would enhance the group's chances of success. Larry is an opportunist. It must be said that he was *never* the manager of the group, although he may like to think of himself as one. Larry had this management company called Denmark Productions owned by himself and Eddie Kassner. They had a 10 per cent interest on live gigs and records, but they didn't have any management concerns. They had a piece of the Kinks and the right to place Ray Davies's music. It was a very dangerous thing to do. I only made one mistake and that was getting involved with Eddie Kassner. From Ray's point of view and mine too it was a *very bad* mistake. But all Page had was a subcontracted piece of the action. A lot of people in those days owned different parts of groups.[5]

Page qualifies Wace's comments on his former business partner, maintaining that his role as publisher proved crucial to the group's development:

> Kassner was very good news for them . . . Wace would be selling bloody ties somewhere if it hadn't been for Kassner. Wace knew nothing whatsoever. He came to me, he *begged* me to see the group. Without that they would be nothing . . . You can say a lot of things about Eddie Kassner but without that man the Kinks would still be the Ravens playing in a little pub. Because, he gave me the chance of going out and signing whoever I wanted to, and it was through that that they got their break . . . Ray had a good basic talent, but he needed a lot of coaching.[8]

Davies would probably have broken through eventually, even without the assistance of the charismatic Page. The set-up, however, could not have been more finely balanced. Here was Davies, green as a cabbage, backed by a couple of managerial novices and a young Denmark Street entrepreneur whose powers were still held firmly in check. The question of which party masterminded the group's career from this point onwards remains a tantalising question. In spite of what Wace maintains, there is strong evidence to suggest that Page's influence at this stage was greater than anyone admits. Not surprisingly, Page is indignant at the suggestion that his partners had any control whatsoever and his perspective of the contractual agreement seems decidedly one-sided:

> There weren't three managers, there was only one manager and that was me. The other two knew nothing about the music business, didn't interfere and at that stage of the game left everything to me. It was only when the money started appearing that the problems arose. They were going to sit back and bathe in the reflected glory. Their contract was with me and *my* contract ensured total control, otherwise I wouldn't have touched it. I wouldn't have got involved with a couple of Hooray Henrys, as they were, unless I controlled the situation.[9]

Sam Curtis seems equally dismissive of the Collins/Wace team, though he acknowledges their undoubted influence on the deb circuit:

> Collins and Wace were just there to make money. All they knew was that people were making money out of it. How they became the Kinks' personal managers, I haven't the slightest idea! They knew nothing about the business, but they had the Kinks play at society dos. Wace booked them to play in a tent for the horsey crowd. I heard him on the phone saying 'Oh yes, darling, you'll adore them. They say things like "fuck" – you'll love them; they're quite crude.' And he was right. They loved it![2]

The primary problem that faced the management in late 1963 was transforming this competent r'n'b unit into a visually appealing, interesting musical act. Their first move was to fire Willett whose image and ability seemed suspect. His replacement, John Stewart, was another older musician, who was destined to remain in the group for only a few short weeks. Larry then instructed Dave Davies to place an advertisement in *Melody Maker* stating 'Drummer wanted for a smart go-ahead group'. Fledgling drummer, Mick Avory, took these ambiguous words literally and when he arrived for an audition at a pub in Camden Head, Islington, his conventional appearance ran counter to the hip expectations of Dave:

> He stood over six feet, in suit, shirt and tie, and had the shortest hair I'd ever seen. 'Ha, he's just got out of prison!' I thought. He looked amazed at my appearance and rather longingly at my shoulder-length hair. 'Have a drink', he said. Then – 'You advertised as a smart group. I thought you meant conventional smart. I went and got all my hair cut off. It was as long as yours. And I bought a shirt and a tie.' We both burst out laughing. Poor Mick, he was really upset.[1]

Dave need hardly have worried about Mick being too straight and conventional for his group. A former rocker and greaser, Mick had previously been employed as a snow clearer, a painter, fireplace maker and an excavator on a building site. His working-class background and generally acquiescent personality appealed to Dave, while his abrasive drumming style proved sufficient to pass the audition. Avory's musical background is particularly interesting. Upon leaving school, he joined a local group, the Hilights, who played regularly in the Hampton Court area. Strangely enough, Mick was also a patron of the Crawdaddy Club and for a brief period he had been rehearsing with Mick Jagger and Brian Jones in a prototype Rolling Stones. The more scholarly rock reader may recall that a certain 'Mike Avery' was listed as a member of the group on the first occasion when they were billed as 'The Rolling Stones' at the Marquee on Thursday 12 July 1962. It would be gratifying to report that Avory was a founder member of the Stones but this is not quite the truth. Ever modest about his ability and achievements, Mick denies that he reached the stage of playing live with the Stones:

> They were rehearsing for the Marquee gig in the top room of a pub, the Bricklayer's Arms. Mick Jagger phoned me and I went along to the audition. I said that I'd do the gig, but, as it turned out, they wanted a full time drummer. I wasn't really available for that as I was still working during the day at that time, so after about two rehearsals I dropped out. That was my big chance of being a Stone![10]

Fortunately, Avory was competent and lucky enough to be given a second chance of achieving success in a potentially first division unit.

With a drummer recruited, Page was free to develop the group's stage act and repertoire. Initially, the Ravens asked Page to find a lead singer and suitable cover material, but Larry provided neither. He argued convincingly that an additional member would mean another split in the profits and reminded the group that self-sufficiency was the key to success. Page's most perceptive idea at this point was utilising the untapped talents of Ray Davies who had yet to evolve as a singer-songwriter. Larry explains the way in which he coaxed Davies into writing some of his finest early work:

> I sat down with Ray and told him that the one thing that would sell records would be riffs. Just riffs going all the way through. The first thing I worked out with him was a number called 'Revenge' . . . We concentrated on trying to write material with stock notes where you didn't need a good singer . . . I based the act on 'Louie Louie'. I was a great fan of the Kingsmen. It was just a riff – that was the whole thing. We'd sit around at the piano and work out ideas.[9]

'Revenge' was far from memorable as a piece of rock'n'roll history, but, in plundering some ideas from the Kingsmen, Page was sowing the seeds for the major hits that would follow later in the year.

While the Ravens worked out their new riffs a deal was finalised with Louis Benjamin of Pye Records with whom Page had been associated over the years. According to Wace, the group were merely offered a standard agreement. The management settled for a low percentage, although having already been rejected by Phillips and Decca they probably had little choice. Thanks to Wace, however, they at least procured the services of a man who would help them create a unique sound, previously unheard in rock.

Shel Talmy was a young, American independent producer who had successfully worked for Decca at a time when freelancers were virtually unknown in the industry. His second production, 'Charmaine' by the Bachelors, was a direct result of the strong link between manager Phil Solomon and Decca's Head of A & R, Dick Rowe. This partnership would later encourage other American producers, such as Bert Berns, to cut records for acts including Lulu and Them. Talmy was determined to establish himself as the first truly independent producer on royalties and was more than anxious to work with an unknown group in order to further his reputation. His break came one afternoon in Denmark Street when he was approached by Robert Wace. Shel recalls the meeting:

> I was in Denmark Street at Mills Music and Robert Wace walked in with an acetate of the Ravens under one of his long arms. He had done some demos with them and was looking for a producer and a deal. I liked what I heard so I brought them to Pye and said this is the act I want to produce.[11]

At this stage, Shel does not appear to have dealt with Larry Page and apparently was not aware that he had already seen the group ignored and rejected by Jack Baverstock and other A & R men. Surprisingly, Talmy regarded Page as a 'hip street-wise type' that the society duo had brought in to improve the Kinks' image. It was only later that Talmy would realise the power and influence that Page wielded. Although Larry supported Talmy initially, the American maintains that the former teenage pop star was intent on usurping him as producer at the earliest opportunity.

Following their signing to Pye, the group underwent a name change, though precisely how the Ravens became the Kinks is a long story. Ray Davies quite rightly credits Larry Page for selecting the new name, though it had apparently been a joke title for a considerable period. The word 'kinky' was a mid-60s catch phrase associated with knee-high boots and popularised by Millicent Martin on television programmes such as the satiric *That Was The Week That Was*. The phrase was first applied to the group when a studio engineer observing Ray Davies's grey pullover, tweed trousers and orange tie called him a 'kink'. The image was reinforced by Dave Davies who began to wear a plastic coat and thigh high cavalier-style boots purchased from a theatrical agency. The sixteen-year-old also began to part his long hair close to the centre, which at the time was regarded as daringly effete. Not surprisingly, the Kinks were frequently invited to play at gay parties and Larry Page immediately realised the commercial potential in exploiting their outrageousness. No doubt remembering the shock value of his rinsed hair during his teenage rage days, Page immediately set to work on revamping the Kinks' image and introducing their name to a larger audience. The recent emergence of the Rolling Stones as a hit act suggested that the public were ready to accept outrageously long-haired groups who did not conform to the style of the smart-suited Beatles. At this point, the Kinks were dressed in leather jackets and caps, a slightly beatnik image that was not quite strong enough visually. Much thought went into creating a new look and Page recalls suggesting something based on his standard 50s uniform of red blazer and dark pants. Eventually, the management ordered some startling new outfits from the classy department store Fortnum and Mason in Piccadilly. The boys were both amused and amazed when they were presented with two sets of green and pink hunting jackets, complete with yellow frilly shirts, black trousers and riding boots. The shock value of the kinky garb was reinforced by the shameless brandishing of riding whips. It was a delightful irony that these staunch working-class boys should don the hunting uniform of the gentry and perform at debutante parties. Posters soon began to appear announcing 'If you like the Stones, you'll rave over the Kinks'. Page even insisted on giving the brothers some rudimentary lessons about projecting their sexuality onstage:

> I taught Ray and Dave how to hold their guitars . . . You hold it as if you're holding your prick – you have it right in front of you and you play it. When the camera comes on you, you grip it so that they can see every little bit of nervous energy in your hand. When the camera comes on your face it's got to be that aggression all the time. And those were the things I went through. Same as their stage act where I put one of them on one side and one on the other and they'd skip into the middle. It was always aggression – the whole thing. It had to be. But it all paid off.[9]

The success of Page's elaborate masterplan continued with an equally effective gigging schedule, which coincided with the Kinks signing to the impressive Arthur Howes Agency in January 1964. Robert Wace rightly perceives the signing as a landmark in the history of the Kinks:

> The Arthur Howes connection was the next major step for them. That came about as a result of a date I got them at the Lotus House in Edgware

> Road. Through that Arthur Howes wanted to sign them to his agency. And, just for the record, Arthur wanted Larry Page out from day one.[5]

According to Wace, Howes felt that Larry wasn't the right person for the Kinks and the society duo expended a great deal of effort actually defending their later adversary. While Wace maintains that Page was fully aware of Howes' objections, Larry insists that he was blissfully ignorant of any such resentment:

> I would say that is wrong, but nothing surprises me in this business. If you've got a chance of dealing with two people, one who knows what he's talking about and one who doesn't then, quite possibly, it's beneficial to deal with the one who *doesn't* know what he's talking about . . . You think how much they know now and how much they knew then. It was very, very little. They were very empty people.[8]

Without doubt, the agency deal was a major coup, since Howes was the most successful pop music impresario in the country. Ray Davies was particularly pleased to be associated with the man who promoted the Beatles. Perhaps the greatest compliment to Howes comes from Ray Davies's frequent contention that the Lotus House gig on 31 December 1963 (Peter Quaife's birthday) represented the formation and professional debut of the Kinks.

By January 1964 the newly christened Kinks had already advanced several steps on the road to success. Page placed great pressure on Vicki Wickham in an attempt to obtain a spot on the influential television pop show *Ready Steady Go*. Many people in the business were suspicious of the Kinks, however, and it was generally felt that Larry Page had gone too far in promoting their outrageousness. Those opinions would be reversed in the succeeding months during which Page watched the momentum steadily grow. The first studio recording by the Kinks took place in January 1964 under strange circumstances. While waiting for Davies to write some suitable material Larry received an urgent phone call from Arthur Howes in Paris where the promoter had just watched the Beatles perform at the Olympia on 17 January. An excited Howes enthused about a brilliant live cut that seemed a sure fire hit. His advice to Page was categorical: 'You've got to get in there straightaway. They did a number last night and brought the house down.' The song was a cover of Little Richard's 'Long Tall Sally' which the Kinks immediately recorded in a blatant attempt to emulate the Fab Four's distinctive style, complete with crashing cymbals and a wailing harmonica. The flip side, 'I Took My Baby Home', also owed much to the sound of Liverpool with some Beach Boys style harmonies thrown in for good measure. Due to the panic, the recording of 'Long Tall Sally' proved unsatisfactory and the final version was achieved by splicing together two alternate takes. The crude editing process proved particularly embarrassing to Dave Davies:

> We signed with Pye and were given a three-hour recording session to do about six tracks – quarter inch tape, that sort of thing. That's when we did 'Long Tall Sally'. Pye weren't actually very willing to spend much money on this bunch of long-haired unknowns so we had to work very fast; in fact, if you're ever unlucky enough to hear that single there's a terrible edit on it. We did two takes and had to cut them together, and it was supposed to cut in right on the beat, but they missed, and you'll hear an extra beat in there somewhere.[12]

Shel Talmy is far less critical of the track which he supported from the outset:

> I thought it would be a good idea to do a standard for the first thing out of the box. We were doing it entirely different from anybody else. It was done quickly but I don't recall an edit. I wasn't knocked out by it – but I thought it was O.K.[11]

Although 'Long Tall Sally' failed to chart, it gained the group some excellent publicity and achieved that much sought after appearance on *Ready Steady Go*.

Strangely enough, it was not until the following month that Wace and Collins (Boscobel Productions) signed the contracts binding them to the Kinks and Larry Page. However, the solicitor chose a curious and unfortunate method of drawing up separate agreements for both the management parties which would subsequently prove contentious. On 12 February, each Kink signed a five-year agreement with Boscobel allowing them to retain 40 per cent of the group's earnings as well as granting them the rights to place their song publishing. Fourteen days later, a separate agreement, to which the performers were not parties, was concluded between Boscobel and Denmark Productions appointing Larry Page as manager of the group on a 10 per cent remuneration for the duration of the previous agreement. The Kinks approved of this new agreement, fully realising that they had simultaneously assigned Kassner all rights pertaining to the placing of their musical compositions. In the cold light of day, it was Page whose position was most threatened by these separate agreements since he was not signed directly to the Kinks and Collins and Wace could legally appoint any person to carry out managerial obligations. It was understood, however, that Page should carry out such duties and the agreements did no more than put into legal form, albeit extremely clumsily, what the Kinks had previously accepted. Page clearly regarded the contracts as watertight, in spite of their unusual form, and proceeded with his managerial plans unperturbed.

For the Kinks' second single, Pye decided to release two Davies compositions. Another of Larry Page's theories was that in order to give a song greater universal appeal the lyrics should put strong emphasis on the words 'You' and 'Me'. In later years, he would carefully select songs with titles such as 'With a Girl Like *You*' and 'Anyway That *You* Want *Me*' in order to provide the Troggs with sizeable hits. After some discussion, he persuaded Ray to write four tunes containing the words 'You and Me' in the title. In April 'You Still Want Me' b/w 'You Do Something To Me' appeared and disappeared with extraordinary rapidity. Shel Talmy had been strongly opposed to issuing the record but his objections had remained unheard amid the cry for new product:

> 'You Still Want Me' was done at the same session as 'Long Tall Sally'. I did not want that to come out. Pye decided that they wanted to release something. It was Louis Benjamin's idea. It was just thrown out.[11]

'You Still Want Me' failed to appear on any album until *The Kinks File* in 1977, while the flip side is still generally unavailable. Mint copies of the original single currently exchange hands for sums in the region of £50 – £75, which testifies to its rarity.

The failure of their first two discs was a major setback for Page who still firmly believed that a 'You and Me' song could provide the required breakthrough. In the Spring, the Kinks were invited by Howes to appear on a lucrative package tour with the Hollies and the Dave Clark Five. The Kinks' set lasted approximately twelve minutes during which they were expected to warm-up the crowd for the two big name acts. Although one ill-informed M.C. introduced them as 'The Kinks from Liverpool', it was evident that their live set was more raucous than the standard Mersey Beat group of the period. The bottom of the bill placing encouraged them to play their heart and lungs out and on at least one occasion the manic enthusiasm proved disastrous for Dave Davies:

> I made a real idiot of myself. We'd just got to the end of a number and I went jumping up and down like we always do, when it suddenly occurred to me that the floor was an awfully long way away. I'd jumped right off the stage and I fell into the orchestra pit. The audience loved it. They all thought it was part of the act. There was blood dripping down my face and yet the audience never did realise that it wasn't supposed to happen.[1]

Apart from the onstage frenzy, the Kinks noticed that one of Ray's 'You and Me' songs was causing a stir. A primitive version of 'You Really Got Me' included a gimmick ending in which the group would sing the words of the title and abruptly announce 'That's all there is of that then'. The Kinks' audacity in seemingly throwing away one of their best songs in the middle of a set disorientated the audience to such an extent that they applauded ecstatically. Watching from the wings, Larry Page was sufficiently impressed to book another session with Shel Talmy in July. By this time Talmy was tired of producing acts such as the Bachelors and Chad and Jeremy and was determined to experiment with new ideas. He spent many hours in the studio recording different guitar sounds using a variety of microphones. The equipment was primitive by today's standards but, fortunately, the sound that Shel was hoping to capture relied primarily on a heavy rhythmic sound. Talmy was aided by the 'Marconi of fuzz' Dave Davies, whose playful destruction of his own equipment inadvertently helped create the Kinks sound. Dave had been increasingly frustrated by the tinny sound of his El Pico 10-watt amplifier and in a fit of boredom he punctured his speakers with a knitting needle. Playing very loud through a single amp Dave was astonished by the distorted sound which he transferred to his regular vox amplifiers. Talmy was suitably impressed by the new Kinks sound, but it was evident that the producer and his group had different conceptions of the end product, as Ray indicates:

> We had a bit of a misunderstanding. The first couple of sessions were okay but when it came down to recording 'You Really Got Me', it was the first thing that was the Kinks. What we wanted to do. We had a lot of trouble getting the record company to even let us record it. They thought it was uncommercial. Shel recorded it once and it didn't work out.[13]

In his determination to cut a hit record, Talmy had used an elaborate production full of echoes and overdubs. The Kinks quite rightly argued that their sparse live version contained enough excitement without the need for such embellishment. Initially, the group met some resistance from their record company who were anxious to release the completed version. An alarmed Ray insisted that the Kinks re-record the song with the intention of retaining the raw in-concert feel that characterised their new sound. Fortunately for Davies, Larry Page also objected to Talmy's production and immediately pressurised Pye Records into reconsidering their decision to release the single. As a negotiator, Page proved irresistible and not even the imposing figure of Louis Benjamin was any match for him:

> I'd already demoed those songs and I didn't like what Shel had done. I didn't think the magic was there. Therefore, I went along and had a meeting with Louis Benjamin and asked him if we could either use the demos or readjust the mixes so that the songs would sound right. And Louis said it couldn't be done because they had a producer who would have to be given credit. I said that didn't interest me at all. All I wanted was the record to be right when it came out. And Benjy refused. So I said, 'At the moment I'm talking to you as their manager. Now I'll talk to you

as a publisher and *tell* you that either the song gets changed or the records don't come out.' And that's what happened because the power of a publisher is such that he can stop it.[9]

Under coercion from Page, Benjamin reluctantly agreed but forced the Kinks to complete the record immediately. A magnanimous Robert Wace also supported the cause of his despairing artist:

> Ray was so sure that the recording of 'You Really Got Me' was terrible and wouldn't be successful that I personally paid for it to be re-recorded at I.B.C. He was saying that if it went out he'd pack it in. The original was flooded with echo and they wanted a much drier recording that was less produced. Talmy thought the original was great as it stood and Pye wouldn't pay for it to be re-recorded. I felt that Ray had a lot of drive and should be given his head. To be honest, I didn't particularly like 'You Really Got Me', but he was totally convinced that it was a smash.[5]

The group entered the Regent Sound studio one night and psyched themselves up for the most spontaneous and important recording of their entire career. Ray Davies vividly recalls the manic energy produced by the group during that memorable session:

> I used to play a lot of lead in those days. When that record starts it's like four people doing the four-minute mile, there's a lot of emotion. It was a great experience standing next to Dave when he played that because I was shouting at him, willing him to do it, saying it was the last chance we had. There's determination, fight and guts in that record. 'You Really Got Me' was, in a way, a computerised version of all we were doing.[14]

Although Talmy admits that a later version was cut, he stresses that the final recording was produced entirely by himself:

> Do you really think that any producer who still has ears is not going to know the difference between what he did and what somebody else did? . . . We recorded two versions. The first version was very much more r'n'b influenced. Ray wanted to try it another way. So they went and cut a demo, probably at Regent Sound. But we cut *the* version at I.B.C. I think Glynn Johns was the engineer . . . Jimmy Page played rhythm guitar, Jon Lord played organ and Perry Ford played piano. The drummer was Bobby Graham. Avory was not involved until after 'You Really Got Me'. There was no slur against Avory. He was a new member and didn't really know the stuff – that's why we used Bobby.[11]

The confusion among commentators concerning the various versions of 'You Really Got Me' has sometimes caused Jimmy Page to be credited erroneously for the lead guitar work of Dave Davies. This incorrect assumption became a matter of bitter controversy in later years when the myth grew to increasingly alarming proportions, in spite of consistent denials from the Davies brothers. The rumour probably stemmed from Jimmy Page's revelation that he had played as a session man on various recordings by the Kinks (and the Who). However, Talmy fully supports Davies's later testimony that Jimmy's involvement did not extend much beyond contributing tambourine and rhythm guitar to a few cuts on their first album. In fact, Talmy says the only reason he brought in Page was because of Ray's own insecurity about his abilities as a guitarist, a view which Talmy did not share.

'You Really Got Me' was released in August 1964 and within a matter of weeks it soared to the top of the charts. It was a distinctive first hit, as well as being one of the most strikingly original records of 1964:

> 'You Really Got Me' as a record was a different record for that time, there was nothing around like it. I remember I used to go down to the Marquee and everyone was close to making a record like that. The Yardbirds thought they'd do it, but we did it first.[15]

The Kinks have often been accused of being derivative and it is something of a critical commonplace to point out the similarity between 'You Really Got Me' and the Kingsmen's early 1964 hit 'Louie Louie'. Even Page confesses that he based the act around the 'Louie Louie' riff, as is demonstrated on several of their early recordings. Of course, the Kinks were not alone in plundering old riffs and revamping them for their own purposes. Even in creating the 'Louie Louie' riff, the Kingsmen were reviving an obscure r'n'b number first recorded by its composer, Richard Berry, in early 1956. Moreover, a similar riff appeared at least three times the following year in such hits as the Who's 'I Can't Explain', the McCoy's 'Hang On Sloopy' and Sam the Sham's 'Wooly Bully'. It is no wonder that Ray Davies acknowledges 'Louie Louie' as 'the best rock'n'roll song ever written'. Without that riff Davies might never have got the Kinks off the ground. Strangely enough, the Davies brothers have always downplayed the Kingsmen comparisons, perhaps because the idea was originally conceived by Larry Page rather than themselves.

According to the brothers, the inspiration for 'You Really Got Me' came from their interest in the blues-orientated forms of French jazz. Apparently, the original version of the song was a light jazzy tune bearing little resemblance to the final recorded version. Dave Davies recalls discovering the riff after seeing a film of the Montreux Jazz Festival in which Jimmy Giuffre and Gerry Mulligan played the seminal 'Train On The River'. It would be intriguing to hear this original version in comparison to the Kingsmen influenced recording that was finally released.

Rock historians are apt to pinpoint the Kinks' combination of feedback and an archetypal riff as the earliest source of heavy metal music. Like many innovations, however, this creation of a musical sub genre was almost purely fortuitous as Ray Davies is too willing to admit:

> All these things happen by accident. Look at the Beatles thing of going 'ooh'. That was an accident, I'm sure. They were probably trying to get the sound that Little Richard gets and ended up with their own sound instead.[16]

If 'You Really Got Me' was an innovation because of its sound, the lyrics were also a contributory factor to its success. The grammatically incorrect song title offended an older generation in the same way that the Stones' '(I Can't Get No) Satisfaction' was to cause controversy in 1965. What most critics failed to observe was Davies's deliberate attempt to break away from the false trappings of romanticism that permeated the teenage love songs of the early 60s. The sentiments of 'You Really Got Me' were direct, intense and carefully pointed at a generation that Ray Davies considered too cynical to accept the romantic songs that he had loved as a child:

> 'You Really Got Me' was an earthy love song without all that moon and June stuff. A lot of people thought it was boring, but it's something we all felt. I think the fans felt the same. Teenagers could never say, 'I Love You'. They want to express their feelings in an unsentimental way.[16]

When the Kinks finally hit the number 1 spot they were heavily featured in the music press. Many critics of the period were suspicious of the group and concluded that their long hair and studiously rebel image were merely calculated attempts to imitate the Rolling Stones. As a result, the promotional posters comparing the Stones and the Kinks were hastily discarded and Page forced Ray to employ all his rhetorical skills in fending off his detractors:

> Okay, so we've got the hair and all that, and some people even say the same attitude, but – well, come to that you could ask 'Aren't the Stones another Beatles group?' because of the hair, couldn't you? Mind you – okay, so it's true. There's a bit of the rebel in us. But we are not doing a Stones. And we don't play r'n'b. That's best left to people like Muddy Waters, who know what it's all about. I call our stuff more *expression*. It's an outlet to us. I know it probably sounds corny to say it, but you feel, when you're standing up there, that you want to get something out of your system. Everyone's got it somewhere – the expression and the need for an outlet. The audience want to experience it. So we help them. Doesn't that sound right?[17]

Davies's sermon was impressive though the contention that the Kinks did not play r'n'b does not appear to make sense. Perhaps feeling that his tone was too apologetic, Ray ended his defence of the Kinks with an emphatic attack:

> I challenge anyone to come and see us onstage, then they'll know what the Kinks are like. We entertain, see. Whether we succeed or not is beside the point. But we have a go. We love theatres, when you have a rave![17]

For all their flippancy, the Kinks never saw themselves as a short-lived fad dependent upon a stylised sound. Indeed, as early as August 1964 Ray Davies was discussing the group's probable development during the next four years. Without a hint of exaggeration he informed reporters that the Kinks would eventually be augmenting to form a band in order to keep ahead of changing fashions. This was no idle boast but an uncannily accurate prophecy of the Kinks' development during the 70s. In an age when pop groups formed and folded in frequent succession, the Kinks were determined to defy critical expectation and survive.

THREE

Kings of the Road

In order to cash in on the chart-topping success of 'You Really Got Me' the Kinks instantly set to work on their debut album. Incredibly enough, the album was conceived and completed within a matter of days as Dave Davies testifies with some amusement:

> The first album we did, we had a week to do it – I don't know how we managed. There were only about six original songs on that L.P. because of the time, and the rest were things we knew and could do very quickly in the time. As I remember, the last sessions for that album, there were actually people hammering on the door to get in because we were running a bit over time.[12]

Shel Talmy places Dave's story in a more realistic perspective by reminding us of the standard recording procedure during the 60s:

> We certainly had time to finish what we had. It was all ready. Benjamin wanted the album out to capitalise on the single, so we finished it quickly. It sounds terrible – it only took a week! The way it sounds is that we rushed it. We didn't. We're only talking about three tracks. How elaborate could you get? That 'knocking on the door' story is a slight exaggeration![11]

In many respects *The Kinks* was a typical mid-60s debut, relying heavily on the r'n'b covers that were highlighted in the group's set. Competent reruns of early Chuck Berry ('Too Much Monkey Business' and 'Beautiful Delilah') were placed alongside more adventurous r'n'b workouts including a raucous version of Don Covoy's 'Long Tall Shorty' and the obligatory 'Got Love If You Want It'. At this point, Ray's songwriting was still in its infancy though he apparently had enough material in reserve for an album's worth of songs. In 1964, however, the chances of a new group completing an album of their own songs was virtually non-existent, as Talmy indicates:

> For a first album I thought it would be a very good idea to do some non-original stuff. On one hit song Ray was hardly established as the great songwriter that he is. Besides this, in the early 60s the singer-songwriter was not yet something that the public had latched on to . . . Early on,

Robert Wace felt that we should be doing somebody else's stuff and Ray saw sense in that. Nobody disagreed with the material – there were no great traumas – nothing like that.[11]

In helping the group select new material Talmy was astute enough to grab a piece of the action by including two of his own compositions, 'Bald Headed Woman' and 'I've Been Driving On Bald Mountain'. Both numbers were blues based folk songs registered as 'public domain' which ensured that Talmy could gain some publishing and songwriting royalties with a minimum of creative effort. Of the Davies compositions that were included, only two merit special attention. 'Just Can't Go To Sleep', with its slightly risque lyrics and Beatle-influenced chorus, remains an undiscovered gem. Much the same could be said of 'Stop Your Sobbing' which was finally recognised by the general public when successfully revived by the Pretenders in 1979. Not surprisingly, 'You Really Got Me' remains the stand-out track, but it is interesting to hear the same prototype 'Louie Louie' riff in Larry Page's 'Revenge', a number that was later adapted as the theme music for *Ready Steady Go*. *The Kinks* was a credible debut and, though overburdened by r'n'b covers, showed enough eclecticism and interesting ideas to suggest greater achievements in the future.

While Ray Davies was swiftly emerging as the major talent in the group, his younger brother was far from idle. It is generally not known that Dave was a prolific songwriter at this point and, but for the fear of experimentation, might have adapted his unusual compositions for possible inclusion on the Kinks' debut album:

It was mostly sort of folk stuff, Dylan influenced I suppose, written on acoustic guitar, and you'd get into the studio and we couldn't really do them. No, not we couldn't do it, but it wasn't really right for the group then, so it got pushed into the background. I admire Ray a great deal and I think he's a genius in his own way, and I think when you're working with someone who's that talented you've got to let them have their head, haven't you.[12]

Dave's reluctance to promote his own material would remain a constant throughout his recording career in the 60s and 70s.

In October, the all-important successor to 'You Really Got Me' was prepared for release. 'All Day And All Of The Night' was the classic paradoxical follow-up in the sense that it was both distinctly similar to its predecessor and completely different. The Kinks were now plagiarising their own work, a trick that was beyond the one-hit-wonder Kingsmen. 'All Day And All Of The Night' narrowly missed the number 1 spot, but provided rock music with another memorable riff. Four years later, the Doors adapted the distinctive chord changes and scored their only British

Top 20 hit with 'Hello I Love You'. The recording was a fitting tribute to the longevity of the number.

Having established themselves as potentially consistent hit makers, the Kinks gradually phased out the gimmicks that had brought them to the public's attention. The whips were discarded but the colourful hunting jackets seemed too distinctive a trademark to abandon until later in their career. Although they appeared to be tempering their outrageousness, their current stage act revealed familiar riotous scenes. Jim Rodford (who was destined to join the Kinks fourteen years later) recalls a 1964 package tour featuring such stars as Marianne Faithfull, Kim Weston, Bobby Shafto, Gerry and the Pacemakers and Gene Pitney. As a new member of the bottom of the bill, Mike Cotton Sound, Rodford was unprepared for the remarkable scenes that ensued when the Kinks closed the first half of the show:

> There was Dave down on his knees playing his guitar to the ceiling. The kids had never seen anything like it before – they didn't know how to react. So they rioted. Every night. That power . . . it was animal.[18]

The Kinks' uncompromising stage act frequently placed them in danger of physical assault. At Basildon New Town, Essex, an estimated 1,000 teenagers stormed the Locarno Ballroom stage in an attempt to devour their heroes. The bouncers looked on helplessly while young Dave Davies was hauled into the crowd by the rapacious fans. The pandemonium worsened when officials knocked down several girls in their anxiety to recover the errant guitarist. This would not be the last occasion a live performance by the Kinks drew the attention of Fleet Street. Ray and Dave Davies were far from frightened of their rioting fans and seemed to wallow in the chaos. Road manager Sam Curtis recalls one occasion when the younger brother intentionally set out to cause a sensation:

> We did a show in London where Dave deliberately went onstage with his bollocks hanging out under his guitar. He was holding his guitar in front of him pretending he didn't know. But before he went onstage he pulled his trouser zip down and pulled his bollocks out to hang over his trousers.[2]

When I enquired as to whether the members of the audience were fully aware of this unusual action, Curtis answered incredulously:

> Were the audience aware of his bollocks hanging out? If you were two feet away from a guy with his bollocks hanging out, could you see them? And it was all girls! Because the stage was only small – it was only about eight foot from the back to the front of the stage.[2]

The Kinks had evidently taken Larry Page's hints about stage presence and sexuality to heart!

In order to increase their Christmas record sales the group rush-released their first E.P. *Kinksize Session*. The disc was most notable for the inclusion of 'Louie Louie' which was a nice touch given the comparisons with 'You Really Got Me'. Equally ironic was Ray Davies's assertion that the Kinks were in the midst of musical experimentation:

> The public might get tired if we stuck to the same formula all the time so we've been trying out different types of guitars and amplifiers, looking for something new. I've found that by using a lot of distortion on my amplifier and then using even more distortion in the recording booth we can make my guitar sound like a whole group of violins.[19]

Davies's words were a sobering reminder of the need for progression in order to survive. In retrospect, it is easy to assume that with two classic hits such as 'You Really Got Me' and 'All Day And All Of The Night' the Kinks must have been the most celebrated new group of the year. This, however, was not the case. 1964 was one of the most competitive years in the history of British rock music. The Mersey boom had spread outwards and the Kinks were not the only non-Liverpool group shooting for number 1 hits. The Rolling Stones outmanoeuvred the Kinks with two consecutive chart toppers ('It's All Over Now' and 'Little Red Rooster') while the Dave Clark Five, the Animals and Manfred Mann each emulated the feat of 'You Really Got Me'. Even in terms of originality, the Animals' 'House Of The Rising Sun' was generally accepted as the most innovative single of the year. For all the publicity and chart success, the Kinks still had a long road to travel before they would be accepted as one of Britain's premier rock groups.

The phenomenal success of the Beatles in America proved to be a crucial factor in the development of the Kinks in 1965. Realising that the beat boom was not restricted to Britain, Larry Page was determined that the Kinks should break into the international market. During the next few months the group were to embark on a rigorous schedule, devastating in its consequences. In retrospect, Page's desperate make or break gamble seems to have been premature considering the relative naivety of the group who were still recovering from the excesses of 1964. On the other hand, the situation was made doubly urgent by the unprecedented slide of the Mersey Beat groups. Gerry and the Pacemakers, Billy J. Kramer and the Dakotas and even the Searchers were suddenly foundering in the face of new competition, while the Rolling Stones and the Animals seemed destined for world-wide success. Although the Stones had virtually a year's start on the Kinks, their Stateside promotion was inexplicably low-key and their current British number 1, 'Little Red Rooster', was not even given a U.S. release. Page clearly realised that if he moved quickly the Kinks might cash in on their two recent U.S. Top 10 hits and oust the Stones as the much touted antithesis of the Fab Four.

While American negotiations were underway the Kinks visited the South of France to appear in a movie destined for the annual Montreux Film Festival. The Kinks opened the film walking down a Marseilles street, playing guitars and miming to their recording of 'Too Much Monkey Business'. Even more impressive was a shot of the group performing 'All Day And All Of The Night' aboard the aircraft carrier *U.S.S. Saratoga.* After filming was completed, the Kinks set up their equipment in the hangar bay and gave a live show for the American crew, using the ship's amplification equipment. The Kinks were heard in every part of the ship until Pete Quaife yelled into the microphone: 'Action stations' upon which everyone scuttled off to their duty posts.

The French visit was succeeded by an attempted Kinks conquest of Australia. The tour kicked off in Perth where Dave Davies was astonished to discover that the inhabitants could be as vocally appreciative as their British counterparts:

> The audience were marvellous to us on our opening night. They yelled just like they do in England. At the end of the show they stood up and clapped, a sort of special thank you and we felt quite moved. When we got back to the dressing-room we were very quiet, each scared to say how we felt in case we sounded soft.[1]

By the time they reached Melbourne, the scenes of Kink mania were all too familiar. Members of the audience would run down the gangways and religiously throw wild heather on to the stage while proclaiming: 'We love you, Kinks'. In spite of this magnificent response, the group were annoyed to discover that their thunder had been effortlessly stolen by some old rivals:

> . . . it was Stones, Stones, Stones every time you picked up a paper and all they said about us was, 'The Kinks Are Coming'. We were disappointed about the lack of publicity, but I think our shows were bigger successes than theirs.[20]

The Australian sojourn proved tiring yet rewarding and paved the way for further achievements later in the group's career. For Ray, in particular, the trip had meant a happy reunion with his favourite sister, Rose. Ray also spent much time discussing life in the old country with Rose's husband, Arthur – who would later be immortalised in a series of Davies songs.

Without stopping for breath, the Kinks then flew to the United States in order to promote their new single, 'Tired Of Waiting For You'. This latest disc was slower than the previous two rockers but retained a distinctive hook line and had yet another ingenious adaptation of that old 'Louie Louie' riff. The number was originally intended as an album cut until Shel Talmy took it to Pye's Head of A & R, Alan Freeman (not the disc jockey!)

and championed its immediate release. It was evident that Ray Davies's songwriting had noticeably improved for he was now confidently playing with lyrics, gradually constructing a song from the repetition and elaboration of a single phrase. Once again, the lyrics were not those of a romantic love song. They concentrated instead on the narrator's neurotic aversion to his lover's tardiness. It was probably the most anti-romantic love song since 'Blue Suede Shoes'. Although the Kinks had yet to book a U.S. tour, they managed to slot in a couple of television appearances including the obligatory *Shindig*. As a visual act, the Kinks were exceptional, and American teenagers sat transfixed by the outrageously long hair of Dave Davies and his bizarre V-shaped futurist guitar. Ray, of course, was almost equally extraordinary. Here was a pop star who looked as uncertain, bemused and vulnerable as any of his audience – he even had a gap between his teeth just like ordinary mortals. In the days when pop stars were gods whose human frailties were obliterated by plastic surgery and cosmeticians, Ray was already emerging as the classic rock anti-hero. Even in his earliest interviews Davies refused to accept the manufactured pop star image and was heretical enough to question the permanence of fame:

> I'm a collection of loose ends. I don't want to be a pop star. I think that this is just a part of my life which will come to an end. I feel like there are other developments in my life. For example, I should very much like to produce a film. Something artistic that would convey emotion and reaction.[21]

Ray's distaste for plastic perfection offended the fashion conscious teenage magazines and *16* refused to take a photograph of the gap-toothed wonder. Pressure was placed on Davies to improve his looks by undergoing dental treatment and although the image-makers almost won the day, the uncompromising pop star recanted at the last minute:

> You know, at the beginning the people told me in their transatlantic accents: 'You can't be a pop star with a gap in your teeth'. And they sent me to a bloke to have it filled up. And just as he was going to get the thing to cut the teeth I said 'No, I'm not having that'. It's the most important decision I've ever made.[22]

The Kinks left the States with 'Tired Of Waiting For You' firmly implanted in the Top 10, their third consecutive hit. A few months before their second album release an additional work, *Kinks Size*, was rushed out in the States in order to take full advantage of the nation-wide publicity.

Having travelled to two continents, the group were allowed the comparative luxury of a thirty-six hour sojourn in Singapore on the way home. By this time, the Kinks were so exhausted that they hardly had the energy to frolic around in their hotel swimming pool. Dave complained of an infected ear made worse by his failed attempts as a diver, while Ray moped about like some ageing colonial still suffering from memories of a recent war. Ironically, it was during this period of post-tour exhaustion that Ray received a message which heralded a triumphant homecoming:

> One of the happiest times I had was in Singapore when 'Tired Of Waiting' got to number 1. We'd been on a world tour and I was really homesick being on the road. And the *Daily Mirror* or one of those papers phoned me up to tell me the record was number 1 in England. I was really lonely. So I got a bottle of champagne and I got the waiter who brought it in, who couldn't speak English, to have a drink with me. That was one of the happiest times. Just that moment.[23]

The success of 'Tired Of Waiting For You' was significant because it established the Kinks as the most consistent chart act since the Searchers. For a moment it must have seemed as though they might replace the Stones but unforeseen disaster was close at hand. Without a break, the Kinks returned to the live circuit punishing themselves with another series of package tours and club dates, while Larry Page carefully plotted that all-important big tour of America. Looking back at that crucial period, Ray Davies remembers the horrors that awaited the Kinks at their regional gigs:

> In those days you arrived at the ballroom, the promoter and his bouncers grabbed you and locked you away in the dressing-room, which was usually no more than a big cupboard, and then they'd come back and unlock you when it was time to go on. It was terrible, but you had to put up with it, and it led to a few strange scenes.[24]

What Davies fails to mention is his own responsibility for those 'strange scenes' and the absolute necessity of ensuring that the Kinks were safely locked away in separate dressing-rooms. The main problem in the chemistry of the group was not merely the rivalry between the brothers but the subordinate role forced upon Quaife and Avory. While the music press extolled the virtues of the fun-loving Kinks, Sam Curtis observed a growing rift between the brothers and their rhythm section:

> Ray and Dave had nothing in common with Mick and Pete. The attitude I saw was that they had them along simply because they needed a bass player and drummer. They were just a couple of geezers . . . The Kinks could be together for a hundred years, but the drummer and the bass player could never have a chance. Whoever they're using now can only be employees. Of that I'm certain. They would never be shareholders – not even in the bus fare.[2]

The Davies's condescending attitude was already causing headaches for

Larry Page, but their cruellest gibes were reserved for Mick Avory. Sadly, Mick's acquiescent personality ensured that he was the obvious target for the bullyboy tactics of the brothers. Larry Page describes him as an easily exploitable character who seemed a born victim:

> Mick would do whatever you told him. He just sits there thumping away like mad. But he was no problem. Mick was like a little puppet. He'd do what you told him to do and that was it.[9]

The Davies brothers took a perverse delight in antagonising the quiet Kink at every opportunity. Curtis recalls one recording session during which Mick was allowed to carefully set up his drum kit before being laughed out of the studio while a session man took his place. Even back at the hotel, Dave loved to pick fights with the drummer and the spilling of blood was apparently not unusual. No sane-minded human being could tolerate such taunts indefinitely and even the good natured Avory frequently found himself frustrated to the point of retaliation. Although Quaife found his loyalties divided, he studiously avoided confrontation in a way that was beyond Avory. Sam Curtis made the following assessment of the contrast in their reactions to the psychological warfare:

> It was the brothers against Mick. Peter Quaife I don't include – he was just *there*. He wasn't the type of guy to get involved in aggravation . . . Peter was of a different background, a different class. He had no experience; he was just a nice guy trying to find his way. You'll notice that in none of these controversies will you find Peter Quaife. The only whipping boy was Mick Avory. He also came from quite a nice family. . . I think he was naive. There was nowhere for him to go in the world other than where he was . . . You could insult him and treat him like dirt and it still didn't matter. He would just tolerate it.[2]

Such personality differences were either played down or ignored by the mid-60s music press, although Dave Davies once came very close to admitting the truth:

> . . . we hated the sight of each other. We would fly into a temper at the slightest provocation. I suppose, in a way, it was only natural when we spent so much time together. I think every group getting a big hit for the first time must suffer this. We were dashing around the country doing one-nighters. We were tired out so much of the time after a long drive. We lived on sandwiches and snatched meals.[25]

While the Kinks' touring schedule was being extended their second album, *Kinda Kinks* reached the Top 3. It was another uneven piece of work built almost entirely around their recent number 1 'Tired Of Waiting For You'. Most of the songs such as 'Wonder Where My Baby Is', 'Got My

Feet On The Ground' and 'Naggin' Woman' revealed the group's continued interest in the blues. 'So Long' was perhaps the one oddity – an acoustic song about leaving the past, probably inspired by the current folk rock boom. An uninspired cover of 'Dancing In The Street' seemed a conscious filler and even two of the better cuts, 'Don't Ever Change' and the haunting 'Something Better Beginning', were reminiscent of the Drifters' 'Save The Last Dance For Me'. In spite of its commercial success one could not escape the impression that the Kinks had once again been rushed into the studio in order to cut an album's worth of very average songs. At the time, of course, such expediency was forgivable. As long as the Kinks could continue to produce classic singles their future would be assured.

Inevitably, the slackness evident on their album cuts eventually permeated their single recordings. 'Everybody's Gonna Be Happy' was superior to the majority of the songs on *Kinda Kinks* but far below the standard of 'Tired Of Waiting For You', 'All Day And All Of The Night' and 'You Really Got Me'. Shel Talmy clearly felt that as a follow up to a number 1 hit the song lacked distinction:

> 'Everybody's Gonna Be Happy' was a single I did not want to put out. Ray did – I believe. He was in love with the song. I didn't like it – I didn't think it was a single. It was the lowest chart record we ever had.[11]

The single was only a middling Top 20 hit and as a result the sides were reversed in the States but 'Who'll Be The Next In Line?' was even less impressive and failed to reach the Top 30. During the same month, the Rolling Stones dominated the U.K. number 1 spot with one of their finest singles, 'The Last Time'. The short-lived battle for chart supremacy between the two bad bands of pop had been resolved. While the Stones prepared for their American onslaught with an ace card called 'Satisfaction', the Kinks were left in total confusion.

In order to keep the boys in shape, Larry Page and Arthur Howes lined up a Scottish tour for April. Unfortunately the excellent efforts of Page and Howes were thwarted by a series of illnesses in the group. The first victim was Dave Davies who was smitten by a severe attack of bronchitis. Far more serious was the state of brother Ray, who suffered a physical breakdown due to extreme exhaustion, no doubt worsened by the constant bickering between himself and the other members of the group. Emotionally distraught, he bundled all his money into his socks and ran the eight miles from his home in Muswell Hill to his song publishers in Denmark Street. Incensed and frustrated, he took a swing at his publicist, ran out of the office and was eventually pursued along a Soho Street by his manager and a doctor. The story was confirmed by Larry Page:

> There was nothing unusual about that. It was like having afternoon tea

with Ray. I can remember the incident with publicist Brian Sommerville because his office was next door to us. I can remember the havoc.[9]

Sam Curtis is equally dismissive and refuses to acknowledge the possibility of Ray succumbing to a 'nervous breakdown'. Robert Wace confirms that the breakdown was short-lived and Ray was quickly snapped out of this frenzy by his anxious management team. Not to be outdone by his colleagues, Peter Quaife completed this triumvirate of breakdowns in equally dramatic fashion. Despite feeling exhausted and ill he had gone to the Muswell Odeon in order to see the spy film, *The Ipcress File*. Venturing to the toilet after the show, Peter suddenly felt faint, collapsed and smashed his head on the stone floor:

I don't know what caused it. Probably that bit of the film where Michael Caine grips a nail in his clenched fist so he won't break down during the brainwashing. There was a lot of blood – and that may have turned my stomach over. Anyhow, I wandered out into the cinema foyer and asked if I could have a drink of water because I'd just fainted when a woman behind me starts having hysterics. Apparently, I had blood pouring from the cut on my nut.[26]

Fortunately for Pete, Mick Avory happened to be in the cinema at the time and he arranged for an ambulance to whisk the hapless guitarist to the local hospital where he was given stitches. A vacation and a brief period of reconstruction before the U.S. tour of the summer would perhaps have been appropriate. At this stage of the game, however, their ambitious management team were in no mood to offer the Kinks a reprieve. In spite of the arduous touring schedules, Larry Page maintains that the group were not unnecessarily overworked:

At that time they were one of the very first English groups and I think what you had to do was to make the impact there and then. If we'd left any country a little bit later, someone else would have been in there and they'd have been the new Beatles or the new Rolling Stones. They *wanted* it. They wanted to work.[9]

At the end of April, the Kinks embarked on an important British tour supported by the Yardbirds and Goldie and the Gingerbreads. It was another gruelling schedule taking in nineteen dates in under three weeks. Still weary from their recent illnesses, the Kinks struggled on while backstage bickering and nervous tension mounted. The atmosphere was probably not helped by the presence of the Yardbirds who, at that point, were one of the most innovative groups on the scene. To what extent Davies felt jealous or resentful of their popularity seems indeterminable though on at least one occasion he apparently attempted to sabotage their act. Sam Curtis recalls a classic example of behaviour bordering on the irrational:

We did a show and the Yardbirds were on and they were going down bloody well. And what did Ray Davies do? He went into this lovely dressing-room with beautiful tiled showers, tore all the metal work off the wall and threw it onstage during the Yardbirds act.[2]

Meanwhile, backstage the friction between Avory and the brothers continued unabated. By the time the group arrived at the Capital Cinema in Cardiff on 19 May, the spurious spirit of cameraderie was all but destroyed. Curtis was forced to place them in separate cars and dressing-rooms for the duration of the tour in an attempt to prevent trouble. However, it was inevitable that the good natured Avory would eventually explode, and as Curtis explains:

These guys could provoke the Pope! They didn't need anything. They would come down in the morning to go off on tour and when they'd see him they'd say, 'Morning cunt'. How would you feel? If somebody says that to you in the morning you just feel like going out on tour with them, don't you? But then, if he didn't he'd starve because he couldn't do anything else. What was he going to do, become a star on his own with a drum kit?! He's got the personality of a cucumber sandwich . . . [2]

That night in Cardiff, Mick finally reached the end of his tether. Stage hands looked on in amazement as the Kinks bounded on from separate sides of the stage like bulls and matadors in a crowded arena. Shortly after opening the first set, Dave Davies wandered across to Mick Avory and, after exchanging a few words, kicked his prize drum kit across the stage. The 2,500 teenagers packed into the auditorium howled with delight at what they assumed was a well rehearsed example of Kinks theatricalism. Suddenly, the mood of the evening changed when Mick emerged from his dishevelled drum kit with a cymbal and gashed Dave across the side of the head. While Ray attended his injured brother, a panic-stricken Avory fled the stage. Sam Curtis takes up the story:

Fortunately, Dave managed to step out of the way slightly because if he hadn't moved that thing would have gone through his head down to his neck. Those cymbals are *sharp* . . . Mick thought he'd killed him and ran out of the theatre. Can you imagine the scene? This guy wearing the hunting jacket and frilly yellow shirt running through the streets of Cardiff with hundreds of girls chasing after him because he's one of the Kinks. And he's running *for his life* because he thinks he's killed someone.[2]

While Dave was taken to the Cardiff Royal Infirmary for treatment and the M.C. announced the cancellation of the second show, Curtis was scouring the streets for the frantic drummer. Eventually, he located Avory in a nearby cafe where an anxious woman was offering him solace. According to Sam, the boy was in such a state that he didn't seem to know what was happening. Realising that Mick was in no fit state to be interrogated, Curtis acted quickly. He instructed Avory to hide in the waiting room of Cardiff station and board the first train, irrespective of its destination. In the meantime, police officers were searching the group's hotel to question Avory on what looked like being a very serious charge. Although the other three Kinks refused all interviews, several journalists realised the seriousness of the Mick and Dave incident and pestered Curtis for an official statement. Under some duress, Sam provided the following grim perspective of the affair:

> This looks like the end of the road for them. I think the group must break up now. I've seen this coming on for a long time. They've been all tensed up and something had to break.[27]

Curtis's analysis of the situation was remarkably accurate, as Larry Page is only too willing to concede:

> That was the *end* of the Kinks. There was no way that they were ever going to play together again. The police were putting out bulletins for Mick Avory who ended up with me, still in his stage suit. They were looking for him, and it was *very* serious. It was the end of the Kinks.[9]

Having persuaded Dave not to press charges, Page set about reforming the group against seemingly impossible odds. Without informing them of his motives, Larry phoned each member individually and invited them all to his office one Friday afternoon. Each member duly turned up expecting to see Page alone:

> As you can imagine when they all sat in the room, it was dynamite. I didn't mess around. I just said OK – there's an American tour starting – and I didn't give them time to ask anything. At the end of it I just said, 'Any questions?' And Mick Avory said he needed new cymbals because he'd smashed them over Dave's head.[9]

Even Robert Wace conceded that Page had successfully stage-managed a reconciliation between Mick and Dave in a surprisingly impressive way. Page's belief in the importance of the forthcoming American tour remained undiminished and it was probably the most important factor in saving the group from premature extinction. He was convinced that a well planned promotional visit and extensive tour would provide the perfect opportunity for achieving permanent international success.

In order to pacify the press, Larry set about instructing Avory in the art of public relations. Between them they concocted a story that was designed to cajole journalists into restrospectively reporting the onstage confrontation as an 'accident'. Fortunately, Avory's explanation for his aggressive behaviour was so ridiculously unconvincing that some papers seemingly believed him:

> It was part of a new routine we had worked on for our song 'You Really Got Me'. The idea was that Dave should wave his guitar at my drums and I should pretend to hit him with my cymbals, but I really did hit him. When he fell over and everyone rushed onstage I felt such a fool, especially when I realised I had injured him.[28]

Amazingly, Page even managed to suppress Ray's filial prejudices and ensured that his words were invariably diplomatic: 'I'm sorry about my brother and also that Mick's been upset'. Not surprisingly Dave Davies remained consistently quiet about the affair. In retrospect, Dave maintains that the clash was primarily a result of the continual pressures of life on the road, coupled with his own emotional immaturity:

> I was only sixteen or something at the time and I think that from the age of thirteen to seventeen I was very big-headed anyway, it was a period of my life that I had to go through. I think that during the first year of our success I really abused myself. I was willing to do absolutely anything that was going, excessive drinking and things like that. Then I started to realise what I was doing wrong when Mick and myself had a big punch-up onstage and I smashed up all his drums. At this particular time I wasn't writing or anything and I was thinking even less. I only started thinking when I was seventeen or eighteen. From then on I could still do a lot of things I'd done before but with reservations.[29]

Following a brief period of convalescence, Dave resumed his place in the Kinks who were herded into another series of live performances. By this point Ray Davies was sick of playing fifteen-minute sets along with half a dozen other groups and approached his agent, Arthur Howes, with the revolutionary idea of presenting a complete one-act show. Davies received short-shrift from Howes who suggested that the concept was impractical and required further thought. Although Davies's objections to the archaic package tour system failed to alter their stage performances it was significant that as early as 1965 he was thinking in terms of a theatrical presentation. Peter Quaife explained Davies's ambitious plans and strongly hinted at changes in the future:

> We thought it would be great if we could tie the whole thing together and do sketches in between numbers and then have a finale with everyone coming on at the end and singing and jumping around . . . The only trouble was that it would need a tremendous amount of rehearsing to put a show like that together and since we were coming out here to Paris and

> everyone else was tied up until the two days we'd set aside for rehearsal, we had to leave it this time. But this is a definite 'thing' we've got into our systems so we're hoping very much that our next tour will take this form.[30]

What Quaife failed to mention was that Ray's elaborate plans had become largely irrelevant in the face of a hotel ban that was effectively preventing the Kinks from touring Britain. Their name had become synonymous with breakages, and of all the British groups only the Who matched them for wilful destruction. Probably the last straw for Britain's hoteliers occurred in Glasgow when some bright spark made the mistake of allowing both groups into the same establishment in quick succession. Sam Curtis recalls the effect of this particular stay:

> God forgive 'em! The Who had taken the front doors off – the Kinks smashed them. Between the two of them they had to almost rebuild the place. There wasn't a single hotel in the country that would allow them in. That's why they couldn't tour. You couldn't come home to London every night. Word went out. The minute I went to book them in – 'No way'. Who wants blood all over their carpets or equipment torn off the wall?[2]

As a result of the ban, the Kinks at least had time to cut a new single. 'Set Me Free' was a conscious return to the style of their earlier hits and though no all-time classic it proved sufficient to take them into the Top 10. In spite of their success, the portents for the future looked relatively bleak for a group who had worked non-stop throughout the year. All their efforts had been geared towards maintaining their grip on the top of the charts, but suddenly the effortless production of number 1 hits had vanished. The pressures placed upon Ray Davies to write a chart topper between package tours were proving intolerable. The situation was not made easier by his evident fear of failure:

> I start worrying the moment I get an idea for a number. I take so much notice of my own criticisms. I may produce three or four versions of the number. Then I get the others to listen to them – and promptly worry over what they have said. When the number goes out on disc, I worry over whether it will make it. Sometimes I go a couple of days without eating. But if my worrying helps us to stay on the scene, I guess that's worthwhile![31]

Davies may have been playing a dangerous game with his health but in other respects his life seemed relatively more stable. He had recently married a Kinks fan named Rasa who had ventured backstage during one of the group's shows only to emerge with a pop star husband. Not surprisingly, Ray's wedding was not without its memorable moments. Larry Page remembers the day with affection:

> I drove Ray overnight from Oxford to Bradford. And there was this little terraced house. We were sitting on the arms of the couch having the breakfast luncheon. The press were there. We had Ray's family in one room and her family in the other. Finally, the priest stood up and said how wrong he'd been, he'd misjudged groups totally, and what wonderful boys he'd found Raymond and David to be and now he'd like David to say a few words. And David stood up and said, 'Well, I'm too pissed to say anything really'. Magic. It was unbelievable.[9]

Page, however, would not have many more happy memories to look back on.

FOUR

Eve of Destruction

The Kinks finally set out on their U.S. tour towards the end of June 1965. It was an arduous schedule taking in New York, Texas, Hollywood and Honolulu and the group were well aware of the stamina-sapping road work that lay ahead. While English journalists talked of sight-seeing and exotic surroundings, Peter Quaife sarcastically reminded them of the bad food, sleepless nights and frequent exhaustion that were part and parcel of life on the road. Almost inevitably the Kinks caused so much chaos that they were eventually forced to leave the States in disgrace.

The problems that were destined to produce an extraordinary series of court cases had actually begun prior to the group's departure. There was apparently increasing dissension between Collins and Wace and Larry Page, no doubt exacerbated by the latter's ever-growing influence over the Kinks. Shel Talmy, in particular, was not impressed by Page:

> He was trying to wind up with the band without Collins and Wace and without me. He wanted to be head honcho.[11]

Shel's statement must be qualified by his own admission that he purposely avoided the managerial wranglings and knew few details first hand. There may be much truth in Talmy's general accusation against Page but there is little doubt that Collins and Wace were equally anxious to oust Page. Indeed, at this point, Page claims that he had the perfect opportunity to terminate the partnership but chose not to exercise such power, even in the face of provocation:

> The Hooray Henrys were starting to say 'We're paying Larry Page this 10 per cent, it's a lot of money. Do we really need him?' You could feel the friction. Now if I'd wanted to I could have rowed them out. I could have taken them out, but I'm not like that. To me fair is fair. If we have an agreement, then we stick to it. But I could have taken them out with no trouble at all.[9]

Page believes that his chance came and went during a meeting with Ray Davies at the Kassner office when the money conscious pop star expressed concern about the amount of commissions being paid out. However, it seems strange that Page should feel such loyalty to a couple of 'Hooray

Henrys' who were taking 30 per cent of the cake between them. Perhaps he realised that a *coup d'état* could not be achieved without the full support of the Davies brothers, who were unlikely to be swayed by either faction. Page was probably biding his time in the firm belief that his commitment and industry would finally be rewarded. At this point, he seemingly held the ace cards. After all, he had successfully promoted the group and more recently prevented their almost inevitable break-up following the Cardiff debacle. The Kinks relied heavily on Page who must have felt extremely confident about his role as preparations were finalised for the American invasion. Unfortunately for Page, Ray Davies was already proving unreasonably awkward and increasingly demanding. With Collins and Wace seemingly plotting a managerial comeback, the last thing Page wanted was opposition from Davies. At such an important point in the Kinks' career, however, Ray was intent on playing the *prima donna*, with all the maturity of a spoiled child. Page recalls Davies's reluctance to sign his contract as a typical example of such behaviour:

> We got the contracts sent from America. These were standard agency contracts. Bear in mind that groups were a new thing. I went round to see Ray, sat there, showed him the contract and said, 'Fine, you've got to countersign them with me'. And I gave him a fountain and I watched him empty the fountain pen on the floor. As he was talking to me I saw the ink dripping out and he said 'Oh, this pen's got no ink in it!' And I said, 'I should bloody well think not, I've just watched you empty it.' Then we got another pen. Then he said, 'No, I can't sign this because it says orchestra leader and they'll expect me to take an orchestra with me.' I said, 'No they won't Ray, groups are a new thing–just cross it out.' There was no way he wanted to put pen to paper to do the American tour . . . Ray just enjoyed being awkward. He really did. You had to coax Ray. You had to treat him like a little boy, humour him, be nice to him and pat him on the head.[9]

Davies's lack of enthusiasm for the projected U.S. tour was not merely bloody mindedness. The previous visit in January had not been enjoyable and Ray was particularly upset by the relatively poor financial rewards. He was additionally apprehensive about the attitude which might be adopted by the American police were there any repetition of the Cardiff incident. Ray was also demonstrating his confusion over who deserved his allegiance. In spite of Page's efforts, Davies was still impressed by Collins and Wace whose family wealth, public school education and brash confidence represented a world that was outside his experience. Page maintains that Davies's dilemma in choosing between his mentors seriously affected the money-conscious pop star:

> He was being hit from all sides. People were trying to influence him

wrongly. He saw the Hooray Henrys as money, as stability . . . but at the end of the day I was the only person in there with any musical knowledge who could have guided them at all.[9]

Robert Wace tells a different story, denying that he was ever in danger of losing the Kinks to the charismatic Page. Less convincingly, Wace implies that he deliberately exploited Page's unquenchable ambition in order to destroy his influence over the Kinks:

> I'm sure Ray saw us as money, stability and background. He had met my father. He knew that the Wace Group was a very big public company. They knew who they were getting involved with. We had the relationship with the band. They knew what we'd done for them. Basically, Larry's an opportunist and he wanted to go to America. I wasn't very happy about that but he pointed out that Eddie Kassner had an office over there. Arthur Howes said, 'Let him go – it should be interesting to see what happens' . . . We wanted them to see how Page would measure up. We felt that he was bad news for the group, being divisive and playing one off against the other. He was also trying to row out Shel Talmy as producer. Everybody was rather bored with Larry Page . . . We'd probably have jacked it in ourselves because we were getting tired of having him around . . . You've got to remember that Grenville and I weren't exactly paupers.[5]

In almost every conversation Wace stresses the fact that Page's day to day involvement with the Kinks was extremely limited. However, it is remarkable that Collins and Wace could be arrogant enough to dismiss his influence so lightly. After all, he was the man responsible for their stage management and public relations, while Collins and Wace were largely restricted to office work. In allowing Larry access to the Kinks they were playing a perilous game and Wace's comment about possibly jacking it in suggests their frustration at his growing influence. Larry maintains that the power wielded by Collins and Wace was virtually non-existent: 'If we ever discussed it with the Kinks at that stage, they were a bit of a joke'. His flippant dismissal of the society duo, however, neglects such factors as Ray's awareness and respect for their pedigree. Moreover, the unpredictable Dave clearly aligned himself with Wace and had supported him strongly ever since the incident with Mickey Willett two years before. But Wace's basic contention that 'Page never had a relationship with the group' does seem surprisingly myopic as Larry explains:

> I was very, very close to Ray . . . I had a good relationship with the group. Come on! I used to be in the [dressing] room when they were screwing around and everything else. Basically, we were all from a working-class background and that was one thing that Wace and

> Collins weren't. They would just show up and say, 'Hello, hello – what! what!' There was no way they could *communicate* with the boys. When there was trouble at Cardiff with the fight onstage I was the one who sorted it out. I was the one who *could* sort it out. There would be no Kinks today if I hadn't sorted them out. Now, if he had such a relationship with the boys, how come he didn't? He couldn't talk to Ray because he would just tell him to 'Get knotted!'[8]

The arguments conflict, but enough has been said to explain the complex relationship that existed between the various parties as final preparations were made for the Atlantic crossing. One way or another, the American tour would provide the solution to all their problems. It gave Collins and Wace ample time to consider their future in the management set up as well as the possibility of pre-arranging further deals without interference from Larry. For the Kinks it presented the golden opportunity to establish themselves internationally while also allowing Page to reach the peak of his managerial career. Inevitably, such logical reasoning proved vacuous when placed in the context of Ray Davies's peculiar rationale. For here was a man capable of sacrificing his career prospects for the egocentric gratification of making life intolerable for his manager. Sam Curtis points to Ray's bitterness and fear of exploitation as symptomatic of his undoing during the forthcoming weeks:

> No matter what you did he would make sure there were problems. He wanted to be contrary. And the reason he was contrary was because he knew that anybody who spoke to him was only speaking to him for one reason – to make money. Nobody *ever* spoke to Ray Davies because they liked him! Nobody spoke to Ray or Dave Davies because they got pleasure from talking to them! People dealt with them to make money. In that position why shouldn't he say, 'You want money – work for it – I'll be as awkward as I can'.[2]

Davies's attitude might have seemed more reasonable had he reserved his awkwardness for the ambitious Page. Unfortunately, other employees received equally derogatory treatment, not least their efficient and respected road-manager:

> Sam could have been due for a nervous breakdown I don't know how many times! He did a good job, a tough job, but he was treated like a bloody slave by them.[9]

The Kinks' ignominious behaviour was not restricted to employers and employees but extended within their own ranks. Since the Cardiff incident, they had virtually refused to speak to each other and segregation was enforced by Page in order to avoid confrontations. In the back of everyone's mind, however, was the nagging suspicion that further fights might occur live onstage in America. Page apparently acted like a stern schoolmaster in disciplining the Kinks, but that recalcitrant pupil, Ray, continually displayed behaviour that bordered on the irrational. Larry recalls Ray's unusual sense of humour with some perplexity:

> During this stage everybody wants to punch the life out of everybody else. It's my job to act as referee. I had to keep them to one side all the time . . . Ray, of course, was enjoying it all and provoking it all . . . Imagine me on the bus with the two of them at each end. I'd hear a little movement and I'd look round and he'd say, 'I'm just stretching my legs!' Then he'd run down the bus . . . and go to me, 'you cunt, you cunt', and then he'd go back again. That is schoolkids stuff, you know. When I used to come home I used to have to count my underpants and count my socks . . . But then again, as they say, possibly a true talent is very very close to the border of insanity. I don't know whether he was before his time, whether he was after his time or where he went.[9]

Page remembers other equally eccentric behaviour from Ray as the tour progressed. On one occasion Larry noticed that his glasses were missing, but later that evening he was astonished to discover Ray wearing them. Upon requesting their return, Ray apparently informed his manager that he had bought the spectacles for his own use. Page was forced into a long argument with Davies before the problem was resolved. Although this seems like an innocent and amusing jest on Davies's part, Page almost seems convinced that Ray genuinely believed his own story. Ultimately, however, Page refuses to provide any final judgment on Davies's strange actions during this period.

Ray's wayward behaviour coupled with a series of unforeseen setbacks proved a sufficient recipe for disaster. The Kinks' debut took place at New York's Academy Of Music, a venue whose name suggested opulence and splendour. When Curtis and the group arrived they were depressed to discover an old auditorium covered in dust and totally lacking the excellent facilities they had optimistically expected. Relations between the Kinks and the theatre's employees were also noticeably cool. The stage hands openly showed contempt for the rock'n'roll business and were extremely unsympathetic towards these obnoxious long-haired English pop stars. While the boys were settling in, the ever industrious Page was horrified to discover a billboard proclaiming the arrival of 'THE KINGS!' Realising that Ray Davies would refuse to perform if he even saw that title Page hastily hustled the theatre management into making the necessary changes. A second and more serious problem manifested itself following the Kinks' arrival that same afternoon. The supporting acts on the programme, the Supremes and the Dave Clark Five, were each under the impression that they were topping the bill. Following a heated discussion, contracts were exchanged each revealing a clause promising headlining status. Each act was ready to lynch promoter Sid Bernstein until it was discovered that one of his relations had died suddenly. The dispute was eventually decided by the toss of a coin. When the Kinks finally took the stage Page stood at the back of the theatre like a proud parent:

> Really, it was very emotional for me. I remember the old tears running down my eyes. For this little band I'd 'found' to be opening in America was sensational.[9]

Page's tears of happiness quickly changed into sobs of grief following the opening chords of 'You Really Got Me' when an electricity cut plunged the theatre into darkness. Amid the stunned silence, Larry bolted backstage where it took all his efforts to revive the Kinks and rekindle that all-important nervous energy. When the lighting was restored the group returned to give a reasonable performance. Fortunately, Page had structured the set so as to gain the maximum impact from their most memorable U.S. hit, 'You Really Got Me'. The Kinks teasingly opened with a few bars of the song, then abruptly played a different number while the audience waited in hungry anticipation. In mid set a complete version of 'You Really Got Me' would be performed and repeated as an encore number. It was excellent strategy by Page and helped save the day at the Academy Of Music. Unfortunately, at later gigs, Ray Davies would exploit Page's stage dramatics for a very different effect.

While Page was attempting to stabilize the Kinks he encountered problems with various promoters. Much of the group's money had already been lost in commissions which was hardly unusual in the mid-60s. What frustrated Page was the constant wrangling required to obtain money that had already been promised in writing. According to Curtis, several of the places they played were run by Mafia style gangsters who would display their firearms at the slightest provocation. It was an entirely different league for the street-wise former teenage rage, but he met his adversaries with unflinching arrogance. A gig booked by a radio station was mysteriously cancelled on the grounds that it had been organised by individuals who were no longer connected with the broadcasting company. Eventually, Page was forced to accept a severely modified deal or lose an entire evening's pay, not to mention air fares and hotel expenses. Larry backed down, but he was already preparing a lawsuit to recover the lost revenue. It later transpired that the reason for the cancellation was due to the promoter's foolishness in booking the group into a 20,000 seater stadium on the same night as the long-awaited rodeo show hit town. Depressed by the poor attendance, the Kinks streamlined their set from forty to eighteen minutes, an action that the promoters later used as justification for the cut in pay. Sam Curtis recalls the exploitation and bad organization that dogged the tour:

> The place was empty . . . so they gave me $1,000 instead of $2,000 and promised the rest at another booking in Sacremento. When we got there Sonny and Cher were on the bill. It was a school armoury! It was only a small building, so they could only pay me so much. This went on all around the country. The promoters knew they'd made mistakes and bad bookings and they didn't want to pay.[2]

When Ray Davies learned that the Kinks were not receiving all the money due to them, he decided to take the law into his own hands. Although Page was successfully instigating a lawsuit, Davies could not resist causing further trouble for his overworked manager:

> We were getting situations where promoters were refusing to pay us because we'd only done forty-four minutes instead of forty-five. The following night it would be for the same promoter, and I'd say to Ray: 'They're refusing to pay us, don't worry we're going to fight it'. The next night Ray would do forty-six minutes, but all he would play would be 'You Really Got Me'! Now that's O.K., you're telling the promoter what to do, but it's not fair on the fans.[9]

Curtis confirms that there was an extended version of 'You Really Got Me' included, but stresses that it did not constitute the entire set! The problems with lost revenue increased Ray's cynicism for the rock business as well as encouraging a cautious attitude towards money that was to remain a distinctive trait throughout his career. This tendency to take the law into his own hands by voicing his objections sometimes went too far. On one occasion, the Kinks entered a club in a small American town and were immediately greeted by a standing ovation while the house orchestra played one of the group's better known hits. It was an affectionate gesture, obviously requiring extra work and rehearsal and Curtis, in particular, was extremely moved by the spectacle. As the Kinks were being escorted to their reserved front seats, however, the mood of the evening abruptly altered. Ray stopped, reached into his pocket, pulled out some loose change and began throwing it around the room shouting, 'Is this what you want? Is it my money you're after?' The clapping immediately stopped as the audience looked on astonished at Davies's outburst and no doubt horrified by his boorish behaviour. Ray's fear of exploitation probably saved him from the bad deals and extravagances that destroyed many 60s acts but his criticisms were not always just. Years after this incident, Davies wrote a song called 'The Moneygoround' in which he documented the avarice of his former managers. For Larry Page, it must have seemed one of the most hypocritical statements ever voiced on record:

> When I hear 'The Moneygoround' I can't believe it! That should give you a good insight into the way Ray thinks. Ray is the tightest bastard that ever lived . . . I've been in a car with him with Rasa. I've sat in the front and I've heard her say, 'Ray, what about that coat' and he's said, 'No, you can't have it!' . . . 'Oh, Ray, please, it's very cold outside' . . . I'm sitting there listening to all this – 'No, it's a lot of money!' And it goes on and on and on. And at the end of the day he says, 'Oh, all right then . . . driver will you go to Sketchleys!' And it's a coat coming out of the dry cleaners! Now that gives you some idea.[9]

Even at the height of his fame, Ray was apparently reluctant to carry money, preferring the 'Low Budget' persona that would later launch an album:

> The boy was worth a lot of money. But he used to say to me: 'Larry, I want some chewing gum but I've only got a penny. Can you lend me a penny?' And that was Ray. Ray would never spend. He was a very careful person with his money. You never saw him put his hands in his pocket. Ray's pockets were sealed. Ray Davies never got screwed by anybody. *Never.*[9]

Strangely enough, an unprompted Sam Curtis also provided the story of Rasa and the coat, and his account tallies with that of Page. Even Robert Wace conceded that Davies's thrift was a phenomenon previously outside his experience:

> It took Ray five years to come to terms with success. You've got to remember that he made a great deal of money as a songwriter. You know artists that aren't able to handle wealth and he's not one of them. But he didn't have a sophisticated attitude towards money. He's *always* been paranoid about it. He has this vision of himself being a tramp. He used to be the tightest guy with money I'd ever met.[5]

In attempting to determine the cause of Davies's financial fears one might consider his relatively deprived working-class upbringing as a crucial factor. It is not inconceivable that as a young member of a large family Ray was robbed of the security of private ownership. The tendency to worry about even absurdly small amounts of money suggests a lack of maturity consistent with many of Ray's other actions. In the rapacious rock world, however, such reasoning can probably be regarded as both strength and weakness. Wace claims that of all the groups he handled, the Kinks were the most careful and financially independent. Conversely, however, Davies's inability to come to terms with his changed status as a rock'n'roll pop star prevented him and others from fully enjoying the fruits of his success. Such considerations are greeted with impatience by Sam Curtis who remains unconvinced that any such analyses could provide a satisfactory explanation for the general attitude of either of the Davies brothers:

> You can't rationalise the actions of somebody like that . . . Wealth is something they were never able to assimilate. Personally, I don't think they ever will. Even if you told me the Davies brothers had become like the *nouveau riche* I wouldn't believe you. He may be a multi-millionaire now but, to me, Ray Davies will still question the price of an ice-cream. If there's two pairs of trousers and one's £6 and one's £4 he'll see if he can wear the £4 ones.[2]

As the American tour progressed, Page found himself under more and more pressure. Inevitably, there were traumas involving groupies, for the Kinks clearly loved their reputation as one of America's most sexually sought imports. Sam Curtis provides an overview of the sexual interest that followed the Kinks across the breadth of America:

> In New York there were birds in the cupboards, under the beds. They crawled all over the hotel . . . In Hollywood two girls fought over who would make love to Dave Davies and they tore each other's hair out.[2]

Somehow the group survived all this but it was yet another constantly irritating feature of this unforgettable tour.

By the time the Kinks reached Los Angeles the incorrigible Davies seemed liable to destroy Page's publicity work at any moment. Ray's wicked sense of humour was impossible to restrain and even on important television shows he would stretch his manager's patience to the furthest limits. Davies was playing a dangerous game and even Page must have wondered whether it was worth expending the effort required to disguise his protégé's misdemeanours:

> I spent the day trying to save it. I used to stand there watching them go on the screen and die wondering what he was going to say. It was totally unpredicatable. You never knew what was going to happen . . . It's very tough. In L.A. he refused to do a T.V. show because there was a coloured drummer. Now I know Ray's got nothing against coloured drummers, but every day there was a little trauma. Every day he would want to bring to everyone's attention that he was the man in control. We had this throughout the tour.[9]

Tapes of the Kinks' televised appearances in America confirm some of Page's comments. In a brilliant and amusing send up of the 60s pop star interview, Davies and the others adopt public school accents and claim that they were art students who met at university! Prior to the interview, Ray had informed the show's unfortunate host that they were to be awarded M.B.E.s by the Queen on their return to England. The interviewer swallowed this story hook, line and sinker and seems amazed when Davies reveals that they will be returning their medals because they object to 'generals and matrons' being honoured in the same way: 'We feel only pop stars should get M.B.E.s because they're the *only* people who should get them . . . ' The confused interviewer then suggests that the group surely regard themselves as pop stars giving Ray leave to retort that the Kinks are 'expressionists'. Generally, these outrageous parodies worked effectively, even though many of the interviewers were made to look extremely foolish and uncomfortable. For Page it was often an agonising spectacle that threatened to blow up in his face at any moment.

Inevitably, Davies's loutish behaviour finally proved his undoing. Events reached a head during a rehearsal session at an N.B.C. studio when Ray became involved in a fracas. Davies explains the events leading up to his strange outburst:

> We were doing a Dick Clark Show and we'd been there for three days, you know, just standing around. Peter and Gordon were there. They had a changing room that was as big as a shoe box and somebody said, 'You wait until the Communists take over Great Britain!' Well that was just too much for me to take. I just lashed out at him. I wasn't drunk. I mean you just shouldn't say wait until the Communists take over Great Britain; it infuriated me.[32]

Why Davies should have become so incensed about such an innocuous remark remains a mystery. Although the poor guy was probably guilty of sarcasm, his words hardly merited such an extreme and violent outburst. Sam Curtis was not surprised by Ray's unwarranted anger which he regarded as a typical response to such a situation:

> One of the guys working there just said something. You must realise that if these people spoke to the Davies brothers thinking they were ordinary people they were wrong. You could turn round and say something innocent and finish up with the most unholy row. They weren't the type of people you could talk to in an ordinary way if you didn't know them and the guys in America *didn't* know them. Like, I could turn round to you and say, 'Oh, don't be silly, don't do that' and you would say, 'Well, what do you mean?' But if you turned around and said that to the Davies brothers there was a punch up or they'd smash a few bottles or knock a table over. 'What do you mean – you're calling *me* silly! I'm the great Davies!'[2]

The problems apparently worsened when the group encountered further problems with a television and recording union. Slowly but surely, Page's ambitions for the Kinks in America were being undermined by Davies's self-destructive tendencies.

The tolerance of Page during this period of crisis was matched only by his absolute determination to break the Kinks in spite of Ray Davies. Remarkably enough, he still held faith, even though the group's misdemeanours had already blighted their future Stateside success. In Los Angeles, the power game between Page and Davies reached a stupendous climax in which both parties lost. The drama was set on the eve of the Hollywood Bowl concert, a performance that Page rightly regarded as the pinnacle of the Kinks' achievement in the States. In Page's mind the Bowl was no doubt inextricably linked with his vision of the Kinks as a second Beatles. While the Kinks were preparing for the show Larry received a phone call from London asking him if it was true that the boys were refusing to appear. An astonished Page told the caller that such rumours were nonsense. When he reached Ray's dressing-room, however, Larry was greeted by the words: 'I'm not going on!' The reason Ray gave for his latest *prima donna* display was a depressed state brought on by the absence of his wife Rasa. In normal circumstances, Larry might have agreed to fly Rasa over to see the show, but it was an unreasonable demand as he reveals:

> At that stage of the game it was very tough because she was of Russian or Eastern block parentage. The Americans weren't too keen about getting them in, even given time, let alone short notice.[9]

In the event, Larry was forced to play the tiresome game of coaxing Ray into changing his mind. On this occasion, however, his perennial patience with Ray's petulance finally snapped, causing bitter reprisals:

> I spent all day pleading, begging, grovelling – and this was after a very heavy tour . . . It was totally degrading for me. I sat there and thought, 'What's it all about? I've taken these boys, I've given them every bloody thing. Here they are at the Hollywood Bowl, and Ray's refusing to go onstage!' And that was it for me. To me, what am I going to do after that? Where am I going to put them where they won't refuse to appear onstage? And since then any act I've been associated with the minute I see problems, I'm out. I don't work my arse off twenty-four hours a day to come through with people who refuse to honour contracts.[9]

Although it seems likely that Page realised his presence in the States was neither benefitting himself nor the Kinks, the circumstances surrounding his departure remain unclear. What is certain is that on 3 July Page finally succeeded in flying Rasa over, and no doubt felt justified in leaving Ray in her capable hands. The following day, Page abruptly departed, having informed the three other Kinks of his intentions. Apparently, none of them voiced any objections. However, it later transpired that during the final stages of the tour Page was seduced by a new duo, Sonny and Cher, whom he later brought over to tour Britain. The Davies brothers were incensed by this action which they regarded as little short of treason. The fact that Sonny and Cher achieved a simultaneous number 1 hit on both sides of the Atlantic with the infectious 'I Got You Babe' while the Kinks' career floundered, no doubt added salt to the wounds. Even Page was felled by the ensuing events, amid which the struggle for power over the Kinks' management was gradually resolved. Without having to lift a finger, the Collins and Wace team found themselves assuming absolute control of the Kinks' managerial affairs from this point onwards. Robert Wace feels that Larry Page's downfall was mainly due to his inability to win the confidence of the Kinks at a crucial time:

> The point is that management is all about relationships. With due respect, you *don't* leave an artist during their first American tour! While he was in America as our representative he was, to all intents and purposes, the manager . . . He blew his stack . . . He ran into Sonny and Cher and at the first sign of the grass being greener he fucks off . . . We wanted Page out and we gave him enough rope to hang himself. And that's exactly what he did. Dave was particularly upset. They came off the plane and Ray and Dave said, 'Get rid of Larry Page! We don't ever want to see him again. We want *out* of any involvement with Page, Kassner Music, Denmark Productions . . . thank you, goodnight! End of story.[5]

Of course, far from being the end of the story, the American disaster was merely a prelude to further managerial wrangling between Page and his adversaries. In the court cases that would later decree Page's fate, much was made of the allegation that he had left the Kinks 'in the lurch'. Larry still denies that there was any substance in this:

> I'd had enough. If I hadn't left I'd have had a nervous breakdown! . . . Of course I didn't leave them in the lurch. I left Sam Curtis there; I left the publisher there; I left the agent there. They were *very* well looked after. Sam Curtis was a very efficient roadie.[9]

Robert Wace was less than convinced by this explanation:

> That group were capable of anything – you couldn't leave them. They were capable of getting involved in a fight . . . or getting knifed. Grenville and I were on subsequent U.S. tours. If even on one morning we decided to leave and not tell Ray I would not expect to manage them on my return.[6]

It should be noted, however, that Page missed only seven days of a twenty-seven-day tour. Clearly, Wace's conception of managerial duties differed considerably from those of Page. While in the States, Larry saw his role as not merely custodial, but promotional. He expended much effort in helping Kassner with publishing deals, even turning up at Dean Martin recording sessions and attempting to persuade him to record Davies's compositions. Meanwhile, Kassner was working feverishly pushing

Davies's publishing and, according to Page, could even be seen on the streets outside theatres flogging sheet music. With so many important avenues opening, the least of Page's responsibilities was to be a nursemaid. Having completed the more important business in the States, he felt an urgent need to return to London.

Page's viewpoint was supported by Curtis who maintains that the controversial departure was of minimal importance at that stage of the game. Indeed, Curtis went as far as to question the necessity of Page's presence in America and implies that he may as well have stayed at home with Collins and Wace:

> I could see no reason that he had to be there other than that they wanted him at their beck and call . . . Page leaving made no difference at all. They wanted Larry there as a whipping boy, somebody to have a go at, or make problems for. If Larry wasn't there they couldn't make problems. He probably realised that was the situation when he left. He must have realised they were doing this. Ray's attitude was 'You're earning money out of me – have trouble!'[2]

Certainly Page's departure did not open the doors of anarchy within the Kinks camp. According to Curtis, the Kinks were no less stable without their manager's presence and effectively survived the remainder of their tiring schedule:

> Larry could not make them perform better. He didn't have to arrange their transport, or put them to bed at night or get them up in the mornings, or get their meals, I did . . . If there was no Ray causing problems then Larry wouldn't have to sort them out. And if Larry wasn't there, Ray couldn't make problems because there was nobody there to make them to. He couldn't make problems for me because I just ignored them. For example, in Hawaii, the shirts got stolen. And Ray said, 'No way am I going onstage without my shirt'. So I turned around and said to him '*Great* don't go on!' So they went on.[2]

The Kinks' anger with Page was increased at the end of the tour when they found themselves banned for 'unprofessional conduct'. Although Page could hardly be held responsible for the decision, his absence during the crisis was frowned upon. Years after that fateful tour, Davies still seemed uncertain of the precise reasons responsible for the Kinks' exile:

> We were banned for three years by some sort of union – for alleged things we were supposed to have done on tour. Just asking for our pay. People didn't want to pay us and we started lawsuits. America's a strange place. You get involved in that sort of thing; it's like a blacklist. It wasn't connected with the group as such, the former members, it was political,

> and as a result the record sales dropped there, with the exception of two. Then after writing letters of apology to the people . . . I shouldn't really be saying this because they'll probably read it and ban us again. But after various negotiations we were allowed back. The ban was lifted in '68.[22]

Although the group were not given specific reasons for the ban, Page believes that the decision was prompted by a combination of factors stemming mainly from Davies's outrageousness:

> Basically, the Kinks were bad news. If you refuse to appear because there's a black drummer or you go on T.V. and start talking about your sexual habits when you're asked about your hobbies what can you expect? Everybody knew if they booked the Kinks they were in for problems. And the word goes round and no doubt they have their reasons for banning. That really was it.[9]

It is no exaggeration to say that the abortive American tour seriously hampered the development of the Kinks' career. Physically and emotionally they had invested everything in the visit, even slaving away on the British live circuit for six months in order to prepare themselves for the ordeal. The American dream was rendered a fiasco of cataclysmic proportions and to make matters worse, rivals such as Herman's Hermits, Freddie and the Dreamers and Wayne Fontana and the Mindbenders were effortlessly sailing to the top of the U.S. charts. Without the possibility of touring or appearing on U.S. television the Kinks had absolutely no chance of competing, even with less talented opposition. All that was left was sadness, resentment and an unfortunate exile that reduced the Kinks' American reputation to that of a semi-obscure cult group.

FIVE

A Legal Matter

The bitterness caused by the failure to conquer America weakened Page's control over the Kinks and allowed Collins and Wace to shift the balance of power in their favour. Page maintains that the society duo systematically poisoned his relationship with Davies, thereby setting in motion one of the most famous legal battles in pop history:

> The package worked but . . . Collins and Wace did what I could have done. It's as simple as that . . . I think if we'd been able to continue without interference from the Hooray Henrys we would still have been in a very good situation . . . Ray is a fantastic talent. I liked Ray and if I'd had him on my own I could have straightened him out. That I know.[9]

Page's chances of winning back Davies's favour were further damaged by the release of an instrumental album, *Kinky Music*, which consisted of orchestral versions of many of the Kinks' best known songs. Ray was apparently less than pleased with the work. Page, however, regarded the album as an excellent marketing exercise and a tribute to Davies's ability as a composer. Even today, Larry maintains that the instrumental album was a perfect example of his astuteness in enhancing Davies's reputation and he appears incredulous at any alternative suggestion:

> I was out to boost him as a writer. That was the whole idea of *Kinky Music*. It was to boost his melodies. I spent a bloody lot of money doing the album to show to people that apart from the 'You Really Got Mes' he could write beautiful melodies. He got every penny that was due to him.[9]

Unfortunately, without the group's trust Page's chances of continuing as personal manager were virtually non-existent. Talmy seems particularly annoyed about demo recordings that Page produced in the States, even though Larry points out that the release of such material and the choice of product ultimately lay with Louis Benjamin and Pye Records:

> I couldn't do that. We went into Gold Star studios in the States. Ray had some things that he'd done. He wanted to record in the States so we

did it. But we had no power to release whatsoever . . . Shel had a contract. They were signed to Pye. Pye could nominate exactly who they wanted to. But as to 'rivalry', what are you saying? I thought with some of the songs Shel was doing . . . the demos were better. To me, producing is a lot more than being in the studio – it's getting the thing right before you get there, which we always made sure was done.[8]

Obviously, as a manager, and later a producer of the Troggs, Page had forthright ideas about how the group should be handled and recorded. His attitude towards Collins, Wace and Talmy speaks volumes about his ambition and unwillingness to delegate on important matters. The complex power structure that controlled the Kinks' affairs was impossible to tamper with without causing potentially disastrous results. Page evidently realised this, but proceeded to follow his ideas and beliefs to their logical conclusion. Unlike his business colleagues, Page was clearly unsuited to a co-management deal that kept his powers in check. Denied creative control by Pye and contractually restrained by Collins and Wace, Page's only real hope for total control of the Kinks lay in the whims of Ray Davies, who was himself influenced by his younger brother and the other parties. It was an impossible situation and, in retrospect, one cannot help being amazed that this delicate balance was maintained even as long as eighteen months.

Following his return to England, Page assumed that he was still in control of the Kinks, unaware of the plans of the others. For several weeks all went well and it seemed that Wace was reluctant to take immediate action. He visited Larry to discuss various matters but gave no hint that any obligations had been broken by his returning home. Ray also made several phone calls to Page and, apart from a sarcastic reference to his abrupt departure, appeared friendly and cooperative. On 2 August, however, Wace took Ray to see his solicitor, Michael Simkins, who devised a plan by which they could be rid of Page. The following day, an unusual incident happened at Pye Studios where Page was attempting to record one of Davies's songs with Sonny and Cher:

Even as their publisher I tried to make him an important writer. I wanted another Lennon and McCartney in one man . . . But when I did 'I Go To Sleep' with Sonny and Cher at Pye he broke into the studio and said: 'Larry, you're stealing my song!' That was the man's mind.[9]

Ray recalls this bitter outburst during which he revealed the true depth of his disillusionment:

I said, 'Get out of the studio. I don't want anything to do with you – get out of my life', and I just told him I did not want him to steal my ideas any more. I did not say 'songs', I said 'ideas'.[33]

The fact that Davies's temperamental explosion took place during Page's recording of a rival group strongly suggests that one of the major factors causing the break up was jealousy. Although Page was perfectly within his rights to manage or record another group, there seems little doubt that Ray's possessiveness precipitated the final split. Wace fully concurred with this theory:

> Artists are very jealous people, and you could say, 'Hell hath no fury like a woman spurned'. They do not like to think that one of their managers is out having a romance with another act . . . If they're paying somebody, they want attention. They don't want it thrown in their faces.[6]

Following the emotional exchange of 3 August there was clearly no going back for Ray Davies who left the Page problem in the hands of Wace's solicitor, Mr Simkins. On 2 September Denmark Productions (Page and Kassner) received a letter from Simkins on behalf of the three senior Kinks stating that their original agreement with Boscobel (Collins and Wace) was unenforceable because of their then 'infancy'. Simkins added that Collins and Wace had committed a fundamental breach of their contract with the Kinks by entering into an agreement with Kassner and Page on 26 February 1964 without the group's consent. According to Simkins' extraordinary letter, the Kinks had been blissfully unaware that Collins and Wace had assigned management and publicity rights to Denmark Productions, even though these provisions had now been in operation for eighteen months. Meanwhile, a fresh agreement was drawn up between Boscobel Productions and the Kinks stipulating that managerial duties be exclusively provided by Collins and Wace. Kassner and Page immediately instructed their solicitors to write to Boscobel threatening legal action if the terms of Simkins' letter were executed. On 14 September 1965, Collins and Wace duly replied to Denmark Productions' solicitor with a letter that would later prove crucial to the outcome of the court case:

> We received your letter of September 8 and we would like to point out that there is no quarrel between our company and your clients, Denmark Productions Ltd, and as far as we are concerned there has been no breach by us of the above agreement. We have had a letter from Mr Michael Simkins, solicitor, representing the Kinks, stating that our agreement with them is determined, which, in view of the fact that the Kinks have offered to renegotiate a contract with us on much the same lines as the last, with a special clause saying that we must not farm off any of the management responsibilities, we have decided to accept this fact.

Although couched in extremely friendly terms, this correspondence clearly gave notice that Collins and Wace no longer regarded themselves bound by their agreement with Page and Kassner. The gauntlet had been thrown down, but the cost of disentangling the Kinks from Larry Page was to prove greater than anyone could ever have imagined.

Ironically enough, a single they had recorded prior to the American tour was issued in August. 'See My Friend' was probably their most adventurous work to date, even though it had been recorded in only one and a half days after the 'Set Me Free' session. The single was possibly the earliest known example of raga rock, predating the Byrds' 'Why', the Yardbirds' 'Shape Of Things' and the Rolling Stones' 'Paint It Black' by almost a year. Ray had apparently been inspired to write the song after listening to Indian music in his favourite restaurant. Indeed, Davies had a strong interest in Eastern culture and occasionally went to see Indian films in order to assimilate the wailing drone-like sound of the sitar. Although Ray hoped to include a genuine sitar on the single, producer Shel Talmy found it impossible to locate a musician capable of playing the instrument. As a compromise Shel tuned the Kinks' guitars down and double tracked them in order to create the desired effect. Talmy recalls how he stimulated Davies's interest in Indian music:

> I was doing some recordings with John Marc of the Marc Almond Band. He was a great guitarist and had started listening to Indian stuff. He wrote a song based on a drum, raga influenced. It was very melodic and I played it for Ray. The next day he came back with 'See My Friend'. That's how we did it . . . It was way ahead of its time. It was only because it was the Kinks that it charted because it was very much a departure.[11]

Apart from its innovative raga tinge 'See My Friend' boasted some intriguing lyrics that revealed strong undertones of homosexuality in the tale of a jilted guy who seeks alternative companionship. Perhaps in order to avoid the possibility of a radio ban the track often appeared as 'See My Friends' and in the song Davies sings both titles, cleverly maintaining the ambiguity. The single was undoubtedly one of the most original of the year and deserved to scale greater heights than the bottom rungs of the Top 10. Ray may have been relatively disappointed at its chart placing but his comments at the time suggest an almost total disillusionment with the mechanics of the pop world:

> 'See My Friend' could be the group's last single. I'm hoping we don't have to make singles again.[34]

In the primitive pop world of 1965, it was unlikely that Davies had considered albums as a viable alternative so his words were probably a couched warning of the possible break up of the Kinks.

Although the group's sudden spirit of innovation had been largely ignored by the pop world, one person admitted to being strongly influenced by their recent work – Pete Townshend of the Who. In terms of chronological and artistic development the Kinks and the Who were destined to follow a parallel path. Townshend, like Davies, was another of the art school brigade; although on different record labels the groups shared the same producer, Shel Talmy. Neither unit made great headway as a U.S. chart act in the post-Mersey Beat boom; both groups were involved in controversial lawsuits that affected their recording schedules; and they each had lean spells in the singles charts towards the end of the 60s before finally emerging as albums artists. In terms of commercial success, the main difference between the groups was that whereas the Kinks peaked early with three mid-60s chart-toppers, the Who never achieved a number 1 hit but outflanked their rivals with album sales and related conceptual works during the 70s.

With 'See My Friend' climbing the charts and their managers busy dealing with the Larry Page situation, the Kinks embarked on a brief European tour. Incredibly, they managed to create even greater pandemonium than on their recent U.S. visit. In Berlin, they played before a frenzied audience of 20,000 and at one point were pounced upon by fifty screaming girls while security guards looked on disinterestedly. The organisers of the gig had unwittingly created a blueprint for chaos. Since the seats were not numbered, the volatile fans were inevitably fighting amongst themselves in order to secure the best possible view. There were no restrictions placed on the consumption of alcohol and many over-excited punters arrived laden with crates of beer which they merrily drank prior to the groups' arrival. To make matters worse, the Kinks were supported by one of the all-time great lunatics of pop, Screaming Lord Sutch, whose antics made them look positively tame. Sutch had been the scene's most infamous raver since 1960 and had even hit the headlines in the national press in a vain attempt to become a member of parliament representing his self-styled Teenage Party. During the appearance at the Berlin Waldbuhne, Sutch pulled out all the stops. He began the set by chopping up part of the stage with an axe, and during his infamous 'Jack The Ripper' demolished a life-size dummy and promptly set it alight, much to the amazement of the stage hands. He even managed to emulate the Kinks' onstage violence by accidently stabbing his saxophonist. Like Avory's head splitting cymbal assault, Sutch's savagery caused a near riot. By the time the Kinks took the stage, the audience was totally out of control and the opening chords of 'You Really Got Me' pushed them over the edge. Demented fans climbed onstage and attempted to devour their heroes while the more drunken clientele threw bottles indescriminately, injuring a number of people. Following the gig, ambulance staff were left to pick up the pieces while the remaining fans staggered home causing considerable damage to public transport. The papers had a field day condemning the long-haired, rabble-rousing English groups, but little comment was passed on the poor organisation that had precipitated the riot. The noteriety of the Kinks/Sutch amalgam was so great that both groups were refused meals in restaurants. Following the Berlin debacle the Kinks were met by a police escort and driven to a large concrete bunker where they were imprisoned behind iron gates. This, it transpired, was the group's dressing-room and they were only allowed into the auditorium through a complex network of underground tunnels. The authorities had evidently decided on a belated clampdown. In Bremen, the Kinks complained about the heavy-handed way in which the police went about ensuring that the audience remained seated throughout their set, but it was all to no avail. Controversy, irritation and exhaustion dogged the tour, so perhaps it was not so surprising that, on their return to Britain, Ray hinted that the group might split.

Davies's contention that 'See My Friend' could be the last Kinks single remained a distinct possibility until the end of the year. In the meantime, Ray hit the headlines as 'Britain's £100,000 a year songwriter'. With the Kinks in hibernation a number of artists were rushing to record Davies songs including Dave Berry ('This Strange Effect'), the Cascades ('Bet You Won't Stay'), the Majority ('A Little Bit Of Sunlight' and 'Ring The Bells'), Bobby Rydell ('When I See That Girl Of Mine') and the Applejacks, Cher and Peggy Lee ('I Go To Sleep'). Once again, Page's involvement in these transactions should not be underestimated. According to one source, Davies is reputed to have made a quarter of a million pounds from Peggy Lee's recording of 'I Go To Sleep', though that figure remains hearsay. In spite of the prestige and career development offered by such covers Davies apparently resisted Page's attempts to establish him as a major songwriting talent. Shel Talmy who was also responsible for recording Davies's songs with a variety of artists, believes that Ray is still tragically underrated as a contemporary songwriter:

> Had Ray wanted to, he could have been the biggest singer-songwriter from this country as a solo. He obviously never wanted to and needed the security of a band . . . I think he's one of the great songwriters of our time. He should have been right up there with Lennon/McCartney and is not. He never had the publicity that the Beatles had. In the public's eye he was never as revered as Lennon and McCartney. Kassner worked as a collection agency . . . Davies is still basically an undiscovered asset. There are lots of songs there that could be done successfully now.[11]

Whatever the reasons for Davies's failure, the statistics tell their own story. With the exception of Dave Berry, none of the previously mentioned artists managed to place a Davies composition in the charts. As the year drew to a close the press duly noted that the Kinks were slipping and several journalists believed that their days as a chart act were numbered. Such criticism was not unwarranted as the Kinks were suddenly besieged with lawsuits from every angle. In his determination not to surrender his management interests in the group Larry Page issued a writ against Grenville Collins and Robert Wace for alleged breach of contract. The Kinks found themselves in the centre of the crossfire and remained hapless pawns in an incredible power game. While Page contested the Kinks' management, his partner in Denmark Street Productions took action to protect his publishing interests. Kassner claimed publishing rights on all Davies compositions and applied for an injunction to prevent the release of the group's new single 'Till The End Of The Day'. Although Eddie Kassner failed to prevent the disc appearing in November, his efforts sufficiently intimidated the B.B.C. for them to ban the Kinks from performing on the Joe Loss Show. Further bans were threatened by the influential television pop shows *Thank Your Lucky Stars* and *Ready Steady Go*, forcing Belinda to produce court orders in order to save the record from extinction. Fortunately, 'Till The End Of The Day' was a powerful enough single to warrant the bitter controversy. A strident rocker in the vein of 'You Really Got Me', it demonstrated the Kinks' continued ability to produce classic three-minute singles. Although the disc failed to crack the Top 5, it stayed in the charts for almost three months. Considering the five month hiatus, the modest success of the single was probably a relief to every member of the group. Although Davies was still capable of being upset by the negative attitude of the press towards the Kinks' chart placing, he was now mature enough to treat the Top 10 game with cynicism:

> People always say you're slipping as soon as you don't soar to the top of the charts with your newest single. As far as the press is concerned we started slipping as soon as we became popular. But it's when you become less popular that you improve. Maybe we're slipping Pop 50 wise because we're not a 'pop' group in the accepted here-today-gone-tomorrow sense of the word. We are more than that. We play pop music but we are four different personalities who are continuing to improve as a group and that has been our aim all along.[32]

Ray continued his tirade against the press:

> The papers are getting very upset because they built us up and then as soon as we made it, started knocking us. It must be galling somebody somewhere that we're as popular as ever in the ballrooms and theatres. They think they can make you and break you, but if the fans like you, nothing the papers say will stop them coming back.[32]

While 'Till The End Of The Day' was in the charts Ray's wife Rasa gave birth to a daughter, Louisa Claire Rasita. During the same month an E.P. *Kwyet Kinks* was issued featuring a controversial song, 'Well Respected Man'. This was the first example of Davies's satire and heralded a new approach to songwriting that would continue to develop throughout his future career. The song was originally conceived in the unlikely setting of a plush Exeter hotel at which Rasa and Ray were staying during her pregnancy. The posh residents recognised Davies as the lead singer of the Kinks and frequently invited him to play a round of golf. It was Ray's distaste for these sycophants that prompted him to write one of his most scathing compositions of the 60s:

> The 60s was a lie, a total lie. I said, 'I'm not gonna play fucking golf with you. I'm not gonna be your caddy so you can say you played with a pop singer.' So I decided I was gonna use words more and say things. I wrote 'Well Respected Man'. That was the first real word-oriented song I wrote.[35]

The single was a brilliant send-up of the hypocrisy of the aspiring middle-classes and like all Davies songs the tone was sardonic rather than bitter. It is generally accepted among the Kinks' business associates that the song was written about their manager Robert Wace, whom they occasionally dubbed 'Bob the snob'. Probably one of the greatest blunders in the Kinks' career was the failure to release the song as a single. It was not only original but catchy, witty and extremely topical. The sales of the E.P. and the radio exposure received by the song, even in competition with 'Till The End Of The Day', suggest most forcibly that it would have been a pre-Christmas number 1. With nothing to lose in the States the track was issued there as a single in December and in spite of the Kinks non-availability climbed as high as number 13 in the Hot 100.

In the meantime, Ray momentarily distanced himself from the legal hassles by concentrating on his songwriting. He had hoped to complete a lyric for a satirical song about *Ready Steady Go* which he intended to perform on the Christmas edition but it remained uncompleted. Instead, Ray agreed to sing a self-mocking rendition of 'All I Want For Christmas Is My Two Front Teeth'. In more serious moments, Ray discussed his intention of including narratives in the middle of Kinks songs in order to demonstrate his lyrical sophistication. In spite of the traumas of 1965 Davies was even more ambitious and determined to extend the Kinks' musical boundaries:

> I'm trying to take pop music a step further now. We all came to a halt after the Righteous Brothers recorded 'You've Lost That Loving Feeling'. That was the end. It was the perfect pop disc – as far as anyone could go. Everyone has been influenced by that disc . . . I'm working on an L.P. with a jazz pianist friend of mine and we are trying to take the music

further, working on the lines established by the Righteous Brothers. For example, I have a number about an actor who dies. At his death a whole orchestra sweeps in from nowhere.[36]

Ray's conception sounds suspiciously like a prototype rock opera, a notion that even the Beatles had yet to consider. Davies's determination to become the British counterpart of Phil Spector would not be easily achieved, while his emphasis on the importance of composing indicated a strong temptation to revert to studio work:

> I've been half-way to giving up the Kinks on a number of occasions. Then I do a gig with the boys and we see all those kids have a raving time and are enjoying what we are doing so I change my mind, but one day I may get three-quarter ways to giving up and that will be the end for me.[36]

It would take all of Davies's resilience to resist the temptation of retiring in the New Year.

SIX

19th Nervous Breakdown

The Stateside success of 'A Well Respected Man' prompted Ray Davies to announce the imminent release of further E.P.s satirising unconventional trends and fashions. Apparently, this policy was designed to enable Davies to fulfil his new role as social critic without sacrificing the raw spontaneity associated with the Kinks' most successful singles. *The Kinks Kontroversy*, released in January 1966, revealed the group at an important crossroads. Although the album included some slower numbers it was essentially a farewell to the r'n'b style they had employed at the beginning of their career. The one non-Davies composition, 'Milk Cow Blues', was a stunning example of the group's raw power with some exceptional lead-guitar by Dave Davies. The calypso influenced 'I'm On An Island' hinted at more novel work in the future, while 'Where Have All The Good Times Gone?' showed Ray's determination to include an interesting lyric within the context of an old fashioned three-minute rock workout. According to Ray, the album was conceived and completed very quickly and unlike some of their earlier efforts the songs were written specifically for the project. Apparently, the group regarded this as their most unified work to date, but ultimately *The Kinks Kontroversy* emerges as an uneasy transitional work and over the years its contents have all but been ignored by the anonymous compilers of multitudinous anthologies.

One of the reasons for the Kinks' continued success on vinyl was their no nonsense attitude in the studio. Shel Talmy reveals that, unlike many of his contemporaries, he successfully avoided any major confrontations with the Davies brothers:

> I never had problems in the studio. You don't keep beating your head against the wall if you don't get on . . . I like to think that I'm a pro. I go in, I rehearse the band, we rehearse the songs and do the arrangements. I did not get involved in their social life or the bickering they were doing between themselves . . . Ray could be difficult at times; Dave was drinking a lot in those day. But it was nothing terrible.[11]

Talmy's professionalism would sustain his working relationship with the Kinks for a considerable period.

While promoting their album, the Kinks visited Copenhagen and got involved in yet another controversial series of events. During their first date at the Tivoli Concert Hall in the famous Tivoli Gardens (a splendid amusement park in a setting of towering trees and sparkling fairy lights) the Kinks unwittingly caused a riot. Forty policemen were called in as 2,000 fans experienced the now familiar symptoms of Kinkmania. Ray Davies remembers it as a bizarre evening:

> It was total chaos. The only thing that didn't get smashed was a big picture of Jim Reeves! . . . Dave got carried away, about forty policeman had arrived to arrest him. It was a bit of a desperate situation because we were supposed to fly to London for the *N.M.E.* pollwinners' concert the next day so we had to bail him out fast and pay off a huge damage bill.[24]

Upon returning to England, the Kinks discussed their next choice of single. Dave Davies was anxious to record a folk rock song but commercial considerations pressurised them into releasing their projected E.P. track 'Dedicated Follower Of Fashion'. The song was an amusingly cynical riposte directed at the fashion-conscious trendsetters of Swinging London. Like many of Davies's satirical works, 'Dedicated Follower Of Fashion' was inspired by a particular incident that stung the pop singer into songwriting action:

> That song came after I'd had a violent punch-up at a party. All these awful 60s trendsetters would come around and wear the latest fashions and I would have on a pullover . . . Anyway, it was an appalling party and these people were making snide remarks about me, so I had a punch-up with this fashion designer. I said: 'Alright, I'm gonna write a song about him now, the dedicated follower of fashion.'[35]

The novelty appeal of the number, complete with Ray's camp vocal, gave the group their biggest chart hit since 'Tired Of Waiting For You' and earned Davies the dubious title of 'pop's George Formby'. The song was meant to satirise the fops of Carnaby Street, but the deliberately ostentatious persona that Ray created when performing the track led some people to regard it as a gay anthem. Ray was surprised by their interpretation:

> I didn't know I was writing that sort of song. I don't mind gay people, people who aren't gay, people who are unhappy, people who are happy – they can all come to our shows. Don't have to be one type of person to like our band. We even have animal lovers coming.[37]

In spite of all the confusion, Davies chose to revive his camp persona in later years, particularly during the glam rock period of the early 70s.

The success of 'Dedicated Follower Of Fashion' was a lifeline that needed to be grasped with both hands. Inevitably, another series of gigs was organised but prior to a prestigious Belgium tour Ray Davies fell seriously ill with influenza. Rather than cancel the tour Davies agreed to allow Mick Grace of the Cockneys to take his place in the group for the duration of the visit. Grace even managed to front the Kinks on a *Top Of The Pops* show prior to their departure. Fortunately, the Belgians accepted the substitution and the tour passed without incident. Upon returning to Britain, the Kinks expected Ray to resume his place in the group but his condition had worsened. His physical illness was no doubt irritated by the continued threat of litigation from his former publishers. In interviews of the period Ray described himself as 'very neurotic' and explained his eccentricities at some length:

> I worry about everything. One night I went round to Barry Fantoni's flat and then remembered that I'd left the tap dripping at home. It was on my mind all the time – in the end Barry had to run me back to Muswell Hill so I could turn it off. If it's cold I put an electric fire near my pipes to stop them freezing. I get worried about those pipes. I slept next to them once.[38]

While Ray was ordered 'complete rest', Mick Grace continued in his role as an auxiliary Kink for several more weeks.

By mid-April Ray had returned to the fold for a U.K. tour but further problems beset the group when Mick Avory fell victim to tonsillitis. Another temporary replacement was recruited in the form of Clem Cattini. Although a relative unknown Cattini boasted years of experience as a player in such units as Johnny Kidd and the Pirates, the Tornados and the Ivy League. A renowned session drummer, Cattini appeared regularly on Shel Talmy recordings and had recently ghosted for Avory on *The Kinks Kontroversy* for a paltry £9 fee. His appearance at the Nottingham Mecca went unnoticed by the Kinks' fans who were sufficiently distracted by Ray's welcome return.

During his convalescence, Davies had found time to write a staggering number of new songs, several of which were slated for imminent release. A forthcoming E.P. was announced with a track listing comprising 'The Reporter', 'A Girl Who Goes To Discotheques', 'Party Line' and 'End Of The Season'. Although the work mysteriously failed to appear three of the tracks were salvaged for subsequent albums. 'The Reporter', a scathing attack on pop journalists, was the strongest cut of all. Essentially a protest song in Dylanesque style, the lyrics revealed Davies at his most bitter: 'Hey, Mr Reporter, how about talking about yourself . . . I'll *kill* you Mr Reporter.' Fearing a backlash from the mid-60s pop press, the management reluctantly vetoed the song, even though they were fully aware of its quality. The same fate apparently befell 'Everybody Wants To Be A Personality', a satire on film actor, Charlton Heston. Not surprisingly,

Ray's songwriting spree led to a spate of cover versions and requests for demos from a diverse selection of recording artists. The interest of Barry Fantoni ('Little Man In A Little Box'), Leapy Lee ('King Of The Whole Wide World') and the Pretty Things ('House In The Country') prompted bigger names such as David Garrick, the Animals and the Walker Brothers to consider Davies compositions for inclusion on future albums. Ray was characteristically modest about his new found reputation as one of Britain's foremost singer-songwriters:

> I don't look on myself as the star songwriter of the moment. It's just that people used to visualise my songs as impossible for anyone else. But now, because I'm having hits, they realise my songs might be worthwhile for them too. You can say the same about Paul Simon who, as far as I'm concerned, is much more in demand than me at the moment. A year ago when he didn't have hits but was still writing some good stuff, nobody was interested. Now they all fall over themselves to record Paul Simon songs. Dylan's another example.[39]

Davies's reputation as a songwriter increased in successive months, but he was denied the commercial success that Dylan and Simon had achieved with their compositions. The Uglys, the Thoughts, Mo and Steve, Gates of Eden and the Attraction each recorded new Davies songs but failed to make any impact on the charts.

While Davies was selecting fourteen tracks from a shortlist of forty for the Kinks' forthcoming album, his fellow members were voicing their present feelings to the ever inquisitive pop press. Avory admitted that the boredom and lack of enthusiasm evident in recent Kinks' television performances was primarily a result of the frustration of spending seven hours rehearsing and waiting to appear for a three and a half-minute slot. The group's continued criticism of such pop shows as *Ready Steady Go* won them no new friends in the business. If Avory seemed bored, Dave Davies was blasé to the point of arrogance in commenting upon the group's future:

> We don't care about five years time. We'll probably be blown up, that *is* the fashionable thing to answer, isn't it? We've done everything we wanted to do, so it won't matter when we get blown up. We are a hit. What more is there? Changes in pop don't bother us, why should they? We can dictate what we want to do. We don't have to go by public fads any more.[40]

While the comments of Davies and Avory seemed a typical example of self-conscious outrageousness, the tone of a world-weary Peter Quaife was much more alarming. Journalists noted that Quaife suddenly seemed the outsider in the group and there were strong hints that his interest in script-writing was greater than his pop star aspirations. Unlike his fellow members Quaife was all too willing to discuss a possible future as a non-Kink:

> I plan my life in stages. At first I was a nothing. Then I became a Kink. This set me up financially and socially, and people wanted to know me. So I decided to go to another stage in my life and make another career. I have been offered a place at college in California, where they run a two-year course in script-writing. I can't go yet because of my work with the Kinks. But I shall go when that work is over.[41]

Further veiled hints followed in successive weeks as Peter uncharacteristically derided the petty world of pop music:

> What is happening? Are we in the entertainment profession becoming a circle of senile old men and women, gossiping about each other for the sake of it? I'm sure we are. And I feel no one is innocent – members of groups, publicity agents, managers and the press are all guilty, including myself. We nowadays read, write and talk gossip, slander and stupid sarcasm. For God's sake let us stop, and grow up. If not let's get out and leave this business to the real professionals.[42]

Quaife's departure from the Kinks was to be sooner than anyone realised.

The Kinks' perennial problems on the live circuit showed little sign of abating during the spring. A projected appearance at the Edgware Town football ground was abruptly cancelled following a row with the Small Faces over top billing. In persuading the Faces to appear, the promoters had apparently offered them the star spot, much to the chagrin of Kinks' manager Robert Wace who refused to compromise his group's integrity by allowing them to appear as support. Rather than involving themselves in further controversy the Kinks adjourned to the recording studio in early June to complete work on their next album. It was destined to be their most ambitious work to date, an eighteen-track recording with each cut linked by additional sounds and musical interpolations. Thunderstorm effects, bongos, a metronome and a shepherd's pipe were some of the surprises revealed by Ray Davies. Mick Avory also promised his singing debut with a new Davies composition entitled 'Lilacs and Daffodils'. The early recordings were completed quickly and on the first day the group cut 'Fallen Idol', 'End Of The Season', 'Most Exclusive Residence For Sale' and 'Dandy'. In the meantime, their latest single 'Sunny Afternoon' had just entered the Top 30 and was selling faster than even 'Dedicated Follower Of Fashion'. The song had been written around the time of their previous hit following a particularly painful interview between Ray and his accountant. 'Sunny Afternoon' was a classic example of Davies's wit and the best Kinks single for over a year. The song was less critical in its satire than either 'Dedicated Follower of Fashion' or 'A Well Respected

Man' and demonstrated a new maturity in manipulating the listener's point of view. Indeed, Davies almost presents a stoical grandeur in his deft portrayal of the aristocrat who loses his wealth while maintaining a stubborn pride in appreciating the pleasantries of a lazy sunny afternoon. Like all of Davies's satirical compositions the overstatement associated with mid-60s protest songs has been studiously avoided. 'Sunny Afternoon' was coupled with the finest flip-side of the Kinks' career: 'I'm Not Like Everybody Else'. The track was possibly Davies's most intense and emotional performance on record. This sustained attack on institutional conformity began quietly as a plea for individuality and ended as a screaming crescendo. Davies had originally offered the song to the Animals, no doubt connecting the theme with 'We Gotta Get Out Of This Place'. Sadly, Eric Burdon never got to sing what would undoubtedly have been a powerhouse vocal performance.

After five weeks in the charts, 'Sunny Afternoon' replaced the Beatles' 'Paperback Writer' at number 1, an achievement that silenced many of the Kinks' critics. Almost inevitably, the celebrations were forestalled by further problems in the Kinks' camp. The accident-prone Peter Quaife and road manager Peter Jones were seriously injured when their car hit an articulated lorry on the M6 near Warrington. Jones was thrown through the windscreen and suffered severe head injuries, a fractured pelvis, broken nose and the loss of several teeth, while Quaife was concussed with a head wound and multiple fractures of the left foot. Doctors estimated that the injury would prevent Quaife from performing for at least six weeks but that prediction was to prove overly optimistic. While searching for a replacement, the Kinks were reduced to performing on *Thank Your Lucky Stars* as a trio. Lightning auditions followed before a suitable candidate was discovered in John Dalton, a former member of the Mark Four. John had been working as a lorry driver for the past six months and was pleased to accept the offer of four weeks employment in an internationally famous pop group. Dalton's induction proved a baptism of fire as he had to appear on *Top Of The Pops* miming 'Sunny Afternoon', a number he had only heard twice before. John recalls this eventful debut:

> I didn't even have time to come home and change into any new clothes. I had to borrow some from our road managers. It was the first time I'd stood in front of the cameras and I must have looked really petrified.[43]

Further problems were in store for him when the Kinks flew out to Spain for a three-night stint at the Yulia Club in Madrid. Taking advantage of their weak position, the wily proprietor demanded a reduction in the Kinks' fee because of Quaife's absence. The Kinks remained firm and refused to appear, arguing that the manager had been informed of Quaife's injury prior to their departure. Unperturbed, the manager informed the police who promptly confiscated the Kinks' working permits and threatened to arrest Dalton.

When Robert Wace heard the news he feared that the Kinks' next date in Oslo would have to be cancelled. In desperation, he phoned Sam Curtis who was despatched to Madrid in order to pacify the police and escort the boys to Scandinavia. The almost impossibly tight timing forced Curtis to plot an extraordinary route. Boarding a plane from Madrid to Paris the group then returned to Gatwick and transferred to a Dutch Airlines flight bound for Copenhagen. From there a private plane took them to Oslo, blowing a tyre along the way. Curtis recalls the climax of this eventful trip:

> We eventually got to Oslo at 1.30 – 2 00 a.m. and the audience were still waiting! We did the show and we'd been going a good twenty-four hours from Madrid. The show finished at about 3.00 a.m. just as the sun was rising. While I went back to bed shattered, absolutely out like a light, they went down to the beach to go swimming. No matter how tough it was they were young people and they had the energy to do it.[2]

The Madrid fiasco ended with a lawyer suing the Yulia club for £10,000 in another absurd chapter in the Kinks' legal history.

On returning to England the Kinks encountered further criticism when they refused to sing either 'Sunny Afternoon' or 'Dedicated Follower Of Fashion' at Jimmy Savile's Manchester club. Ray argued that these slower satirical numbers could not be integrated into the group's repertoire without seriously affecting the pace of the show. Perhaps to pacify his detractors Davies promised a new style Kinks show in the future, even indicating the likelihood of abandoning clubs and ballrooms in order to concentrate on summer season cabaret. Without a hint of irony, Ray promised to introduce a comedy routine and felt that the future of the group might well lie in pantomime. (Perhaps he was suggesting that the business affairs of the group had been reduced to the level of farce.) The new album, originally intended for release in July, was delayed indefinitely pending the results of a court order. In order to break the deadlock Ray flew to New York and signed a management deal with that renowned trouble-shooter of pop, Allen Klein. The Rolling Stones had already entrusted Klein with their U.S. affairs and Davies was convinced that he was the one man capable of winning the Kinks' battle over their song publishing rights. Robert Wace stresses that Klein's involvement with the Kinks was less significant than his controversial relationships with bigger acts:

> I'd been friendly with Peter Grant and he said that I should bring in Klein because we weren't making a lot of money. We neither made nor lost in the Klein situation. He didn't have *that* much to do with the

> Kassner thing. His real job was to get a hell of a lot of money from Warners in the States. And he never really brought it off. Allen never did anything harmful to the Kinks whereas he may have been a bit more dangerous where the Beatles and Stones were concerned. I think he was rather put off by my and Grenville's background.[5]

While Klein began the long drawn out negotiations with Pye, the Kinks' internal problems remained unresolved. By August, Quaife had still not returned to the group and was reported to be living in Denmark with his girlfriend, Annette Paustian. Rumours persisted that Peter was poised to join the advertising department of B.E.A. as a designer and retire from pop music. The following month twelve weeks of speculation ended with the announcement that John Dalton had replaced Peter Quaife as Kinks' bassist.

The enforced delay of their new album release encouraged the Kinks to accept a selection of continental bookings. However, they ran into further trouble following the cancellation of several gigs in Iceland, Copenhagen, Austria and Switzerland. The Scandinavian Musicians' Union took a dim view of the Kinks' capriciousness and banned them from appearing in Scandinavia in the future. When the group returned to England their agent Arthur Howes announced that he would be accepting no more bookings for the Kinks until the end of the year. Robert Wace took a dim view of the continually disrupted gig schedules:

> The cancellations were very tedious. It was down to Ray growing up. I got very bored and fed up with it. Very often I was angry with them because I don't like letting people down. A couple of promoters were hit very hard. It affected the Kinks' credibility as a live act. There was a period when they were very difficult to book. When their agency agreement with Arthur Howes ran out I had to *convince* Harold Davidson to take them on. He was very reluctant.[5]

With a simultaneous ban on recording and touring, the situation was nothing less than desperate.

Under pressure from the Kinks, Allen Klein pushed hard for an early settlement. In October, the wrangling with Louis Benjamin of Pye was amicably resolved leaving the Kinks free to record a single and release their album in time for the pre-Christmas sales rush. The new work, *Face To Face*, thankfully proved worthy of the delay and for the first time boasted fourteen Ray Davies compositions. The original idea of connecting each track with special musical effects was abandoned, thus depriving the Kinks of preempting the Beatles' *Sgt Pepper's Lonely Hearts Club Band* by a clear year. Nevertheless, the thunderstorms and splashing water were ingeniously included on such tracks as 'Rainy Day In June' and 'Holiday In Waikiki'.

The former was unlike any Kinks track yet recorded and the doom-laden imagery and musical effects were both fascinating and foreboding. The other unusual feature of the album was the extensive use of harpsichord by session man Nicky Hopkins. The album was undoubtedly the group's most diverse work to date, encompassing every aspect of Ray Davies's songwriting skill. 'Dandy', the humorous story of an ageing Casanova, recalled the mild satire of 'Dedicated Follower Of Fashion'. The 'Sunny Afternoon' theme of aristocratic degeneracy was repeated in such songs as 'House In The Country' and 'Most Exclusive Residence For Sale'. The former attacked the amorality of the successful businessman while the latter charted the inevitable decline of the aristocracy into debauchery and alcoholism. In order not to overburden the album with social commentary, Dave Davies was allowed a couple of inspired rockers in the form of 'Party Line' and 'You're Looking Fine'. The raga rock experiment begun on 'See My Friend' was briefly resurrected for the much underrated 'Fancy', while the previously discussed 'A Girl Who Goes To Discotheques' finally emerged as 'Little Miss Queen Of Darkness'. The album demonstrated fully Davies's new role as the Nöel Coward of rock. From this album onwards Davies would bite with the tooth of the satirist while maintaining a polite reluctance to draw any blood.

The new single, released in November, 'Dead End Street', proved the equal of any song from *Face To Face*. Ostensibly, an account of working-class deprivation in England, the song was originally conceived following a visit to New York:

> I had read a book about the life and times of Al Capone, the American gangster of years ago. I felt they were very similar to those we are experiencing today. My feelings were so strong the song emerged.[44]

Without doubt, 'Dead End Street' was Ray's most provocative social comment to date and indicated a possible future as one of rock's political spokesmen. For all his rebelliousness, however, Davies's growing obsession with England's aristocracy and dying traditions suggested that he was less an anarchist than a patriot:

> I hope England doesn't change. I'm writing a song now called 'You Ain't What You Used To Be' which expresses what I feel. I hope we don't get swallowed up by America and Europe. I'm really proud of being British . . . I don't care if a bloke votes Labour or Conservative as long as he appreciates what we've got here. We have so much that is great, compared with other countries, and people just don't realise it. I want to keep writing very English songs.[45]

Davies's jingoistic tirade contrasted markedly with the working-class heroics of 'Dead End Street' but it would be unfair to brand him a hypocrite. In effect, there was no real contradiction between 'Dead End Street' and 'Sunny Afternoon' since the viewpoints presented in both songs are virtually identical. In 'Dead End Street' the participants are portrayed as destitute, without work, money or even the hope of emigration. The situation is not so far removed from 'Sunny Afternoon' and 'Most Exclusive Residence For Sale' in which the aristocrat and the businessman are deprived of all their worldly goods. Davies's tone in all these songs is that of the sympathetic observer and the characters described fail to elicit any strong emotional response from the listener. Just as he respects the stiff upper lip of the aristocrat whose world has collapsed so Davies celebrates, with equal exuberance, the working-class fatalism of the inhabitants of 'Dead End Street'. The aristocrat stoically sips his beer and enjoys what he can of the sunny afternoon while the working-class family cease protesting and simply pour their tea and put some toast on. The contrasting social worlds are mirrored in a self-realisation that Davies appears to regard as quintessentially British.

'Dead End Street' was a solid Top 5 hit and a tribute to Ray's arranging skill as well as his songwriting technique. In recording the song, the group had employed two bass guitars, an electric twelve-string guitar, an acoustic twelve-string guitar, piano, trombone, drums and a French horn. In addition to its musical impact, Ray had taken an innovatory step by filming a video to accompany the Kinks' television performance of 'Dead End Street'. The video which featured Mick as a boy scout and the other Kinks as undertakers was deemed distasteful by the B.B.C. The ban proved particularly upsetting for Ray who had placed great faith in the idea of promotion through film feeling that it was a logical extension from the outmoded tradition of lip sync. It was doubly frustrating to be thwarted from making an apparently relevant observation on urban life:

> I don't like it when people are out of work and hungry, obviously. That's why I wrote 'Dead End Street'. I even made a film to go with the song on *Top Of The Pops*. But it showed slums and poverty and so they wouldn't run it. I guess they prefer films about running around in parks, jumping over chairs. I was upset by the refusal but was pleased to see that when *Panorama* showed a film about the slums they used 'Dead End Street' as the accompanying music. Our trouble at the moment is doing something new. Once you've had a number 1 record you can only repeat yourself. You go on *Top Of The Pops* and stand there and sing the song. We wanted a challenge, something different, which is why we did the film.

It is worth adding that the Kinks included another exceptionally strong flip side to 'Dead End Street' with 'Big Black Smoke', the story of a country girl who falls victim to the lure of the city. The track is most notable for the unusual sound effects such as the opening church bells and the town crier hollas of 'Oh yea' that bring the number to a bizarre close. Shel Talmy maintains that these high quality flip sides were a deliberate policy that Pye failed to exploit in promoting the group:

> We were trying to put out two good songs. If Pye had done their job properly they would have promoted them as double A-sides and both of them would have got up there. Whatever lack of success the Kinks had is strictly to do with Pye. It was a horrible label to be associated with.[11]

With the Kinks re-established as a chart act it was fitting that the year should close with the unexpected return of Peter Quaife. Apparently, Quaife found conventional employment even more soul-destroying than the hectic life of the Kinks and his new found talent as a short story writer proved insufficient to earn a living. His reappearance as a Kink forced Dalton to take up a new occupation as a coalman while saving up for his forthcoming marriage. Fittingly enough, the new Kinks repertoire was rehearsed in the scout hut at the back of Mick Avory's house, just like the old days. The new set included several recent Davies compositions as well as some surprise cover versions, including Bob Dylan's 'Absolutely Sweet Marie' and 'Most Likely You Go Your Way And I'll Go Mine'. What had for so long seemed the most disastrous year in the history of the Kinks with Ray's nervous breakdown, cancelled tours, litigation, injuries and group upheavals finally ended on a happy note. Although even at the end of the year, Ray was still casting serious doubts on the Kinks as a stable recording unit:

> I'm worried about Dave. Really I worry about Dave. I might leave the group but I want Dave to be financially and emotionally secure first. He's just beginning to find his feet.[46]

SEVEN

Silence is Golden

The legal battle between Larry Page and the Collins/Wace partnership dragged on into early 1967 and effectively prevented the Kinks from pursuing any live work. Following the riots and cancellations of the previous year, however, the ban was greeted as a well deserved break, particularly by Mick Avory:

> It's good for us really – having time to think as we have had lately. It has given us time to sort ourselves out. You find that you work so hard in this business, often having to do two shows a night and then travel many miles afterwards that you just don't have time to sit back and work out in your own mind precisely where you are going, and what you are trying to achieve. Having a break like this has given us a chance to discover ourselves, to think about the business side of our work, about the money, and the kind of work we would like to do in the future. We would all like to make a film, and in the future we will probably make just one British tour a year. If you keep going back to the same ballrooms you find you are just repeating yourselves. So now we want to make it an event every time we go back to a town.[47]

While the Kinks were formulating their future, the irrepressible Larry Page was pushing a claim to retain his 10 per cent interest. Since being abandoned by the Kinks, Larry had discovered another unknown group, the Troggs, and in establishing them as a chart act he simultaneously achieved production credits. His independent record label, Page One, was flourishing so the Kinks must have felt some reservations about meeting an adversary at the height of his powers. Eventually, the case was taken to the High Court where it was presided over by Mr Justice Widgery, who later became Lord Chief Justice.

It was an extraordinary case that had no precedent in the pop world. During the early stages of the hearing Page emerged in an extremely strong position. The argument that the original contract was invalid because of the Kinks' 'infancy' was dismissed as the judge felt they were mature enough to sign such an agreement. This, in itself, was a sensational decision very much to Page's advantage. The judge also dismissed the rather absurd suggestion that the Kinks had been unaware or did not approve of the assignments of management and publishing rights to Denmark Productions. Prior to the hearing, several amendments had been made to the defence, including the contention that the contract of 12 February 1964 (and thereby the assignment of 26 February 1964) had ended in April 1965 because fresh agreements had been entered into between Boscobel and the Kinks for tax avoidance purposes. Again, this was quickly dismissed by the judge who was all too aware of the Kinks' reliance on Larry Page throughout this period. It was conceded that Page was the person largely responsible for transforming the Kinks from profitless nonentities into a £90,000 a year group and several allegations casting aspersions on his conduct were deemed 'unfounded and not justified at all'. Page looked to have the case sewn up until Ray took the stand and by his testimony made it clear that a reconciliation was impossible. Davies was particularly acerbic when expressing his feelings towards Page following the U.S. tour:

> I hated him . . . because he made a promise to me, he had broken it, and left the group high and dry and it seems he rushed back making deals everywhere with our songs with other people, and I was disgusted with him.[33]

After considering all the evidence Justice Widgery dismissed Page's £6,000 court bid, decreeing that his contract with the group was 'frustrated' and no longer tenable. Extraordinarily enough, the defence of 'frustration' had only been included in the amendment less than twenty-four hours before the trial. What may have been regarded as an afterthought by the Kinks' solicitors proved the crucial point in Justice Widgery's summing up. The judge recalled the testimonies that had swayed his decision in the Kinks' favour:

> It was not until I saw the four members of the group in the witness box that I began to realise the seriousness of what Mr Page had done. Mr Page knew the group intimately, and could have foreseen their reaction. By his action he destroyed the trust that was vital for the continuance of a relationship between them.[48]

Page still believes that it was Davies's admission of hatred that put the verdict beyond doubt and those sentiments filled him with total disillusionment:

> I was always told in the music business that the artist is always the enemy, they're animals. I was told this with the Kinks as well. And I used to say, 'No, not these boys . . . they're different'. At the end of the day it proved to be right. It did. They were the enemy and they did turn out to be animals . . . The sad thing was I still admired Ray like mad as a writer and performer. And the group too – I loved the boys; I really did. They

were just pricks as human beings. That was the terrible thing. When it came to treating people with respect, they didn't like it . . . People were treated like dirt.[9]

The Kinks' former road-manager, Sam Curtis, fully concurred with Page's opinion in this damning comment on the brothers and their lifestyle:

They always spoke to people like dirt, including me . . . These people, the Davies brothers, are exceptional. *Very* exceptional. They are exceptional for their talent and they are exceptional for their *grossness*. They think that their talent entitles them to live in a world of unconventional disorder.[2]

While the behaviour of the Kinks was a crucial issue in the case, Robert Wace maintains that Page's hopes of retaining an interest in the group were doomed from the outset. More significantly, he stresses that the management clause, so prized by Page, was a red herring employed by Eddie Kassner to retain control over Davies's music publishing:

The crux of the case was that Page broke the fiduciary trust between the parties. The relationship had broken down. There was no good will, trust or whatever between the parties . . . Kassner started the lawsuit because he wished to hang on to the publishing rights. That's what the lawsuit was all about. It had nothing to do with management at all. Kassner would have set aside the claims of commission for live gigs and records. That was peanuts. Music publishing – that's what it was all about. The judge turned round and said precisely that. It took him four days to find out. The penny dropped.[5]

Wace's assessment is largely correct. The transcripts of the case reveal that Denmark Productions were not particularly interested in the 10 per cent management clause, or even claiming the damages. Although as a company they did not obtain any commission from specifically placing Davies's songs with any publisher, Kassner's role as chief shareholder ensured that he stood to make substantial profits from such material if he controlled the placing rights. Page himself admitted that without the publishing clause the 10 per cent would have been unacceptable. Indeed, he had received a largely increased remuneration for handing Davies's songs over to Kassner following the success of 'You Really Got Me'. Of course, Davies was aware that the Kassners were handling his songs and assigned them over one by one himself, making a considerable profit as a result. Although Page feels that he was strongly motivated by the loss of the 10 per cent management interest, there can be no doubt that the publishing clause was the real bone of contention.

The Kinks left the court in victorious mood, but their celebrations were short lived. Page and Kassner were unwilling to accept defeat, even at the hands of a High Court judge, and an appeal was lodged soon after. Page vowed that he would return stronger than ever and argue his case before the House Of Lords. It was a remarkable bid for control over the Kinks' empire and another year would elapse before the final outcome.

Following the dispute with Page, Ray Davies announced his intention of restricting public appearances with the Kinks in order to concentrate fully on songwriting. It was even suggested that he might leave the Kinks permanently and adopt a Brian Wilson-like role as a composer/producer. In the event of such a decision, a substitute would have to be found and all promoters would be informed of the situation. Although this seemed an extraordinary idea, Ray had evidently not forgotten the success of Mick Grace as a temporary substitute during the previous year. Having been absent from the live circuit for some time, Davies was apparently finding it difficult to readjust to the kind of schedule that had precipitated his nervous breakdown. His disenchantment was blatantly visible during the taping of a Simon Dee television show:

> I was standing there – just standing there singing and thinking what a drag it all is. And I'm sure the kids think it's a drag just to watch someone standing there singing. It's got so stale and boring.[49]

But in his final comments there was the veiled hint that a solo project was under serious consideration:

> I still intend to sing on the Kinks' records because my work is written around the group. There is no question of my severing all connection with them. It's possible I may also undertake work of an individual nature as long as it does not conflict with my interests with the Kinks.[49]

When Robert Wace heard about Ray's outburst he immediately denied any rumours of an impending split. The following week Davies retracted his controversial statement and admitted that he had underestimated the practical difficulty in employing a substitute. Nevertheless, his professed policy of undertaking solo projects seemed about to be realised. In a calculated gamble Ray intended to finance, set up and supervise a fifty-five-minute pilot T.V. show that he hoped to sell to one of the major British companies. He had for some time been working on the idea of an entirely new concept in television pop, but was unable to secure financial backing for the venture. Eager to commence work, Ray intended to begin shooting the film at Fulham's Granville Studios upon completion of the final script. Live groups were apparently being approached for inclusion and Ray also required a twenty-piece orchestra in the studio. This ambitious project would be the first in a series of summer ventures that inexplicably failed to reach fruition.

The Kinks' credibility as one of the more innovative groups of 1967 was increased with the release of 'Waterloo Sunset' which reached number 2 in June. The song was one of the most evocative in the Davies canon, a love story enshrined in the unlikely setting of London's Waterloo. The genesis of the song is particularly intriguing. Originally, Ray had intended to name the couple in the song Mabel and George but changed his mind after seeing the movie *Far From The Madding Crowd*. The working title 'Liverpool Sunset' was also reputedly altered when the Beatles suddenly released their own odes to Merseyside with 'Penny Lane' and 'Strawberry Fields Forever'. Ray was impressed with the new version and philosophical about the revisions forced upon him by the Fab Four:

> It happens quite a lot with my numbers. I work on a theme only to find as it nears completion someone else has come up with exactly the same melodic or lyrical idea. I suppose 'Waterloo' has stuck in my mind because I used to walk over Waterloo Bridge several nights a week on the way to art school when I was young. Rasa and I drove up there recently and just sat in the car for an hour or so watching. I've had the actual melody line in my mind for two or three years. If you look at the song as a kind of film I suppose 'Terry' would be Terence Stamp and 'Julie' would be Julie Christie. I've never really thought about the lyrics being sarcastic, but I suppose they are – it's just the way I feel.[49]

Like many Kinks' songs 'Waterloo Sunset' was recorded several times before Davies felt satisfied with the final product. Shel Talmy originally employed Nicky Hopkins again to play some haunting piano work on the track but the results failed to please Davies. A second attempt was even less inspired so Ray secretly entered the studio with the Kinks and laid down a third version which was reputedly used on the record, though Talmy denies this. By this point, it was clear that Davies and Talmy were no longer the complementary forces they had been in the early days of the Kinks. Ray had very precise ideas about the production he desired on particular compositions and frequently found himself in disagreement with Talmy. An amicable split took place when Talmy's contract with the Kinks expired. Shel recalls his feelings about the dissolution of one of the most successful musical partnerships of the 60s:

> After four or five years we decided it was probably a good time to do other things and try other ways. That's basically what happened . . . We needed a break from each other. It would have been nice to take a year off and resume, but that's not the way it happened. There was some talk of us going back and doing some more singles (in the mid-70s) but that never got resolved.[11]

Wace maintains that the departure of Talmy was an inevitable step in the Kinks' evolution:

> The Kinks had their sound and the contribution of Shel was simply to take down the performance. On two occasions he wanted to put out recordings by the Kinks that the act wanted to disassociate themselves from . . . That was part of the reason why Shel Talmy was never respected by the Kinks . . . You see if you don't have confidence in the producer you're working with, then, ultimately, the guy's got to go. I like Shel and I would justifiably say that if he produced the Kinks they'd produce more 'commercial' material . . . But there comes a time when the act resents paying the producer a percentage. There comes a time when they get fed up and want to do it themselves.[6]

Ray's new found freedom as a producer would result in even greater achievements in the near future, but it is also true that when Talmy left part of the old Kinks sound sadly disappeared. Under Shel Talmy's guidance the Kinks notched up ten Top 10 hits in under three years but since his departure they have managed only three more. The statistics reinforce Talmy's much-deserved reputation as one of the most adventurous yet commercially successful producers of the 60s.

While the Kinks set about completing their next album, plans were announced of future recordings and revolutionary changes in their stage act. Reviving an old idea that had once been dismissed by Arthur Howes, Ray promised a revamped thirty-minute stage act consisting of comedy dialogue and speciality numbers. This dangerous move towards the cabaret circuit was a determined attempt by Davies to break into television work. Davies's mid-summer delusions of grandeur were further revealed in his prediction of three simultaneous autumn album releases by himself, his brother and the Kinks. Ray's own album was intended as an essentially satiric work, including a parody of the Beatles' epic 'A Day In The Life' humorously retitled 'A Hole In The Shoe Of'. To add to the confusion there were even promises of a Ray Davies E.P. featuring Jacques Dutronc's 'Et Moi Et Moi Et Moi'. As the summer progressed each of these projects were successively shelved.

While Ray was boasting of his future plans, Peter Quaife ensured that his current activities did not go unnoticed. During his hospitalization following his accident, Quaife had nurtured ambitions of writing a novel and now he was in danger of seriously overreaching himself. Quaife's intended effort was a three-volume work tentatively titled *The Priest And The Physician* in which he hoped to present an argument for and against religion. His presumptousness even surpassed that of Ray Davies whose ideas at least sounded plausible. In an unguarded moment Quaife indicated that, far from working themselves to death, the Kinks were determined to pursue a more relaxed schedule in the future:

> We don't want to push ourselves as a popular group any more. To push

yourself is death. This group has terrific contrasts in personalities and it's part of our success. It's probably one of the most physically violent groups. It doesn't take much to get us going. One wrong word and you walk away with a black eye. We haven't got many friends in show business.[50]

The new relaxed attitude adopted by the Kinks indicated a maturity that many critics had felt was beyond them. Although the Davies brothers remained as different as chalk and cheese, their relationship had considerably improved during the past year. Dave spoke with some candour of the changes that he had observed in Ray's personality and attitude since his lay off:

It's really difficult to talk about Ray as a person because he changes so much. It's almost impossible to say what my impressions of him are . . . he's so changeable. He's more introvert than anything else. And a very deep person, I think. But since his nervous breakdown he had over a year ago, he's been much better as a person. He used to flog himself workwise unmercifully, but not any more. He's eased up and become less tense.[51]

Similar changes in Dave's personality were also noticeable. Since his clash with Mick Avory, Dave had somewhat modified his raucous adolescent behaviour. Ray spoke with great exuberance of Dave's potential as a songwriter and seemed determined to include more of his compositions on future albums. Dave, however, still retained his role as the extrovert of the group. He had recently grown big bushy sideboards and taken to wearing his Noddy hat about the London clubs and this tasteless dress sense was frequently castigated in the music press. But the fraternal flare-ups that had provided such good copy in the past were now little more than tedious comic interludes provided by Ray Davies:

He got very annoyed with me last week when I said he was playing too loud. He picked up ash-trays and things in the dressing-room and threw them at me. Then he knocked me over and tried to kick me. He missed and kicked this iron table and went hopping out of the room holding his foot![49]

Dave Davies's coming of age occurred sooner than anyone could have imagined. During the summer of 1967 his surprise solo single 'Death Of A Clown' zoomed to number 3 in the charts, easily outselling several of the Kinks own hits. The song, co-written by Dave and Ray, was originally intended for inclusion on the next Kinks album until the group persuaded Dave to risk issuing the track under his own name. Ray explained the strange circumstances that inspired this year old composition:

Dave came up to me one day and said 'Death Of A Clown' and I said what a great phrase it was and could he write something to go with it and he came back with 'Let's all drink to . . . ' and we built it from there. The idea of him singing it came one night when we were doing this ballroom date and Dave did the B-side of 'Tired Of Waiting For You'. A girl was standing near me and she said what a good singer he was. I said yes he was, and she said why didn't I let him sing everything then![49]

Although the track was cut in two takes there was an alarming moment prior to the first session when Ray accidently lost the lyrics, which were finally discovered amongst some of his old income tax return forms! The disc proved one of the most memorable songs of an eventful summer with a distinctive haunting melody, captivating lyrics and an unusual nasal vocal style that many critics compared to Bob Dylan. Suddenly, the exuberant Dave was a solo star and received as much press as the Kinks had elicited in their first flash of fame back in 1964. He remained surprisingly modest about his current success and even under severe pressure from the music press scoffed at the possibility of a solo career. While journalists were willing to gamble their reputation on his potential, Dave reminded them that his talents were limited and even admitted his uneasiness concerning the prospect of a solo appearance on *Top Of The Pops*. Dave cast further doubts on the possibility of recording a follow up to his hit revealing that he had no plans to re-enter the studio in the near future. In spite of these denials it was clear that Dave's ego had received a tremendous boost and he clearly enjoyed the grudging respect offered by his former detractors:

I think that if it had been a miss, a lot of people in the business would have been pleased. I've had the feeling for a long time that I was regarded by some people as just coasting along within the group without offering very much. People used to think that all I wanted to do was rely on Ray and the group all the time. This record will change that I hope.[52]

Ray was fully confident that 'Death Of A Clown' represented an exciting new stage in the career of his recalcitrant brother:

I do feel responsible for Dave because he's nervous and completely irresponsible himself. But this record has given him a confidence, I feel he can polish himself up now and he's got to do it himself because he's got a responsibility towards himself. I don't want him to have a bad deal.[53]

The success of 'Death Of A Clown' provided the Kinks with an opportunity to experiment with new ideas without the fear of chart failure. More importantly, the release had relieved Ray of the pressure of producing, writing and arranging the all-important successor to 'Waterloo Sunset'. The Kinks could no longer be criticised as a one man group for Dave's extra-curricular activities indicated the possibility of more eclectic and ambitious work in the future.

The long awaited new album *Something Else By The Kinks* was released in September but, in spite of Dave Davies's recent media blitz, failed to make any dent on the charts. The commercial failure of *Something Else* was a terrible injustice as the work was easily the equal of the impressive *Face To Face*. The musical and lyrical diversity was once more in strong evidence with Ray tackling a number of themes ranging from schooldays nostalgia to sun worship. 'David Watts' was a stunning opening cut, and the most successful example of Davies's near-obsessive interest in schooldays, a theme that would later inspire an entire album. Watts was apparently a former schoolfriend of Davies's and in the song his attributes are exaggerated sufficiently to capture the hero worship phenomenon peculiar to early adolescence. The subtle quasi-sexual elements in the song, both in the narrator's fixation with Watts and the hero's professed aversion to girls in favour of a gay and fancy free lifestyle are typical of Davies's delicate touch. Several other numbers show a similar maturity in presenting characters in unusual social situations. The predicament of Johnny in 'Situation Vacant' stems both from an overbearing mother-in-law, as well as a misplaced faith in the benefits of social mobility. Again, one cannot help noting the subtle way Davies avoids making any potentially reactionary statements by focussing attention on his characters. The power of most of these songs lies in Davies's determination to maintain a universal significance while describing particular incidents. 'Two Sisters', for example, relates the tale of how misplaced jealousy can be accepted and overcome. Significantly, Davies does not bother to name the characters:

> I couldn't put a face to them. It wasn't people that I knew. But I knew people in similar situations. It isn't just a feminine thing either. There were aspects of my relationship with my brother. It's not just a feminine thing. That's the way I like to write. It's interesting that way. To me, it's not good enough to write a song about a situation. I like to relate it to something else. I find that's the only way to get a good, honest statement . . . maybe it's wrong. It's a method I like to use. It's a way of sussing out something that isn't true.[13]

Davies's refusal to indulge in popular fads and his conscious avoidance of hip moral or political philosophising partly explains why his compositions still sound fresh and appealing today. Unlike many of his contemporaries Ray's work never became stylised because he refused to accept the limitations of working in any single musical genre. His delightful vignettes of middle-class life in the 60s were balanced by songs such as 'Harry Rag', a sea-shanty style celebration of nicotine addiction, and 'End Of The Season', a number that would not have sounded out of place in 30s' vaudeville. At the other extreme, 'Lazy Old Sun' with its raga drone and array of musical effects could be classified alongside the best of contemporary psychedelia. And for final good measure there was the Dave Davies example of psychotic humour in the form of 'Funny Face', a tale of a guy who discovers his girlfriend is a lunatic. *Something Else* may have lacked the power and depth of a *Sgt Pepper's* but it showed that Davies was infinitely more 'progressive' than his overrated British underground contemporaries. More importantly, the work revealed the increasing importance of Dave Davies as a songwriting force. With three numbers of surprisingly high quality it seemed likely that the younger brother's efforts would be even more fully assimilated in the future. Sadly, this was not to be the case and the possibility of achieving a balanced selection of material from both brothers remained unrealised.

In retrospect, the failure of *Something Else* is extremely puzzling. After all, the work included the much loved 'Waterloo Sunset' and also cashed in on Dave's solo success with 'Death Of A Clown'. Ray maintains that such inexplicable failures were partly the result of Pye's policy of issuing budget albums of the group's material at distinctly inopportune moments. It seemed that the marketing department at Pye was unable to reconcile the importance of artistic development with the constant need to shift vinyl. Recalling his many years with the Kinks as a freelance producer, Shel Talmy was extremely critical of their record label. His most scathing comments were reserved for former Pye managing director, Louis Benjamin, whom he felt had too tyrannical an attitude towards minor or inconsequential matters. Apparently the staff were so over-awed by the man that they allowed themselves to be distracted from more important tasks. The Kinks' impressive chart success notwithstanding, Talmy maintains that they failed to achieve their full commercial potential with Pye. His criticisms of Benjamin may have some foundation, but it should be noted that under his regime the label flourished. Not only did he sign an impressive number of acts but also pioneered cut price records and television advertising at a time when such ideas were considered financially unsound. Benjamin's aggression and uncompromising ambition may have adversely affected the Kinks at times but he always allowed them control over their product. Whether they would have achieved greater commercial success on a bigger label, as Talmy implies, remains debatable. Robert Wace provides a less emotive analysis of the Benjamin/Pye set up:

> On a personal level I like Louis Benjamin. My comments on Pye are unprintable. As a record company, they didn't handle the Kinks badly. But their whole attitude to artists explains why they haven't got a record company today. You can't take all the cream and not pay the artist well. And that's what they did. Consequently, while they had a thriving record company with Petula Clark, the Searchers and Sandie Shaw, their cheapskate attitude meant that all their artists were trying to get away

from them . . . Our deal got extended in order to get a higher royalty rate, which was probably a mistake, in hindsight. The Kinks were not earning a phenomenal amount of money as a group. The original deal was 2 per cent and the improved deal was 8 per cent. They were not a really big band sales-wise. We never had as much clout as we would have liked.[5]

The long overdue follow up to 'Waterloo Sunset' had still not appeared by the end of September. A new song titled 'The Interview' (presumably a re-titled version of 'The Reporter') was intended for release in October, but this satire on pop journalists failed to appear. Instead, another number originally begun the previous spring was at last completed and released as 'Autumn Almanac'. Originally entitled 'My Street', the song was described by Ray as a 'possessive love song' celebrating his affection for Muswell Hill. The catchy tune and clever lyrics were sufficient to take the song as high as number 3, completing a run of eight consecutive Top 10 hits. A successful year was concluded with another Dave Davies hit, 'Susannah's Still Alive' which reached number 20. The song, complete with risqué sexual allusions, was based on a book Dave had read 'about a bird who never had any luck with the blokes'. Although Dave failed to record his projected album of cover versions or complete his much touted solo work, his latest hit provided strong hopes for a New Year L.P. release. Dave gave the following reasons for his failure to complete an album's worth of songs in 1967:

Ray can sit down and write a number, I can't. If I sit down with my guitar and intend to write something, I can never usually finish it. I've got lots of unfinished songs around. But if I just mess about I come out with something. Ray writes about things that happen, I write about how I feel about people by going out and getting drunk and what have you. It takes me away from show business and brings me back to reality. I don't write anything deep or psychological, I try to write something that is simple.[54]

Dave's down to earth songwriting style was the perfect foil for Ray's subtle satires and social commentaries. While the younger brother spoke of drinking sessions and escapism, Ray ended the year with a number of introspective musings that ultimately presented more questions than answers:

I don't really feel I'm an artist of any kind. I mean sometimes writing songs gets a real bore. And then suddenly something happens and I'm filled with excitement and I really want to get it down . . . I am such an honest person people think I'm difficult to talk to and get along with. But more important is that I'm *me*. I don't put on an act to make myself

> more interesting. I can't. I never understand people who do, just like I don't understand people who say if they had their life to live again they would do everything the same. If I could live over again I'd change every single thing I'd ever done.[55]

Davies's philosophical ramblings at least suggested that after a long period of exploitation and uncertainty he was at last coming to terms with his role in the pop world.

EIGHT

Those Were the Days

The Kinks' first release of 1968 was *Live At Kelvin Hall* (Glasgow), which appeared in late January. The album was recorded back in March 1967 and scheduled for autumn release but failed to appear presumably because of either a legal dispute or a belated realisation that a live work might affect the sales of *Something Else*. According to reports of the previous year the second side of the album was to be taken from a gig at the Paris Olympia on 23 April though whether this occurred seems unlikely. The album captures the raw spontaneity of a 1967 Kinks concert, though the recording quality leaves much to be desired. Indeed, far more attention has gone into recording the audience's response than anything else, and as a result, the songs are engulfed by the sound of screams which continue throughout the entire show. The unselfconscious amateurism of the Kinks is fully exposed in the off-key vocals and out of tune playing that dominate the set. No attempt is made to overdub the errors and even the track listing on the record erroneously credits 'All Day And All Of The Night' instead of 'Tired Of Waiting For You'. As a live album the work provoked a mixed response, though it has frequently been championed as an excellent example of garage group enthusiasm overcoming technical imperfection. In general, it is the more raucous songs that best stand the test of time, particularly the opening 'Till The End Of The Day' and Dave's plodding 'You're Looking Fine'. The quieter tracks such as 'Well Respected Man' and 'Dandy' are drowned by screams, while 'Sunny Afternoon' is surrendered to the audience as a singalong. The highlight of the set, however, is the unique closing medley which combines 'Milk Cow Blues', 'Tired Of Waiting For You' and the 'Batman Theme' in an ingenious arrangement. *The Kinks Live At Kelvin Hall* remains a valuable artifact, brilliantly documenting a period of pop when audience participation replaced musical finesse as the primary considera-tion. Even Ray Davies looks back at the work with a mixture of mild embarrassment and great affection:

> I think I'm trying to justify that album now. I think it was a good example of what it was like at a rock concert then. I think it may have 'historic' value. You've got to understand that for two or three years I never heard myself playing. No monitors . . . and with the audience, it was just a wall

> of sound. I got back from a world tour after the first three hits with this infected ankle . . . sticking out like elephantitis. I got off the plane and we were rushed straight into a recording studio to record our next album. The pressure was enormous. It's all pressure and it's called show business. I thought I was lucky to be working, being a musician. I'd probably do it now . . . and I am doing it now to a certain degree.[15]

Although the old pressures of non-stop gigging had been reduced by early 1968 the Kinks were still encountering hauntingly familiar problems. In February, Pete Quaife broke his wrist following a fall at his North London home and was forced to struggle through a series of engagements in Belgium shortly afterwards. For all their experience as a live act, the Kinks consistently failed to live down their image as an incompetent performing group and it was only their impressive chart appearances that maintained their status as a headlining act. Their major U.K. tour of 1968 boasted an impressive support cast including the Tremeloes, the Herd, Gary Walker and the Rain and Ola and the Janglers. Reviews of the period severely criticised the Kinks for their poor stage presence, inaudible vocals and inability to provide a climactic conclusion to the evening. Despite a seemingly non-stop medley of hits, the Kinks apparently failed to generate the excitement that characterised their performances in previous years. Dave Davies recalls those gigs at which the Kinks' 'old age' was first pounced upon as a potential weakness:

> Yes, I remember that tour in '68 – the Herd were on it and in a way it was a badly organised tour because they were the 'new faces' of '68 and people didn't know if we were the 'old faces' of '66 or what. I don't think we were that big at the time. There were also some internal problems in the band. We were at the stage where we didn't really want to work much. Ray was really into writing and creating and when we did do live appearances they weren't really that rehearsed.[56]

In order to coincide with the tour two singles, by the Kinks and Dave Davies respectively, were scheduled for release during the second week of April. It was a ludicrous situation but after some negotiations with Pye Dave's effort was successfully postponed. It was the Kinks' projected single 'Wonderboy', however, that Ray had most wanted to drop as he maintained that it had insufficient commercial potential. Although the cut would have fitted nicely on to an album it lacked both the satirical bite and the distinctive melodic quality of their recent singles. Davies's objections proved well-founded and, in spite of the tour, 'Wonderboy' became the Kinks' first Top 30 failure since 'You Still Want Me' in early 1964. While the Kinks narrowly missed achieving their thirteenth consecutive hit, Dave Davies's solo career also ground to a halt. His much vaunted solo album had been put back indefinitely while his latest single was re-scheduled for release, then mysteriously withdrawn. Recoiling from these setbacks, the Kinks set out on a European tour playing the principal outdoor stadiums in Italy and Scandinavia. When they came home towards the end of June their follow up single, 'Days', was receiving strong airplay and subsequently returned them to the Top 20. The song was another vision of an idyllic lost past and this theme would soon be extended over an album's worth of material. Although 'Days' had failed to set the chart alight in the spectacular fashion of previous Kinks hits, Ray remained surprisingly unconcerned about its minimal commercial success and seemed more worried about maintaining the group's artistic integrity:

> I still have a lot of faith in our single 'Days'. If we like a record and like making it, it becomes a successful venture. After it's finished we're very proud of it – but we never pretended to know anything about the sales or promotional side of music. Each disc is a separate chapter and segment in a chain of things. Some releases are slow, and perhaps this is one of them. At any rate, I don't think our image or position is altered by its moderate progress in the charts. What is a pity is the chart requirement for getting on a television programme. I don't want to push myself into writing faster and churning out single after single so we can remain in the public eye via T.V., radio and the charts. There are large gaps between our records because we like to take time to concentrate and to do other things we enjoy.[57]

Ray's growing disenchantment with the apparent importance of chart singles would be a crucial factor in the development of the Kinks as an albums band. At the same time, his refusal to concentrate his powers on singles material would prove the greatest threat to the group's survival over the next few years.

The indignities of a chart flop and badly received tour were small beer in comparison to the Kinks' other major headache – Larry Page. As promised, Page took his case to the House Of Lords. The outcome was crucial to all parties for Denmark Productions were not only claiming publishing rights but 10 per cent of all monies received by the Kinks since 1965. The Court of Appeal sat from 25 March to 1 April, returning for further sessions from 1–3 May but still failed to reach a verdict. The proceedings were concluded on 28 June amid bitter controversy. Although Lord Justices Winn, Harman and Salmon finally reached the same verdict, they were in substantial disagreement over certain issues in the case. As before, much of the preliminary evidence went in Page's favour. The basis of Justice Widgery's findings the previous year were deemed 'somewhat obscure'. In particular, the argument that the Kinks' contract had been 'frustrated' was unanimously overruled. The doctrine of 'frustration' was applicable to contracts which became impossible of performance due to some supervening event, such as war, flood or famine, for which neither party was responsible. However, since Collins and Wace had introduced the Kinks to their own solicitor, Michael Simkins, they had actively sought to determine the contract and rid themselves of Page. Under such circumstances, the doctrine of 'frustration' could not be relied upon. This new ruling led to a long argument over the seemingly crucial issue of whether Page's return to England on 4 July 1965 really did constitute a breach of contract. Justice Winn supported Justice Widgery's conclusion on this matter arguing that if Page had been in direct contractual relationship with the Kinks they would have been entitled to dismiss him because of his conduct in the States. Winn opined that Page should have anticipated a reaction from the Kinks, or at least Ray Davies, which would have been extreme enough to destroy their relationship. Wace agrees that this was the decisive error that nailed Page's coffin:

> I would take the view that where Larry made his mistake was not telling Ray he was going back. I think that was the *fundamental* mistake . . . I think if Larry had stuck it out in the States it might have been a different case . . . But he wasn't capable of handling the group. I'm not saying it's easy. The kind of problems that Ray posed for somebody were considerable and Larry had never been confronted with them on a day to day basis. It got to him. It reached him. And he cracked. He couldn't wait to get away. Maybe he did do a lot for the Kinks but, at the end, he couldn't get them to do what he wanted.[6]

Larry did, of course, fulfil his obligations during the tour. As the Kinks' manager he was arguably in a position that demanded a degree of respect. If Davies chose to sabotage his manager's plans by playing the *prima donna* then, arguably, Page was within his rights to retaliate by refusing the role of 'gofer' and concentrating on more important business. Wace does not subscribe to this viewpoint:

> You don't talk about respect! It's either there or it isn't . . . Either you can stand the drama that goes along with being the manager of a band or you haven't got the stomach for it and you cave in . . . You can't come back to Denmark Street and play the wheeler-dealer. They're not just a commodity – they're artists and they are temperamental . . . Being a manager can be a remunerative business and you have to put up with being the whipping boy.[6]

Wace's opinion would probably be laughed at by many of the important and aggressive entrepreneurs that dominated mid-60s pop. Clearly, Page's philosophy of management does not even entertain the possibility of being a 'whipping boy':

No fucking way. Not me. And that, no doubt, answers your question as to why Wace stayed on for another four years. If that is his theory of what a manager is then that is it! . . . Why did he stay? Because they could manipulate him to do things the way *they* wanted. Don't ask me how? You're talking about Ray Davies, so you're talking about something that is completely beyond logic.[8]

Although Wace's objections were partly supported by Justice Winn, Page had his own champion in Lord Justice Salmon. In a long summing up, Salmon noted that all the complaints against Page had been rejected and the original case stood or fell on the controversial departure from the States. Clearly, Justice Widgery had concluded that this event was such a fundamental breach by the plaintiff company of its obligations that it constituted a repudiation of the whole contract. But what did Page's conduct amount to? He was, as Widgery had found, under no obligation to stay to 'the bitter end of the tour'. Moreover, he had told every member of the group, other than Ray Davies that he was returning home. The only Kink questioned about this in court was Mick Avory who claimed that he did not object to Page's departure and felt he had important business to attend to in London. Ultimately, the one valid criticism of Page, as Wace admits, was that he failed to tell Ray of his intentions for fear of a temperamental outburst. While accepting this fact, Lord Justice Salmon was unconvinced that such an action could justify the termination of contracts:

I find it very strange that this can in reality constitute a fundamental breach of contract in any event, and, in particular against the background of all that Mr Page had done for the group.[58]

Lord Justice Salmon also noted that Wace's letter to Page's solicitors on 14 September 1965 clearly indicated that Boscobel Productions placed no blame on the plaintiffs. Indeed, even Wace's solicitor, Michael Simkins, had not assumed that Page's conduct amounted to a breach of contract otherwise he would not have put forward the ridiculous grounds for termination that had been set out in his letter of 2 September 1965. Salmon concluded that there never was a breach of contract by Page, a ruling that must have caused some consternation to Collins and Wace:

It is very difficult indeed for me to accept a finding in the defendants' favour that there has been a fundamental breach of contract by the plaintiffs through Mr Page when the defendants, knowing all the material facts, by their letter of 14 September 1965 negatived any such breach, and when the evidence does not, in my view, appear to establish any such breach . . .

I am not satisfied that there was any real breach unless one puts the obligation upon the plaintiffs as high as an absolute duty to ensure that

> Mr Page should retain the goodwill and confidence of the Kinks – and this I am not prepared to do.[58]

Page must have felt that the case was won, particularly when Lord Justice Salmon dismissed the emotionally charged admission of 'hatred' that Davies had previously voiced to such effect:

> I think that almost anything a manager might do, however harmless or trivial, could induce hatred and distrust in a group of highly temperamental, jealous and spoilt adolescents.[58]

Wace regarded the summing up as the words of an old man who had failed to understand the pressures and personalities of creative people battling for survival in a treacherous business. Yet, in many respects, Justice Salmon's brilliantly perceptive description of the Davies brothers still sounds as impressive today as it did sixteen years ago.

Although Page's conduct in the States had been placed in a new perspective by Lord Justice Salmon, this finally proved of little consequence to the outcome of the case. Both Lord Justice Salmon and Lord Justice Harman agreed that Boscobel Productions had, with the full approval of the Kinks, repudiated the agreements by their letter of 14 September 1965. This repudiation was unjustified in Lord Justice Salmon's opinion, and Denmark Productions should have claimed substantial damages for wrongful dismissal. Unfortunately, they had chosen instead to fight for the publishing rights and 10 per cent of the Kinks' earnings for the past three years. Of course, it has long been settled that if a man employed under a contract of personal service is wrongly dismissed he has no claim for remuneration due under the contracts after the repudiation. For example, if Page had been earning £10,000 a year as personal manager on a five-year contract, he could not simply bask in the sun and draw a salary on the basis that he was willing to serve as manager! His sole claim would be for damages, which were not properly pursued in the Kinks' case. The claim for an injunction to restrain Collins and Wace from placing the Kinks' musical compositions with anyone but Denmark Productions was also misconceived on the grounds that neither Page nor Kassner derived any direct benefit from the exploitation of those rights. The object of their claim was to enrichen a third party. The fact that the third party was Kassner himself was irrelevant to the terms of the contract. Salmon and Winn, in spite of their contrasting arguments, agreed that the appeal was misconceived and ordered that Denmark Productions be paid 10 per cent of the group's earnings from 30 June 1965 to 14 September 1965. Justice Harman concurred with this ruling though his argument was based on the 'lamentably clumsy' terms of the original agreements which had placed Page in a position where the Kinks were not bound to accept his services. The complex arguments fully demonstrate how Larry Page's hopes were scuppered by a flawed contract and a misconceived action against his former partners. Had Denmark Productions sought straightforward damages rather than an account of the Kinks' publishing and management the outcome might have been very different. Yet, even after receiving the rulings of Justices Widgery, Winn, Harman and Salmon, Page and Kassner were still determined to continue the fight for another year. However, on 9 October 1968, the Appeal Committee of the House Of Lords refused Denmark Productions' petition of appeal and closed the book on what was probably, in contract law, the most spectacular court case in pop music history. For the Kinks the court case was a costly and troublesome affair, but at least they were at last free from the machinations of Page, an adversary whose determination and entrepreneural skill was all too frequently beyond their imagination.

The big news of July concerned Ray and Dave's announcement of their intended joint production company. Ray's stated policy was to launch new talent rather than capture established artists from their present labels. Davies pinpointed the failure of the majors to allow artists sufficient time to develop their talents as the reasoning behind the venture:

> Somebody gets hold of a new group, looks at the chart, and says, 'Let's make a record like that! Then we'll have a hit. But we'll put some trumpets in there.' So they turn out another trendy record. A record which is not really representative of the group – it's not really them. They're glad to get a record anyway, but more often than not it fails to become a success. So it's a big drag, especially if the group really does have talent. We have lots of new ideas we want to try out. We'll produce the record ourselves. Other than the Kinks records, I did a few little jobs about three years ago that turned out reasonably well. I didn't have any hits with them, but people asked me to go to sessions and supervise them. Now we've formed this record producing company and have put our money into it.[59]

Although several major companies showed interest in distributing Ray and Dave's new products the brothers failed to secure a deal whereby they would be given their own label. It would be many years before they would achieve the autonomy they desired.

The summer of 1968 was another confusing period in the Kinks' recording history. So many projects had been delayed, abandoned and sometimes resurrected that it was impossible to determine what might be released. In August, the twice withdrawn Dave Davies single 'Lincoln County' finally appeared and was greeted with reasonably favourable reviews. One critic expended much effort explaining its allegorical association with the Jesse James legend, while others noted similarities with Donovan's 'Hurdy Gurdy Man', mid-period Dylan and traditional country music. Dave clearly regarded the single as the most important release of his career and spoke with a note of desperation about the possibility of failure:

> I want people to know what's in me. I want to be taken seriously, but people never will. It's hard to say that to anyone, but you know the sort of things we do that people don't like. This record is all I've got in me, if people don't like it . . . do you think people might not like it? They *must* like it because I'm a normal person and it's a normal song. I will give up if people don't like it. If it gets into the Top 20, that'll be O.K. Even if a few people I like play it, I won't mind. This is the first record I've done on my own that I've really believed in.[60]

Davies's worst fears were realised in the succeeding weeks. The single received little or no airplay and quickly disappeared. It was a bitter blow to Dave who had set his heart on completing the elusive solo album for pre-Christmas release. The failure of 'Lincoln County' not only undermined his own confidence but severely lessened Pye's interest in future Dave Davies material.

The Kinks' current recording situation was even more confusing than the non-appearance of Dave Davies product. They had recently begun work on an album tentatively titled *Four More Respected Gentlemen* which, according to Ray, was a satire on English social etiquette, featuring songs about table manners and outmoded customs. Eventually, some labels were printed with the track listing of *Four More Respected Gentlemen* as follows: 'She's Got Everything', 'Monica', 'Mr Songbird', 'Johnny Thunder', 'Polly', 'Days', 'Animal Farm', 'Berkeley Mews', 'Picture Book', 'Phenomenal Cat' and 'Misty Water'. The interesting point here is that none of these songs satirise social etiquette which suggests that Ray's original concept had either been abandoned, or the record company presumptuously compiled a probable collection of songs from completed demos. Such an action may seem unlikely, but there is a precedent with the Beach Boys' *Smile* for which sleeves were printed long before the completion of the tracks, many of which remained in fragmentary form. Whatever the truth, *Four More Respected Gentlemen* failed to appear but most of the above tracks were included as part of a new double album concept based on Dylan Thomas's *Under Milkwood.* In the third week of September *The Kinks Are The Village Green Preservation Society* was released as a twelve-track album and received a major review in the *New Musical Express* by Keith Altham. Strangely enough, the album was withdrawn shortly afterwards and a new improved version appeared complete with a different cover, altered running order and revised selection of tracks. 'Mr Songbird' was deleted along with the single 'Days' and replaced by

'Animal Farm', 'Big Sky', 'All Of My Friends Were There', 'Last Of The Steam Powered Trains' and 'Sitting By The Riverside'. It was a bizarre situation that confused both the music press and the record buying public.[61]

The Kinks Are The Village Green Preservation Society is a remarkable album and remains one of the most underrated of its era. Before phrases such as 'concept album' became hip, Davies was already laying down a series of songs based loosely around a single theme. The album was Davies's version of Dylan Thomas's *Under Milkwood*, a day in the life of a village seen through the eyes of the narrator and various other characters. Like Thomas, Davies succeeds in investing his work with an elegiac quality, partly through the characters he portrays, but mainly in a near obsession with the past that permeates almost every cut. Even in celebrating the preservation of the village green, Davies appears to perceive that its continuance is an anachronism. The idea of basing an album on such a theme might seem pretentious and potentially tedious but Davies meets the challenge by colouring his work with different moods and employing some masterfully contrasting musical arrangements. 'The Village Green Preservation Society' and 'Village Green' demonstrate these points most forcibly. The former is a rather quaint listing of the various institutions that need to be preserved. Davies is cast in the role of the saviour of our threatened British culture, though the inclusion of Donald Duck alongside village greens and cricket suggests that the ideal has already been bastardised. The cloying sentiment and smug attitude are fully conveyed through the inane singalong chorus. Thematically, 'Village Green' covers the same ground with its simplistic glorification of daisies, clocks and steeples. However, the tone is modified in order to create a markedly contrasting effect. The solemn vocal style sounds defeated and the sense of loss conveyed through focussing on the past creates a strong feeling of pathos. The over use of the harpsichord dramatises the effect further, totally negating the spurious optimism of the title track. The same technique can be observed by comparing 'Picture Book' and 'People Take Pictures Of Each Other'. The former describes a pleasant browse through a photo album recalling happy memories, while the latter satirises this very process and ponders upon the absurdity of photographic representation as a means of proving one's existence. Davies expressed his ambiguous feelings about his subject in this revealing statement:

> . . . I like these traditional British things to be there. I never go to watch cricket any more, but I like to know it's there. It's like not being able to read *Eagle* any more. And it's bad for people to grow up and not know what a china cup is – or a village green. In other words, I'd rather have the actual things here not just pictures of things we used to have. It all sounds terribly serious, but it isn't really – I mean I wouldn't die for this cause,

but I think it's frightfully important.[62]

Like many songs on the album 'People Take Pictures Of Each Other' was inspired by an everyday occurrence:

I was at a wedding. It was only a little wedding in the country . . . We walked back from the church. The guy was in the navy . . . and he put a flag up in the back garden . . . and they all stood there and they took a picture. And then she got the camera and took a picture of him . . . and he got the camera and took a picture of her . . . that's strange. That's where that came about. I just got the line and then built on that.[63]

The remaining songs dwell on a lost Golden Age and are equally varied in musical style and mood. 'Last Of The Steam Powered Trains' employed a blues riff not dissimilar to Howlin' Wolf's 'Smokestack Lightning', but what better way of enhancing the strong mood of past glory than adapting such an archetypal blues riff. 'Do You Remember Walter' is another of the album's highlights and its neat characterisation brilliantly conveys a loss of almost tragic proportions. Arguably, a superior rewrite of 'David Watts', Davies this time presents the idealised adolescent hero demythologised in adulthood. The myth can be maintained only through memory, which sounds like a damning comment on the entire village green preservation ideal.

There are many more thematic couplings on this most distinctive of Kinks albums, each demonstrating Davies's growing maturity as a writer/arranger. 'Sitting By The Riverside' and 'Animal Farm' are songs of pastoral bliss, the latter again using Nicky Hopkins' harpsichord to delightful and unusual effect. 'Wicked Annabella' is Hansel and Gretal revisited with an opening riff reminiscent of the Doors' 'Light My Fire' (the ultimate irony) and some effective feedback by Dave Davies. 'Phenomenal Cat' is even more unusual; a haunting flute and tambourine backing prefaces a tale that might well have been adapted from the pages of Edward Lear or Lewis Carroll. 'Starstruck' and 'Monica' provide an Acapulco-style beat, indicating Ray's continued interest in calypso as a form of musical relief from his more serious moments. 'Monica' is particularly interesting as an example of Davies's apparent coyness in understating his theme. The song, which may have been partly inspired by the character Polly Garter in Thomas's *Under Milkwood*, relates the tale of a prostitute. Ray explained his reasons for presenting the theme so modestly:

I think there's something in underdoing things because they're much better when they work than the things that are overdone . . . I like the way I did 'Monica' and I think that I explained it enough to me and to various other people . . . I didn't actually say she was a prostitute . . . so it can apply to a lot of other people . . . If you say somebody is a prostitute or a hooker you're restricted. Like 'Miss Straight-back' who goes to work in the morning and doesn't do anything else isn't affected by it. I suppose that if you don't say that she's a prostitute she might see little things in the song about herself.[63]

Although most of the album is a visual representation of life in an English village, occasionally the lyrics touch on larger issues. Some critics, for example, interpreted 'Big Sky' as an allegory about God. Ray remains predictably uncommunicative about this possible interpretation:

I'm always wary about talking about God because I was told that I'm not religious because I don't go to church. I was told that at a very early age. But I think I'm quite religious even though I don't go to church. So I just don't talk about it. If God's an influence on something, I don't want to tell everyone about it. If the influence is there, it'll come out without mentioning it.[13]

The Kinks Are The Village Green Preservation Society makes a strong claim as the group's finest album. The variety of musical styles employed over the fifteen cuts is often quite staggering and the juxtaposition of contrasting instruments and sound effects from harmonica to harpsichord and flute to feedback shows the Kinks at their most innovative. Having completed his *meisterwerk* Davies was shattered by both his record company's inexplicable failure to promote the album and the lack of interest shown by the general public:

I was upset because people didn't get a chance to hear it. I know when I write a good song and I really thought there were good numbers on it. It just had to be thought of in modern terms and presented in a proper way.[64]

Unfortunately, Pye's promotional department were not geared towards pushing unusual albums. The Kinks had always been regarded as a singles group whose albums were quickly recorded and rushed out to cash in on their chart success. A new policy was needed to ensure that their transition from a singles group to an albums band was greeted by the public as an exciting proposition. Instead, Pye continued with their mid-price re-release campaign of old Kinks material which effectively distracted interest from the group's current work.

Perhaps as a reaction against the failure of *The Kinks Are The Village Green Preservation Society* the group immediately moved into cabaret work. In October they made their debut at Stockton Fiesta followed by such legendary club dates as Spennymoor Top Hat and Chester-le-Street Garden Farm. In summing up the group's current attitude Mick Avory sounded like an ageing pro, resigned to the anonymity of life on the Northern club circuit:

> You have to get out into a new field. Mostly, on the performing side, we work abroad and now we've broken into the cabaret field up north. It pays well and it's given us a new challenge – you have to routine a new kind of act which will go down with different kinds of audience.[65]

The Kinks were in a sad state, but Ray Davies remained characteristically ambitious and hoped to turn current circumstances to his advantage. He approached Pye with the idea of promoting a cabaret version of *The Village Green Preservation Society* to be performed in selected clubs. It was an incredibly imaginative concept for 1968 when the gap between pop and theatre had yet to be successfully broached. Unfortunately, Pye refused to finance the project and instead unsuccessfully attempted to persuade Davies to write a Christmas hit single. As 1968 drew to a close, the only good news concerned the lifting of the three-year ban that had prevented the Kinks from touring the States. The group's U.S. record company Reprise reacted quickly, paving the way for a possible visit with a promotional campaign bearing the slogan 'God Save The Kinks'. An album, including eighteen songs from various stages of the group's career, was made available on mail order for a bargain $2. The marketing technique proved effective and resulted in several critics re-evaluating the Kinks' past work. Ray spoke with renewed optimism about the possibility of a U.S. comeback and appeared confident that the group would reverse the events of 1965 and complete the long delayed American breakthrough in the New Year.

NINE

He Ain't Heavy He's My Brother

The lack of single success and the failure of *The Kinks Are The Village Green Preservation Society* might have destroyed the group's confidence at an earlier stage of their career but by 1969 they were ready to gamble with their future, deferring the release of the next Kinks 45 in order to concentrate on improving their live act. Rehearsals now took place three times a week and Davies even abandoned his luxurious house in Elstree in order to seek songwriting inspiration in his native North London. Davies's professionalism encouraged a more mature approach to live performances and he appeared content with the group's progress:

> We're working a lot better together now than ever before – we've at last reached an understanding between ourselves onstage. It's taken us a long time, I suppose, but we've developed very naturally . . . we've made a lot of mistakes as a group since we started, but I think of all those mistakes as successes because we've learnt from them. That's the thing about this business – there isn't a school where you can go to learn to be a pop group. It's not like going to art school, for example, to learn to be a painter. Obviously you can't learn that, but they give you certain things, and at least you can react against them. But the only way you can learn about being a pop musician is from actual experience from the mistakes you make and then putting them right.[66]

The new maturity in the Kinks' attitude could even be detected in the actions of Dave Davies. His latest release, 'Hold My Hand', was prefaced by confident plans for a solo tour rather than tirades against the press and record-buying public. Cabaret plans were suggested, with Dave performing solo material and selected Kinks songs, accompanied by a small backing group. Having almost completed his solo album, Dave was ready for such an ambitious venture, but sadly his plans remained unfulfilled because the single flopped. Without a chart hit, Pye were reluctant to release a Dave Davies solo album and the work remained on hold before finally being withdrawn. In spite of this major setback, Dave accepted his fate stoically and committed himself to his brother's future projects. Meanwhile, fellow Kink Peter Quaife was developing his songwriting talent and composing material in the vein of Simon and Garfunkel and the

Association. Whether such folk/rock influenced songs were appropriate for a Kinks album was a question that would trouble Quaife during the succeeding weeks.

In March, the long awaited new Kinks single 'Plastic Man' was released, for the first time boasting vocals from all four members. The song was another example of Davies's satire, though lyrically it lacked the subtlety and wit of 'A Well Respected Man'. Some commentators felt that the humour was too obvious and heavy handed, but Ray was surprisingly defensive about the composition:

> This record has outgrown what a pop record can be. This record has more love for people. Sometimes you love a person so much. But he's got himself in a hole, and the only thing you can do is to kick him to get him out of it. People have had a go at me for using the word 'plastic'. But it's the only word you can possibly use. You couldn't call a man a pathetic man . . . Certain people dislike it because they get certain truths about themselves. Nobody likes truth. But I admit the truth. It's probably not the greatest song I've written and not the greatest song I'll ever write. But it's the only song I could have written at this time. Even though I hated it when I first heard the acetate! But I think it could be a hit. It does bother me if I don't have a hit. But only because I feel I've made something wrong. But then I listen again, remember why I did it – and then I know I'm not wrong.[67]

The novelty value of the disc appeared to ensure its commercial success and such was the initial response from disc-jockeys that Ray felt sufficiently confident to pursue an important Stateside trip during which he negotiated a deal to produce the next Turtles album. Prior to his departure, Ray learned that 'Plastic Man' was about to enter the B.B.C. chart and he hastily produced a promotional film for inclusion on *Top Of The Pops* during his absence. Upon his return, however, Ray discovered that the B.B.C. had banned the disc on television because the lyrics contained the word 'bum'. The situation struck him as absurd:

> It's ridiculous, but you're in the hands of a B.B.C. monopoly. I'm surprised about this thing with *Top Of The Pops* really because the record had had good airplay on the radio. 'Plastic Man' is selling steadily – I suppose it's doing as well as any record could be expected to do that's been out four weeks and hasn't had a television plug.[66]

The lack of television promotion arrested the progress of the disc, which failed to climb higher than number 31. After an absence of eight months from the charts it was hardly an emphatic comeback. The Kinks' disappointment was partly relieved, however, by the news that Granada had commissioned Ray to write a full length pop opera titled *Arthur* for scheduled transmission on the new I.T.V. colour service in the autumn. But even that heartening news was swiftly rendered inconsequential by the shock revelation that Pete Quaife was again quitting the Kinks.

Although Quaife had indicated his disillusionment with 'playing pretty bubblegum music', it was generally hoped that the decision to quit might be averted. Even following his announcement the Kinks' management refused to confirm his departure which left Quaife exclaiming to sceptical journalists: 'I don't know why everyone's playing it down. I'm leaving. And that's it.' The reasons for Quaife's departure were summed up in the old cliché 'differences over musical policy'. It was obvious that Peter was tired of playing in the shadow of Ray Davies and felt a growing need to establish his own musical identity outside of the Kinks:

> I'm sick of standing onstage and just playing two notes per bar. I want to do something more productive. There's no enmity. It's just that musically our tastes are not the same. I couldn't stick playing 'Sunny Afternoon' forever. I want to do something more than just produce sounds. I can play that commercial stuff standing on my head . . . I'm leaving the Kinks on good terms. But I'd rather go to prison than play with them any more.[68]

In spite of his ambitions, Quaife's post-Kinks career was surprisingly inauspicious. Following his departure he formed a group called Maple Oak and released a flop single 'Son Of A Gun' followed by an equally obscure album. Disillusioned, Quaife abandoned the rock music world and returned to his former occupation as a commercial artist. Eventually, he settled in Copenhagen, with Annette Paustian, now his wife, the daughter of a millionaire impresario at whose club the Kinks had once performed. Peter would later move to Montreal where he now resides.

Predictably, Quaife's replacement as bassist was his former substitute, John Dalton. Dalton had been musically inactive since leaving the Kinks apart from a brief stint with John Rogan of the Roulettes in Pastime. Although the Kinks might have recruited a more actively professional player, they realised the value of a musician who could reel off their old hits from memory. The first new Kinks release featuring Dalton was 'Drivin'', released on 21 June. The song was another very commercial ditty presenting working-class escapism via the temporary bliss of a country drive. At the time of the record's release Ray indicated that, unlike the narrator of the song, he had never learned to drive though it later transpired that this was not quite correct:

> I took some lessons and I took my test. I swear this is the truth – I knocked an old lady over on my test. Fortunately, she wasn't injured. They failed me on lack of consideration for other motorists. I haven't driven since. I

went back and locked myself in my room and I sobbed for a day. I felt rejected by the world. I really did.[69]

The Kinks' celebration of Sunday driving was also rejected by the general public and the record failed to enter the Top 50. It was now becoming disquietingly obvious that the Kinks' impressive run of chart hits was perhaps at an end.

The summer of 1969 was another industrious period with Ray promising the imminent release of *Arthur* as well as an anniversary album to celebrate the Kinks' fifth year as a recording group. He even hoped to complete work on a book recalling the behind the scenes story of the Kinks from 1964 to the present. Like so many of Davies's ideas, these projects failed to materialise, but at least his excursions into the film world were proving fruitful. Ray had already written the title theme for the movie *Till Death Us Do Part* and it was hoped that he might record the track as a single. Unfortunately, Ray's sensitivity about being typecast as a solo singer precluded this excellent possibility of promotion. Instead, Davies wrote several songs for *The Virgin Soldiers* as well as composing the incidental music for Romy Schneider's *Hushabye*. His film work led to a B.B.C. contract for *Where Was Spring?*, a six-week satire series starring Eleanor Bron and John Fortune. It was an arduous schedule, requiring Davies to write a new song every week with only two days' notice. Ray admits that occasionally the results were surprising:

I tried to use topical ideas. Enjoyed writing one about Malcolm Muggeridge. It was around that time when he'd resigned as Rector of Edinburgh University. I think, because of the students' attitudes to sex and drugs. I read up quite a bit about him but I couldn't write anything against him for some reason. I just felt he was getting on. So I wrote 'Could Be You're Getting Old'. Never named him but Muggeridge was who it was about.[70]

Work was also completed on the Turtles' *Turtle Soup*, which appeared towards the end of July. Ray had spent less than three weeks working on the record while staying at the Hollywood Hawaiian Hotel where he could be found drinking lots of beer and devouring copies of *Playboy*. The Turtles were more than impressed with Davies's production work and provided a fascinating and flattering testimonial:

We let him totally influence our music . . . We still buy every album of his that comes out and pick out the best parts and still believe that there are very few people with his vitality and sense of humour. What his albums lack in commerciality they expand in eccentricity. He hasn't cared for ten years whether he sells records, and for that I applaud him. He's a good guy and he knows what he's doing. He's a genius, he's *obviously* the middle-class genius of the 60s, the 70s – and the 80s too.[37]

Davies's impressive spate of extra-curricular activity attracted the interest of a music press that clearly viewed him as an eccentric pop genius. He was regarded as a solipsist, lost in dreams of an archaic world where English middle-class values were still upheld. For Ray, however, the everyday realities of life as a pop star were too immediate to be reduced to the level of fantasy:

> It's not a little world any more. It started off a little world but there are infiltrators in my little world. When you say 'little world' it kind of makes me think that I'm mentally not all there. It would be great for me to be actually mad. I've got a terrible feeling that I'm not. That's the whole pity of it all.[13]

As autumn approached, the details of the projected *Arthur* play were released to the public. Apparently, Ray had hoped to collaborate on the project with Poet Laureate, John Betjeman, but the script was eventually offered to novelist/playwright Julian Mitchell. The story-line centred on Arthur Morgan and his wife Rose who live in 'Shangri-la', a house situated in London suburbia which they share with their children and grandchildren. As the story opens, they are all about to emigrate to Australia. The action takes place on their final day in England, during which they talk about the state of the country and Arthur recalls, with mixed feelings, a life of conformity that has brought financial reward but spiritual impoverishment. Although it is generally assumed that Arthur was a figment of the Davies imagination, created specifically for the television play, this is not the case. Ray adapted the characters of Arthur and Rose from the lives of his eldest sister and her husband, who emigrated to Australia years before the Kinks were formed. Davies recalls the many parallels between his late brother-in-law and the central character of his 'pop opera':

> I was very close to Arthur; he was a very strict man. He was a welder in a plastics factory, a simple man, but he realised the British Empire was fucked. His brother was shot and killed in the war. Arthur realised that it was futile, that you could never get a break in the British Empire. He was such a frustrated man, and I wrote the album partly for him. He just died recently – he died of tension – but before he did, he said, 'I loved the album you did about me'. A lot of people in the family thought that he was a bitter man, but he was just frustrated. A lot of people gave up their lives and their youth for the war. They had been promised a new world, and what did they get? Motorways and concrete.[35]

Davies had enormous faith in the *Arthur* project and he was therefore greatly upset when midway through production, the play overran Granada's budget and was dropped. Despite the threat of legal proceedings, the television company refused to screen the play. So, after all the hopes and plans, there remained only the album, *Arthur Or The Decline And Fall Of The British Empire*, which was released in August.

The album was reasonably well received in the music press, but proved a poor seller. In retrospect, it is not too difficult to see why. The work was unfavourably compared with the Who's recently released *Tommy* merely because both albums were touted as rock operas. There was also some suspicion that Davies had been inspired to write a rock opera after hearing about Townshend's intentions though, the informed critics realised that both groups had been individually working on their albums at the same time. What inevitably destroyed *Arthur's* chances, however, was its peculiarly uninviting subject matter. Who else but Ray Davies would have had the nerve to compose an entire album of songs about the aspirations of a working/lower-middle-class family headed by an arch-conformist? The concept was anti-heroic, but, instead of a rebel without a cause, there was a conformist without a care. Although Davies occasionally satirises Arthur, in the same unmerciful way as that well respected man, his general approach is so sympathetic, and apparently unironic, that the album could almost be interpreted as a glorification of working-class fatalism. Davies's celebration of the mundane was far removed from the studious iconoclasm of *Tommy* and its successors. The traditions of celluloid rock from *Privilege* to *The Wall* through *Stardust* and *Breaking Glass* reveal a continued fascination with the notion of the performer as a Messiah. Ken Russell's extravagant *Tommy* captured this hackneyed theme most forcibly in its often gratuitous use of destructive imagery. In comparison, a big screen version of *Arthur* would have seemed the equivalent of an Ealing comedy. Its commercial limitations notwithstanding, *Arthur* achieved some cult status in America as a great undiscovered work. Even here, however, it is important not to be over-sentimental about its worth. Ultimately, *Arthur* was a far less interesting album than *The Village Green Preservation Society*, in spite of its unity of design. The political songs sound particularly unconvincing, with Ray uncomfortably emerging from his normally subtle satire to openly parody such figures as Churchill and Montgomery. Several other numbers, including 'Yes Sir, No Sir' and 'She Bought A Hat Like Princess Marina', are too superficial to be of anything other than cursory interest. Ray remains defensive about these songs, maintaining that they were an accurate reflection of the mood of the times:

> Well, obviously I wasn't around when that was happening. But I know people who were. And I can remember Churchill being Prime Minister. The idea was like in 'Yes Sir, No Sir' . . . to make people feel important to the cause . . . and make them interested so that they give their all . . .

> everything they've got. That's what I think was going on. I think people who were there say that was great because we had Mr Churchill and good old Churchill told us what to do. And Montgomery and Mountbatten . . . You see films of Mountbatten poofing around the Far East in airplanes and swimming with Douglas Fairbanks and everything. And it's all very nice . . . [63]

In spite of Ray's defence, the songs lack the characteristic wit and musical depth of the group's better work. Perhaps the fact that several of the songs were tailored to the central theme of the Fall Of The British Empire explains why they sound so dull and laboured. Although there are some exceptional cuts, such as the strident 'Victoria', the arrangements are generally less adventurous than on *The Village Green Preservation Society* while the lyrics are disappointingly simplistic. Only 'Shangri-la' rises magnificently from the mire to stand as one of Davies's greatest compositions. The delightfully ironic title and the dramatic slow/fast arrangement fully convey the mock heroic splendour of the theme, increasing the satirical bite in each successive verse as Davies collates the rewards and calculates the price of conformity. The Kinks wisely released an unedited version of 'Shangri-la' as their next single, but their previous ill-luck was compounded by its surprise chart failure.

The public rejection of *Arthur* and *The Village Green Preservation Society* must have left the Kinks wondering whether there was any point in continuing as a recording unit. Fortunately, their recent disappointments were alleviated by a six-week tour of America in October including dates in Boston, Chicago, Detroit and Hollywood. Although the visit was not envisaged as a promotional trip, the timing coincided with a resurgence of interest in the Kinks among the underground rock press. Ray Davies was pleasantly surprised to discover that the Kinks had not been completely forgotten during their three-year exile:

> The Americans seem to understand the feeling behind the album and Arthur himself just as well as the British. There's a lot of interest in it and I've been approached with three very exciting possibilities to expand *Arthur*. I really thought nobody would know anything about our records in America. But audiences now show a much greater appreciation of everyone's music.[71]

It was not only the American audiences and critics who were intent on celebrating the Kinks' U.S. return, but also their record company Reprise. A bizarre series of promotional tactics were considered, most of them embarrassing and ridiculous, yet extremely inventive. At one point, the P.R. department toyed with the idea of recruiting several thousand young teenagers to converge on Kennedy Airport on the day of the group's arrival, in an attempt to emulate the mania of the Beatles' first landing in 1964. Reprise would conveniently equip the fans with hundreds of placards proclaiming 'Welcome The Kinks' and, while the fury raged outside, the group would attend a press conference with representatives from every teenage magazine on the market. Further posters would be produced for distribution at New York's Fillmore East and other prestigious venues on the group's itinerary. The radio blitz was to include a seductively voiced English girl intoning 'The Kinks Are Coming' while excerpts from *Arthur* were played in the background. In order to play on Dave Davies's rebel image, false arrests for the possession of marijuana were planned, not to mention gang-rape and the filing of multitudinous paternity suits. In every city on the tour a series of minor arrests were to be concocted for such offences as loitering, impersonating an officer and income tax evasion. As a finale, it was hoped that the Fillmore East might be closed midway through the Kinks' set under the pretext that they were destroying the hearing of the nation's youth. Not surprisingly, Ray dismissed their ideas as cheap hype and the promotional visit passed without incident. However, without spending any money, Reprise had ingeniously used the false promise of extravagant publicity as a means of attracting press attention. Their super-hype self parody was an ironic gesture worthy of Davies himself.

The U.S. tour ended with a memorable four nights at Hollywood's Whisky A Go Go. There the group played before a hard core of Kinks devotees, many of whom attended all four sets. Although concentrating heavily on selections from *Arthur*, the group was careful to include several hits and a sprinkling of rock'n'roll classics, including 'Rip It Up' and 'Milk Cow Blues'. Critics noted with some surprise that Dave Davies sang most of the songs while Ray seemed content to play rhythm guitar and contribute occasional verses. Although Ray found this U.S. visit tiring, his enthusiasm was fuelled by the encouraging response and plans were immediately formulated for extensive touring in the New Year.

TEN

Leaving on a Jet Plane

The beginning of 1970 was a crucial period in the history of the Kinks. The previous two years had seen a decline in their popularity. The Kinks were perplexed by this but were nevertheless determined to establish themselves as an albums group. Ray remained self-critical and ever vigilant about the need to develop his songwriting skill and, although he felt that his writing had improved, particularly during the past three years, he was aware of the danger of losing direction by compromising the Kinks' music:

> I'd like to be fully in control of my music. To be honest I'd like to know what I'm good at, but unfortunately I'm not clever enough. If I did know I probably wouldn't write the songs the way I do.[72]

What Davies needed was a new audience, ready and willing to accept concept albums as well as his commercial singles. Fortunately for the Kinks their reputation remained high in the States where nobody took them for granted. Many Americans regarded them as a link with the mid-60s British beat boom, lately replaced by post-hippie superstardom. In spite of their seeming irrelevance, the Kinks had much to offer to a nation increasingly nostalgic for the innocence of Swinging 60s Britain. Already, the evergreen Troggs were discovering rich pickings as a live draw, while the defunct Zombies had achieved a 'posthumous' U.S. number 1 hit with 'Time Of The Season'. The Kinks were in the perfect position to take America by storm and spared no effort in trying to achieve this.

The first leg of their 1970 Tour Of The Americas was progressing towards its climax when Mick Avory suddenly fell ill. As a result, the Kinks were forced to cancel the remaining dates, including a prestigous weekend at the Fillmore East that would have elicited strong interest from the rock press. While Dave, Mick and John returned disappointed to England, Ray remained in New York for talks regarding a re-scheduled visit in June. The rigours of the American tour convinced Ray of the need for instrumental augmentation, particularly on the album cuts that had featured the work of session pianist Nicky Hopkins. Back in England, manager Grenville Collins was searching for a suitable player via his contacts in the music business. Following up a tip from ace rock journalist, Pete Frame, Collins contacted John Gosling, a Royal Academy student with an impressive knowledge of classical, folk, pop and rock music. Gosling was puzzled by Collins' offer of a place in a recording group called 'The Kings' and claimed that he'd never even heard of them. An incredulous Grenville explained their pedigree and, finally, realising that the combo were the legendary Kinks, Gosling uttered the classic: 'The Kinks . . . are they still going?' An audition was hastily arranged at Morgan Studios and John cut half a dozen tracks including the chord sequence of a number that later emerged as 'Lola'. Amazingly enough, Davies retained that recording which was used on the single, even though the chords clashed with his vocal line. Gosling passed the audition with flying colours, assumed his nickname, John the Baptist, and accompanied the group on their next Stateside visit. The Kinks opened at the Depot in Minneapolis, a venue run by Danny of Danny and the Juniors fame. For Gosling, it was a frightening debut as his equipment broke down three quarters of an hour into the set. Characteristically, the group played on oblivious of his panic, while the roadies desperately tried to repair the damage. Although it was their longest U.S. tour, Gosling adapted to the exhausting circuit of Holiday Inns with surprising ease and even indulged in the frivolous and sometimes dangerous group escapades which included setting fire to hotel rooms and smashing television sets.

While the Kinks were assaulting the States for the second time in three months, problems arose delaying the release of their current single, 'Lola'. The original lyric included a reference to 'Coca Cola'. Anxious to avoid a ban by the B.B.C. because of advertising, Ray flew 6,000 miles to London during a 24-hour break in the group's itinerary, in order to alter the reference to 'cherry cola'. A further disaster followed when the master tape, insured for £10,000, was mysteriously lost somewhere between London and New York. Eventually, the problems were resolved and this incredibly expensive recording was released in June towards the end of the tour which proved to be the Kinks' most successful yet. An exuberant Dave Davies recalled scenes reminiscent of mid-60s Kink mania:

> We played at Vancouver where we'd never been before and the kids almost tore up the place. One place that we played in America they weren't quite sure what to expect. I think they thought we would be dressed in suits and very, very smart. A lot of people didn't even know we existed but the reaction we got was very good all round.[73]

On returning to England, the Kinks were greeted with the news that their single 'Lola' was heading for number 1 in the *New Musical Express* chart. The single was another Kinks classic, with a riff almost as distinctive as the seminal 'You Really Got Me'. The lyrics were both clever and amusing, and the intentionally risqué theme almost invited a radio ban from the B.B.C. Despite its suggestiveness, however, 'Lola' was sufficiently ambiguous to keep the radio programmers smiling and even during interviews Ray refused to be manoeuvred into admitting that Lola was a transvestite:

> Lola is a real person and a very good friend of mine, a dancer actually. I'm not going to tell you what sex the person is, though. It's a joke song but it's very real. I think that sex is very unimportant in friendships. That's why I wrote the song.[74]

With Lola Ray had found a character far more intriguing to the general public that the fatalistic Arthur. Clearly, if he had chosen to base his rock opera on the decadent nature of the pop business commercial success might not have been so elusive. Having watched the Kinks decline in popularity, Davies suddenly found himself on the front page of the music press beneath such headlines as 'Sex Change Record – Kink Speaks!' Overnight this one single had re-established Ray as one of pop's leading personalities and his comments on 'Lola' revealed a new confidence:

> When we first did the song I had the cameramen blowing kisses at me from the floor. The song is actually meant to show that things aren't always what they seem. In such realms, you could think one thing and something else would be hidden, lurking in a shadow. I like writing songs with stories about people. I live in a strange world to some, but I think the world is a lot stranger. Everything is really a great comedy with a stage manager somewhere watching the whole thing going along. I'm the one who treads dangerously, but if you read into the lyric, you'll see the song is only about friendship . . . I'd been thinking about writing 'Lola' for a long time, as it was an interesting subject. I like people – even the ones without much character. In fact, those are usually the ones that have the best personalities; the others have to replace it with an act. My whole intention was to build a complete record. The L.P. we're doing has a story-line and 'Lola' is part of that too.[75]

In many ways the minor controversy surrounding 'Lola' was extremely gratifying for Davies since it indicated that the public were at least listening to his songs. The success of 'Lola' ensured that Ray Davies was once again a bankable commodity for the filmscore market. Unfortunately, the offers he received invariably seemed to be connected with tasteless projects, conceived primarily by businessmen in search of a current chart act. Probably against his better judgment, Davies agreed to write the score for *Percy*, a sexual comedy on the unlikely theme of a penis transplant. Ray would have been better advised to exploit the Kinks' recent chart-topping success with an extensive British tour, but apart from an appearance at the Yorkshire Festival of Jazz, Folk and Blues, they remained inactive.

While the group were recharging their batteries, following the Stateside trips and British television appearances, the ever-industrious Ray was working on another play. Such was the intensity of his schedule that, for a brief period, he considered employing the services of an outside producer on future Kinks' records. His latest idea was a football musical but, in spite of two months' solid work, the project was shelved. Suddenly, it seemed that Davies was once again falling victim to his own imagination. Although his songwriting was apparently as strong as ever, his talents were being diffused over an increasing number of abortive projects. Many ideas might well have developed into concrete album concepts but for Davies's restlessness and boredom. Instead of exercising discipline over his craft he was constantly writing new songs at every opportunity. Increasingly he became aware that his obsession with the importance of composing was developing into a neurotic habit:

> I have to keep writing. If I had it all my way and had a country cottage to get it together in, I'd write lousy songs and maybe make a lot of money. But I've given up trying to get rich. I'll do the things I want to do. If I were Prime Minister, I think I'd carry a tape recorder around with me everywhere I'd go and record it all. Each of my songs has been a proper record of what I thought to be happening at the time. I want to record for history every man that walks down the street – every little incident that takes place. I want to lie a little to help the truth, use some fantasy. I'll keep writing until I get stabbed in my bed . . . I'm tired and exhausted but I've got to keep moving.[76]

One project that did reach fruition was Alan Sharp's television play *The Long Distance Piano Player*, featuring Ray in the role of a pianist driven on by a fanatical promoter to break the record for non-stop piano playing. As I recall, the play was more than adequate, but television critic James Thomas tells a different story:

> If this was a play for today, heaven help us tomorrow . . . It could take the prize as one of the most palpable non-events to be seen on T.V. in a long time.[77]

The play included two songs, the unreleased 'Marathon' and 'Gotta Be Free' (which appeared in slightly different form on the next Kinks album).

The long awaited results of Davies's songwriting summer were revealed in *The Kinks Part One – Lola vs Powerman And The Moneygoround*, an ambitious project chronicling the group's disillusionment with the pop industry. The album was Davies's most bitter work, though much of the vitriol was couched in humour. Essentially, the work was divided into songs satirising the music industry and documenting the effects of rock star life. The satirical numbers were easily the most successful, containing a verbal wit and musical invention often the equal of his finest work. 'Denmark Street' was a humorous excursion into the rapacious world of Tin Pan Alley, complete with an appropriate music hall inspired backing. 'Top Of The Pops' and 'The Moneygoround' took the satire to its furthest extreme, with some bitter comments on Davies's personal experiences in the rock business. The former was a brilliant imitation of the Kinks' early style, complete with old-fashioned riffs which recalled such songs as 'Louie Louie' and 'Land of 1,000 Dances'. In parodying the Kinks' archetypal riffs, Davies was sending up those critics who had once criticised the group for their derivative style. The final irony came several years later when the television show *Top Of The Pops* played the Kinks song while celebrating its 100th broadcast. If 'Top Of The Pops' pricked the sensitive skin of the rock business, the scathing 'Moneygoround' tore into its flesh unmercifully. In damning the money-grabbing sharks that inevitably infest the business, Ray even had the audacity to name his three managers, Robert Wace, Grenville Collins and Larry Page. His major complaint against Page concerned a foreign publishing deal in which Ray apparently lost half his money. However, there is not a shred of evidence to suggest that his former managers were guilty of duplicity. In reality, Davies's complaint was a far more generalised one against publishing deals of the period. Page reminds us of the rules of the game:

> That was normal publishing procedure. If you have an overseas publisher you have a 50/50 deal with that overseas publisher on cover records. Even today, a deal you'd set up would be 75/25 and 50/50 on covers. It was a normal publishing practice. But the way he worked it out was that we were all giving his songs away. You're not giving *anything* away.[9]

Collins and Wace were equally disturbed by the sentiments of the song, as Robert recalls:

> I didn't see the funny side of that at all. Grenville and I were very upset about some of the lyrics on the album because, by and large, they were untrue. The fact was that Grenville and I never earned a dime from his songwriting. There's no doubt that that album severely soured our relationship with Ray. There are deep-seated things that lurk and linger. The opening lines of 'Moneygoround' were funny and amusing – but they didn't happen to be true. I accept that part of the song is about giving Denmark Productions placing rights on publishing. But we never made anything from his bloody songs.[6]

What is most intriguing about 'The Moneygoround' is the carefree tone with which Ray delivers his autobiographical tale of avaricious publishers, writs and nervous breakdowns. Whereas most writers would have sung the song either as a dirge or an angry protest, Davies stands back and smiles sardonically at the absurdity of his situation in the pop game.

The remaining tracks, dealing mainly with the problems produced by the rock singer role, were less impressive, but still good. The rigours of flying ('This Time Tomorrow'), the insecurities of life on the road ('A Long Way From Home'), the power of the unions ('Get Back In Line') and the horror of the pin-stripe brigade ('Rats') were some of the themes covered in the Kinks' full frontal attack on their chosen profession. It would have been a depressing catalogue but for the characteristic flashes of Davies humour. Apart from an original uncensored version of 'Lola', the album contained one of Ray's most expressionistic songs, 'Apeman'. On one level this was a novelty number, complete with Davies's affected West Indian vocal, but there were also more serious undertones. The inspiration for the song stemmed from Ray's art school days when he spent much time in the monkey house at London Zoo staring reflectively at an ape. In meditating upon man's apparent lack of civilisation and the problems produced by over population and pollution, Davies humorously invoked primitivism as an ideal state. The number succeeded both as an amusing singalong and an effective pop translation of Eugene O'Neill's *The Hairy Ape*. Perhaps the one criticism of Davies's writing might be that, though he talks about the importance of personal and political freedom in society, there are never any possible solutions offered. On the other hand, his conscious avoidance of hippy utopianism and his willingness to parody his own idealism in 'Apeman' indicated a songwriting ability the equal of Randy Newman.

By late 1970, the heavy metal riffs of Dave Davies were producing almost as much interest as his brother's lyrics, particularly among young Americans in search of an old fashioned British beat group. The American response was so promising that the Kinks arranged another tour of the States for November. It was their most impressive series of gigs to date including stints at the Fillmore, supported by Love and Elton John, and a celebrated performance at Carnegie Hall during which they were presented with special commemorative plaques. The group played diverse sets at a number of different venues, occasionally catering for older audiences as well as the younger fans. After playing a very straight set at an obscure club in Grand Junction, Colorado, Ray was accosted by a woman who remarked that the Kinks were the only 'underground' group she admired. Having just performed such songs as 'You Are My Sunshine' and 'She's My Ladylove', Davies was somewhat perplexed that the Kinks should be regarded as pseudo-heavy:

> I think it's a little strange when people say we're an underground group. I'd feel more at home being called a performing troupe of players . . . I think underground in its truest sense is a heavy sound like Grand Funk.

> And I think underground was a very good thing when it came out. It brought to the surface things that had been hidden and as a result people who were not normally heard of became popular. And that's how I think we got into that because we weren't heard of. Although our records were released, no one would play them. That's how we were regarded as an underground group, perhaps. I don't think the Kinks will ever change.[22]

During their tour of the East Coast the Kinks gave a performance at New York's Philharmonic Hall that is still regarded by many as their most outrageous of the decade. By the time Ray took the stage he was apparently drunk and his manic movements were almost frightening to watch. Half-way through the set, with his body movements out of control, Ray stumbled backwards towards Dave, who neatly sidestepped and watched his brother crash into the amplifiers. It was a hilarious yet pathetic scene with Ray still singing into a microphone that had long since gone dead. For many groups that would have been the end of the night, but the audience saved the evening by climbing onstage and assisting their fallen hero. It was a glorious moment for Ray, reminiscent of the old Bill Haley movies of the 50s, in which the combo would leave the stage to be replaced by their followers, who would pick up their instruments and play. After years of fleeing from fans Davies joked about the need to break down the barriers between the Kinks and their audience. This stress on the empathy between the man in the street and the entertainer would later be used as the basis for a play and two albums. Although the Kinks' outrageous performance encouraged the Philharmonic to slap a ban on many rock groups, Ray maintains that the gig provided an important lesson, which ultimately proved extremely valuable:

> I think it was a lucky thing that happened because I realised then they could see I was in trouble and they wanted to help me. That taught me quite a lot. It was that people . . . they like you for your weaknesses too; you don't have to go up there and be in control of everything.[78]

In spite of the controversy surrounding the Philharmonic gig, John Gosling remembers it as relatively innocuous and stresses that there were far more outrageous scenes elsewhere both onstage and off, including fistfights and general mayhem. For much of their stay, the Kinks were plagued by transvestites who would tirelessly pace hotel corridors waiting for one of the group to emerge. When this occurred, the results were often hilarious, as Gosling testifies:

> I remember Dave fleeing in terror down the corridor pursued by this huge, coloured man dressed in suspenders and a wig. It was a frightening sight. A lot of these transvestites claimed they were 'Lola' – and even believed it![79]

The Kinks visit to the West Coast was less controversial and their return to Hollywood's Whisky A Go Go was greeted with plaudits by even the most sceptical critics. As if to testify to the Kinks' sudden emergence as a heavy group they were supported by Black Sabbath. This incongruous coupling at least provided some cynical humour from Dave Davies who sat in the audience rudely yelling 'Play "Temptation" or "Albatross"' throughout the Sabbath set. For Ray, the rigorous touring schedule was once more becoming an inevitable fact of life, and he described the Kinks in terms of a commando of entertainment officers:

> We follow quite a general pattern on tour. For the first couple of weeks we don't talk to each other, now Dave's finally getting round to talking to me, and me to him – so we've got over that period. It's like being in the army I think, although I don't really know what the army's like – but I imagine it must be like this.[80]

Although they had neglected Britain for much of 1970, the Kinks ended the year with another impressive chart hit when 'Apeman' climbed to number 5 in December. This welcome hit might easily have gone unheard had the B.B.C. realised that Davies had sung 'fucking' rather than 'fogging up my eyes' on the record. Ray's jest was no doubt prompted by the B.B.C.'s unnecessary television ban on 'Plastic Man' the previous year. Davies's determination to cajole radio stations into playing risqué songs did not always meet with success however. In Australia, the Broadcasting Control of Commercial Broadcasters imposed a total ban on 'Lola', from its release date on 28 November. Luckily, radio stations felt they could overcome the ruling by fading out the last verse which had caused the controversy. The edited version was sufficient to project the single to the number 1 spot for four weeks over Christmas and it was not until January that the Board finally removed the disc from Australian programmers' playlists. After so many lost battles in the past, Ray was at long last having a laugh at the pop business.

Having spent the best part of a year flying to and fro across the Atlantic, Ray perversely refused to settle down for a pre-Christmas vacation. In December, he flew from Heathrow to Los Angeles but the sole purpose of the £300 return flight was to incarcerate himself in the air in order to complete some compositions for the next Kinks album. Davies's obsessive song-writing was clearly getting out of hand although he tried to rationalise his eccentricity:

> I don't really like flying but I can't concentrate on the ground. There are too many distractions like strikes and things. The only way I can finish these songs is in the air. I'm not sure when I will be coming back but I certainly will be back for Christmas to see Walt Disney on television, and

> I have to be in this country in any case. I've got to have all these songs finished by Christmas and I can't see any other way of doing it. When you are flying you are nowhere at all – and that's the best place to be for concentration. It's very hard to adjust oneself after a long period of touring, so instead of adjusting myself I am going away again. I won't be taking any luggage, just a small hold-all. It's no different from people who work in an office instead of at home. My office is in the plane where I can work better.[81]

Sceptics could be forgiven for thinking that this Christmas transatlantic flight was designed primarily to grab some press attention. Whatever the truth, Davies must have been extremely pleased to read of his idiosyncrasies on the front page of *Melody Maker*. Although many people had been ready to write them into history at the beginning of the year, the Kinks had ended 1970 on a triumphant note.

ELEVEN

He's Gonna Step on You Again

By 1971, the Kinks' seven-year stay with Pye Records was about to end. Although the company had allowed them time to pursue elaborate projects such as *Arthur* and *The Village Green Preservation Society*, they continued to release mid-price Kinks albums without the group's support. Ray was also displeased with the Kinks' royalty rate, and a clause that forced them to pay for their own recordings. The final Kinks release on the label was the soundtrack of *Percy*, which had been premiered in February. In the film Ray's songs were cut to pieces and thrown in between suitable breaks in dialogue. The album was predictable movie soundtrack fodder, padded out with six instrumentals of dubious quality. Amid this hotch potch of cuts were some unusual songs that are often overlooked by Kinks collectors. 'God's Children' was the highlight, a plea for a return to Edenic innocence, featuring Ray on acoustic guitar backed by swirling strings. Originally, the film-makers had requested Ray to write a bouncy, amusing song about penis transplants, but finding the subject-matter nauseating, Ray rebelled and composed this serious and surprisingly impressive protest against the wonders of modern science. 'Dreams' was another reasonable track, possibly taken from the uncompleted football musical written in the summer of 1970. There were other surprises too, including 'Willesden Green', a bizarre 50s/country'n'western pastiche sung by John Dalton. In retrospect, Ray admits that he treated *Percy* with the contempt it deserved. Most of the songs sound derivative, 'Moments' recalling 'Days', while 'Animals In The Zoo' seems a re-write of 'Apeman'. Perhaps the saddest aspect of the album was revealed in 'Just Friends', which begins with an unusual arrangement, including a music box, harpsichord and orchestration before degenerating into a novelty number. The poor quality of the material was an insult to the punters, but at least Pye managed to extract four of the cuts for inclusion on a maxi-single. Unfortunately, 'God's Children' received little airplay and failed to reach the Top 50.

While *Percy* was being released, the Kinks were already mid-way through another world tour which saw them booked into the summer. A brief U.K. tour in February was followed by a Stateside visit and a series of dates in Europe. The tour culminated in Australia taking in Brisbane,

Sydney, Canberra, Melbourne, Adelaide and Perth. It was an unwelcome tour for Dave Davies and more particularly John Gosling, who disliked long flights so much that he resorted to alcohol and sedatives. The group zoomed from one city to the next in the space of a week, during which they were saddled with lousy equipment and amateur organisation. While on tour the Kinks neglected to release any new product and Ray, having seen the group survive chart failures in the past, seemed unconcerned about the failure of 'God's Children':

> We went through a period when there was little success chart-wise but all that is relative. I don't believe there is any success without failure. If you are a success in your business life you can be certain it is going to mess up your private life somewhere. No one can be successful all the time and we proved it but I've never doubted the Kinks' ability to come back.[82]

For most of 1971 the Kinks were locked in negotiation with R.C.A.'s president Rocco Laginestra, legal representative Steve Fisher and A & R head Mike Everett before a long term contract could be finalised. Ken Glancy, manager of R.C.A.'s U.K. division, greeted the signing with relief and he spared no adjectives in expressing his hopes for the future:

> This is a triumphant day for R.C.A. – it is the biggest deal the company has been involved in since becoming independent five years ago. We are delighted to welcome the Kinks to R.C.A.[83]

On being asked why he had chosen R.C.A., rather than any other company, Ray Davies replied in a deadpan tone that he had always wanted to share the same record label as Chet Atkins. During the autumn of 1971, the Kinks set to work on a new album which Ray originally conceived as a double. Eventually, R.C.A. vetoed the idea using the same argument as Pye Records by stressing its impracticality, particularly for the American market. Ray had intended to complete a television special to coincide with the release of the album, but once again the project was aborted. The sudden inactivity of the Kinks was welcomed by Ray Davies who spent most of his nights listening to bad English country'n'western music at North London's Archway Tavern. After the musical upheavals of the mid- and late 60s this unpretentious, derivative material was pleasant listening and Ray remembers the period as one of his happiest times.

In order to celebrate their recent signing R.C.A. held a party for the Kinks at the exclusive L'Etoile restaurant in New York. It was a bizarre affair with a guest list close to 500, including such luminaries as Keith Moon, John Entwhistle, Lou Reed, Andy Warhol and Alice Cooper. Apart from the large quota of stars, R.C.A. had assembled an intriguing cross section of the American press ranging from radical writer Jill Johnston to

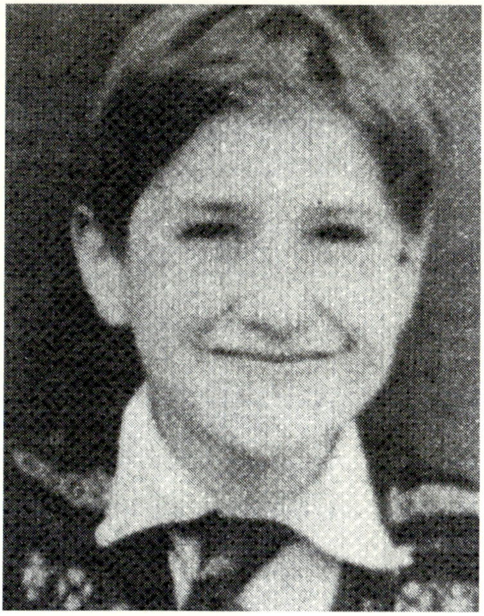

Ray Davies, aged 8

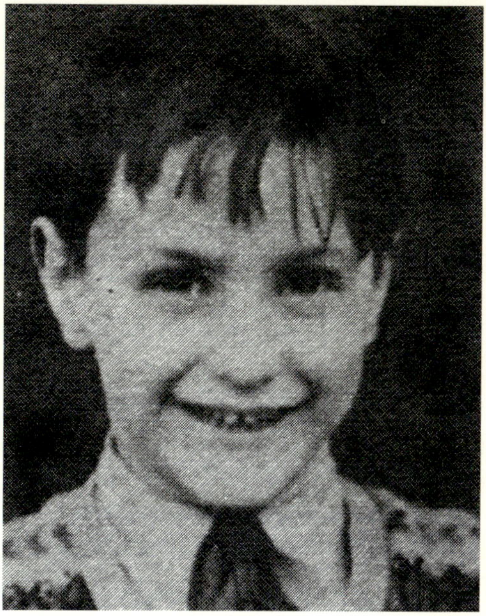

Dave Davies, aged 8

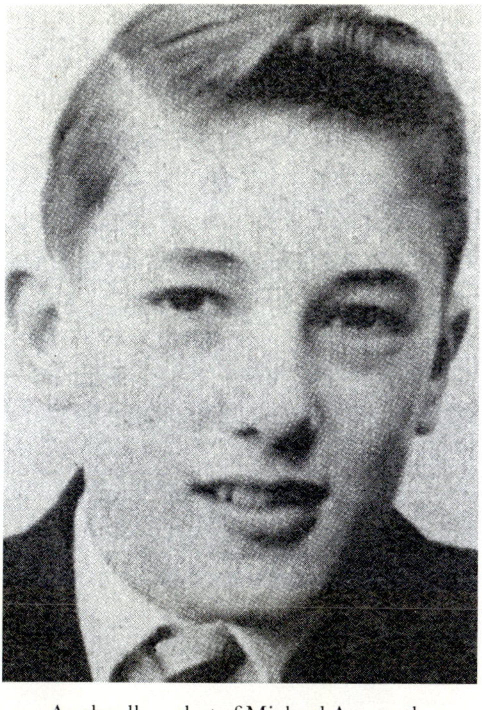

A schoolboy shot of Michael Avory, the Brylcream boy

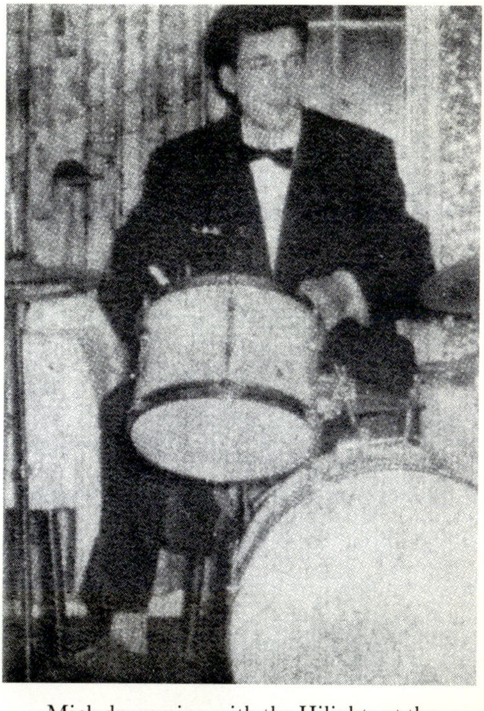

Mick drumming with the Hilights at the Osterley Hotel

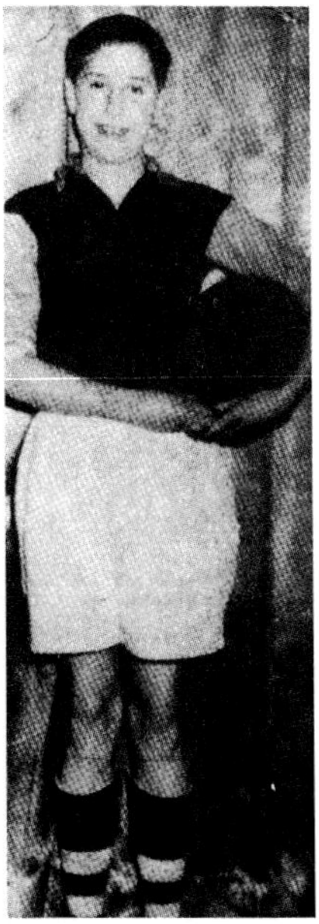

Ray as a teenage football star

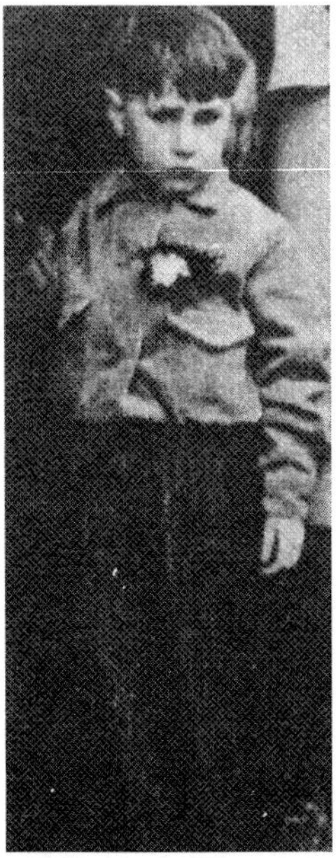

Ray as the archetypal 'mean, moody and magnificent' young kid

On the rooftops of London.
Left to right: Avory, Ray, Dave and Quaife

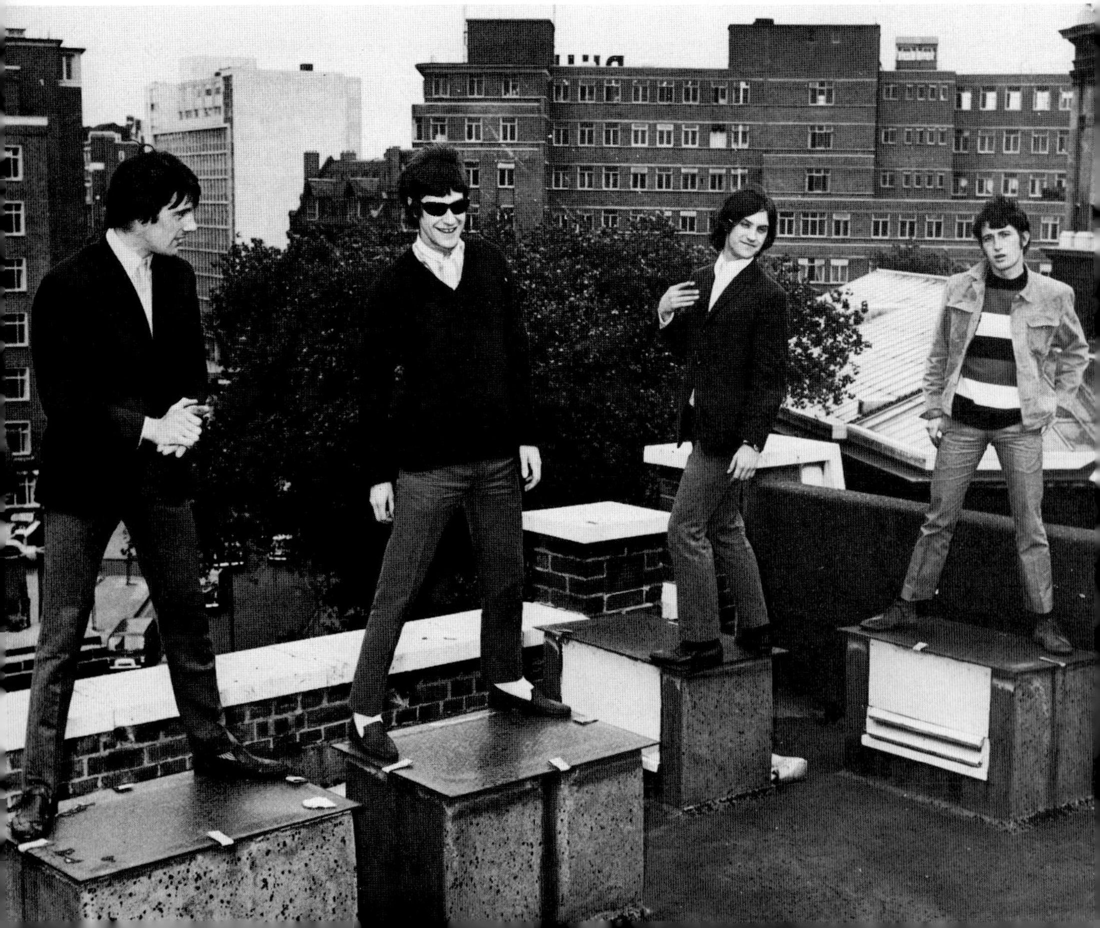

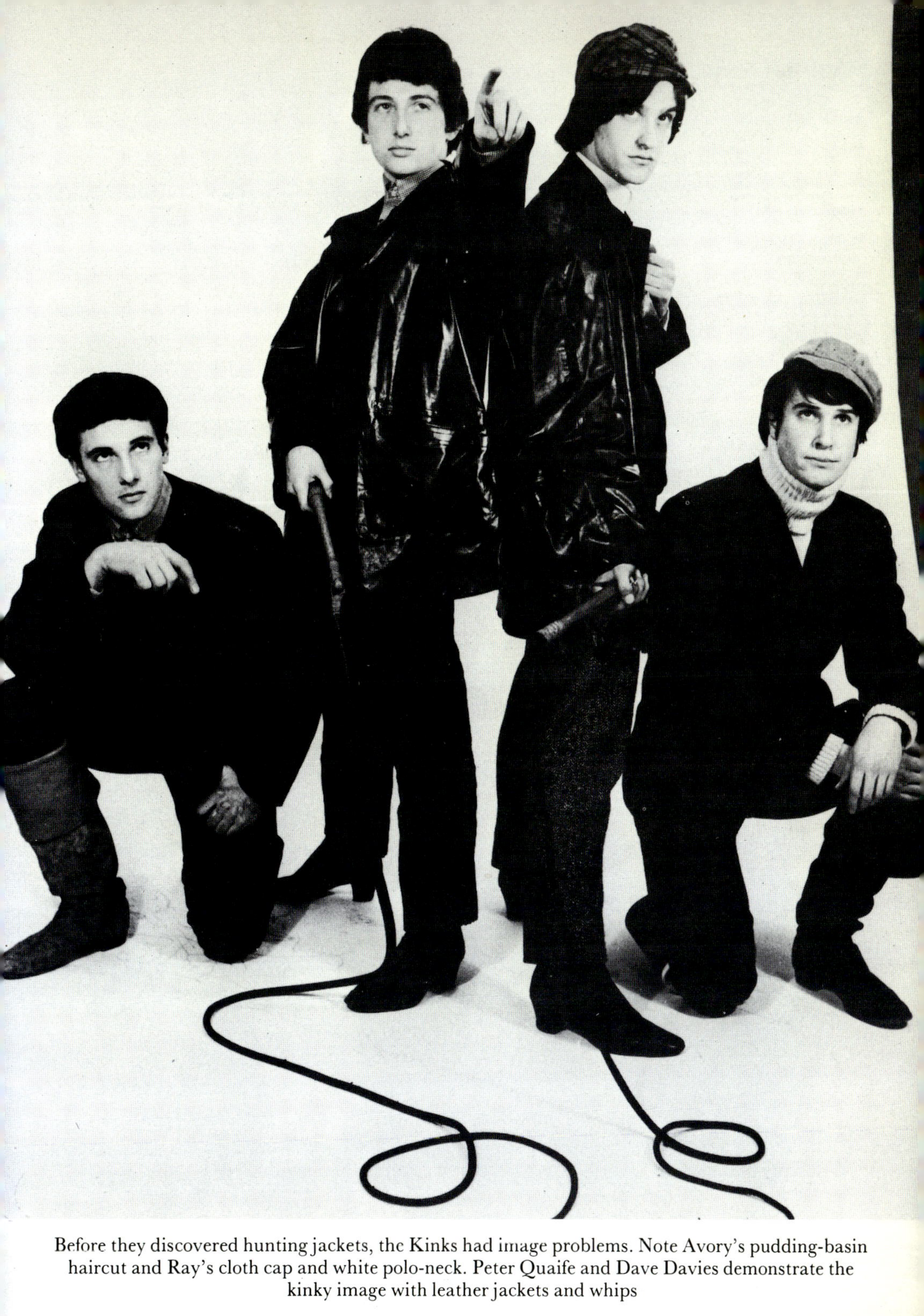

Before they discovered hunting jackets, the Kinks had image problems. Note Avory's pudding-basin haircut and Ray's cloth cap and white polo-neck. Peter Quaife and Dave Davies demonstrate the kinky image with leather jackets and whips

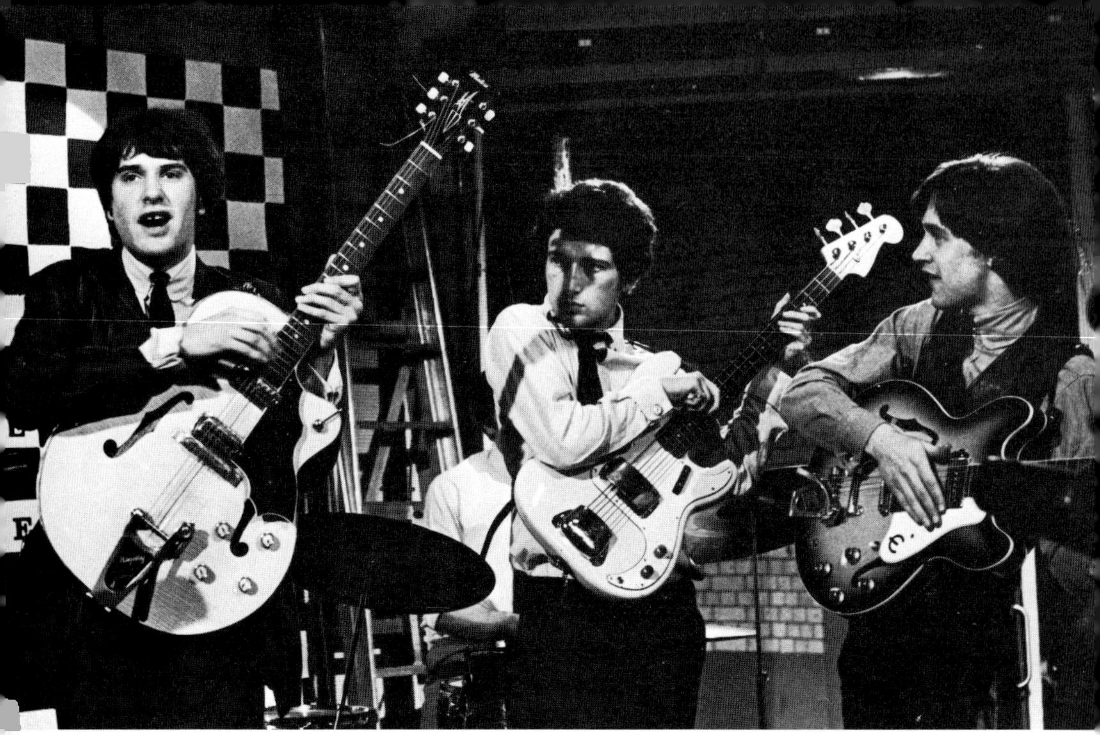

January 1964. The group performing 'Long Tall Sally' on their *Ready Steady Go* debut

One of the earliest posed shots. Although the whips have been abandoned, Dave promotes the group's 'kinkiness' with thigh-high Cavalier boots

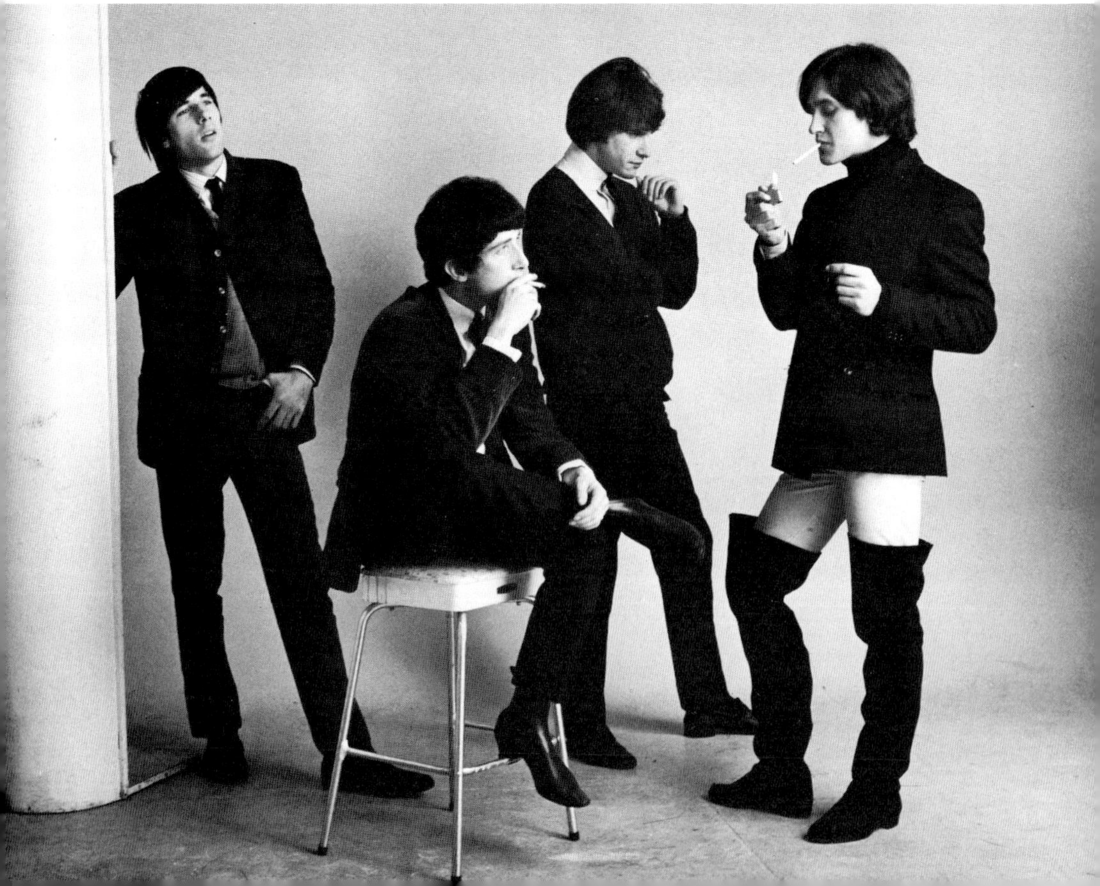

Desperately trying to look cool outside a hairdresser's salon. Avory prefers to ponder the meaning of life

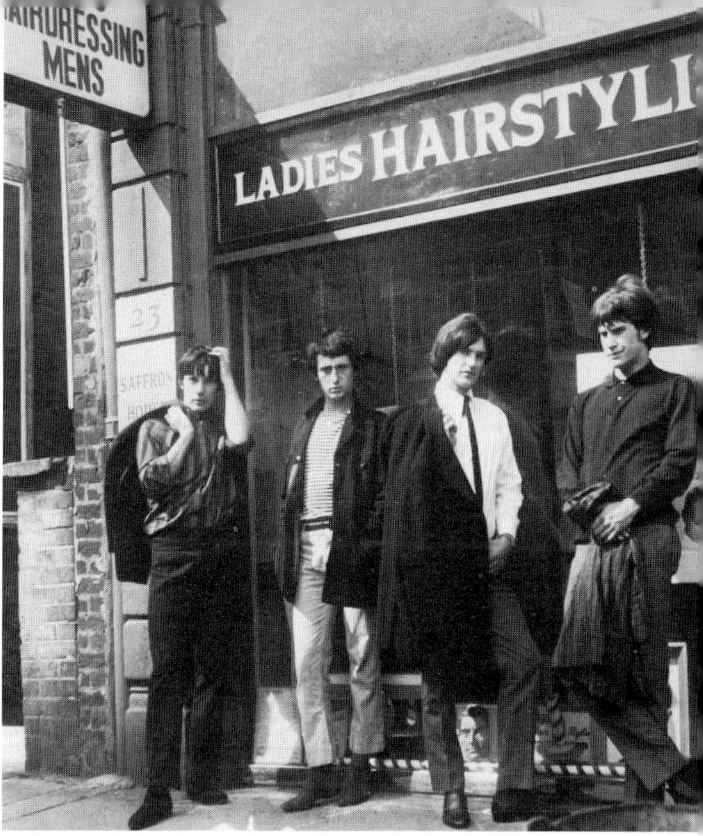

Dedicated followers of fashion, resplendent in their hunting jackets and frilly shirts

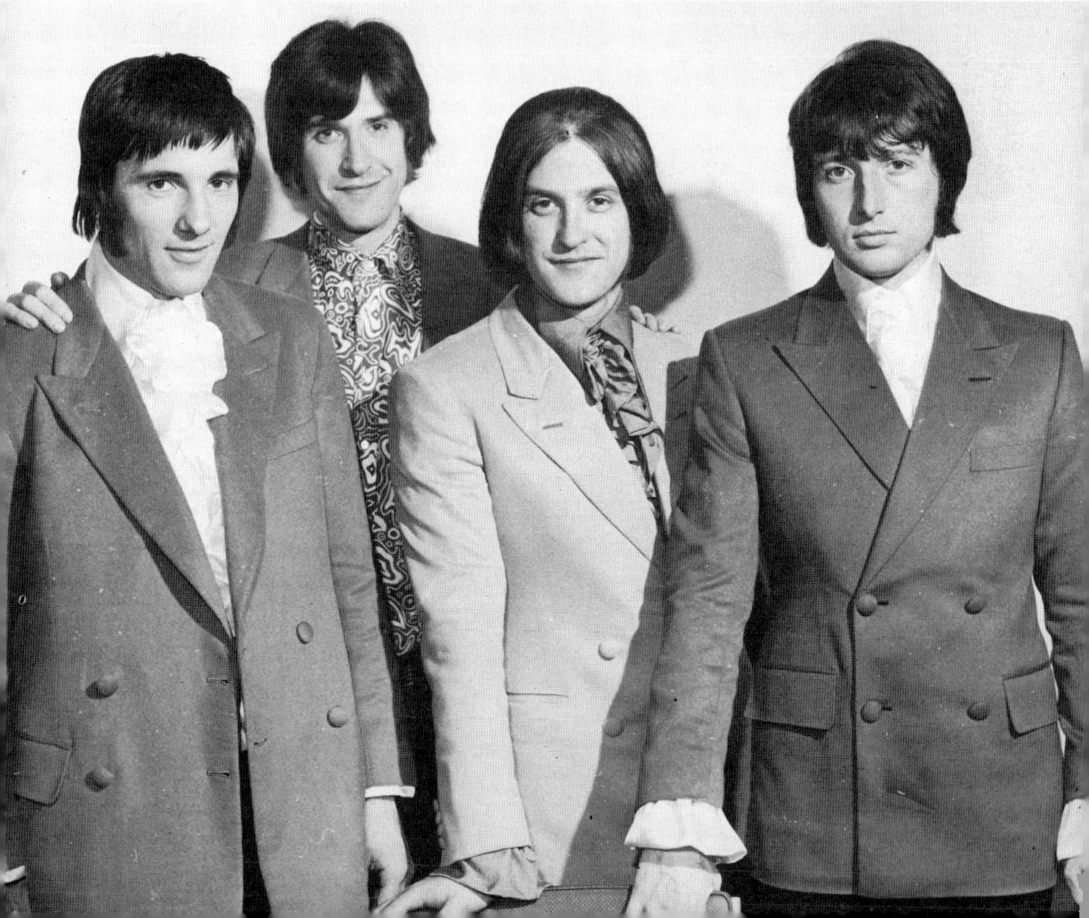

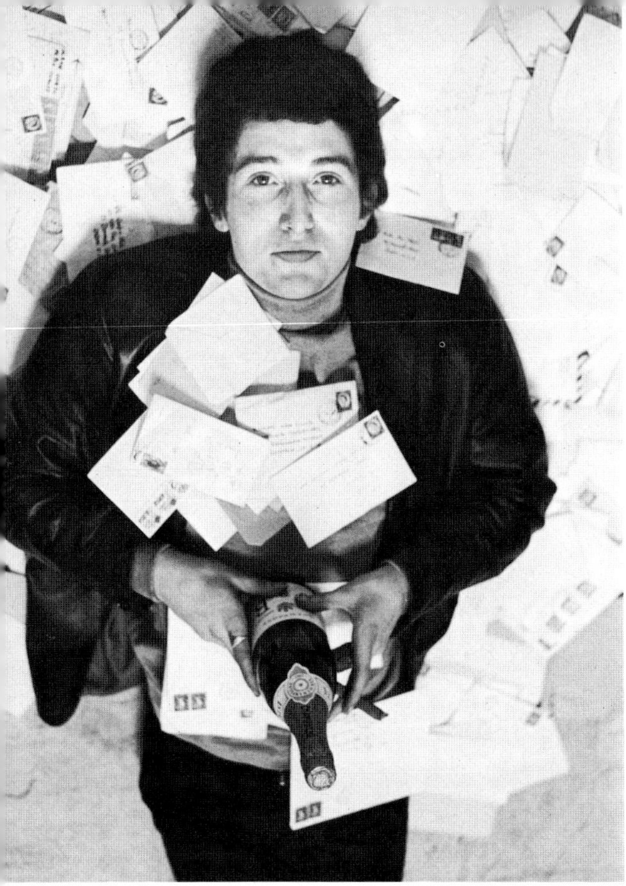

Peter Quaife celebrates his 21st birthday

'You're calling me silly — I'm the great Davies!'

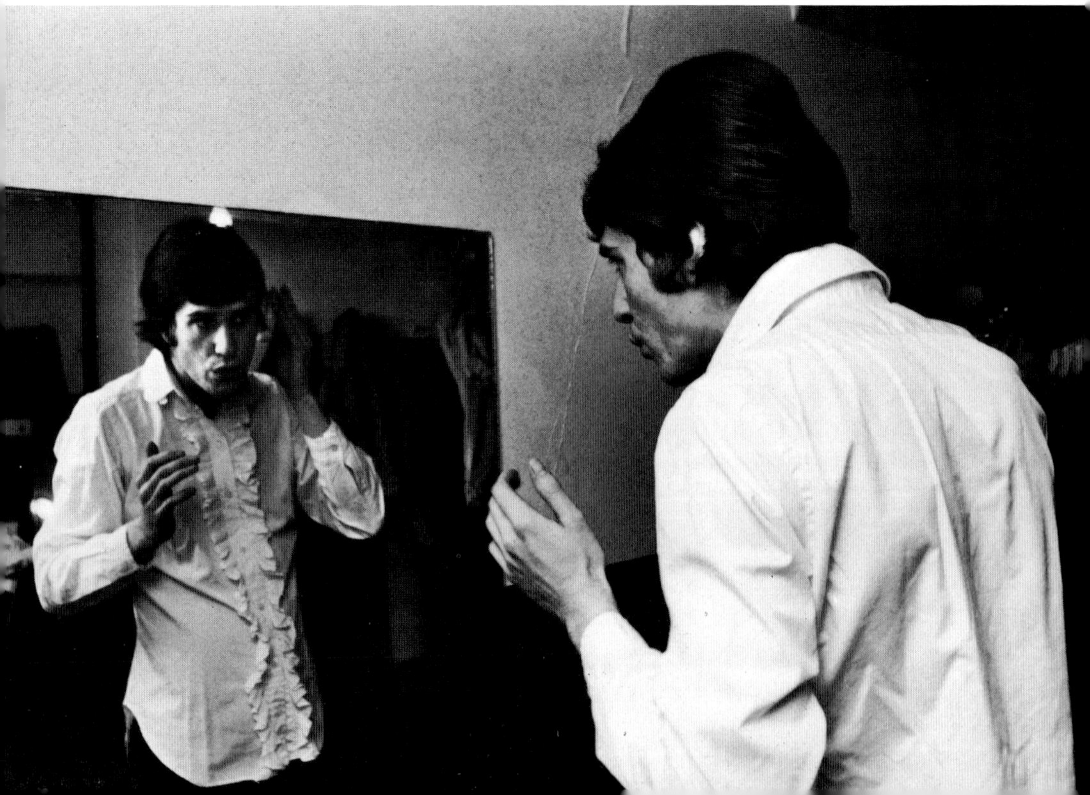

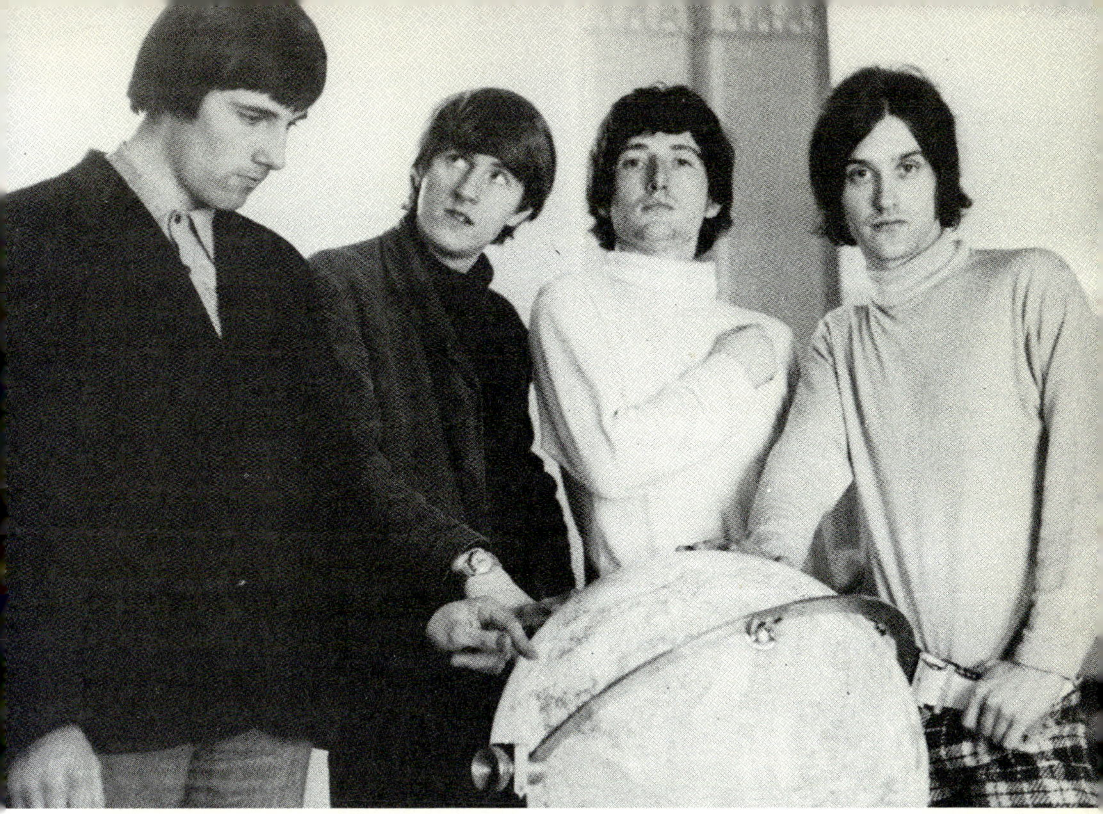

March 1966. The month that Ray Davies was replaced in the group by Mick Grace (*second from right*)

As this shot demonstrates, Peter Quaife had the most photogenic face in the Kinks

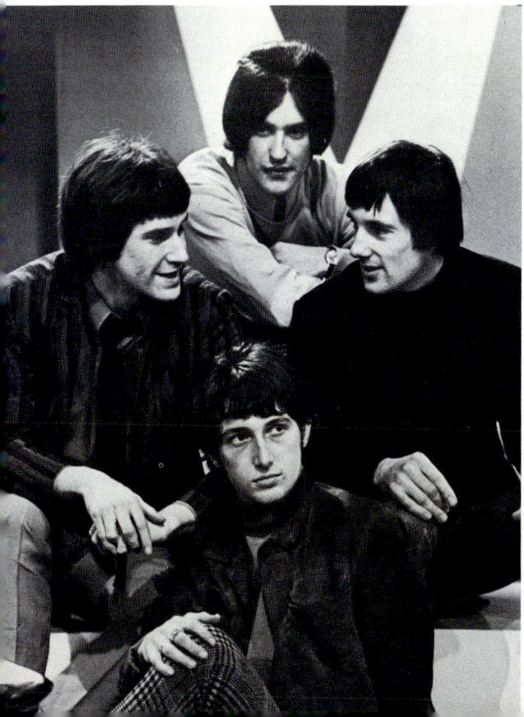

1967: an unconvincing attempt to pass themselves off as stoned hippies. Ray's moustache was equally short-lived

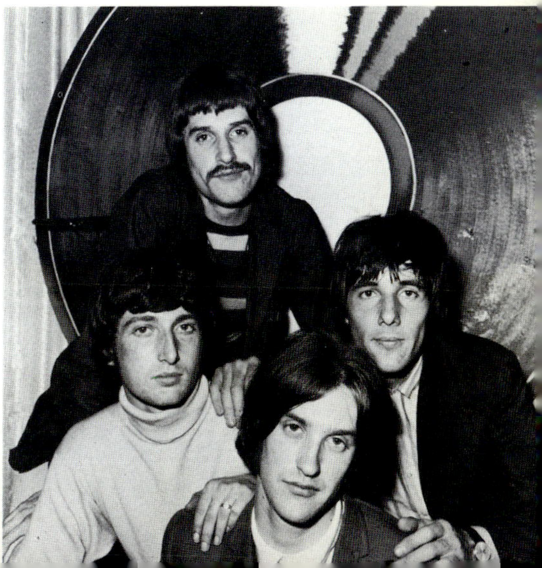

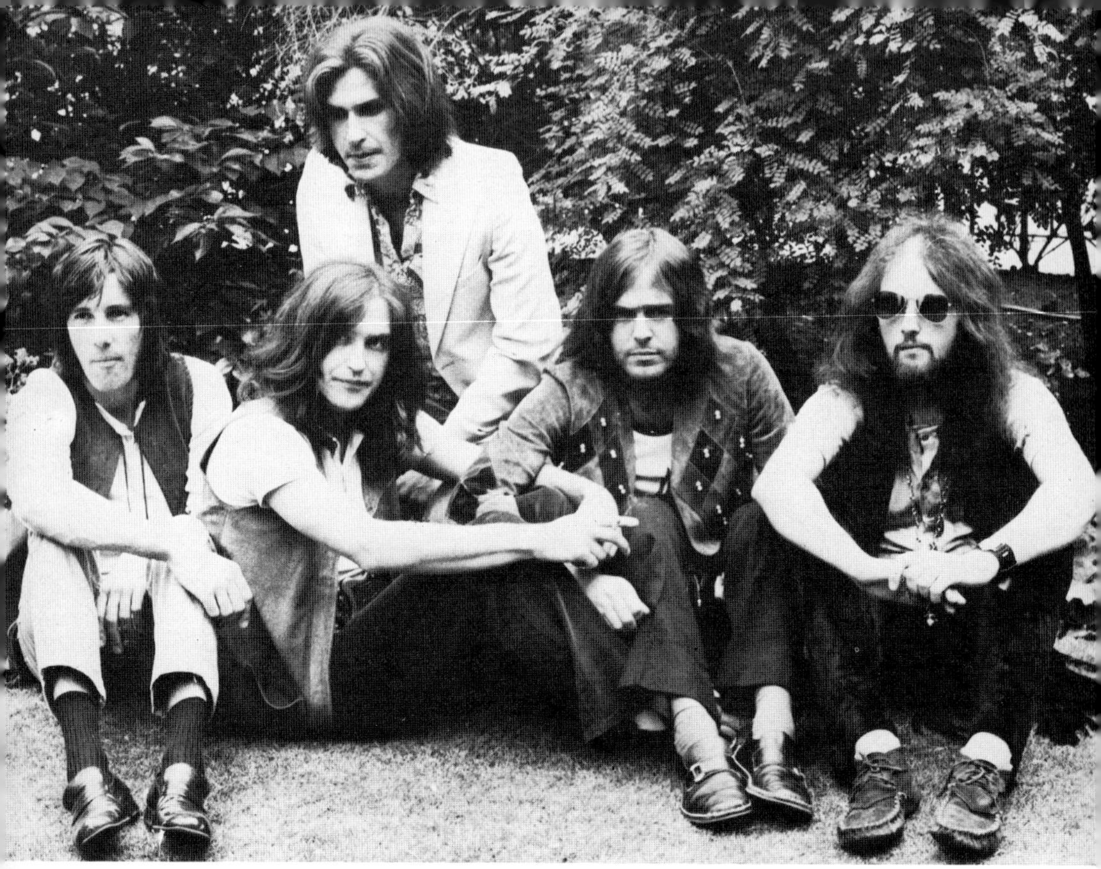

The long-standing 1970s line-up. *Left to right:* Mick, Dave, Ray, John Dalton, John Gosling

Even after two decades they can still smile. The Davies brothers – a study in group dynamics

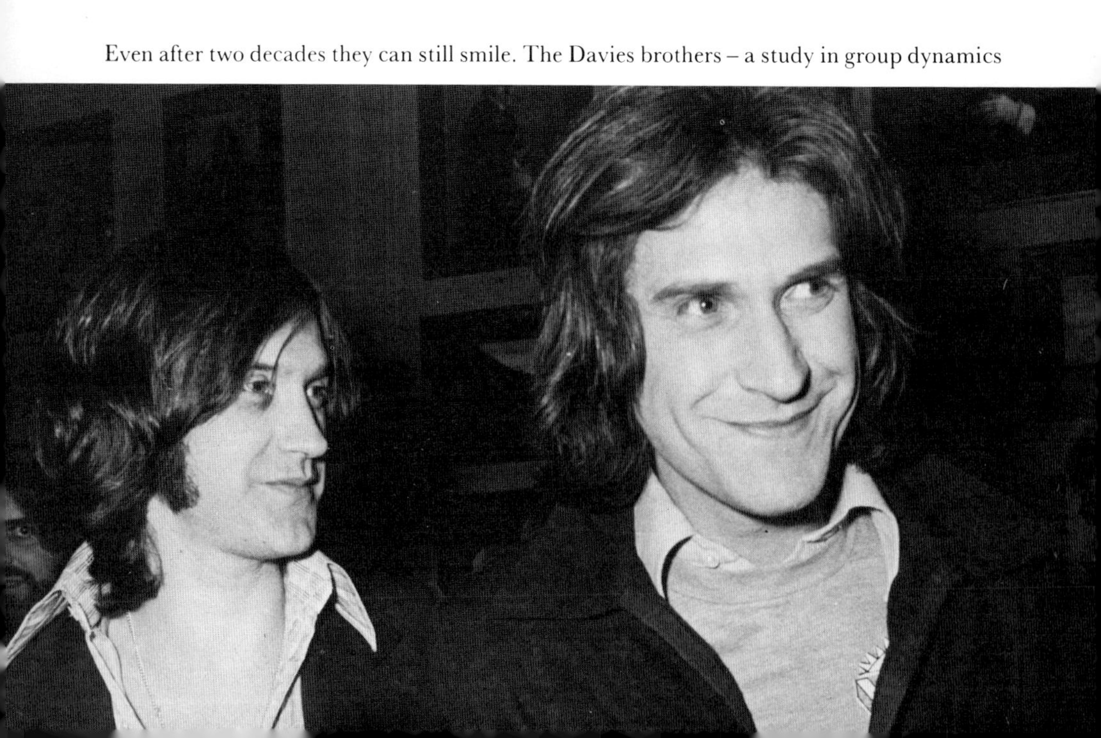

theatre critic John Simon. The highlight of the evening was the entrance of the Cockettes, a group of female impersonators who Ray was apparently anxious to meet. Their camp cavorting ensured that the party was well publicised, both in the States and Britain. The liggers returned home flattered by R.C.A.'s extravagance which had included an all expenses paid stay at the plush Plaza Hotel in New York. The decision to splash out $5,000 on a launching party demonstrated R.C.A.'s confidence in the Kinks' potential as a major U.S. draw.

The first Kinks R.C.A. album, *Muswell Hillbillies*, was another landmark in the group's history, indicating their incorporation of a three-man brass section, the Mike Cotton Sound. This unit would gradually play an increasingly important role on successive R.C.A. albums as well as forthcoming tours. What *Muswell Hillbillies* also represented was Davies' most pertinent statement on the perils of living in present day society since 'Dead End Street'. Almost every track was concerned with ordinary working people struggling in the modern world – from the alcoholic who has deserted his wife, to the anorexic girl and the Muswell Hillbilly boy lost in fantasy. The gatefold album sleeve brilliantly portrayed the scene, with its unflattering photograph of the Kinks drinking in the Archway Tavern and cavorting around the corrogated iron fencing of North London's Retcar Street. In the background, the dark satanic towers of Highgate Hill's Whittington Hospital were pictured alongside the green trees of a barely visible Dartmouth Park Hill. Seldom has an album sleeve captured the effects of urbanisation so vividly and unpretentiously.

Musically, *Muswell Hillbillies* was a determined attempt by the Kinks to restate their importance to 70s rock through the synthesis of British music hall with American-tinged country rock. It was a bizarre and often unsuccessful fusion, yet this unfashionable sound, complete with conventional brass imitating Salvation Army cadences, proved extremely effective in a satirical context. Tremendous effort was expended in achieving the precise sound envisaged by Davies. His first trick was intentionally speeding up the arrangements of fast songs and, similarly, dragging the tempo of the slower numbers in order to create a distinctive aural effect. Live vocals were recorded and played back, but Davies was constantly frustrated by the inevitably slick sound produced in the studio. Following the advice of engineer, Mike Bodak, the expensive and extremely sensitive studio microphones were traded in for some old fashioned radio mikes that had not been used since the early 60s. The P.A. system, with a microphone attached, was then set up outside the studio while Ray used a separate mike for his vocal. The double-feed effect produced the strangely archaic live sound that Davies had long been hoping to rediscover. Within the context of *Muswell Hillbillies* these old fashioned recording techniques were to prove particularly appropriate.

What Davies appeared to be doing was combining his lyrical ideas with a distinctive yet dated sound in order to conjure up visions of a decaying urban setting inhabited by social inadequates. In many respects, the album was theatrical, but unlike Davies's later conceptual works, the naive social commentary occasionally struck home. Perhaps the main reason for the album's partial success was Davies's abandoning of personae in favour of a narrator with views and experiences similar to his own. Ray stresses the autobiographical elements that permeate the album and provide the songs with additional force:

> For that L.P., *Muswell Hillbillies*, I really had to get inside . . . That whole L.P. was a story about a person who was thrown into an environment and had to come to terms with it, and went through depressions, nervous breakdowns. That was what it was all about.[84]

Although Davies followed his usual habit of sympathising with his characters on tracks such as 'Uncle Son', 'Oklahoma U.S.A.' and 'Have A Cuppa Tea', there were other tracks that revealed a darker humour. 'Skin And Bone' and 'Acute Schizophrenia Paranoia Blues', for example, dealt with anorexia and mental illness in a flippant tone that barely concealed the cruel laughter. Here, Davies was apparently singling out the misfit and holding him up to ridicule in a style similar to that of Randy Newman in such songs as 'Fat Boy' and 'Short People'. Of course, Davies's black humour was essentially a defence against the absurd pressures of modern living that had frequently plagued him over the years. Before dismissing these numbers as distasteful, it is worth noting the therapeutic value of his satirical songs and the need to place his own neuroses in a humorous context. In analysing the inspiration behind *Muswell Hillbillies* Ray remembers moments of sudden panic and disorientation that can be appreciated as delightful mixtures of comedy and pathos:

> There are all sorts of these little comedies taking place. Last time I did an interview at the B.B.C. – and it took me a long time to learn how to do interviews at all – I went in and it took three hours to do the thing. When I came out, I couldn't find a cab – I was standing there in the street with £100 in my pocket and I couldn't get anywhere. I just stood there and cried. But it isn't depressing – just more comedy.[85]

An inability to cope with the technological age was most vividly presented in '20th Century Man', another of Davies's pleas for a return to Edenic bliss. Unlike 'God's Children', however, the tone was more urgent, even desperate, as Ray screamed his protest against the negative aspects of contemporary life. In discussing the album, Ray's comments were once again alarmingly similar to the rantings of his paranoid narrator:

> I'd like to be free of all the chaos; I'd like to be free of money too. I like to

make people happy – but it isn't possible to just prance about all the time. When I have these bad periods I try not to let them come out in the music – but they do.[85]

Although Davies claims that he was unable to suppress the bleakness and depression that pervades the album, this is not the entire truth. What he frequently achieved was an ironic perspective that prevented the album from becoming a document of despair. The most harrowing track, originally titled 'Suicide', was later revamped as 'Complicated Life'. In common with 'Here Come The People In Grey' it presented the complications of living in a bureaucracy as the real threat to the ordinary working man. When composing these songs, Davies deliberately employed a mundane, anti- heroic subject matter to offset the serio/comic personal commentaries about schizophrenia, anorexia and alcoholism:

> The songs were about trying to live, getting up every day and problems like writing letters and paying bills. These are real problems to me, actually getting them done. I just don't know how other people deal with these problems, but that's what I was trying to get across on the album. Complicated life isn't about big business deals or having lunch with Rothschilds bankers; it's worrying about the electricity bill and petty things that are always there.[86]

The closing title track, 'Muswell Hillbilly', was the most parochial on the album, full of references to Davies's North London home. Rosie Rooke, for example, was an eccentric lady who lived in the Camden Town area during the Second World War. According to Ray she was renowned for her ostentatious hats. He elaborates on the legendary Rosie, with obvious affection:

> She used to be my mother's best friend when they were about sixteen. They used to walk up the Holloway Road, and all the boys whistled at her because she was very big and well-endowed and nice and shapely. She had a very sad life, and she never felt fulfilled as a person. On the original demo for the album there was a whole song called 'Rosie Rooke'. Leaving Rosie Rooke behind is like leaving everything behind. She symbolised all that for me. She was what it was like and I didn't actually know her.[87]

Davies's often deliberately obscure allusions to old institutions and working-class traditions highlighted his sense of the declining community spirit in London. In discussing *Muswell Hillbillies* Ray blamed both council redevelopment plans and working-class aspirations towards social and geographical mobility as the chief cause of this social malaise:

> It's about people being moved out of the city and moved into this new

environment that they can't comprehend. There are thousands of people, and it's the same thing that they're doing to sort of, hillbillies. Are there hillbillies any more? A few mountain people, and they go to big cities. And cockneys are going out. I think that in ten years time there won't be any cockneys left, because they'll all be taken out of London and brought into the country, into new cities. And that's what the inspiration behind it was, because I've seen it happen to people, forced on them really.[84]

Muswell Hillbillies is far from the greatest Kinks album, but it remains unusual enough to be interesting. Although the satire on modern society is ever present, it is clear that on several tracks Davies allows the mask to slip in order to reveal his personal impressions of contemporary life.

It is only through close examination of each track, clarified by Ray's own comments that the full import of his statements are conveyed. Even a seemingly innocuous Davies ditty, such as 'Have A Cuppa Tea' or the mildly satiric 'Here Come The People In Grey', take on personal significance for the writer since they were originally inspired by his ninety-year-old grandmother's enforced removal from her Islington home to an anonymous block of flats. Another of Ray's family appears as Uncle Son, though, once again, the relationship is underplayed and the character emerges, like Arthur, as a symbol of everyman rather than a flesh and blood figure. Davies's recollection of his uncle reveals a character far more pathetic than the one presented in the song:

Uncle Son was an uncle of mine who worked on the railway. Most of the people I know in life are just ordinary people like Uncle Son. They're not extremely talented. I can't remember talking to him but he came to see me when I was very young, just before he died. He had T.B. from working on the railway and he died because of his job. He drew me a picture of a train. He couldn't draw, but he thought he was giving me something by drawing a train for me. I never really spoke to him, but, like Rosie Rooke, he symbolised something to me.[87]

Although it would probably prove extremely maudlin if Ray had related the above tale in song, one cannot escape the feeling that his deliberate suppression of emotion is frequently counter-productive. Potentially powerful compositions are often generalised to such an extent that their impact is severely lessened. Even when trying not to appear self-conscious Davies succeeds in conveying a tragi-comic effect that is at once arresting and frustrating. Moreover, in combination with the unorthodox musical style these songs are enough to demonstrate precisely why Davies is regarded as one of the great eccentrics of British rock music.

Characteristically, Ray ended the year with news of elaborate plans for another television spectacular. Granada had apparently offered Ray the opportunity to write the music for a play about a social misfit dominated by his friends and unable to discover his own identity. Although the project was not completed, Ray once again developed the idea into a series of songs that would be discarded and re-written during the next few years. Content with his songwriting productivity, and his new record label's plans for future promotion, Ray spoke optimistically about the Kinks' possible development as a 70s group:

> We could break up next week, but I don't think we will. We are developing all the time. We are going on to new things and keeping the old songs as well. We do it to live and I get a certain feeling from the songs I write. I like to think that other people get a feeling from the songs I write, and those are the people who really understand the Kinks.[86]

TWELVE

John, I'm Only Dancing

Although the Kinks had established an impressive long-term deal with R.C.A., they lost the services of their managers, Collins and Wace, in 1971. Collins had switched from managing the Kinks to administering the affairs of his wife's country estate, leaving Wace in total control. However, even the faithful Wace was growing tired of Davies's obduracy and fickleness. The relationship between the parties had been strained since 'The Moneygoround' which Robert regarded as a cruel, inaccurate and unwarranted attack on his managerial reputation. The final straw came following a delay in the payment of outstanding monies to Wace. Unhappy with such treatment, Wace abruptly resigned, leaving the Kinks to manage their own career. Looking back at those often troubled years, Wace feels that the group lacked sufficient drive to achieve their full potential:

> The Kinks as a group never worked as hard as the Who or the Rolling Stones. I mean *graft.* This was part of Ray, I suppose. They were unreliable in those days, cancelling tours and all those sort of things. There was too much worrying, bickering and in-fighting . . . Ray once described the group as being like a football team that's always on the brink of relegation to the second division but somehow just does enough to avoid the drop by getting a hit record. They never wanted to be as big as the Beatles or the Stones. They could have been, but they ran away from it.[5]

Even former Stones' manager, Andrew Oldham, felt that Ray's talents remained untapped:

> Why doesn't somebody get Ray Davies into something good? I'll tell you the reason. He's connected with people only interested in working nine to five, and there are so many people in the business who have no connection with what's happening at all.[88]

It might be possible to turn some of Oldham's criticisms against Collins and Wace, but, in many ways, this misses the crucial point. The fact that Ray has continually avoided capitalising on the group's early successes betrays his own ambivalent attitude to fame that would have thwarted the efforts of most managers. Perhaps he required the services of a Svengali figure or an aggressive entrepreneur to control his career development, and it is interesting to consider the probable fate of the Kinks had they been in different hands. Larry Page has already indicated the managerial shortcomings of Collins and Wace but his perspective covers only their first eighteen months in the business. By the end of the 60s, the duo had been involved with a number of acts, including Marianne Faithfull and the Small Faces, and Wace later put that experience to effective use by catapulting Stealer's Wheel and Sailor to chart success in the 70s. Whatever their initial limitations, Collins and Wace had undoubtedly proved their loyalty by successfully managing the Kinks for many years after Page's controversial departure. One is left with the impression that Wace perhaps deserved more respect from Davies than he was ever given. Although the Kinks were already in decline as a singles group, the surprise success of 'Lola' notwithstanding, Robert Wace feels that their subsequent chart record indicates a serious loss of direction, part of which may be attributable to his absence. Indeed, if we are to believe Wace, his selection of hits was a crucial factor in the Kinks' success and without his advice Davies fell victim to a tunnel vision that still blinds his commercial instincts today:

> The personal motivation of the artist is to come up with the right song. But it's also a question of spotting it and making sure he locks on to the potential of the song that has the special magic that maybe twenty others he's played haven't got. 'Lola', for example, was recorded three times until it was done to my satisfaction. In other words, if you've got somebody who's not in the group but has a relationship with them, he becomes an outside arbitrator. He's able to say 'that's good' or 'that's terrible'. Ray needs that because not everything he does is good. Some of it is really awful. He's with a bunch of musicians who are not enthusiastic about what he does. They couldn't give a toss. You need somebody there, who's an enthusiast, who'll say 'that's terrific' – so that he's almost making a record for you. And I was able to make reasonable criticisms that he would accept.[6]

In effect, Wace had partly filled a role left vacant by the successive departures of Larry Page and Shel Talmy. Each departure was a disaster. Without Page, the dream of assailing the Stones had vanished. Minus Talmy, the string of seemingly guaranteed Top 10 hits had run dry, and the loss of Wace meant that there was nobody left to pick up the pieces. Lacking any managerial guidance, the Kinks looked to America and placed themselves in the erratic hands of Ray Davies. For the next few years their fortunes would be decidedly uneven and their reputation at home all but forgotten.

The five-piece Kinks opened their first U.S. tour of 1972 in Florida on 25 February. The itinerary also included two dates at New York's Carnegie Hall (2–3 March) which were to be recorded for possible inclusion on a live album. It was a memorable performance featuring Ray at his most mischievous. Mid-way through the set he began singing an impromptu version of Connie Francis' 1958 chart topper 'Who's Sorry Now?' Forgetting the words, he suddenly turned to Dalton and exclaimed 'Sing It Nobby!' forcing the quiet bassist to give a rare and unrehearsed vocal performance. Soon Ray decided to expand the Kinks line-up to include the brass section that had played on their last album:

> This is something I've wanted to do for some time. In the past I've written a lot of material which has included the use of brass on our records – as, for example, our present *Muswell Hillbillies* album in which we used the Mike Cotton Sound. But when we perform live without the brass, the songs lose a lot of their character.[89]

The instrumental ensemble included clarinet, saxophone, trombone and trumpet, all of which would be used to great effect on their forthcoming album.

Although the Kinks were already a big draw in the States, they chose not to imitate their contemporaries by restricting their performances to giant football stadiums. In certain towns, where their pulling power ensured a crowd of 20–30,000, the lure of the stadium would prove irresistible, but the group generally preferred to play a more arduous series of 4,000-seater gigs. Mick Avory argued convincingly that the Kinks' sound system was not adequate for the stadium shows, and the other members agreed. Ray had also recently seen Elvis Presley perform before an enormous crowd and was so frustrated by the impersonal atmosphere that he vowed to retain small club dates during the Kinks' current tour. For all their ambitious ventures, it was evident that the Kinks still regarded themselves as a people's cult group in certain quarters. Ray Davies's attitude could clearly be seen in his idealistic comments on the Rolling Stones:

> Initially people distrust us. And it's not because we'd be playing in a small hall, or somewhere that only held 2,000 people . . . I think people think I should stand on a golden stage all the time, with fantastic lighting. I believe that the Rolling Stones are only good when they play in a little club that holds about 300 people, that's the only way they'll be truly great. That's why I like the Rolling Stones.[90]

Unfortunately, certain promoters equated Ray's idealism with unprofessionalism and there was still much suspicion about this group who were once notorious for disrupting their own shows through bickering and physical assault.

The audience response that the Kinks generated during their Stateside tour was encouraging, but the reviews were mixed and sometimes contradictory. Only the Central Park gig that had been recorded for their next album was greeted with universal praise by the critics. Some of the reviews were so partisan that they spent paragraphs raving about the outbreak of Kink mania and relating apocryphal tales of near riots. Apart from the tracks that were destined to appear on their album, several other numbers were hailed as classic, including a driving version of 'Milk Cow Blues' and a particularly moving rendition of 'Waterloo Sunset'. Davies's showmanship was apparently reaching new levels of camp excess as he wiggled around the stage, hands on hips, pouting at the crowd. At one point, he climbed the stage scaffolding followed by a white spotlight which revealed him tip-toeing his way between the monitor speakers. Abruptly, he opened a can of beer and sprayed it over himself and most of the front row of spectators. Soon, this routine during the Kinks' elongated version of 'Alcohol' became all too familiar to the audience who reacted in kind. At one concert, the Valley Stream branch of the Kinks Appreciation Society came armed with confetti, paper planes and cans of beer and succeeded in transforming the show into a near carnival. New York rock scribe, Lillian Roxan, noted the proceedings with interest and spent much time describing the reactions of the attendant cult figures including Bette Midler and Candy Darling. While these East Coast reviews made flattering press cuttings, the critical reaction in California was less enthusiastic. The Kinks' performance at the Berkeley Community Theatre provoked serious questions about Davies's attitude towards his songs, his audience and his standing in rock. Greg Shaw concluded his critical drubbing by suggesting that Davies might be more at home recording a *Live At The Talk Of The Town* album. Such critical castigation was apparently not unreasonable given the nature of the Kinks' Berkeley performance. The group opened dramatically with a strident version of 'Till The End Of The Day' but abruptly concluded the proceedings after two verses and satisfied their egos by answering the shrill cries for multitudinous numbers from different members of the audience. 'Dead End Street' was also rendered redundant by the absolute lack of an effective guitar accompaniment. Many other songs were treated equally irreverently, and the once memorable 'Sunny Afternoon' was reduced to an applause baiter. Although it had been a common feature of Kinks' concerts to entice the crowd to sing during the chorus of 'Sunny Afternoon', Ray was now demanding much more. Parodying the worst aspects of showbiz shlock, he encouraged the spectators to sing virtually the entire song, unaccompanied by either group vocals or instrumentation. Instead, Davies would stand coyly, with his hands on his hips, occasionally demanding applause for his gyrations and commenting on the structural beauty of his backside. While burlesquing his own material, Davies carried his parody even further by increasing the number of camp cabaret pastiches such as 'You Are My Sunshine', 'Baby Face' and the bizarre 'Banana Boat Song'. Even the magnificent 'Lola' was squandered and used as a vehicle for Davies's pseudo gay persona, complete with a mock striptease. Many critics rightly observed that Davies seemed intent on climbing aboard the glam rock bandwagon and using the Kinks' repertoire in order to cash in on the success of artists such as David Bowie, T. Rex, Sweet and Alice Cooper. Greg Shaw went one step further by interpreting Davies's theatrics as a form of artistic condescension, resulting from the bitterness of commercial neglect. It was a theory not without foundation, for the Kinks had spent several years observing their best work die a commercial death while inferior product effortlessly succeeded. The Kinks were now in a position of power, though their audience consisted predominantly of post-'Lola' fans who were more interested in rock'n'roll boogie than social commentary. It was small wonder then that the Kinks should pander towards the lowest common denominator by perverting their finest work into cheap audience pleasers. By this point, John Gosling was already questioning the inclusion of the brass section during the performances of the Kinks' old hits:

> I didn't think the brass was right. The sound of a three-piece brass section playing 'You Really Got Me' didn't gel. It was almost a travesty! We used to laugh a lot about being like the Billy Cotton Band Show.[79]

Although the Kinks were having fun, some of the shows were embarrassingly sloppy. John Dalton recalls many occasions on which Ray's 'spontaneity' came dangerously close to unprofessional condescension. The long tours of the U.S. were often so boring that the group took to frequent jamming with nameless support groups. During one drinking session a blues pastiche was hastily conceived bearing the unlikely title 'Shoe Without A Lace'. According to Dalton, Ray played a private joke on the Kinks and their audience by using the song as a new opening number:

> One night we were waiting to go on while the audience were shouting 'We want the Kinks'. Ray suddenly said 'Let's go on and do "Shoe Without a Lace"'. We thought he was joking but he insisted, even though it was terrible. The American audience thought the song was really deep because it started with the words, 'Shoe without a lace, banana without a skin'![43]

Given such antics it was hardly surprising that the critics were beginning to comment adversely on Davies's attitude towards his audience. Yet, plausible as it seemed, the idea that Davies was ironically sabotaging the Kinks' concerts in order to show disdain for his new audience was a rather extreme interpretation of his motives. His comments about rock during this period reveal none of the cynicism one might have expected from a seasoned showman:

> The things I do are all I've got; I work hard at what I believe is an art – the people who say rock doesn't matter are crazy. It isn't *that* important, but it is a way of saying something. If I work really hard and my work has a good effect on somebody in Cincinnatti, it doesn't matter what it's done to me. It is a battle but the results are worth it and I enjoy it.[85]

The true reason for the Kinks' tacky performances was probably an extension of Ray's cabaret concept. He had always wanted to transform the group's concerts into a theatrical performance and now the introduction of the brass band had allowed him to concentrate on his acting. Although some of the more puritan U.S. critics dismissed Davies's latest efforts as indulgent he was determined to produce a glittering spectacle rather than a mundane rock'n'roll show. While on tour, Ray decided to film the Kinks as part of a personal documentary of their life on the road. It was during a particularly wild party in Los Angeles that Davies became fascinated with the reactions of the various liggers and hangers on who were determined to appear in his documentary. As soon as the cameras were introduced, an array of bright young things would leap into action and perform embarrassing stunts in order to immortalise themselves on celluloid. On witnessing the proceedings Mick Avory casually remarked: 'Everybody wants to be a star'. What had begun as a home movie gradually took on greater significance as Ray perceived the possibility of producing a soundtrack centring on the show business aspirations of everyman. Confident that such an album could prove an enormous seller, Ray attempted to persuade R.C.A. to finance a film to promote the record. According to Ray the powers that be at R.C.A. retorted: 'We're not in the talent business, we're in the record business'. Depressed by their lack of enthusiasm, Davies decided to finance the project with his own money and work on the songs as though he were writing a soundtrack. Although the group initially felt self-conscious about being constantly filmed off stage, they soon became used to the presence of the cameras and some highly entertaining scenes were apparently captured on celluloid. By the end of the tour 6,200 feet of film, totalling over six hours, was neatly edited to a forty-five-minute documentary. Unfortunately, R.C.A. still could not find an outlet for the video but it was hoped that an American or British company might purchase the work. After several months of tentative approaches, however, Ray was forced to admit that another ambitious venture had failed to reach the masses.

Having returned from the States the Kinks set about completing work on their forthcoming album. When the press heard about this latest Ray Davies inspired work they began to speculate on his increasingly dominant role in the group. The suspicion that the Kinks had merely become a passive vehicle for Ray's elaborate ideas was emphatically denied by his brother Dave:

> No, it's by no means a dictatorship. It's just that he has a lot to say. And when it comes to recording most of the songs are his, and when he writes a song he obviously knows how he wants it to sound. To work with him you must respect his ideas. But then you've got to be flexible. He can get upset, but he will compromise, otherwise there would be no working relationship at all.[91]

Mick Avory's analysis of Ray's dictatorial tendencies was equally diplomatic though he hinted very strongly at Ray's lack of flexibility:

> Well, if Ray's got an idea he puts it forward to the rest of us. Then he's open to suggestions. If you have your say he sometimes looks like he isn't listening. But he is and he reconsiders. Ray isn't completely dominating. But a lot of the ideas and concepts come from him because they are usually to do with his writing. Everyone understands that. He's so good at writing songs that it's silly for anyone to come out with an idea that's completely disconnected. You have to contribute what you can . . . If you can't come up with better ideas than Ray then what he says goes. He thinks about the group a lot more than anyone else anyway.[92]

In later years, Ray's singlemindedness would cause at least one member to pursue his interest outside the Kinks.

In May, the Kinks returned to the U.K. charts with the calypso-influenced 'Supersonic Rocketship'. It was to be their last Top 20 single for eleven years. Following a brief three-week tour in August, the group came home in time to promote their double album, *Everybody's In Showbiz, Everybody's A Star*. This half-studio, half-live effort was strangely erratic in quality, though not without its strong points. 'Top Of The Pops' opened the Carnegie Hall recording on an impressive note, with Dave borrowing even more heavily from the 'Land Of 1,000 Dances' riff. Unfortunately, the remaining tracks consisted of irrelevant snippets from Davies's cabaret act including 'Mr Wonderful', 'Baby Face' and 'Banana Boat Song', placed alongside a disproportionate number of songs from *Muswell Hillbillies*. Of the recent material only the melodramatic 'Alcohol' proved fully satisfying. The audience participation is a joy to listen to and, inspired by their involvement, Ray slurs his vocals and drags out the verses in a performance of oscar-winning quality. Ray's convincing persona during 'Alcohol' sometimes led reviewers to assume that all the Kinks' shows were a drunken shambles. Ray refutes this:

> I'm not necessarily drunk onstage. I drink very little. I'm not a great

> drinker, that's why I get drunk. I have one drink and I get tipsy . . . I like pubs but that doesn't mean to say I'm a drinker. I like pubs because I like the people who go to them . . . I guess you could say that the stage is my kind of pub.[31]

As a collection, the *Showbiz* album was rather unrepresentative of a Kinks concert and the noticeable lack of classic rock songs was disappointing. The studio side had slightly more cohesion, many of the songs being inspired by Ray Davies's experiences of touring in America during the last few years. The opening track, 'Here Comes Another Day', was a reasonable tune and the lyrics detailed the obsessive nature of touring with an ironic slant. Several of the other tracks described the excesses produced by life on the road, often expressed through Davies's preoccupation with food from 'Maximum Consumption' and 'Motorway' through 'Hot Potatoes'. This theme was elaborated in the remaining songs including 'Look On The Sunny Side' and Dave's 'You Don't Know My Name', both of which described the alienation resulting from the rock star lifestyle. Although these tracks ranged from mediocre to reasonable there were only two undeniable Kinks classics – 'Sitting In My Hotel' and 'Celluloid Heroes'. The former was a brilliantly accurate portrayal of the depression produced by rock star hedonism. Davies adopted a serio/comic tone in cataloguing the illusions that can ensnare those whose lives are lived as metaphor. While the 'genius is pain' school of 70s singer-songwriters were narcissistically bemoaning their fate with romantic allusions, Davies was refreshingly self-castigating and honest about his personal inadequacies. Rather than deifying the rock star, Davies stressed his inferiority in relation to the ordinary man. The singer remembers his former existence and his old friends with affection and, in a self-mocking tone, derides his effete posturings and absurd fantasies as pathetic. Underlying the humour, however, is the realisation that in spite of his perception, the rock star cannot escape from his fantasy world. For Davies, the song expressed ambiguous feelings about his own depressions and escapist nature:

> I think life is a series of peaks and pinnacles . . . the ultimate pinnacle is when you go. Well, I hope it's a very grand day when I go. Although I did write in my diary the other day, 'I hope it will be soon . . . and alone'. I was very upset . . . People think that I'm strong, and I'm not. I'm weak. I get the feeling that people think I'm strong. If I hadn't done all this I think I would have gone to the other extreme and gone to the Outer Hebrides to live, and been a sculptor or a painter and hid under a pullover . . . a big pullover.[31]

The closing studio track, 'Celluloid Heroes' was probably the best Davies composition in several years. The song was a tribute to the Hollywood stars whose lives had been mythologised on the silver screen. Again Davies acknowledged the wish-fulfillment fantasies of everyman, but his glorification of Hollywood life was loaded with ambiguity. Despite their 'immortality', Davies's array of stars are portrayed as real people whose human frailties are all too evident. After years of writing about life in Britain, Ray had finally composed a memorable tribute to America's most famous institution. Although the album failed to reach the U.K. charts, it rose steadily in the American Hot 100, paving the way for more successful works in the future.

During the winter of 1972, the Kinks completed a short tour of the U.K., culminating in a performance at London's Rainbow Theatre on 22 October. They also made a surprise appearance in the Fleet Street press when Ray was reprimanded for an incident in the B.B.C. bar where he was reported to have poured a pint of beer over a member of a well-known pop group and become involved in a fracas with their manager. The facts remain unclear, but Davies maintains that the entire affair was exaggerated by sensation-seeking reporters:

> It was an absolute joke . . . people don't realise what happens. Within five minutes I'd had somebody come over and say they didn't like my record. Somebody else said, 'Oh, we're suing you for a lot of money' and then somebody came over and touched me up. Five minutes later I find myself being throttled by some manager. A week or so later I read that I've attacked a group of people. All right I'm six foot and a bit and I might look quite strong, but I'm not capable of beating up five or six people. I don't think I could even beat up their manager. Then all these ridiculous stories come out and I wouldn't say anything because it was all so ridiculous.[93]

In spite of Ray's publicity, the Kinks' 'Celluloid Heroes' failed to restore them to the singles charts. According to Ray, he was fully aware that the elongated version of the single would suffer the same fate as the excellent 'Shangri-la', but released the number because of its undoubted quality. Surprisingly nonchalant about its failure, Davies added that number 1 hits no longer provided any lasting satisfaction for him.

The gigging year ended with several small dates including a stint at the University of London's Imperial College. The Kinks were supported by Peter Barden's Camel, an interesting coupling when one remembers that Peter and Ray once played alongside each other in 1963. One reviewer, high with expectation following U.S. reports of Kink mania, was so disappointed with the gig that he savaged the group unmercifully. Ignoring his detractors, Ray immersed himself in work and spent the entire Christmas period formulating plans for the Kinks contribution to the Fanfare For Europe concert in the New Year. Rumours suggested that

Davies was planning a music hall show including a selection of songs from *The Village Green Preservation Society*. Four years after its chart failure, Davies was still not ready to forget his most aesthetically pleasing work.

THIRTEEN

Goodbye Yellow Brick Road

For once Davies adhered to his impossible schedule and completed arrangements for the Kinks' appearance at Drury Lane Theatre on 14 January 1973. In many respects, the concert was a turning point for the group and the addition of six brass players, six backing vocalists and a film backdrop indicated the direction Davies intended to travel in the future. Prior to the show there were some backstage nerves as rehearsal time had been short. Considering the speed with which the production was organised, the results were surprisingly impressive. Using *The Village Green Preservation Society* as a vague framework, the Kinks presented a potted musical history of their own career, with a sprinkling of hits including 'Sunny Afternoon', 'Waterloo Sunset', 'Victoria' and 'A Well Respected Man'. These were interspersed with a selection of numbers from the forthcoming *Preservation* project. The synthesis of old and new material was demonstrated most effectively at the end of 'Where Are They Now?' when the affirmation of the permanence of rock'n'roll was punctuated by the dramatic emergence of Dave Davies, who leapt from behind a column of speakers and burst into the unmistakable chords of 'You Really Got Me'. Ray contributed to the fun by singing an impromptu version of the Troggs' 'Wild Thing' and reeling off a string of names from pop's golden years including *Ready Steady Go*, Cathy McGowan, the Merseybeats, the Swinging Blue Jeans and Gerry and the Pacemakers. Although the gig was an undoubted success, Ray found the project exhausting as well as exhilarating. The ambitious Davies learned that even a comparatively low scale performance could provide organisational headaches. Despite the fact that he was effectively promoting *The Village Green Preservation Society* album, his former record label failed to supply any old photos of the group for the projectionist. Although some shots were eventually procured from another source, the projectionist's machine broke down during rehearsals, and there was no time left to run through the numbers. In addition to these setbacks, Ray found himself under severe pressure to modify his original concept in order not to alienate his audience. Caught between the desire to present a fully fledged theatrical show and the need to include a series of Kinks greatest hits, Davies made what he later considered an unhappy compromise by combining the two. Stung by his own indecision, Davies vowed to take the *Preservation* project to its logical extreme:

> At Drury Lane, we were doing our regular set with a few new ideas thrown in. But really, that's the last time I want to perform last year's show. We're now working on a new repertoire with a few surprises. I think we'd like to present even more of a visual performance. Perhaps we can take a light show around with us and present dialogue as well as the usual delivery.[94]

Inflamed by his own rhetoric, Davies added that an elaborate show would be staged in New York and various parts of the Continent. He even promised a unique presentation of the *Village Green Preservation Society* in selected small halls in rural England with a maximum audience capacity of 2,000. Although the press, the public and the other members of the Kinks took Davies's notions with an obligatory pinch of salt, his gargantuan plans were no idle dream. The group worked industriously on an album, which was completed in March, but the perpetually perfectionist Davies voiced dissatisfaction and scrapped the project until later in the year.

With touring commitments to fulfil, Ray was spending every spare moment reconstructing the *Preservation* idea, but the strain of overwork was gradually sapping his energies. The average Ray Davies day began at an hour that most rock stars have seldom seen. He would rise at 7 a.m., eat a breakfast of raw eggs, complete several hours work and then briefly return to bed. His succeeding actions were even stranger:

> Then I get up again and have a little worry and cry and get that out of my system and try to do a bit more work. The day goes very quickly.[95]

Without realising the consequences of his behaviour, Ray was pushing himself too hard. The effects of his work and personal life would soon be revealed in one of the most dramatic announcements of the rock year.

The Kinks' appearance at the Royal Festival Hall in June was reasonably well received in the music press, but Ray Davies's personal problems were now becoming increasingly obvious. Towards the end of the month his wife, Rasa, fled from their home taking their two daughters to an undisclosed address. The following week Davies was still in a state of shock. It was time for a long lay off but, ever perverse in his professionalism, Davies decided to appear at the White City Stadium for a gig supporting Edgar Winter and Sly and the Family Stone. The show was a shambolic affair, made worse by Davies's growing conviction that his music had become an uncontrollable monster that had distracted him from his home life and destroyed his personal relationships. Although Ray looked haggard and ill onstage, his performance was the usual blend of theatricalism and humour. His nephew, Phil Palmer, joined the Kinks onstage and towards the climax of the set Ray kissed Dave affectionately on the cheek. With a beer can perched precariously on his head, Ray looked directly into the audience and with the P.A. half-drowning his words, announced that he was sick of rock music and intended to quit. The shock revelation reverberated around music circles and the following week the press carried banner headlines announcing the retirement of one of rock's most revered elder statesmen. Ray's closest friends expressed some doubt that he would abandon the live circuit forever, though provisions were taken to ensure that the Kinks would continue with brother Dave assuming leadership. The group's press secretary, Marion Rainford, was hounded by the music papers but in a press statement refused to concede that the Kinks' demise was at hand:

> One has to understand that Ray is in a very emotional, confused state. Two and a half weeks ago his wife Rasa left, together with Ray's two children – and she hasn't been heard from since. Ray is naturally a very worried man. He hasn't eaten since she left, he hasn't slept – it's a miracle he got through the gig. He feels that touring and gigs have contributed to the situation. And don't forget Rasa had a nervous breakdown . . . and Ray knows all about nervous breakdowns. But I must say that neither the Kinks nor I believe for one moment that Ray will really quit the business. He's a grieving man and he made an emotional statement.[96]

Not all of the other Kinks shared Marion's optimism; John Gosling was evidently confused enough by the announcement to fear the worst:

> It was a funny atmosphere. He suddenly said he was retiring . . . I don't know whether it was a stunt but I took it seriously. I was quite upset that it happened that way rather than before the gig. We could have done it as a big farewell gig . . . I don't know to this day whether he meant it. It was a big mystery to me.[79]

During the succeeding weeks Ray apparently drowned his sorrows, while Rasa filed for a separation which eventually ended in divorce. In the meantime, the Kinks waited, uncertain of their future. John Gosling recalls weeks of silence, finally broken by a telephone call demanding his presence in the studio. Gosling was pleasantly surprised to find Ray back in action, even though he still looked wan and unhealthy. According to Ray he spent several weeks convalescing with his brother Dave and, although they initially ignored any discussions about music, the guitars were eventually brought out, some Chuck Berry riffs were exchanged, and the Kinks' future was reconsidered. At the beginning of September, Ray provided the press with a detailed account of his plans and explained the reasons behind his 'retirement':

> Several weeks ago I wrote a letter to the world; it turned out to be a letter to

me. But I do feel that I made a decision, whether emotionally motivated or not, to change the format of the band. The White City was not a good place to say goodbye. The sun wasn't shining, my shirt was not clean, and anyway rock festivals have never held many happy memories for me personally. The Kinks are close enough now to be able to work as a team in whatever they do, and anyone who thinks they are only my back-up band is very mistaken. There are still things to extract from the Kinks on an artistic level – whether or not it turns out to be commercial remains to be seen.[97]

Davies's statement suggested most strongly that he was determined to continue experimenting with the Kinks' music, irrespective of commercial success. In the meantime, the group began converting a former warehouse into a new studio (later dubbed Konk) for the modest sum of £70,000. Ray was determined to achieve total autonomy for the group and it was expected that this new venture would eventually release them from the financial restraints of endless re-recordings in expensive studios. An impressive amount of equipment was delivered to the Tottenham Lane warehouse including a sixteen-track control desk, a sixteen-track tape recorder, a noise-reduction unit, microphones, speakers, and a baby grand piano. In order to create a pleasant atmosphere special lighting was also installed plus a sizeable snooker table and plush furnishings. The financial outlay would be partly offset in the future by leasing out the studio to other musicians during the Kinks' absence. In retrospect, the Hornsey studio was a sound financial investment that would prove beneficial to the Kinks in successive years.

In the wake of the White City shake-up Ray showed few signs of altering his workaholic lifestyle. His comments on the necessity of a constant work schedule were alarmingly obsessive:

> I like to get drunk sometimes, but I don't use it to cover anything. When I wake up scared in the night I start working. When I'm working it's my life, everything. I don't care if we're on the radio or something or we have to play a concert. I work so much that it's ridiculous and I don't have any life other than that. What actually takes my mind off working is being on stage. I know I'm singing my own songs but I forget in the moment. I go on as an artist – as a performer. It means going on tour is like a holiday.[98]

Even when Ray attempted to avoid the insulation of rock star life by spending his time in the National Gallery and frequently travelling by bus and tube, his actions were deemed eccentric. During one interview, Davies arrived off the street, clutching a bag containing an overcoat and pullover to protect him from the cold. Despite his wealth Davies still felt genuinely concerned about unnecessary extravagances. Journalists duly noted the contrasts between Ray and the other Kinks and the often contradictory viewpoints held by the Davies brothers. Although Ray frequently smiled at the madcap antics of his younger brother, there was a genuine element of envy in his attitude towards him:

> He worries about himself physically more than I do. He doesn't worry about himself mentally. Maybe he doesn't give as much as I do. Or maybe he *gives* as much – but I take more from myself by subtracting, by fighting inside. I think Dave's got more taste for living . . . Dave's got a nice car whereas I've got a battered rusty old thing in the garage which I can't drive. After all these years I should have learned. What happens is that Dave'll drive down the street in his Mercedes – and pass me on a bicycle.[98]

In spite of their differences, Dave and Ray were working together effectively, though there would be frequent clashes over the next few years.

The delayed *Preservation Act I* album was finally released in November in the hope that it might pick up some extra Christmas sales. The work was a prelude to the stage presentation featuring songs by a number of characters including 'the people', Johnny Thunder and Flash and the Tramp. The album presented problems for the critics, who were forced to judge the work on its merits, while realising that it was designed as part of a larger structure. Unfortunately, as a collection of songs, *Preservation Act I* was only partially successful, even though some of the material was reasonably strong. Perhaps unconsciously Ray allocated the finest songs of the show to the enigmatic tramp, a forlorn figure lost in memories of a golden past. 'Sweet Lady Genevieve', one of the Kinks' most popular numbers of the period, was a moving song about lost love, while 'Where Are They Now?' served as a paean to the heroes and villains of the 50s and 60s. 'Sitting In The Midday Sun' was almost equally successful, retreading the 'Sunny Afternoon' theme from the tramp's perspective, while the resurrection of the Village Green's Johnny Thunder in 'One Of The Survivors' gave Davies leave to sing a stunning 50s style rock'n'roll workout. The remainder of the album suffered from the vaudevillian overkill that had first been heard on parts of *Everybody's In Showbiz, Everybody's A Star.* The vocal ensemble was used to some effect on 'Daylight', a song almost recreating the opening scene of *Under Milkwood,* but on other cuts the results were disappointing. The girl choruses and overbearing brass section sounded so stagey that the work sometimes seemed like a surrogate *Jesus Christ Superstar.* The overtly theatrical 'There's A Change In The Weather', 'Demolition Man' and 'Money And Corruption', complete with Davies's affected vocals, sounded extremely grating when heard outside of the *Preservation* concept. Even 'Cricket', which boasted some clever lyrics was firmly rooted in the music hall tradition and seemed tangential to accepted Kinks' work. Overall, the album was a diffuse work, incomplete in itself and almost impossible to categorise in any particular genre. It was almost akin to reviewing snatches of a movie soundtrack having never seen the film or heard the completed score. The work presented a number of aesthetic problems which most critics felt could not be resolved until after the release of *Preservation Act II*.

The idiosyncratic nature of Davies's latest work inevitably alienated the record buying public and *Preservation Act I* was a flop sales-wise. Ray found it difficult to suppress his disappointment at the negative reaction shown towards the work:

> I suppose I was disgusted – I worked really hard on it but maybe that's a reward in itself. I was unhappy when people hadn't heard it. That's all I care about really . . . I'm not concerned that people buy it, they don't have to walk around with a copy under their arms. But I would like them to *hear* it.[98]

For many artists such a rejection might have encouraged greater compromise in the future, but Davies was determined to continue with the *Preservation* concept irrespective of critical or audience disapproval. Ray's belief in the implicit quality of his work was unshakable and he even boasted of further plays, including an hour long television play based on *Muswell Hillbillies*. The revamped plot apparently centred on a schizophrenic Irish country'n'western singer, resident in Camden, who gradually falls victim to his onstage cowboy persona and ends up in a *High Chaparral* style shoot out with London policemen. It was another bizarre project, never to be realised, but the perennial theme of the fantasy star entrapping the mind of the ordinary man would be successfully dramatised in the future.

While Ray distracted himself from plummetting record sales with talk of future record projects and television plays, his brother Dave was threatening to complete his long awaited solo album. Five new songs were apparently in the can, though Dave spoke of the need to overdub keyboards and brass on certain cuts. These latest sessions sounded particularly promising and, apart from the expected rockers, Dave promised a series of songs reflecting his love of folk music. At one point, he even considered recording a couple of Hank Williams songs, though these were eventually discarded in favour of pursuing his own work. Unfortunately, Dave lacked the songwriting discipline of his elder brother and appeared content to sit around waiting for 'inspiration'. By Christmas, the album remained half-completed and, weary of the sessions, Dave finally abandoned the project.

FOURTEEN

Gonna Make You a Star

Although Ray Davies had never written a hit musical his talents were still in demand from producers in search of new ideas. One enterprising company even offered Davies the leading role in a play on the life of Aubrey Beardsley, which was an amusing comment on the rock singer's decadent persona. Unfortunately, plans to pursue the project were shelved when the Kinks embarked on a U.S. tour. Prior to their departure, work was completed on a pilot single from the soon to be released *Preservation Act II*. 'Mirror Of Love' was a strong number that deserved to chart but the Kinks' unavailability in the U.K. hampered its chances. In spite of its quality, the disc was actually taken from a Ray Davies demonstration tape following a failed attempt to record with the entire band. Apparently, Ray had entered the studio, written the song, added piano and drums and finally passed it over to Dave who overdubbed the mandolin and brass parts. Although it was not unusual for Ray to control proceedings, his increasing tendency to use the Kinks as a silent vehicle for his own rigid ideas was becoming increasingly alarming. During the succeeding months individual members would see their contributions becoming less relevant as rock'n'roll was superseded by full blown theatricalism.

A spring U.S. tour featuring *Preservation* was arranged by Ray even though he realised that the project was unlikely to be a commercial success. Davies was so intent on staging the show that for once he was willing to sacrifice personal financial gain:

> The only people who are going to make money are the people making wages. The roadies are going to get more money than I will. But I want to do it. It's what I've said all along. It's good to have a big success and try and get things like this going to make money, but you wouldn't be able to do it otherwise. And I've got to do it, I'm determined to do it.[99]

A further reason for the tour was Ray's need to communicate with an audience. Recently, he had noted that his insulated lifestyle was adversely affecting his writing and it was hoped that the Stateside trip might provide the necessary inspiration to complete his half-written songs. Before finalising the American tour Ray had been approached by Granada Television with the idea of writing a contemporary late night musical play focussing on the way in which Davies set about composing new material. It was a vague proposition requiring Ray to present his ideas as 'an experimental dream'. Such a script might never have been attempted but for a sudden illness during the group's Chicago date. Confined to his bed by an insistent doctor, Ray attempted to alleviate his boredom by watching afternoon soap operas on the television. Amused by the plastic perfection of the leading male actors he concocted the idea of the 'Starmaker' – an image builder who would search for the most boringly normal person in the country, take over his personality and transform him into a superstar. It was an extension of the 'Everybody's In Showbiz' concept refined into a tight script which Ray completed in his hotel bedroom. Following the tour, Ray returned to England with a full scenario and set about recording the half-hour show in late June. It was another arduous work schedule which barely gave Ray enough time to learn his lines. On the last day of recording he even added a new song to the script, much to the amazement of the director. Impressed with his latest television venture, Ray spoke confidently about a future in film work:

> I don't know whether I want to direct, produce, or what – I just want to make films . . . I think there's a lot to be said about people that still hasn't been said. I'd like to make films about people, deep people. Everyone these days thinks you have to have some kind of fast action, like a car chase, but I just want to make films about people.[100]

In addition to the television plays, films and new recording studio, Davies was also launching a new record label, Konk. Claire Hamill was already signed to record an album and it was hoped that a small rostrum of artists would gradually be recruited in successive years. Sceptics could not help observing that Davies was again taking on too many enterprises for his own good.

The release of *Preservation Act II* in June presented two more sides of Davies's musical, making it the longest rock opera to date. However, *Preservation* was also the least ambitious of its *genre*, in complete contrast to Townshend's bombastic work. Instead of centring on one figure as Townshend had done in both *Tommy* and *Quadrophenia* Ray had created a number of vague character sketches in *Act I*, almost consciously imitating the plotless structure of *Under Milkwood*. By the time he had completed *Act II* the original concept had substantially altered. Figures such as Johnny Thunder and the Vicar, who had been allocated key songs in the first act, were nowhere to be seen in part two in which Davies reversed his earlier technique by presenting a rigid and simplistic plot line relating the clash between Mr Black and Flash. Emerging as a socialist reformer, Black first allies himself with the Festival of Light do-gooders in order to overthrow the degenerate and corrupt Flash and his cronies. Several songs are devoted to unravelling the character of Flash from his origins as a second-hand car spiv to his personal defence in 'Scum Of The Earth' where Davies humorously adapts some lines from Shylock's 'Hath not a Jew eyes?' speech in *The Merchant Of Venice*. After a brief interlude devoted to Flash's relationship with his special floosie, Belle, the arch villain is captured by Mr Black, whose latest alignment with a mad scientist reveals him as a meglomaniac. In the end, Flash is brainwashed and society transformed into an Orwellian police state.

The album both puzzled and disappointed the critics in 1973, and even a retrospective piece on Davies in 1977 noted, somewhat harshly, that the work had failed to produce even one decent song. Ian MacDonald of the *New Musical Express* penetratingly summed up Davies's failure:

> The plot's obvious, the method is at best hit-and-miss and the words are a shade on the shlocky side, as well as being badly sewn together . . . Davies's facility for creating beguiling tunes dies the death in the face of his doggedly unimaginative lyric requirements and ponderously low-profile dramatic aims . . . in attempting a rock equivalent of *The Threepenny Opera*, Ray Davies has merely created a drawn-out sequence of socio-political platitudes couched in the tritest lyric formats and supported by music of little overall cohesion, and no individual personality whatsoever. In short, what started out as a worthy project has failed on every conceivable level – which must at least be some sort of record in consistency.[101]

MacDonald's criticisms were well-founded. Although *Preservation* transcended the normal rock criteria in some respects, since it was never intended solely as an album but an audio/visual/theatrical package, the individual songs still needed to be judged in some context. It is all too easy to excuse Davies by arguing that bad songs are acceptable in a musical if they contribute strongly to the development of the plot, but even on this level, *Preservation* can hardly be deemed successful. Ultimately, Davies is pitting himself against the likes of Rodgers and Hammerstein and Rice and Lloyd Webber by veering towards the rock opera/pop musical *genre*. Unfortunately, *Preservation* fails to provide the melodic ingenuity that is a functional necessity for such a project. Of all the writers performing in the rock field, Davies seemed the most likely to exploit the pop/rock musical by producing a full blown theatrical work with an album full of memorable songs. The sad result was a series of grandiloquent failures, each more frustrating in its adherence to an original idea gone stale.

Despite the shortcomings of his theatrical ventures Davies's determination and absolute refusal to concede defeat was a worthy quality in the 70s rock world. Although he abandoned projects almost every week, his more serious or ambitious efforts were invariably taken to their logical conclusion. In July, for example, a new version of 'Mirror Of Love' was released, complete with the full Kinks line-up and additional girl singers. Once more the single flopped, leaving Davies feeling resigned but not bitter:

> Well you know you put a single out and it doesn't sell. It's really a drag every time that happens. Right from the beginning I've hated that because what I've done I always felt was the best thing ever. But the me that thinks of the idea really doesn't care about anything because I've got my own standards. That's a bit conceited but I've got to be like that or I'll get shot down all the time.[99]

Two months later, Ray finally broke into television drama when *Starmaker* was screened nationally. The play, co-starring Ray and June Ritchie, combined dialogue and song in an ingenious manner, preceding Dennis Potter's *Pennies From Heaven* by several years. The plot was simple but effective. An ordinary person named Norman, believing himself to be a rock star, sets out to write a concept album based on his mundane lifestyle and as the play progresses dream and reality become increasingly confused. Norman exclaims 'I'm a star and I've got the press cuttings to prove it' but his rock star persona is bludgeoned into submission by his wife's unrelenting practicality: 'First it was a painter and a footballer and ever since 1965 you've had this fantasy of being a pop star'. The thirty-minute play concluded with Norman wandering into the audience eating crisps and watching the Kinks, led by Dave, closing the show. Although the project had been rushed, Davies was sufficiently pleased with the play to promise an album based on the *Starmaker* theme in the New Year.

The Kinks returned to the U.S. in the late winter for another *Preservation* tour. The improved show included several segments of film shot in England, six additional songs and special screen projections. Realising that the entire recording of *Preservation* would run for approximately two hours, Ray edited the show to an hour and a half, concentrating on the Mr Black and Flash confrontation and jettisoning the Vicar's sermon about cricket and other less relevant material. Although Ray seemed reasonably content with the reception afforded the show in those early days, the tour was not without its problems. Every new venue brought a different sized stage which created organisational havoc. On the first night of the tour, for example, the group had opened at a university where no stage was provided. A makeshift platform was hastily erected which proved too large, so a second was constructed at great effort and expense. By the time the show reached Chicago, however, there was a noticeable improvement and the theatrical touches were very much in evidence. During 'Money And Corruption' pictures of leading world political figures were flashed on to the screen followed by an image of Ray in his Mr Black disguise. With

Dave Davies striking up the chords of 'Here Comes Flash', backed by the full chorus, Ray appeared in his Flash outfit, followed by his cronies Mr Twitch (Dave), Big Knob (John Dalton) and Big Ron (Mick Avory). During Flash's assault on society various landmarks were projected on to the backdrop including the Empire State Building and the White House. Another clever touch was the inclusion of Victorian pornographic photos during the puritanical tirade 'Shepherds Of The Nation'. The Kinks also included a new song in the form of 'Slum Kids' backed by a film showing scenes of poverty in contemporary Britain. This may well have been the same film originally used as part of the 'Dead End Street' promotional campaign. The finale of the show was the transformation of Flash and his cronies into robots, complete with rods protruding from their heads. Several performances during the Stateside visit received good reviews, which augured well for the forthcoming U.K. leg of the tour.

Returning to Britain, Davies organised the customary Kinks climactic Christmas celebration. The 1974 edition consisted of three performances of *Preservation* at the Royalty Theatre in London. The show was championed by Robin Denselow of the *Guardian* in a surprisingly favourable review in which he expressed a firm belief in the aesthetic validity of the project:

> It has been an uphill struggle, but with *Preservation* it seemed he would at last produce a significant work. The tragedy is that he has, but it ran so briefly, and the lack of promotion was matched by the shambling, cheap production. And yet *Preservation* has all the making of a major success, if only it was carefully staged and put on at, say, the Roundhouse for a couple of months.[102]

Few of his fellow critics shared Denselow's view, and the other reviews offered Davies little solace as he prepared for further shows in the New Year. Although he might easily have lapsed into a depressed state, Davies remained stoical about the Kinks' current status in the rock world:

> I feel much better about myself. Now, after a show I feel like I've done a good day's work, like I've actually achieved something at the end of the night. *I'm not unhappy* – it's just that I'm unhappy that people *think* I'm unhappy. I'm really happy. I felt that I was on top of the world the other night. When I was onstage I was the biggest star in the world. When I tried to balance the beer can on my head. In the old days, we'd just go onstage and play the hits. We've done our *loose* shows, like the Philharmonic, and I like that, but it doesn't really give me a buzz at the end of the evening. I don't think I could have ever toured again if I hadn't been able to do *Preservation* . . . do the concept shows.[103]

FIFTEEN

Bohemian Rhapsody

By 1975, the Kinks were on a conveyor-belt that was becoming increasingly wearying. Endless tours of the States were punctuated by album releases and further theatrical concepts of dubious quality. For John Gosling, in particular, the move away from the old Kinks style was proving frustrating and the unnecessary inclusion of an American cast of thousands seemed farcical; he likened it to being a member of an amateur dramatic society. The spring 1975 U.S. tour indicated that the punters were tiring of Ray's rock theatre experiments. Attendances at several of the gigs was sparse, though the group were still capable of drawing capacity crowds at prestigious venues. The latest shows mixed a short set of old hits with Ray's *Starmaker* concept, now retitled *Soap Opera*. As usual, the Kinks introduced a new stage garb, this time appearing in absurd Afro wigs. There were also a large number of props employed including a vertically placed bed and gigantic ducks introduced to accompany the number 'Ducks On The Wall'. The Americans responded vociferously to the show and, when the star finally reverted to his mundane life as Norman the accountant, many spectators yelled 'No! No! You're Ray Davies'. For most, the highlight of the performance took place during a dramatic moment when Norman desperately attempted to maintain his fantasy by exclaiming 'Wait a minute, I'm Ray Davies I made this . . . ' following which he burst into 'Sunny Afternoon', 'Well Respected Man' and 'Dedicated Follower Of Fashion'. It was a perfect synthesis of the old and new Kinks and sadly all too short lived.

The release of *Soap Opera* in May was generally greeted as a distinct improvement on Davies's recent conceptual endeavours. The work included three tracks released as singles: 'Holiday Romance', 'Ducks On The Wall' and 'You Can't Stop The Music', none of which made any chart impact. However, critics breathed a sigh of relief that Davies had toned down the music hall elements in order to concentrate on his favourite theme of suburban life. 'Rush Hour Blues' and 'Nine To Five' were further comments on the rat race reinforced by 'Have Another Drink' in which Ray pinpointed the friendly local as the opium of the people. Perhaps the most interesting song of the bunch was 'You Make It All Worthwhile' a humorous piece of melodrama during which Norman placates his wife having rejected her shepherd's pie. There are few songwriters other than Davies who could successfully tackle such a pathetic theme. Following the release of the album, however, Ray spoke with mixed feelings about his ambitions and songwriting talent:

> I'll never make it as a songwriter. Well, I think if I make it I'll give up. The reason I keep going is that I haven't achieved what I set out to do . . . I am honest about the things I do. I mean *Soap Opera* is good. It's a step and it's a progression. In many ways it may be the best thing we've ever done even though some of the lyrics and some of the music aren't as good as others. It's an overall thing, the play, whatever. It's a step in the right direction. And I'm going to get there eventually.[104]

Although Ray admitted that *Soap Opera* was the type of theatrical project he should have been tackling three years before, it was difficult to resist the temptation to expand *Preservation.*

In effect, Davies decided to reconstruct the origins of his favourite villain, Flash, beginning with his schooldays. The album, *Schoolboys In Disgrace*, released in November, less than six months after its predecessor, was surprisingly good in spite of the restrictive nature of the concept. The ambitious sleeve work showed the group dressed somewhat ludicrously in school uniform, and the jacket notes detailing the album's plot must have scared off even more potential buyers. Essentially, the subject matter dealt with a naughty schoolboy who gets a girl pregnant, receives a public caning and is finally ignominiously expelled. Although it hardly sounds rivetting, Davies's most colourless concept to date actually spawned several half decent songs. The opening cut, 'Schooldays', was one of Ray's best nostalgia numbers recalling the power of 'Do You Remember Walter?' in its sad acceptance of a lost past. Several other songs on the first side were clever pastiches of late 50s/early 60s pop music in a satirical style not dissimilar to Frank Zappa. 'The First Time We Fell In Love' showed influences from the Poni-Tails and Elvis Presley to the Shangri-las. Even more successful was the hilarious 'Jack The Idiot Dunce', a brilliant recreation of 50s rock'n'roll. Ray explained the genesis of the song:

> It was based on a real person in England who failed all his entrance exams but didn't try to commit suicide – he just got kicked out of home. I was amazed when I heard that; I didn't think people did that any more. He turned up at a relative's house. He said, 'Can I stay here? My father's thrown me out'. Like Victorian times. His father really had big ambitions for him and he just didn't make it. But the guy who was a dummy in school ended up a rock'n'roll dancer and a world famous *character*. I was like that – bad in school but a dancing fool. I guess you could say Jack was me.[103]

The second side of the album featured a contemporary Kinks sound with some extended guitar work by Dave on 'Headmaster' and 'The Hard Way'. 'No More Looking Back' completed the proceedings, with Davies coming to terms with his nostalgia and romanticism. The overall strength of *Schoolboys In Disgrace* stemmed from Davies's ability to write several songs that transcended the severe limitations of his concept. Unfortunately, the work also included numbers such as 'Education', 'Headmaster' and 'The Hard Way' that were firmly entrenched in the *Schoolboys* theme, but devoid of any universal appeal. It was an unhappy compromise that proved sufficient to damn the record in the eyes of the public.

Although Ray had over twenty-one outtakes from *Schoolboys In Disgrace* he decided not to continue the theme. Originally, he had considered writing a sequel, documenting Flash's late adolescence and gradual decline into a life of crime, but a growing disenchantment with R.C.A. halted the project. Ray felt that the promotion of recent Kinks product was half-hearted and so, in early 1976, he began negotiations with several other companies in the hope of moving to a new record label. The *Schoolboys In Disgrace* road show continued in the States and opened for three weeks in Britain on 27 February. By this time, however, Ray was beginning to meet strong resistance from his fellow Kinks who were growing weary of being part of a stylised dramatic society. John Gosling summed up the feelings of the Kinks during this troubled period:

> The dressing up was good fun. It was in the Kinks' character. We dressed up in clubs as clowns, gangsters and schoolboys. We all liked theatre and the movies, but it went too far. It was a hassle to do the things. We did two shows in Los Angeles . . . we'd get to the theatre at two in the afternoon, and leave at two the next morning. A twelve-hour shift for one gig! After all that we still got cries of 'rock'n'roll' from the audience. They didn't take it to their hearts as Ray had hoped. I suppose we were all upset . . . we all had our say, but Ray was hell-bent on doing it.[79]

Although he eventually stressed the need for the Kinks to return to their rock roots, Ray did not entirely accept Gosling's criticisms of the theatrical years:

> In a way I think I neglected the music and concentrated too much on the lyric form, but I don't think it was overdone. To me the albums were musical plays. I don't think I'm being big-headed when I say that it worked.[105]

Even former manager, Robert Wace, who had been around for Davies's finest theatrical venture, *The Village Green Preservation Society*, had little sympathy for such work:

> Ray was always trying to write those wretched rock operas . . . Part of the problem was that he always thought he was a better writer than Townshend and, subconsciously, he started trying to compete with him.[6]

While the Kinks' contractual future was being decided, there was a notable lack of product, and, indeed, the group would fail to release a new album in 1976. Realising that they were poised to lose the Kinks from their rostrum, R.C.A. decided to emulate Pye by issuing a presumptously titled *Kinks Greatest Hits*. When Ray heard the news he immediately phoned the marketing department and warned the company that they were in danger of infringing the Trades Descriptions Act in Great Britain. Eventually, R.C.A. compromised and retitled the album, *Celluloid Heroes – The Kinks Greatest*. The one hit single achieved by the Kinks on R.C.A., 'Supersonic Rocket Ship', was inexplicably excluded from the compilation. However, the work did include alternate and remixed versions of original recordings and a previously unreleased live cut, 'Here Comes Yet Another Day'.

As the months passed, the Kinks' low profile was reflected in minimal press coverage. The lack of hits and the eclipsing of the group by Ray's conceptual works had led to many misconceptions about the Kinks, which Davies was at pains to correct:

> Perhaps the Kinks have been a little under exposed. But maybe it's a good thing not to be in the limelight all the time. A lot of people think we haven't done anything for three years. When I worked two days a week, everyone thought I was working seven. Now I *am* working *seven* days a week, people think I'm not working at all.[105]

On 23 June, the Kinks' future was settled when a press release from Arista Records revealed that they had signed the group to a long term contract. Ray's official announcement to the press indicated the obligatory optimism expected after such long negotiations:

> This all came about because Clive Davis, Elliot Goldman and myself were having lunch. I was having a simultaneous conversation with both Clive and Elliot – Clive asked me if I wanted to sign the contract and Elliot asked me if I wanted any tossed salad. I said yes. As a result I have made my first and only decision of 1976. I was overwhelmed by the interest expressed by various record companies with respect to the Kinks and I would like to take this opportunity of thanking all the other companies for the interest shown in us. I met Clive Davis on two or three occasions during our career and always felt that some phase of our recording career would be spent with his company. Arista seems to be an exciting new company and the emphasis on the Kinks' music is on the future. I feel that this could be an exciting and successful combination.[106]

Arista president, Clive Davis, also waxed eloquent about his admiration for the Kinks and stressed the tremendous contribution to music they had made before delivering what must have been the worst concluding speech of his executive career:

> I couldn't be happier that they've chosen Arista as their new home and am confident that the future of the Kinks lies very much in front of them.[107]

The Arista signing was immediately followed by the reopening of Konk studios. The latest additions to the building included a new soundproof booth capable of accommodating up to a dozen brass players and a wealth of recording equipment comprising a custom Neve desk, quadro monitoring via JBL 4350s, Dolby noise reduction, Ampex MM 1100 multitrack and AC 440 two-track tape machines plus Studer A80 four-track and two-track machines and four Ameron DC 300A monitor amps. Session drummer, Nick Trevisick, who used Konk frequently in his appearances on albums by Dave Davies and the Kinks, provided an interesting assessment of the studio:

> I think it's one of the best studios in town. I think it's very well equipped, plenty of room. There's a main studio, a vocal booth and piano booth. There's limitless possibilities there – it's already computerised. They'll develop it as far as modern technology increases. I think it's one of their major investments.[108]

For the remainder of the year, the Kinks worked on their Arista debut. The lack of new record releases, however, ensured that Davies's personal life was once more a hot topic for gossip. Relentless journalists from the dailies questioned him about such matters as his 1974 divorce, a subject which the incredulous Ray regarded as not only out of bounds but irrelevant:

> Look, my marriage is over, finished, and that's it as far as I'm concerned. It's not part of my life any more, so there's nothing more to say about it.[109]

One writer tackled Ray about his onstage limp-wrist routine and backside wiggling. Davies's reply was characteristically humorous:

> Well, it's had a hard time lately, it's not at its best, but its still a pretty good ass . . . Haven't had much chance to keep it in shape . . . [110]

Ray described the stage persona as a study in narcissism:

> I don't think it's necessarily gay. I think on certain occasions the character may be so in love with himself that he gives that appearance to an outsider. Conceit really. It's just . . . my wrist is *loose*.[103]

Perhaps in desperation for some new insights into the private world of Ray Davies, one magazine presented 'Words from a script of statements by several people who know Ray Davies well'. It was a sycophantic piece of nonsense, seemingly concocted to present an image of Ray as an eccentric romantic:

He's just a super – an *over* sensitive guy. Really affected by adversity of others. He has a hard time being happy if there's any misery around him. One time we went to a topless bar and Ray offered the girl his sweater because he thought she was cold. He was genuinely concerned. He's a lovable sort of person, a little fucked up, but then who isn't? People love him because he's endearing, he's adorable, he's so caricatureable. But he's a very intense guy: he tends to get moody and emotional about things. I remember one interview I sat in on, with some kid who was obviously more groupie than journalist. After a while Ray hissed out of the corner of his mouth: 'Get rid of him!' Next day he turned to me and said, 'What ever happened to that nice boy? He never came back.'[103]

In December 1976, the press finally found a story involving Davies that was worthy of editorial comment. The group Cafe Society, featuring Tom Robinson, had apparently been signed to Konk Records for two and a half years during which time they had released only one album, much to the disappointment of Robinson. Nick Trevisick, Cafe Society's drummer during this period, expressed his view on the long delay:

I think Ray gets these ideas but then he gets bored with them. He didn't realise how difficult and how much time it would take to run the Konk label.[108]

In his frustration, Tom Robinson had taken to performing 'Tired Of Waiting For You' dedicated with sarcastic comments to Davies. On one Saturday night at London's Nashville Rooms the private disagreements between Robinson and Davies became a public issue when Ray was heard railing against his protégé from the audience. Trevisick recalls the embarrassing episode:

I was in the middle – I took no sides . . . Ray came down to see what Tom was up to and they started their slanging match and I walked off stage and refused to come back until it had died down.[108]

According to press reports, the fracas ended with Davies aiming V-signs at the group before leaving in a flurry. John McCoy, the first manager of Cafe Society, quipped: 'Davies couldn't run a luggage label, let alone a record label'. There was much truth in this assertion as Konk Records ceased releasing material shortly afterwards. Davies's grand conception of a burgeoning record label had ultimately proved over-ambitious.

The episode involving Robinson evidently upset and embarrassed Ray sufficiently to cause problems in future interviews. A journalist from the *New Musical Express* happened to mention Robinson in passing during a conversation and met with a fiery reception from Davies who immediately terminated their discussion while threatening, ' . . . if you wish to pursue that line I'll go to every length I can to have this tape bought back – I swear to God, I'll do it'. It was an extraordinary reaction to an almost totally innocuous question, but once again underlined Davies's remarkable sensitivity about certain issues.

SIXTEEN

Way Down

Prior to the release of their Arista album, news filtered through that John Dalton had quit the Kinks. He had actually left in November 1976 having completed work on virtually all the cuts on the new Kinks album. His departure after seven years was a shock to Kinks fans, but those close to the group hardly found the news unexpected. During the previous year, Dalton had voiced his disenchantment with the rigours of touring and the continued need to commute between Britain and the States. In common with John Gosling, he was tiring of the theatrical shows and had hoped that Ray would revert to rock'n'roll. Although Davies intended to pursue this route, the decision apparently came too late for Dalton who returned to the quiet life in Hoddesdon. It would be a considerable time before he even thought about playing bass guitar again.

Dalton's replacement in the Kinks was Andy Pyle, a respected pro who had already gained a sizeable reputation playing in such units as the Alvin Lee Band, Savoy Brown and Blodwyn Pig. Pyle was the first established player to join the Kinks and his induction procedure was unusual to say the least. He received a phone call from Brian Wilcox, former tour manager of Savoy Brown, informing him that Ray Davies required some session work for the forthcoming Kinks album. Pyle completed work on a couple of tracks, following which he was officially invited to join the group. He later discovered that several other bassists had been invited to play during the same period, which suggests that the sessions were part of the audition procedure. Apparently, Pyle gained great support from John Gosling who had been aware of his reputation since the days when both musicians played in separate groups in Luton. Davies's peculiar reluctance to make important decisions about new members ensured that Gosling's support was a crucial factor in determining Pyle's appointment. While Andy was helping the Kinks to complete the seemingly endless sessions for their Arista debut, he noted some strange occurrences in the recording studio. The mood of the musicians was unlike anything he had previously encountered:

> At the time I couldn't understand why whenever we were in the studio Dave, Mick and Baptist would be there with their heads down all day. Not a word would be spoken by anybody. The reason I couldn't

> understand this was because the minute we'd finish in the studio, we'd go to the pub, Dave, Mick, Baptist and myself, and it'd be pints and a good laugh. Then we'd go back into the studio the next day and not a word would be spoken! And I'd say 'Come on boys . . .' I was feeling really up – working with the Kinks seemed wonderful – I used to like the Kinks. But Mick and Baptist kept warning me, 'You'll find out when your time comes'.[111]

Andy paid little heed to the warnings of his fellow Kinks and failed to perceive any reason for their discontent. The time of reckoning, however, was closer than Pyle could ever have imagined.

In February, the *Sleepwalker* album was finally released. The main reason for the long delay had been Davies's difficulty in moving away from thematic concepts. During the early sessions Ray felt that he could have easily composed five L.P.s and, by December, the group found themselves with thirty compositions from which to select an album. Twenty of these were eventually recorded, leaving Davies with the unenviable task of choosing nine for the album, the majority of which had to be edited from lengths of seven minutes and more. After such time, care and industry one might have reasonably expected an album of musical complexity and lyrical density. Davies's determination to avoid the pitfalls of theatrical experimentation, however, encouraged a ruthlessly minimalist approach to recording. Much of the studio time was spent cutting out overdubs and strings as well as simplifying his songwriting method:

> I had to change my attitude to writing, cut down on things. Basically, I've tried to say something in one line and then use the next three for repetition instead of using four lines and saying something different in each one.[112]

Arista were satisfied with Davies's work and *Sleepwalker* was widely touted as proof positive of a Kinks renaissance. Minus the promotional hyperbole, the album was an average piece of work, but in spite of the pedestrian and derivative nature of several cuts it was still refreshing to hear the Kinks playing straight rock music again. Most of the songs were lyrically inferior to the theatrical work of the past few years, but the occasionally distinctive riffs were sufficient to generate a modicum of public interest.

The opening cut, 'Life On The Road', was an amusing guided tour of London from Abbey Road to Praed Street and Pimlico. For Ray, it was one of those songs that could easily have spawned another conceptual work:

> The song is about eighteen months old. It was not written specifically for me; it is not autobiographical. Although there are bits of me in it, I wrote it for another character. It's a song I would have liked to have done a whole album about. Some of the lines are true.[113]

Although there were some other interesting lyrical numbers on the album such as 'Brother', most of the cuts relied on predictable licks for their effect. The title song clearly fell into this category but Davies was evidently anxious to explain its significance:

> It's about a vampire, but not the bloodsucking kind. It's more somebody who feeds off of people's lives rather than people's blood – somebody who feeds off their stories. It's like a writer going around getting people to talk in their sleep and then coming out with all of the things they say in their subconscious. I tried to think of other titles for it, but I just wanted the riff. It's an instrumental, really. It was too easy to work out as a song. I feel close to it.[113]

Ray's desire for riffs provided brother Dave with an excellent opportunity to show his abilities as a lead guitarist and he was also allowed the luxury of lead vocals on 'Sleepless Night'. Apparently, Ray had originally intended to sing the number until Dave appeared with his own rendition. Although unspectacular, there were evidently some extremely good one liners in the original lyrics that were eventually deleted for possible use at a later date. Another member who received a shot at glory was Andy Pyle, whose bass work can be heard on 'Mr Big Man'. Once again, however, editing was necessary to prune the song to a suitable length. Pyle recalls the original session with some amusement:

> I remember playing the bass and Ray would say, 'Go on Andy, play loads of things, anything you like'. and then he snipped all the best bits together. It was a very funny approach recording with the Kinks – and not always in a jocular way.[111]

Pyle's account indicates that Ray approached the *Sleepwalker* project with tremendous but misplaced energy, since his efforts probably robbed the album of much of the spontaneity at which he was aiming. On reflection, Davies admits that the album was far from a complete success:

> There wasn't the commitment, the conviction in that album that is the absolute essence of what the Kinks are really all about.[114]

In spite of its limitations *Sleepwalker* was a sizeable U.S. hit, reaching as high as number 21. With everything to play for, the Kinks set off on another memorable U.S. tour, taking in ten cities and securing important television spots including one on N.B.C.'s *Saturday Night* on 26 February. Meanwhile, Pyle had almost forgotten the Cassandra-like warnings that Avory and Gosling had voiced during the Kinks' pre-Christmas sessions. Several dates into the tour, however, Andy learned the reasons behind them:

> My time came in Chicago. Then I knew what it was all about . . . When it came my time to be accepted as a member of the band I received this devastating attack on my person from Ray. Absolute devastation. He gave a real belittling speech out of the blue. You know, 'Who the hell do you think you are, cunt?' It was completely out of the blue wheras an hour before it was 'Another pint, Andy?' I can remember this real tirade in the dressing-room in Chicago and at first I thought the bloke was joking. I'd seen him do this before with other people, airline pilots and people like that. For no reason at all he'd pick on me and lay into me in not a very nice way. I didn't think he could be serious because I hadn't done anything . . . I packed the bass up, clonked down the stairs and went to the hotel. And we didn't speak to each other for another fortnight. The boys all went, 'There you go – told you'. They had *all* experienced it.[111]

What Pyle had witnessed was hardly revelationary or even unexpected. Davies's psychological tactics and *prima donna* displays were strikingly reminiscent of his childish conduct during the 1965 tour. Andy was merely receiving a small dose of the behaviour that had made Larry Page's life a nightmare twelve years before. Worse was to follow when the Kinks resumed the onstage aggression and petty silences that had come so close to destroying them in the old days. In spite of their frequent claims that they had mellowed and matured over the years, the Davies brothers continued to display a sibling rivalry that should have died in the school playground two decades before. It was an unpleasant experience for the other members of the Kinks whose loyalties were inevitably divided. John Gosling was reticent about the problems that were tearing the group apart from the inside:

> We had fights onstage. It was part of the Kinks thing. It was almost expected of us. Dave and Ray never really saw eye to eye on anything. It was very difficult to take sides with either of them. Mick was always the middle man. It was an awkward situation, not always easy to work with.[79]

The new recruit, Pyle, was finding that the conflicting loyalties expected from him were impossible to meet. Verbal intimidation and schoolboy bullying were par for the course on a stage that was beginning to resemble a battleground. Andy recalls the unsubtle way in which he was manipulated by the brothers:

> In tandem with Ray asserting his control, you had Dave asserting his . . . There were periods when Dave would say, for example, 'Come out to the mike and sing the choruses'. One of the reasons I got the job in the first place was because I could sing – which I can't! Dave would say

'Come out and join me on the choruses of "Lola",' but he'd say that to me without Ray knowing. So I might venture out, and then at the next soundcheck there would be a monitor put in front of me to prevent me going out again. Dave would say something to me and Ray the opposite. At other times I'd be encouraged by Ray to play what I liked because I think he had a certain respect for me as a bass player. But while I was playing, Dave would come up and I'd feel this belt in the shin and this screaming in my ear, 'What are you doing, cunt?' We'd be playing a song in C and he'd scream in my ear 'Give me an E flat *now*.' And this would be in front of an audience.[111]

The individual members of the Kinks were merely pawns in a tiresome and pointless game between Ray and Dave Davies. For a professional musician such as Andy Pyle, the tragedy of the Kinks was the failure to take control of their own artistic destiny. In a group with a fifteen-year history the main concern should have been the music, but what Pyle most remembers about his stay can be summed up in the numerous accounts of petty squabbling and clashes of ego. Looking back at that period, Pyle is filled with frustration at the enormity of the lost potential:

The crux of it is that you've got two blokes who are extremely talented. I've got a great respect for both of them as writers, musicians . . . If only they could work together. The reason they're not up there with the Beatles, the Stones and the Who is because of their silly arse games. They've got the world at their feet and they're throwing it away. And that pisses me off.[111]

It is quite possible that the Kinks provides a means of cathartic aggression for the Davies brothers. Ray Davies admits that hatred and unpleasantness are the primary sources for his songwriting inspiration and without them he would probably cease composing. Perhaps the psychological warfare and childish tantrums are other methods by which Davies maintains his interest and occasional excitement for the rock'n'roll game.

Whatever the truth, the Kinks live performances during 1977 were becoming increasingly shambolic. Returning to England, the group played a one-off gig at London's Rainbow Theatre on 24 March which received a scathing reception in the music press. The ever-perceptive Nick Kent of the *New Musical Express* described the show as 'the pits of mediocrity', no doubt aggravated by Davies's oafish smugness, a selection of dire material and a perfunctory performance that barely masked the group's total boredom with the entire proceedings. In an effective summing up, Kent pinpointed the lackadaisical attitude of a once interesting group that had apparently fallen into self-parody:

When a band who've been around for ten years or more fail to present their audience with new inspired material then that's one problem. But when said band is seemingly incapable of handling even their own established masterworks with any dint of respect or authority then that's just too much to take.'[15]

Kent's hostility should not distract attention from his genuine concern about the group's apparent fall from grace. Even the Kinks were losing their confidence. Wary of undertaking a full U.K. tour they restricted themselves to a couple of television appearances, including a forty-five minute *Old Grey Whistle Test* special in which they played six of the nine songs from *Sleepwalker*. Ray could also be seen on I.T.V.'s *Supersonic* playing alongside an all-star line-up including Marc Bolan, Elkie Brooks, Dave Edmunds and John Lodge. A brief trek to the Pink Pop Festival in Holland only brought more vitriolic abuse in the shape of reviews declaring Davies a tragic has-been. Shunned by their homeland critics, the Kinks probably looked on the next U.S. tour as a welcome relief.

Unfortunately, the onstage bickering that had marred recent Kinks performances continued unabated. At times there were some hilarious scenes, such as the New York gig when Gosling carried Ray on his back during an encore, following which Davies reappeared without his trousers to sing the closing number. Too often, however, seemingly innocent onstage antics would turn nasty. During a gig at the British Ambassador's house, the Kinks set degenerated into a brawl following which Ray found himself alone onstage:

At the end of the show I was just standing there. Mick got fed up and kicked his drum kit over, there I was strumming my guitar saying, 'Well I'd like to play this number', realising it would have to be a solo job. I was about to go into 'Juke Box Music'. I thought, 'No, I can't do it without a group'.[15]

It was small wonder that many punters began attending Kinks gigs in the firm belief that they might be witnessing the group's final performance. Remarkably, the members somehow managed to stay together and despite the crude and violent behaviour onstage, differences of opinion were subsequently reconciled. In many respects the individual members of the group were conned into believing that these fights were consistent with the Kinks' character, and therefore justifiable. Pyle retains ambivalent feelings about the Kinks, even in the face of extreme provocation and physical violence:

You can have all this chaos going on but there is a certain wonderful feeling when you're onstage and 20,000 people are singing along with you. You feel good for five minutes until you get another kick in the shins! Drums are kicked over and people are spat on. Dave went around

> and spat at everyone in the band. This was at the Santa Monica Civic. We came off and got an encore and Baptist said, 'I'm not going back on with that cunt'. And Ray said, 'Either you go back there or I'll knock you out'. And then 'bop' – he was out! Ray ran on all smiles and played the keyboards. But Ray's clever . . . because after awhile, for some reason, you think, 'Ah, it's not so bad after all'. But it *is*.[111]

Davies's almost Machiavellian cunning in promoting disorder and restoring unity at the eleventh hour was proving an increasingly dangerous game. Yet, as Pyle testifies, Ray frequently succeeded in preventing members from leaving the group merely by reverting to his Noel Coward, Mr Charming persona. His extreme changes of mood from the polite gentleman to the iron-fisted dictator were somehow sufficiently disorientating to quell the unrest. Already, however, Pyle was beginning to notice a change in his own behaviour and attitude towards the Kinks. In every other group with which he had been involved over the years, the onstage performance was the highlight of the day. Suddenly, Pyle realised that instead of building up to the gig and winding down afterwards, the group were performing the opposite function. Almost every night, Mick, John and Andy, often accompanied by the girl singers and horn players, would return to the hotel and join the house group for a selection of Buddy Holly or Chuck Berry numbers. If the house group weren't available, the boys would hit the town, frequently appearing in obscure clubs alongside local combos who were pleased to perform Kinks covers. This extra-curricular activity was probably the most important factor in keeping the group together, as Andy now realises:

> You mustn't think that it was *all* bad. We had some fun, but it was never when the two brothers were together. With the Kinks the gig was the low point of the day. The attitude was 'Let's get it over with, let's get it done'. Onstage at the hotel *that* was the high point. I remember once we played four gigs in a day. And that was our compensation. It was sad.[111]

As Pyle indicates, once the Davies brothers were separated the pressure on the Kinks as a unit was greatly alleviated. In fact, Andy struck up a reasonably good working and social relationship with Dave. He recalls staying up half the night on a number of occasions having intense conversations with the younger brother. Pyle described these non-conclusive metaphysical musings as 'the sort of discussion you have when you're out of your brain at nineteen'.

By the winter of 1977, the Kinks were still in one piece, but the cracks in the relationship were increasingly obvious. Even the placid Mick Avory was apparently close to quitting, though according to Pyle this was nothing new:

> Every tour was Mick's last tour. Every tour. Baptist's first tour was meant to be Mick's last. Once a week he would put his sticks down and say, 'Right, I'm not having any more of this'. And he's still there because . . . living on the road with these people, it gets a bit difficult. You finish the gig and go back to the hotel and you get a call from one of them at five in the morning.[111]

In an attempt to save the group from extinction Ray entered the studio and began work on a new album. However, the commitment of the members was apparently so low that Davies was forced to consider employing new musicians. For a while he may even have threatened to embark on a solo career, but his own insecurities prevented the whim from being realised. With Avory's interest close to an all-time low, session drummer Nick Trevisick was recruited to work on several of the new songs:

> Mick was a bit disillusioned. Basically, the whole band was in disarray. Ray called me to do some tracks. It wasn't behind Mick's back – he was there at the time. After that Ray asked me to do the entire album but I couldn't because I was working on an album with Andy Desmond. I was a great friend of Mick's. After I'd done those tracks Mick told me he'd asked Ray to include my name on the album. I think Mick's a very good player, but it's difficult to sustain an interest over twenty years when there's a lot of tension around. I think Mick retreated a bit from it.[108]

Trevisick's opinion is almost certainly a classic understatement. Former members of the group maintain that Mick is evidently far more interested in playing golf than drums these days. His love of playing and dedication to the Kinks no doubt died many years ago amid the petty squabbling and personality clashes that have plagued the group since its formation. Andy Pyle recalls his failed attempt to rekindle Avory's love of playing in the Kinks line-up:

> I said, 'Let's be one of the best rhythm sections, let's get good, let's get tight.' And Mick would say, 'All right, we'll try . . . ah, but it doesn't matter does it?' And he was right. It *doesn't* matter with the Kinks. Mick's got a good feeling for the drums and he's a good listener. He listens to what other people do and plays accordingly. He could have been a good musician, but he's been there too long. Heaven help them if a drummer's drummer had been in there instead of Mick . . . Mick's not allowed to play drums. He's a mediator. He's the Henry Kissinger of drums.[111]

Without Avory, it seems likely that the constant rivalry between the brothers would have destroyed the Kinks years ago. However, in accepting the role of peacemaker Avory may well have blighted his own professional career. It is difficult to imagine him easily slotting into a new group if the

Kinks suddenly folded. A dramatic move was not only desirable but necessary many years ago, but it is now probably too late. Larry Page saved a great rock group when he reunited the Kinks after the Cardiff incident of 1965, but, in retrospect, it might have been more humane to have allowed Avory his freedom following his one great gesture of defiance.

SEVENTEEN

Angels With Dirty Faces

The internal problems suffered by the Kinks during 1977 ensured that work on the new album was proceeding painfully slowly. On 25 November, a compensatory Yuletide single was released in the form of 'Father Christmas', a delightfully ironic Davies attack on the commercialisation of the festive season. Unfortunately, the single flopped, in spite of some additional publicity provided by the flip side 'Prince Of The Punks'. This scathing comment on New Wave posturing has often been interpreted as a satire on Tom Robinson, who severed his connections with Davies's Konk label amid great acrimony. At the time of the single's release, Davies stressed how close he felt to Robinson, even venturing as far as to describe his role in the affair as paternalistic. His presentation of himself in the role of hurt party was so heart-rending it almost sounded convincing:

> I wanted to patch it up a month ago, but it got to the stage where he refused to meet. I'm a soft touch really. I'd be silly if I said I wasn't upset. I have to pretend I'm thick-skinned, but I'm a very creative person myself. I'm not a solicitor.[116]

Six months later, however, Ray had no reason to couch his criticisms in sentimental rhetoric:

> I don't put people down for taking my ideas or my style and finding something of their own. But I don't think he [Tom Robinson] has found anything original yet. He's only saying things that I said in *Preservation*. I don't think there's anything original there.[117]

Tom Robinson may be far from a great artist, and nobody could reasonably place him alongside the old master. Yet, few could disagree that he deserved better treatment in his career development than Davies ever offered in his role as Konk label manager. The long drawn out public slanging match was a final bitter comment on the total failure of the Davies brothers to establish their late 70s version of Apple.

Meanwhile, back at Konk studio, the elongated Kinks sessions were taking their toll on the group. Andy Pyle sounds like a victim of the *Invasion Of The Bodysnatchers* in his description of the insidious process by which the Kinks robbed him of his love of music:

> After about a year I was in the studio for the first time since *Sleepwalker*. After about three or four weeks I suddenly realised that there I was getting up in the morning, driving to the studio and sitting in silence until it was the end of the day and we'd go to the pub. I'd *become* like the others! Within the space of a year my enjoyment of going to work and playing had gone . . . It was a gradual process. Everything else was fine but I didn't like playing . . . If it wasn't for the fact that I knew I was getting worse as a bass player I'd probably still be there.[111]

Although staying a Kink meant steady work over a long period, Pyle felt increasingly frustrated by his inability to enjoy playing and finally approached Ray about leaving. Andy chose an opportune moment between tours in order to give Davies sufficient opportunity to find a replacement. Instead of accepting the situation, Davies apparently placed Pyle in a position where he was virtually forced to remain in the Kinks. Andy would be requested to attend sessions during which he would play only four notes for hours on end. While more time was wasted in the studio, a pre-Christmas U.S. tour had been arranged which was somewhat unwise and premature given Pyle's obvious disenchantment. But Davies was determined to stabilise the Kinks, even though Pyle was proving difficult. One possible alternative was to jettison the Kinks and form a new group with established session men. However, this would probably have resulted in Ray embarking on a solo career, a move he has always chosen to avoid. In the event, such considerations were unnecessary as Pyle agreed to remain a Kink for a while longer. His reasoning was less pragmatic than sentimental, for Andy knew that if the U.S. tour was cancelled the group would be deprived of their Christmas bonus:

> They were my mates, and still are, but Ray put me in that position. So we went on tour, and I got nothing from it . . . I just continued what I was doing with Baptist, writing songs and going into Konk when I was needed.[111]

Although Ray had been informed that Gosling and Pyle were contemplating a project outside of the Kinks he took no immediate action against them.

The Kinks ended 1977 with a unique Christmas show at London's Rainbow Theatre. Ray had originally voiced the possibility of presenting the gig as a History Of The Kinks, with John Dalton and Peter Quaife returning for a few songs. He may well have intended this to be the last Kinks concert, though how close Ray really came to dissolving the group may never be known. The reviewers sat on edge during the show half expecting a White City style retirement speech as Ray teased the audience with hints that this could be 'the last time'. Critics spoke of the strange atmosphere of celebratory finality as Ray presented selected hits from every era of the Kinks' long career. The presence of B.B.C. disc-jockey, Alan Freeman, in the role of Master of Ceremonies and historical narrator, prompted further suspicions of a grand finale. In the end, the critics' speculation was to prove only partially correct.

Following the Christmas show the Kinks went into semi-hibernation as Pyle and Gosling continued work on their own project. Andy never saw Ray again after the Rainbow concert and his public status in the group remained unclear until he was officially 'fired' in April. During the same month John Gosling terminated his employment with the Kinks, following a discussion with Davies. The reasons for his departure have never been made entirely clear but it appears that there were a number of factors involved. Ray complained that Gosling was not giving the group his full commitment and had the audacity to suggest that he had never been accepted as a member of the Kinks:

> We never communicated and to be in a group you must communicate. That's why it's so good now with the people we have got. Everybody's chipping in ideas and everybody's happy. John used to get depressed about things.[115]

Although Gosling admits that he, Dalton and Pyle had always been uncertain about their status in the group, he regards Ray's comments on his eight-year stay as somewhat less than convincing. Gosling clearly did communicate with Davies on a musical and personal level and though he may have failed to voice his criticism of the rock musicals loudly enough, it should be remembered that there was little opportunity for constructive dissension. Gosling found Davies's point about the need for individual members to 'chip in ideas' amusing to say the least, considering Ray's normal overbearing presence in the studio:

> Ray knew what he wanted. If you're a writer you know exactly how the song is going to sound. Certain writers will compromise their ideas in order to make it a group sound. But with Ray, I don't think he was willing to compromise. He was producing the stuff as well and it all became a little wearying. He couldn't see the wood for the trees. Everybody else was chipping in ideas but I don't think he really wanted to know . . . Dave used to get quite frustrated. Often Ray would end up telling Dave the solo note for note.[79]

Gosling's exit was precipitated by Ray's desire to sign him to a long term contract, presumably as a means of preventing his extra-curricular work with Pyle. After eight years without a contract, John declined the offer, realising that in doing so his departure was now imminent. The final conflict took place following a ludicrous twelve-hour session during which

Davies obsessively demanded infinite re-recordings of 'Get Up' for the forthcoming album:

> In the end, I don't think he knew which was the best version. I counted sixty-three takes of the one song. He went back the next morning and said, 'Do you think we could try that song once more?' I just exploded. I was worn out – I'd had enough. It seemed that certain songs got washed and dried of their original melody and emotion because we'd done them so many times. To me the last three albums sounded like a lot of bored people. It was a shame – a lot of the spark had gone.[79]

Davies's perverse perfectionism was insidiously destroying the Kinks' morale. Avory had been forced to watch the proceedings from a booth while a session drummer filled his role; Dave's spontaneity was squashed by demands for note perfect reproductions of his brother's melodies; Pyle had been reduced to playing four notes on a different finger at every session and Gosling had lost every iota of inspiration. Something had to crack and, in the wake of Pyle's departure, Gosling offered the parting comment, 'This isn't the Kinks any more'. Although they would rise again, even Davies recognised that these latest departures represented the end of another era in the Kinks' history.

Having played in such a well-known group as the Kinks, one might reasonably assume that an experienced musician such as Pyle would have made a financial killing. Unfortunately, this was not the case. During 1976–7, Ray's no frills attitude was all too reminiscent of those ascetic days of the 60s when Larry Page marvelled at his frugality. Pyle was unimpressed, though surprisingly unconcerned about the wages situation:

> What you get depends on how Ray feels on the last day at the end of the tour. What bonus you get depends on what side of the bed he got out of. The bonuses varied so much from tour to tour that it was a joke. The basic wage was about the same as I'd get as a motor mechanic, which is what I used to be . . . I earned a lot more money with other bands. Alvin Lee, for example, was paying me twice as much as the Kinks paid me. In fact, I got twice as much from Savoy Brown five or six years before! . . . But I don't do this thing for money, it doesn't enter into it. It didn't bother me at all. Even if I was making a fortune with them I'd still have gone . . . If I got ten times the amount it would have been compensation for all the shit I had to put up with.[111]

While many professional musicians would have pushed Davies for more money, Pyle maintains that such an action would only have created greater friction in a group already beset with problems. Surprisingly, he harbours no real resentment and prefers to remember his Kinks days as one long farce.

Following their departure from the Kinks, Pyle and Gosling formed a new group, United. The line-up, including Ron Berg, Dennis Stratton and Dave Edwards, was forged from the remains of Remus Down Boulevard, a popular group who had frequently played at London's Bridge House. Eventually, United became Network, losing Stratton and Edwards along the way, who were replaced by guitarists Gary Pickford Hopkins, Dave Tedstone and Graham Foster. Following a series of gigs in Germany, the group recorded an album at Morgan Studios which was scheduled for release on Phonogram. Sadly, an unprecedented purge by the record company blighted the hopes of many aspiring acts including Network who were dropped from the label, while their completed album remained unreleased. Pyle moved on to Chicken Shack while Gosling retired from full time playing in order to concentrate on managing his music shop in Berkhamsted.

The Kinks' long-delayed follow up to *Sleepwalker* was finally released in May. *Misfits* was a great improvement on its predecessor indicating Davies's desire to combine his songwriting powers with the Kinks' musical muscle. Although the album lacked consistency, its high points ranked alongside some of the Kinks' best work. Some critics suspected that *Misfits* was a deliberate riposte to Tom Robinson and a reminder to the rock world that Davies was the true master of social commentary. Unlike his New Wave left-wing counterparts, however, Ray remained characteristically apolitical. In interviews of the period he denied allegations of having jumped on the late-70s protest bandwagon and frequently derided soap-box rock for its blatant insincerity:

> I do get angry about things. I want to say things, and my music is my vehicle for saying them. But I won't put myself on a platform and tell people to do this and to do that, and have control over them. I think that's wrong. There are still a lot of things that need to be said. There are still a lot of frauds around that need to be exposed. I'm not saying I'm going with any one side. I want the truth to come out, and you can't get the truth if you adopt that one-legged attitude.[117]

For Ray the 'truth' was to be found in a confused vision of everyman that he had created in characters such as Arthur. The lower middle-class was the group that Davies apparently identified with most strongly since, like his eponymous hero, their political allegiance was uncertain:

> There's one section of the population that doesn't seem to have a voice, that doesn't have songs speaking its mind, I'm talking about ordinary people, the ones who're not part of any movement or fashion. That's who I write for because that's me.[118]

Davies criticised England as an intolerant country and voiced concern about supposedly extreme left-wing groups manipulating the unions and paving the way for totalitarianism. In the midst of an economic recession Ray's liberal musings sounded suspiciously conservative. In spite of Ray's occasional angry commitment, the tracks on the album were relatively innocuous, and centred more on personal insecurities than political concerns.

The title track, 'Misfits', was one of Davies's best lyrics for ages with an excellent arrangement, spotlighting the inspired Spanish guitar accompaniment. The number was so quintessentially Kinks that many reviewers latched on to it as the key to the entire album. Although Ray denied that he had any particular concept in mind while writing the work, he accepted that 'Misfits' may have provided an unforeseen thematic unity:

> It wasn't meant to be a concept album, because the idea was to make it a lot of tracks that didn't fit in with a concept. But as it wore on and I actually got down to writing lyrics to 'Misfits', things changed. The lyrics and the music to the first verse came out at exactly the same time, and it wasn't until I got into writing the lyrics for the rest of the song that I realised that it was the key track that could tie the whole thing up: it could say a lot about the band, a lot about me, and a lot about the album . . . So really, though it wasn't intended to be a concept thing, it ended up one purely and simply because it was tied together by one track. If we'd taken that one track off, the rest of the album wouldn't have fitted together. It wasn't intended to be a story album.[119]

Like all of Davies's best songs 'Misfits' revelled in its own ambiguity, recalling the mood of such numbers as 'Celluloid Heroes' and 'Dead End Street'. The same equivocal stance could be observed more clearly on the other standout track, 'Rock'n'Roll Fantasy'. Ray had begun writing this number in his Manhattan apartment one evening after observing a person in another block who apparently spent his entire time playing records. The song served as an affectionate tribute to Kinks fans though there was also an implied warning of the dangers of surrendering to fantasy. The importance of maintaining contact with his working-class London roots had been a constant theme in Davies's work and, even during the first flush of R.C.A. extravagance, he had chosen to write *Muswell Hillbillies*. The dangers of falling for the American Dream, as exemplified in the self-analytical 'Sitting In The Hotel' may have suddenly seemed closer than ever during Ray's Manhattan sojourn. What began as a personal statement took on greater significance when Elvis Presley died during the week that Davies was completing the composition. Although Ray was not a great Presley fan, he confessed that the shock news influenced the writing of 'Rock'n'Roll Fantasy'. One critic described the number as Davies's swan-song and it is difficult to think of a more suitable epitaph. Arista wisely issued the song as a single backed with a new number, 'Artificial Light', and although it failed to chart in Britain, the American release provided a surprise and well-deserved Top 30 hit.

The remainder of the album was a mish-mash of themes from the quasi-didactic 'Live Life' and 'Get Up', to a series of humorous songs dealing with racial equality ('Black Messiah'), tax exiles ('In A Foreign Land') and image makers ('Permanent Wave'). Davies even attempted a re-write of 'Lola' in 'Out Of The Wardrobe', a tale of husband and wife transvesticism:

> Sexuality's something I haven't worked out yet. People's roles get confused at a very early age because they have this sexual thing thrust on them. You're immediately pigeon-holed. You might be a normal person pushed to extremes because you've been crushed by rules, by whatever other people call you. And you might be having a rebellion against what you really are. You see the guy in 'Out Of The Wardrobe' – it might be a phase, a rejection of something that happened at the office. He might not be that way permanently.[120]

The problem with most of these songs was their inconsequential nature, especially when you consider that Davies had spent about a year carefully recording them for an album. Most of the songs dated back several years which suggests that the album was a distillation of Davies's finest available material. Even Dave Davies had six songs in reserve from which the passionate rocker 'Trust Your Heart' was selected. For all the work that went into the album, however, the dividends were surprisingly low. Who else but Ray Davies would bother to write 'Hay Fever', a tiresome ode to middle-class psychosomatics? And who else would waste so much time and energy in pointless re-recordings of such an absurd and uninteresting song? John Gosling found Davies's dogged persistence in the face of plainly mediocre material hard to comprehend:

> 'Hay Fever' we did over and over again. We did it with John Dalton on bass, and then Andy on bass. We did it in E, we did it in C, we did it with backing vocals, without backing vocals . . . It was incredible.[79]

Some reviewers credited *Misfits* with having a pseudo-political stance. This was seized upon by Arista and incorporated in the promotion of the album. Clearly the press department realised that a new image was crucial and the possibility that the group could be touted as important social commentators was an opportunity not to be missed. Their initial approach was to present the current work as 'The Misfits Album' as opposed to 'the latest Kinks L.P.' Adopting a Ray Davies caricature, they conceived the notion of Mr Misfit, a rebel without a cause, a man without a movement, and a loner with a 70s image. Stickers and advertisements were designed with cryptic quotes such as 'You don't have to be white to be God' and 'You don't have to be a chick to wear suspenders', subtly alluding to 'Black Messiah' and 'Out Of The Wardrobe'. It was even hoped that a Mr Misfit cartoon strip could be used in such magazines as *Private Eye* and *Time Out* as an effective and unusual form of advertising. Andrew Bailey of Arista worked closely with Ray Davies in manufacturing this new image which he firmly believed could restore the Kinks to their cherished role as socio-political commentators:

> The existence of Mr Misfit gives Ray a specific topic to base his P.R. approach on. Ray will become known as the spokesman for the misfits of today, the people who don't want to be labelled as punks or left-wing protesters, but who still don't feel like giving up the fight. Ray believes this whole idea is strong enough to pass on to the U.S. office for them to consider using it as a basis of back-up advertising for the L.P. over there. One could imagine the cartoon strip appearing, for instance, in magazines like *Rolling Stone* and *Cream*.[121]

In spite of the ambitious plans, the cartoon idea was never sufficiently developed and whether such hyping would have ultimately helped Davies's credibility is debatable. In certain quarters, the socio-political stance of Ray Davies was already being questioned. His New Wave posturings were dismissed by John Lydon as blatantly hypocritical, and in a scathing reference to 'Live Life' the former Sex Pistol observed:

> What can you say about patronising, prattish, ill-conceived, calculated token gestures of 'understanding the scene maaan' like this? Just hear the thing and find out for yourself because I can't put into words readable my disgust with this and would it be worth the effort?[122]

Following the release of *Misfits*, Davies found replacements for Pyle and Gosling in the form of bassist Jim Rodford, a former member of Argent and Phoenix, and keyboard player Gordon Edwards, who had recently quit the latter day Pretty Things. Gigs were hastily arranged in Birmingham, Manchester and Liverpool but the Kinks failed to appear due to insufficient rehearsal time. As compensation, Davies agreed to perform at a special benefit concert for the Roundhouse Club in Chalk Farm where the Kinks played before an 800 strong audience. Ray explained the apparently sudden decision to play at the Roundhouse as an inspired idea:

> I seriously regretted having to postpone those concerts but it was just too early for the band. Now the Kinks are really working well and itching to play on stage. As we're an English band I feel it's only right that we should debut here in England so when I discovered that the Roundhouse had a

> free day this Friday I felt it was an ideal opportunity to play a concert which would also help the theatre.[123]

Davies's sincerity should not mask what may well have been a pre-planned publicity stunt. A full month before the album's release, Bailey had sent out a memorandum with the revealing line: 'Interest in London will be stimulated by faking a sudden decision to do a one-off club date during the week of the L.P.'s release'. Arista were obviously determined to use every promotional trick in the book in their efforts to put the Kinks back on the rock map.

EIGHTEEN

The Winner Takes it All

The latest Kinks recruits, Rodford and Edwards, were immediately exposed to the group's temperamental nature during the five-week U.S. Spring tour of 1978. The Davies brothers maintained the aggressive stage behaviour that had become a hallmark of their performances over the years. For some American critics, the Kinks were the archetypal British punks and their insulting exchanges onstage were a joy to behold. When questioned about the continued bickering, Ray seemed uncertain about his brother's true feelings:

> It's just one of those things. We sometimes look at one another. I wouldn't want to destroy him or anything like that. He sees bits of me that he hates. And it just starts. I don't know how much of it is serious from his side. Me, I try to look at it light-heartedly and say it's a joke. I get the feeling from him it's for real. Because Dave is a real tight guy, and he can turn just like that.[69]

While on tour Davies spoke confidently about his plans to transform *Preservation* into a movie, part of which he hoped to film in Cleveland, Ohio. It was the usual Davies exaggeration and following his return to England the idea remained undeveloped. Instead, Ray found himself distracted by a new project when his secretary read him the following letter: 'Dear Mr Davies, You have been chosen to write some songs for an Aristophanes play'. Ray could hardly believe his luck. For years he had been trying unsuccessfully to fuse theatre and rock and now he was being offered the chance of contributing towards an Athenian comedy. The playwright, Barrie Keefe, already had a list of credits to his name, including the *Gimme Shelter* trilogy and the controversial *A Mad World My Masters*, which had included satirical sketches on several media figures from newscaster Angela Rippon to members of the Royal Family. More significantly for Davies, Keefe had written a television play called *Waterloo Sunset* and obviously had a strong affection for the Kinks' music. Davies and Keefe scripted a play for production at the National Theatre based on their conception of what Aristophanes might have written had he been born in the twentieth century. Essentially, they adapted the old 'play within a play' idea but with a new twist. The setting of their play was the National itself, and the central character was director, Peter Hall. The action sprang from Hall's determination to stage an all-male *Lysistrata* and *Oresteia* in the face of a woman's revolt. It was a novel idea, but the satire proved too biting for the National who eventually rejected the script. Although disappointed by the failure of another grand scheme, Ray was pleased about his work with Keefe and looked forward to the possibility of further collaborations in the future.

While the Kinks' reputation in the States was improving, they had yet to be rediscovered in their home country. Those nouveau mods the Jam had waxed a faithful reproduction of 'David Watts', which climbed into the Top 30 in the summer of 1978, but no one seemed willing to champion the Kinks as the great unheralded British rock group. On the contrary, their November appearance at the Hammersmith Odeon brought further criticisms from the *New Musical Express* whose reviewer dismissed them as 'a second rate heavy metal band' and described the performance as 'a travesty of rock'n'roll'. Their old work was dismissed as 'criminal' and Davies's apolitical stance and sentimentalised ideals of individuality on tracks such as 'Misfits' were derided as: 'Selfish, insular and thoroughly reactionary'. Within a few months of this attack, however, Davies was close to being accepted as an honorary member of the New Wave. His luck changed when the Pretenders revamped an even older and almost forgotten Kinks classic, 'Stop Your Sobbing', for another Top 40 hit. Suddenly it was recognised that the Kinks had been slogging away on the live circuit for years without achieving the mega-stardom of such contemporaries as the Rolling Stones.

The Kinks had changed very little during the past few years and apart from a new haircut and the occasional name-dropping of artists such as the Residents and Pere Ubu, Davies's interviews were the same as ever. Instead of blasting Ray for his reactionary stance, the *New Musical Express's* Charles Shaar Murray now listened intently as Davies explained that he was neither socialist nor capitalist but supported 'anarchy with order'. Another critic might have questioned Ray over his fashionable use of the term anarchy, especially in the context of such an apparently contradictory and meaningless statement. Murray, however, was obviously in search of a new angle since his article eventually emerged as an unconvincing attempt to glorify a 'born again Ray Davies'. Perhaps the most amusing of Murray's statements was his opening gambit in which he glamorised Davies's frustration when faced with the necessity of buying a round of milkshakes. Ray fumbled through his pockets in the vain hope of finding some cash, but was eventually reduced to asking his manager to lend him ten dollars. This was strikingly reminiscent of similar requests to Larry Page fifteen years before. Old eccentricities die hard, but who would have believed that by 1979 Davies still felt himself a victim of his fictitious

'Moneygoround'?

The renewed faith that some critics were placing in Davies was partly vindicated by *Low Budget*, the best Kinks album for a considerable period. Prior to its release Ray sounded unusually relaxed and even said: 'The time I spent writing and recording this has been the happiest time ever for me'. Suddenly, the Kinks were reaping the dividends of all those American tours of Holiday Inns and *Low Budget* effortlessly achieved their highest U.S. chart position since the mid-60s. The album marked a return to Davies's all-time favourite theme, the plight of the common man in modern society. From problems with the National Health to petrol shortage, Ray probed the mundane worries of everyman. Part of the charm of tracks such as 'Pressure' and 'Attitude' came from the listener's belief that they might be autobiographical accounts of Davies's own lifestyle. Ray explained his interpretation of 'Pressure':

> The pressure is something that you hand on . . . I thought if people get a bit of pressure and talk to somebody else about it then somebody else would go off and worry about it. I thought it would be a nice idea for a play – somebody has a bit of pressure and it gets passed on and eventually gets to the president. It's like a disease. The first verse could be about V.D. I wrote it about pressure but it could be about anything else. I love that lyric . . . I'm proud of that song.[124]

The release of 'Pressure' in the States as a single indicated Arista's faith in its commercial potential. After years of overdubbing and re-recordings, Davies had produced this latest hit with the kind of spontaneity that Gosling and Pyle would have admired:

> It was recorded first take. I was pointing to my guitar, pointing out the next chord they would play and they were changing as I was pointing. They didn't know the chords. I said to Mick, 'Just keep drumming until I say 'stop!' I'm so proud of that backtrack because I get to play lead guitar at the beginning which is really bad if you listen carefully.[124]

Another factor in the album's success in the States was the American orientation of tracks such as 'Catch Me Now I'm Falling' with its references to comic book hero Captain America and, of course, '(I Wish I Could Fly Like) Superman'. The latter was another sizeable hit which Ray revealed as his favourite number in the current Kinks set. Unlike 'Pressure', however, Davies took considerable time completing work on the cut:

> That's an interesting track because I got Mick to play a really tiny bass drum. We laid bass and drums down first and built everything around it. I didn't know what the guitars were going to sound like. It

was a lot of trouble to get the guitar mixed into the track. I mixed it about ten times.[124]

Overall, the album was a suprise success, effectively combining *Sleepwalker* style riffs with the melodic and lyrical strength of *Misfits*. Having abandoned his angry young man pose, Davies settled more easily into a new persona as the Woody Allen of rock'n'roll. His semi-autobiographical songs were both amusing and refreshing in their self-effacing honesty. 'Low Budget', for example, was a humorous portrayal of an absurdly penny-pinching individual, a victim of 70s economic recession who bore more than a passing resemblance to Ray. In interviews of the period Ray admitted to travelling by tube, ignoring to pay his television licence and refusing to take taxis because they were too expensive. While his low-budget lifestyle obviously had negative effects it also served to keep him in touch with ordinary people and prevented his falling victim to the decadent aspects of stardom:

I've never been into the celebrity trip. I did go into Studio 54 in New York once, and I actually asked Bianca Jagger to dance. She told me to clear off. I'm a fairly anonymous person, and hardly anyone ever recognises me. I've stood at the bar at places where the band have been playing and I've heard people talking about the Kinks, but to them, I'm just a guy having a drink.[125]

Following the release of *Low Budget*, the Kinks found themselves yet another new keyboard player, Ian Gibbons, a young and relatively inexperienced player still in his twenties. It was generally hoped that he would stay longer than Gordon Edwards who had quit prior to the recording of the album, leaving Ray to take the keyboard credits. The latest line-up seemed potentially more stable and a series of well-received gigs encouraged Davies to record a number of concerts for inclusion on a double live album. During the same period he was approached by *Time/Life* to record an in-concert video cassette to promote the album. Ray refused unless he was offered the role of associate producer which was eventually granted. As well as featuring most of their gig at Providence, Rhode Island, the videotape included rare footage from a 1965 edition of *Shindig*. The video received an official preview on 7 July at The Roxy Club in Los Angeles and the Bottom Line in New York. The general reaction from the critics was mixed and according to press reports many long-time Kinks' fans were disappointed by what they saw as Davies's unimaginative use of the medium.

On 18 July 1980, the double album *One For The Road* hit the racks, preceded one week earlier by a surprise E.P. containing four of the best cuts: 'David Watts', 'Where Have All The Good Times Gone?', 'Attitude' and 'Victoria'. The twenty-track album was a reasonable selection of

Kinks material and, not surprisingly, climbed into the U.S. Top 30 almost immediately following its release. Davies carefully selected songs ranging from archetypal Kinks ('Where Have All The Good Times Gone?') through memorable covers of 'Celluloid Heroes' and 'Victoria' and no less than six cuts from *Low Budget*. The latter were the great weakness of the album, for although these versions were effective, the songs were too recent for revival and smacked of opportunism. Nevertheless, the wily Davies had seen fit to revive 'David Watts' and 'Stop Your Sobbing', as if to prove the Kinks' versions could live alongside those of the Jam and the Pretenders. Even more surprising was a strong chunky version of 'You Really Got Me' that betrayed no sign of boredom on the part of the participants. After sixteen years, the Kinks could still play their first hit with love and conviction, a fact that even surprised Davies:

> The really weird thing about 'You Really Got Me' is I don't think about it. It's like getting up in the morning. It would be like cutting off an arm not doing it. It's really important to me. At one point in my life I put everything on that song.[69]

Although no classic, *One For The Road* was an interesting document of the Kinks in concert at the end of the decade. What it revealed most clearly was that after years of sloppy performances, the group could still produce a tight set without unnecessary frills. Their London performances during the summer were favourably received by a music press that had at last taken the Kinks back to their hearts.

Returning to the States in the winter, the Kinks played to capacity crowds in almost every town they visited. In spite of their new found professionalism, however, the group still found themselves surrounded by incident. During a performance in Seattle one punter who failed to purchase a ticket, plummetted through the roof of the auditorium into the 6,000 crowd injuring three fans who were immediately taken to hospital. The intruder escaped unscathed! More drama followed at the airport in Portland, Oregon, where Davies was arrested on an alleged fraud charge. It was, of course, entirely unjustified. Police believed he was the San Francisco swindler who had been hiring limousines, borrowing money and checking into hotels under Ray's name before running up an unpaid bill. The bogus Kink had even received an advance from an unnamed record company on the vague promise of a future album! It took a couple of hours questioning before the Portland police finally accepted that Ray was the *genuine* rock star but their suspicions were at least a positive comment on his 'common man' persona.

Within a month of the release of *One For The Road* the rock world was taken aback by the arrival of *PL13603* – otherwise known as Dave Davies's long- awaited solo album. After thirteen years of abortive attempts and broken promises, the younger brother had finally completed and released a work that many believed would never appear. Dave attempted to explain his reasons for finalising the project in 1980:

> I dunno. It's bizarre isn't it? Why bother now anyway? But because the Kinks are now where I think they should always have been in America, it makes me feel right to do a solo project. I suppose really I've been a bit lazy, and in a way I couldn't dissipate my energy too much as we've learnt from bitter experience in the past. If you try and do too much, you end up doing nothing. But now we've got more freedom, and none of us are getting any younger.[126]

Dave had actually begun compiling material for the album during the summer of 1979. Drummer Nick Trevisick and bassist Ron Lawrence, fresh from the *Misfits* sessions, helped Dave complete the album in ten days, though much of their work was eventually scrapped when the errant guitarist chose to play all the instruments, sing all the vocals and produce the work. Although Trevisick was disappointed by Davies's decision to delete his work, there were apparently no personality problems or fights in the studio:

> It was O.K. working with Dave. He's very single-minded though . . . it's the same with Ray. He wants a robot really. He wants ideas, but in the end he prefers to do it himself.[108]

PL13603 sold approximately 150,000 copies in the States but it was undoubtedly a great disappointment to those fans who had waited thirteen years in the hope of quality material to rival such past gems as 'Death Of A Clown', 'Susannah's Still Alive' and 'Funny Face'. Although the album included a couple of interesting cuts, most notably the anti-doctrinal 'Doing The Best For You', too much of the remainder consisted of clichéd heavy metal riffs of dubious quality. According to Trevisick, Dave was determined to record a non-melodic, guitar-orientated work:

> He wanted to make the ultimate heavy-metal album. At one point we hired a massive drum kit and put it in the stone hall at Konk to get the heaviest drum sound you could get. It was even heavier than the old John Bonham Led Zeppelin sound.[108]

Like several heavy-metal exponents, Davies had also supposedly taken a sudden interest in black magic. Tales of musicians playing inside a pentagram chalked on the studio floor and white witches waiting in the wings were some of the reputedly strange happenings. It was all a far cry from the tentative days of 'Death Of A Clown' when Dave recorded what may have been a far superior album to this 80s heavy metal tribute.

In order to promote the live album and Dave's solo, the Kinks embarked on another U.S. trek, returning to England in December 1980 for a short tour, including a date at London's Apollo Theatre (a.k.a. the New Victoria). There they played alongside Pimlico based trio, the Gas, a young group whose unpolished spontaneity and boundless energy compared favourably with the old master's studied nonchalance. One might have expected the Davies brothers to show some warmth and friendliness towards a young group eager to succeed in the music business. Unfortunately for the Gas, the cameraderie that they had previously felt with other musicians on tour was all but suffocated by the determined aloofness of the brothers. Lead singer, Donnie Burke, recalls some of the restrictions that the Kinks imposed on the support act:

> They seemed paranoid about their position and paranoid about their future. We were denied access to their kitchens and told that we had to cater for ourselves. You couldn't even walk in during a soundcheck . . . They were like schoolkids. The most entertaining thing was watching the evening's argument. It was like a soap opera. I saw guitars being thrown across stage and Ray giving Dave the two fingers! It seemed like Ray and Dave were always on the verge of exploding. There seemed to be a lot of jealousy as if they still had this argument going after twenty years! You could understand this in 1964 but in 1980 they were still like a bunch of sixteen-year-olds.[127]

Observing the power struggle between the brothers, Burke was perplexed, like others before him, by a group set up in which the subsidiary members were continually placed in an uncomfortable position:

> I don't see how you can run a group like that with the kind of love-hate relationship that was going on between the brothers. The rest of them seemed to be pandering towards their whims. But what's Mick Avory going to do – get up and say, 'Look, I've had enough of this!'[127]

Like many of his contemporaries, Burke's opinion of the Kinks was ambivalent. Prior to the tour he had some admiration for the group, but their hackneyed professionalism and petty squabbling was a painful reminder of the dangers implicit in continuing a partnership for too long. By the close of the tour Burke and his fellows had strong feelings about the Kinks' career development:

> They should have stopped. Those guys for their own dignity should have stopped ten years ago and Ray should have carried on as a solo and become an enigma in his own right. The band were, quite frankly, going onstage and living on their name. Bringing their dirty washing out in public is perhaps excusable in the gossip columns, but onstage . . . I was

embarrassed. I was embarrassed I ever liked the Kinks. They're a bunch of shitbags.[127]

But in spite of the suspicion and hostility shown towards the Kinks by certain members of the New Wave establishment, the fans showed little hesitation in turning out in large numbers to support one of Britain's oldest institutions.

NINETEEN

(Just Like) Starting Over

With the Kinks in top gear, Ray decided to break away from group activities and concentrate his attention on theatre work. During the early months of 1981 virtually all his time was spent working with playwright Barrie Keefe on a revamped version of the Aristophanes adaptation that had been aborted three years before. Keefe's recent work had proved surprisingly controversial – the play *Gotcha* had been banned from a repeat showing on television following the intervention of the crusading Mrs Mary Whitehouse, while Lord Lew Grade's company had dropped *The Long Good Friday* because of its portrayal of gangland life in London, although it was later made. The Davies/Keefe collaboration contained some potentially offensive material about the Royal Family. The plot of *Chorus Girls* was centred on a government attempt to close the Theatre Royal and turn it into Britain's biggest job centre. While preparations are underway, the chorus girls are organising one final show for the visiting dignatory, Prince Charles. Unfortunately, their performance offends the royalist local policeman, Sniffer, who attempts to close the show. In the ensuing debacle, Prince Charles falls through a trapdoor and suffers amnesia while Sniffer assumes that he has been abducted. Therein begins the siege of Gerry Raffles Square. The plot, of course, recalls Aristophanes *The Poet And The Woman*, in which the Athenian women take hostage Euripedes' servant Mnesilochus, following which the tragedian attempts a series of daring rescues, parodying the action of his own plays. In the original, the leading female figure was a patronisingly presented Amazonian Puritan, replaced in *Chorus Girls* by a feminist. The feminist angle was a necessary addition in Keefe's view, adding force to the political thrust of the play which was deliberately set in a deprived area of London. Although Davies would not be drawn on the subject of politics, he expressed satisfaction with the songs written for the script. Keefe was even more effusive:

> This is someone whose heart and soul is in rock'n'roll that's coming into a theatre in a theatrical form. It's not the same as a group of theatre people trying to create a rock musical. That's like putting on make-up. This is the real thing. You can tell the difference.[128]

The play proved reasonably successful and seemed a far better vehicle for

Davies's talent than the severely limited *Preservation* shows of the early 70s.

The Kinks received further vicarious attention when the Pretenders hit the charts with a surprise cover of 'I Go To Sleep'. After sixteen years, a forgotten Davies's classic had finally been accepted by the British public. Although Chrissie Hynde of the Pretenders was a well known Kinks fan, many people were surprised to read that the couple had been enjoying a secret romance for a year as well as sharing Davies's home in Muswell Hill. The popular press latched on to the story following the revelation that Chrissie was named as a correspondent when Ray had been divorced by his schoolteacher wife, Yvonne, in September. The usually reticent Chrissie was extremely forthcoming about the affair:

> Obviously I'm besotted with him . . . It's a major part of my life. I mean, I've got the band and then I've got my relationship or whatever you want to call it with him. Did you see that movie *Last Tango In Paris*? You know how he met that girl and they had that affair and they never spoke to each other for a long time? It was a little like that. We were so relieved, like two kids who leave the room where the adults are . . . [129]

As if to punctuate their uncloseted affair, the duo appeared onstage together at a Kinks concert in Los Angeles where they sang Jackie Wilson's 'Higher and Higher' to one another in true show business fashion.

By late 1981, Ray Davies seemed more satisfied than ever with his role in the rock world. While Pete Townshend continually questioned the relevance of the Who in the modern world and Mick Jagger became a rock'n'roll athlete in order to preserve his physique, Ray appeared blissfully free from such mental and physical pressures. The Kinks' enormous success in the States allowed Davies the luxury of speaking out against his New Wave critics and championing the last of the last survivors:

> I think people should give groups like the Stones and the Who more credit, and not write them off as being the tired old men of rock. These bands started in the 60s and are still going. Overseas people see certain aspects of Britain being ridiculed. But our rock music is still regarded as the best in the world. America and Europe always look to Britain for the new influences. We are an export . . . We've gone to America and proved the British critics wrong.[130]

Davies's vision of the Kinks as old warriors carrying the British flag abroad sounded remarkably similar to Sir Harold Wilson's promotion of the Beatles in the mid-60s. In spite of his love for the past, however, Davies carefully avoided the pitfalls of nostalgia. Ever imaginative, he spoke with confidence of the Kinks' ability to exploit the visual aspect of rock by emerging as the forerunners in the video revolution. Ever since the 1966 film of 'Dead End Street' Ray had been anxious to present what he termed 'visual records'. Although there was much talk about the Kinks releasing a video disc, most fans found it difficult enough to obtain a vinyl copy of their latest album. Review copies of *Give The People What They Want* had been duly despatched in September but successive delays and postponements prevented the album from reaching the British public until January of the New Year. Prior to its release there was some speculation about the album's content, especially among those gullible enough to accept Davies's professed plans following the release of *Low Budget*:

> The next album I'm going to do will be a blues album. I'm going to go to New Orleans, live there for a bit and write it there.[124]

Of course, *Give The People What They Want* was a very different proposition, predictably retreading the territory charted so well on *Low Budget*. Although a reasonably solid work, *Give The People What They Want* revealed the Kinks veering towards a younger American audience weaned on heavy rock and hackneyed solos. Songs such as the title track, 'Around The Dial' and 'Back To Front' displayed a heavy-handedness verging on the tiresome. Davies's more perceptive British critics had little doubt that he was pandering towards the lowest common denominator of public taste, but Ray disagreed:

> I don't want people to get the wrong idea. I don't think we're at all heavy. We're just loud. I think there is an actual musical difference in heavy metal playing, a different attitude towards playing. Rock'n'roll's got this sloppy, laid back feel and I think we tend more towards that than heavy metal. Although Dave is kind of a hard, heavy guitarist.[131]

Less than convinced by such explanations, several reviewers concluded that the album title was a deliberately ironic comment on the Kinks' current musical policy. Ray argued that it was actually a criticism of radio programming, while the sleeve design had been inspired by a riot that had occurred near Konk during the recording of the album:

> That's how we came about to do our album sleeve, it's our studio window, and the police told us to block it up because there was going to be a riot in Turnpike Lane which was just down the road and they put wood over it and painted it and I sprayed 'Give The People What They Want' on the wall. What I'm trying to say is that what is happening has an effect on my work.[131]

The heavy riffs, notwithstanding, *Give The People What They Want* included a varied selection of bizarre themes in the old Kinks tradition and though the craftsmanship often left a lot to be desired. Davies's imagination and humour remained intact. 'Destroyer', for example, went beyond

'Out Of The Wardrobe' by not merely reintroducing the old transvestite theme but resurrecting Lola. Davies even cheekily borrowed the 'All Day And All Of The Night' riff for extra effect. At one stage, Ray considered deleting his creative plagiarism but changed his mind on hearing David Bowie's number 1 hit 'Ashes to Ashes', a sequel to the 1969 hit 'Space Oddity'. Impressed by Bowie's sense of his own history Davies completed 'Destroyer' with a clear conscience.

There were many other surprises on the album, not least the controversial 'Killer Eyes', written on the day Pope John Paul was shot. The Kinks were travelling on their coach from Edinburgh to Glasgow when Ray heard the news and read the newspaper reports. While completing the song on the coach, Ray also recalled the publicity surrounding the trial of Yorkshire Ripper, Peter Sutcliffe, and the worldwide shock produced by the recent assassination of John Lennon. Davies explained the genesis of the song, beginning with his portrayal of the Pope's assassin:

> There were some quotes from his mother . . . he was a poor boy and he was always strange, and she always knew that he was going to do something bad one day. I took that attitude in the choruses . . . There's also an element of the Peter Sutcliffe thing. I saw his parents being interviewed on television. And imagine what Sonia Sutcliffe, his wife, must have gone through, not knowing he was a murderer. There's this madness, this attention people want in the Sunday papers. 'Sonia's Terrible Torment.' But they didn't give a shit about Sonia Sutcliffe, she's just good copy.[35]

Ray's concern with senseless violence was continued in 'A Little Bit Of Abuse', a damning comment on wife-beating. Davies was treading dangerous ground by taking up the feminist banner, but his sincerity was never called into question by the music press, although militant activists on the *Chorus Girls* set had voiced criticism. In defence of his lyric, Ray indicated that the inspiration had come from childhood memories rather than any sudden fashionable flirtation with the Women's Movement:

> I used to live down the block from this woman, in Muswell Hill, where I grew up and her face always used to be cut up. But I was too young to realise what it was. Her husband used to come home pissed every night and they were always shouting and fighting. But she stayed with him . . . until one day she couldn't take it any more. It's so common. I really wanted to write that song and I'm proud of it. I know there'll be criticism from feminists who'll say, 'Who are you that you can write a song like that?' There's also a lot of mental battering that husbands take. It works both ways.[35]

With Davies tackling so many controversial contemporary issues, it was little surprise that most critics interpreted 'Art Lover' as a study in paedophilia. Unaware of the underlying connotations presented by his portrayal of a lonely man watching 'little girls' playing in the park, Ray explained that the number had been written following his daily jogging workouts. According to Davies, the song conjured up memories of his own estranged wives and family:

> I run in Regent's Park and it's lovely and I believe in beautiful things and I'm divorced – I have two little girls who I don't see; I'm not allowed to contact them but I can write to them. So I have a lot of feeling for people in that situation, and I want to write for them. I want to write for waitresses and divorced people.[35]

Amid the more uninteresting songs on the album were a couple of fine singles, neither of which achieved chart success. 'Better Things', released prior to the album, was a sequel to 'Days', a song of optimism for the future as opposed to a tribute to the past. The follow-up single, 'Predictable', was an amusing and accurate description of Davies's feelings about himself, the Kinks, and the recent music scene:

> Everything I say is a cliché. Everything is predictable. That's the thing about the world now, it's so predictable. The predictability of something like television is a joke. I'm sure that's why people like to watch the Olympics because it's unreliable – like us. We're so unpredictable that we're predictable. They say that popular music should have an air of inevitability about it and that's true but there's not a lot that's human about it.[132]

Davies's comments indicate a probable realisation that *Give The People What They Want* betrays the same predictability of which he complains. Remembering the Kinks' past, however, it seems unlikely that they will surrender themselves to a safe formula for the remainder of their days. Their next task will be maintaining a growing American following while gradually experimenting with new musical ideas rather than relying on hackneyed riffs and old melodies. The pitfalls of complacency remain the greatest threat to the quality of their future work.

TWENTY

Let's Dance

While *Give The People What They Want* consolidated the Kinks' position in the U.S. charts with a four month run, the group continued to play larger venues. Successful appearances at the Boston Garden and Madison Square Garden in the winter of 1981 led to several hastily arranged New Year gigs including a tour of the East Coast. Amazingly, even at the height of their American success, the Kinks showed few signs of maturity and several gigs were marred by the predictably schoolboyish behaviour of Dave. The presence of Ray's constant companion, Chrissie Hynde, waiting in the wings, did little to relieve the tension. During an outdoor gig on the West Coast, Ray mischievously ushered Chrissie onstage instructing the audience to welcome 'The Greatest Female Rock'n'Roller In The World'. Incensed by such presumptuousness, Dave threw down his guitar, left the stage, and returned moments later to spit in the face of Ms Hynde, in a grotesque parody of punk oafishness. At Nassau Coliseum, Long Island, Dave criticised Mick's drumming and, on this occasion, the ever tolerant Avory snapped, threw his sticks at his tormentor and stormed off. An unperturbed Ray casually announced to the shocked audience: 'I think our drummer's just had a phone call'. That particular date apparently culminated with Ray throwing curry at his brother during the subsequent backstage shenanigans. Needless to say, Avory was placated for the umpteenth time and life in Kinkdom continued as abnormally as ever.

For the remainder of 1982, the group continued their regular touring schedule and Dave surprised everybody with a second solo album, *Glamour*. The days of endlessly abortive attempts were long past as Dave effortlessly adopted the mantle of an 80s heavy-metal kid. For those disappointed by *PL13603*, *Glamour* must have sounded even more cacophonous. In spite of some success in the U.S., it was clear that Dave's solo career was hardly setting the world on fire. Leaving R.C.A., he approached several other labels but was given a cold response by record company officials wary of signing a soloist who was also committed to a big name group. Eventually, Dave secured a deal with Warner Brothers and immediately got to work on a third solo album. *Chosen People* finally appeared in late 1983 and came as a surprise to some fans and critics who had written off the younger brother as an ageing heavy-metal kid.

Although the album included some obligatory hard rock workouts, there were also some impressive ballads. The quasi-religious title confirmed Dave's growing interest in New Age spirituality, complete with credits to the Mystical Order Of St Peter. The album was dedicated to Sir George Young, who, in 1954, founded the Aetherius Society after hearing a voice telling him to 'Prepare yourself! You are to become the voice of interplanetary parliament'. It was all a long way from 'Death Of A Clown', but at least Dave had recorded an almost half decent solo album. Whether he can overcome his predilection for heavy metal and produce a melodic, carefully structured work remains a tantalising proposition that may one day be realised.

With Stateside tours increasing in popularity the Kinks seemed to be moving further away from their British roots. By the summer of 1983, however, their fortunes in the U.K. would dramatically alter. The champagne began flowing as early as February when Chrissie Hynde gave birth to Natalie, another Davies daughter. Further festivities seemed likely following rumours that the Kink and the Pretender were finally ready for marriage. Instead, the ever unpredictable duo went through a series of confusing interludes that merely highlighted their comic indecision. The wedding was booked at a registry office near London, but minutes before the ceremony was due to commence the couple had a dramatic change of heart. Ray recalls the ensuing events:

> We just talked and thought that we couldn't be any closer than we are now. So we backed off. But then we talked some more and we decided that we would go through with it after all. So we went back to the registry office a second time, but the registrar wouldn't marry us because we'd missed our wedding time. Now we have decided that we don't need to be married to stay together and be happy. But it was a very close thing.[133]

The 'on-off' marriage of Ray and Chrissie was hardly a surprise to those who had followed the activities of the leading Kink over the years. For Fleet Street, however, this proved an excellent opportunity to rediscover Davies's legendary eccentricity and old familiar tales were told with glee. A deadpan Ray described his strange habit of spending hours watching commuters disembarking at Waterloo station. Was he trying to remember what everyday life held for the average Londoner, or was this latest activity an extension of his favourite nightmarish excursion on the Underground's never-ending Circle Line? Even while journalists were pondering these questions, Ray would interject with news of his plans to make a movie about mortuaries! The brevity of these interviews and the often strange replies suggested that Ray had lost few of his old insecurities. But, surely, top selling U.S. albums, regular concerts and prestigious appearances at

Madison Square Garden ensured that the thirty-nine year old Kink was finally free from his financial phobias? Amazingly, this was not the case and in spite of an unshakable belief among his contemporaries that Ray Davies is an extraordinarily rich man, the money conscious Kink remains cautious:

> Mentally, I'm still sixteen although I've got more experience. I've always lived simply. Early in our career we got into contract problems so we're not as rich as we might have been. I think I'm one of those people who's fated not to be rich. I don't think I'd enjoy it.[134]

Davies has always used his eccentric lifestyle to good effect, and even his strange habit of watching commuters partly inspired 'Waterloo Sunset'. Now, he has gone one step further and fulfilled an old ambition by writing and directing a play based on the same theme. *Return To Waterloo*, scheduled for screening on Channel 4, is a fantasy musical based on the imaginings of a commuter travelling the fifty-two-minute train journey from Guildford to Waterloo. While this seems a typical Davies concoction, the ideas are sufficiently experimental to warrant interest. For a start, the central role, played by Kenneth Colley, is silent, and his daydreaming fantasies provide an excellent framework for a number of new Davies songs. Produced by Dennis Woolf, of *Starmaker* fame, the play so impressed Channel 4 that on seeing the first draft, they immediately poured in £200,000. On completion of the script in May 1983, R.C.A. agreed to inject a further £160,000 as part of a videodisc scheme. The £360,000 budget enabled Woolf to recruit a formidable crew including art director Terry Pritchard (*The French Lieutenant's Woman*), director of photography Roger Deakins (*Another Time Another Place*), production manager Paul Sparrow (*Nelly's Version*) and assistant director Selwyn Roberts (*Give My Regards To Broad Street*). The actual filming was done on the train to Waterloo, which apparently caused a number of amusing problems. The final product promises to be Davies's most interesting and remunerative non-Kinks venture to date. The tripartite production credit between Waterloo Films, Channel 4 and R.C.A. will result in two screenings on U.K. television and worldwide release of the videodisc. Should the play prove more successful than Ray's other thespian related projects, then the staging of a Davies musical in London may not be as chimerical as it sounds.

Apart from his drama pursuits, Ray remains involved in the development of Konk studios which now boasts forty-eight-track facilities. The studio has been used extensively by aspiring new talents as well as the rich and famous, and recent clients have included Strawberry Switchblade, the Boomtown Rats, Wang Chung, the World, Rockoco and Vitamin Z. Plans are already underway to refurbish the studio room and renovate the piano and vocal booths. All things considered, the Konk studio is probably one of

Davies's wisest investments and its reputation is likely to grow in successive years.

While Ray and Chrissie continued to provide the gossip columns with odd snippets of romance and large chunks of eccentricity, the Kinks road show soldiered on. A lightning British tour during the Spring of '83 was followed by a series of promotional manoeuvres in the States in preparation for the new Kinks album. The pilot single, 'Come Dancing', had already flopped in the U.K. but radio play in the States proved sufficient to provide a Top 5 hit. After nineteen years, the Kinks had finally found a song that could chart higher in the U.S. than any of their legendary early hits. Strangely enough, the number was not a celebration of American values, but an affectionate paean to a defunct English dance hall. Instead of conjuring up comic book heroes such as Captain America and Superman, Ray had produced a charming autobiographical account of his sister's dancing youth. The failure of the disc in the U.K. was an irony not entirely lost on the Arista publicity department. It's success in the States prompted a re-release in Britain which was accompanied by an appealing video that attracted interest following a screening on *Top Of The Pops*. Within days, the disc entered the lower rungs of the chart, finally climbing into the Top 20 as the summer slowly expired. Only students of ancient history recalled that this was the Kinks' first U.K. hit since 'Supersonic Rocket Ship' back in 1972.

In spite of their surprise hit, the Kinks' standing in Britain seems unclear. Whether a successful follow up can be found remains questionable and as yet there is little evidence to suggest any marked improvement on past album sales. It is a different story in the States where their latest L.P., *State Of Confusion*, has climbed confidently into the Top 15. Solid, if unspectacular, the album shows Davies's astute grasp of programming, neatly combining heavy rock with soft melodic material. The title track lists the familiar, trivial neuroses that Davies has made his stock in trade over the years. The seeming obligatory social commentary can be heard on 'Young Conservatives' and 'Clichés Of The World (B Movie)', though neither cut can approach the grandeur of 'A Well Respected Man' or similar satirical material of the 60s. Only occasionally does Davies reach an impressive peak and this occurs on those compositions in which he seems most involved. 'Property', the tale of a broken marriage has the conviction of personal experience that appears lacking in the throwaway 'Labour Of Love'. Similarly, the two dance songs, 'Come Dancing' and 'Don't Forget To Dance', have a charm reminiscent of some of Davies's best work. Of all the new songs, Ray's personal favourite is the catchy, though unremarkable, 'Heart Of Gold', a tune inspired by Princess Anne's celebrated 'naff off' rebuke to intrusive photographers:

I wrote about it imagining I was a photographer, but really it was about

Chrissie having her first baby. Both she and Princess Anne seem to be quite anonymous people at times.[134]

State Of Confusion has the occasional high spot but is ultimately far too erratic in quality to be compared with Davies's finest material. But what can you reasonably expect after twenty years on the road? As a rock writer and performer, Davies has played his hand, though the public still wants more.

The future of the Kinks has always been unpredictable and as we approach their twentieth anniversary, the old break-up rumours resurface once again. A lucrative U.S. tour was mysteriously cancelled at the eleventh hour due to Dave's inability to perform. Ray was reportedly incensed by the abrupt cancellation and apparently informed the press that the Kinks would be touring the U.S. in the spring of 1984 'with or without Dave'. Rumours spread like wildfire that Dave had officially left the group and was being replaced by Chris Spedding. One U.S. magazine claimed to have uncovered the truth:

> . . . Dave Davies has checked into an undisclosed institution for treatment of a 'serious mental illness', the details of which have been kept mum. It's not known if the hospitalisation was voluntary and brother Ray has been unavailable to shed further light on the situation.[135]

Minus the hyperbole, the truth of the matter was that Dave suffered 'mental fatigue and exhaustion' and according to the Kinks' representative, Ken Jones, was unable to tour. Everything else has been dismissed as 'absolute nonsense' including the suggestion that Chris Spedding lay waiting in the wings. The sensational stories did not subside until Dave appeared with the group.

In the future there will no doubt be further rumours of Ray abandoning rock for theatre work or attempting to relive his middle age by forming a high powered ensemble with Chrissie Hynde. When approached on this question, the Pretender's response was ambivalent:

> . . . I think that would be dangerous. It's bloody hard enough keeping a relationship happening without mixing . . . this is the problem, if you end up working with this person. We *have* collaborated and written a couple of songs, just for fun, and we've even made demos of them, but . . . I don't know . . . I would have thought it was a bad idea in many ways, because we do two different things, maybe they're better off . . . I'm not really opposed to it or for it. I wouldn't want to put our relationship in jeopardy because of it.[136]

The speculation on the personal and creative futures of Ray and Chrissie ended in May 1984 when the Pretender married Simple Mind Jim Kerr.

With so many new creative options in the 80s, it may seem remarkable that Ray chooses to straitjacket himself in the Kinks. Those who know him well believe that, in some strange way, he sees the group as security, both for himself and his wayward brother. And as long as Davies can still produce the odd flash of lyrical or melodic genius, there is little likelihood that the Kinks will ever be unable to record for a major label. Nor are they likely to be demoralised if their albums fail to sell in large quantities or their ticket sales betray a decline in audience interest. Unlike their great contemporaries, the Rolling Stones and the Who, the Kinks have already suffered the indignity of public rejection during the early/mid-70s but have demonstrated their ability and resolve to survive. With their American following continuing to grow rapidly, the Kinks can look back on seven Arista years in which they have proven that the work ethic can still produce financial and aesthetic rewards, even in the fashion conscious rock business.

EPILOGUE

This is a book that begs some form of conclusion, but what can you say to sum up the Kinks? Theirs is a sad tale that becomes more soul destroying with each new interviewee you meet on the road. It is a remarkable story dominated by two talented and often contemptible individuals, Raymond and David Davies. A frequently victimised drummer, Michael Avory, seems to force himself through purgatory just for the hell of it. Other members come and go without ever realising their precise role in the group, or fully understanding the psychological intimidation employed by their malicious mentors. It is difficult to comprehend these vegetarian brothers who are still capable of tearing each other apart at any given moment, onstage and off. It would take volumes of childhood psychology to unravel the origins of a love-hate relationship that shows no signs of abating as the brothers fast approach their forties. Whatever resentment and jealousy lurks within the brothers, however, it is the subsidiary members of the group that have always suffered most, but in spite of all the clashes and psycho dramas played out by the Davies brothers, the former members of the Kinks are still in contact with one another. Perhaps the happiest footnote of this story can be found in a town named Hoddesdon where a group known as the Bulletts can be seen playing the pub circuit. The line-up includes John Dalton and John Gosling, plus a couple of honorary members in the form of Andy Pyle and Mick Avory. The spirit of cameraderie that still exists among them is a testament to the theory that friendship is forged through strife.

In spite of the Kinks' turbulent history there is no bitterness forthcoming from former members. Their perverse affection for the wild days of yore can be observed as they merrily down pints of bitter and wax eloquent on past escapades. Underlying this, however, there often emerges an inexplicable sense of loss and resentment at the scars that still remain. The twinges of latent pain are frequently manifested in occasional asides. Andy Pyle asks about his work on *Misfits* which he has yet to find the stomach to listen to, while Larry Page confides that he cannot watch the Kinks on television without a constant urge to switch off the set. Relating their conflicting emotional responses one is almost reminded of lovers spurned.

Over the years, the Kinks have lost a lot of lovers but maintained a hard core of fans, particularly in America where some devotees will loyally follow an entire tour itinerary. Whatever reservations one may have about the Kinks it is difficult not to be impressed by their ability to survive. The Kinks have struggled on through folk rock, glam rock, punk, power pop and neo-romanticism, occasionally influenced, but never submerged by the sounds of their more commercially successful contemporaries. Their present status in the rock world is even more surprising and confusing. While the break up of the Stones is constantly threatened or pondered by rock scribes and the Who have actually split the often unstable Kinks seem more resilient than ever and look all set for the gay 90s. And despite their disgraceful and obnoxious behaviour over the years there are few people who would not show some regret at the break up of the most notorious and successful fraternal partnership since Don and Phil Everly.

Although the Kinks may eventually become a rock'n'roll version of *The Good Old Days*, Davies at least realises that the 80s will be a challenging decade, requiring an unprecedented capacity for survival:

> If the Kinks are going to go on, we've got to change. We can still be a good live rock'n'roll band, but for me creatively I need more stimulation. I'll always be able to put out a good rock show because that's in my blood, but as a writer, when I get home I need more stimulation.[131]

What Davies is voicing here is the universal plight of the middle-aged rock star who knows, though refuses to acknowledge publicly, that his best work is in his past. Davies will always be haunted by 'You Really Got Me' and 'Waterloo Sunset' no matter what he records in the future. Critics talk of 'timeless classics' but such songs only achieve this status by being written during an artist's golden era and, for the Kinks, that era was the 60s. Davies can still produce the odd melodic gem and the occasional witty line but, ultimately, he is an artist out of time. Past inspiration can be rekindled but the unique qualities of 60s rock *cannot*. At the moment, the Kinks' strongest asset is their own survival but even this fact will soon become a cliché. We are all time's subjects and in spite of the recent U.S. successes, the Kinks may come to realise that musically they have little left of lasting value to offer the world. How much longer the group can avoid becoming a rock'n'roll anachronism is the real endurance test. Perhaps the key to the Kinks' perverse survival can be found in the misfit personality of Ray Davies who after twenty years appears to have retained a disproportionate number of his old strengths and weaknesses:

> In a lot of ways I still feel like a fifteen-year-old kid, walking around frustrated. That person who was as angry and out of tune with the world – misfit if you like – is still within me, I think. I'd probably be much more acceptable as a person if I could not be like him, but he's in me; he's a strong animal, and all the time he's fighting inside me.[137]

Davies's present attitude is not dissimilar to that of the angry young man of

1964 who in one of his first interviews voiced a prophetic warning that needs little revision:

> In 1984 I shall be fighting what I fight now. The same kind of petty authority and pocket-sized tyrants I resent now will be around in 1984.[138]

Notes

1. Dave Davies's fleeting comments on life before the Kinks and the early days of the group.
2. Sam Curtis in conversation with the author. Walsall, 24 August 1982.
3. *New Musical Express* 9 April 1965. Dave Davies interviewed by Keith Altham.
4. John Turney in conversation with the author. London, November 1983.
5. Robert Wace in conversation with the author. London, 15 October 1982.
6. Robert Wace in conversation with the author. London, 25 June 1983.
7. Mickey Willett in conversation with the author. London, 4 November 1982.
8. Larry Page in conversation with the author. London, 24 June 1983.
9. Larry Page in conversation with the author. London, 7 August 1982.
10. Mick Avory in conversation with the author. London, November 1983.
11. Shel Talmy in conversation with the author. London, 17 September 1982.
12. *Sounds* 7 October 1972. Dave Davies interviewed by Steve Peacock.
13. *New Musical Express* 13 May 1972. Ray Davies interviewed by Danny Holloway.
14. *New Musical Express* 20 February 1971. Ray Davies interviewed by Richard Green.
15. *Dark Star* No. 21 July 1979. Ray Davies interviewed by Colin Larkin.
16. Ray Davies commenting on his initial reactions to the public and press.
17. *Melody Maker* 19 September 1964. Ray Davies interviewed by Ray Coleman.
18. *Hot Press* 1980. Jim Rodford interviewed by Jack Lynch.
19. *Record Mirror* 14 November 1964.
20. *Melody Maker* 20 February 1965. Dave Davies interviewed by Chris Welch.
21. *New Musical Express* 16 April 1965. Ray Davies interviewed by Keith Altham.
22. *Melody Maker* 23 January 1971. Ray Davies interviewed by Michael Watts.
23. *Sounds* 7 June 1975. Ray Davies interviewed by Babara Charone.
24. *Zig Zag* No. 27 December 1972. Ray Davies interviewed by Connor McKnight.
25. *New Musical Express* 8 April 1966. Dave Davies interviewed by Norrie Drummond.
26. Peter Quaife commenting to the press on one of his many 'accidents'.
27. Sam Curtis commenting on the Cardiff Incident, 19 May 1965.
28. Official apology from Mick Avory to the national press, May 1965.
29. *Disc* 8 July 1970. Dave Davies interviewed by Brenda Tarry.
30. *Disc* 1 May 1965. Peter Quaife interviewed by Penny Valentine.
31. *Disc* 22 April 1972. Ray Davies interviewed by Lisa Robinson.
32. *Hit Parader*. Ray Davies interviewed by Valerie Wilmer.
33. Ray Davies's comments on his relationship with Larry Page from the transcripts of the court case between Denmark and Boscobel Productions.
34. Ray Davies commenting on the future of the Kinks shortly after severing his connections with Larry Page and Eddie Kassner.
35. *The Aquarian* 7–14 October 1981. Ray Davies interviewed by Jeff Tamarkin.
36. *New Musical Express* 24 December 1965. Ray Davies interviewed by Keith Altham.
37. *Crawdaddy* March 1976.
38. *Disc* 9 April 1966.
39. Ray Davies commenting on his songwriting reputation to the national press.
40. Dave Davies's curt comments on the Kinks' future, *c.* late 1966.
41. The first indication of Quaife's impending departure, late spring 1966.
42. An open letter to the press composed by Peter Quaife.
43. John Dalton in conversation with the author. Hoddesdon, 4 August 1982.

44. A revelation originally published in an obscure teenzine.
45. *Melody Maker* 10 April 1966. Ray Davies interviewed by Bob Dawbarn.
46. *New Musical Express* 3 December 1966. Ray Davies interviewed by Keith Altham. Reprinted in *Hit Parader*.
47. *Disc And Music Echo* 13 May 1967. The Mick Avory Interview.
48. Lord Chief Justice Widgery's concluding comments on Larry Page, May 1967.
49. *New Musical Express* 20 May 1967. Ray Davies interviewed by Keith Altham. In a later interview Ray claimed that the 'Liverpool Sunset' story was a deliberate fabrication.
50. *Melody Maker* 27 May 1967. The Peter Quaife Interview.
51. Dave Davies commenting on his relationship with Ray, early 1967.
52. *Disc And Music Echo* August 1967. Dave Davies interviewed by Penny Valentine.
53. Ray Davies commenting on his brother following the commercial success of 'Death Of A Clown'.
54. *Record Mirror* 9 December 1965. Dave Davies interviewed by Bill Harry.
55. *Disc* November 1967. Ray Davies interviewed by Penny Valentine.
56. *New Musical Express* 8 July 1972. Dave Davies interviewed by Julie Webb.
57. *Record Mirror* 3 August 1968. Ray Davies interviewed by Lon Goddard.
58. Lord Justice Salmon commenting on the relationship between Larry Page and the Kinks 28 June 1968.
59. Ray Davies commenting on the establishing of his production company.
60 *New Musical Express* 3 August 1968. Dave Davies interviewed by Richard Green.
61. The mystery surrounding the original version of (*The Kinks Are) The Village Green Preservation Society* has never been explained satisfactorily. Although I have always assumed that the original twelve-track version was released in late September 1968 I have never located a U.K. pressing. While researching this book I spoke to avid Kinks collectors on both sides of the Atlantic, none of whom could verify the existence of the disc. According to a Pye spokesperson of the period, an unspecified number of copies were despatched, though where they eventually went remains a mystery.
62. *Record Mirror* 10 May 1969. Ray Davies interviewed by Derek Boltwood.
63. *Crawdaddy*. Ray Davies interviewed by Mark Breyer and Rik Vittenson.
64. Ray Davies commenting on the chart failure of (*The Kinks Are) The Village Green Preservation Society*.
65. Mick Avory disclosing the Kinks' celebrated cabaret plans to the American press.
66. *Record Mirror* 29 March 1969. Ray Davies interviewed by Derek Boltwood.
67. Ray Davies commenting on the controversy surrounding 'Plastic Man'.
68. Peter Quaife's parting comments on the Kinks.
69. *Soho Weekly News* 15 June 1978. Ray Davies interviewed by Ira Kaplan.
70. Ray Davies commenting on his work for the B.B.C. series *Where Was Spring*.
71. Ray Davies commenting on the U.S. reception afforded *Arthur*.
72. Ray Davies in conversation with Penny Valentine.
73. *New Musical Express* 1969. Ray Davies interviewed by Richard Green.
74. Ray Davies commenting on the success of 'Lola'.
75. *Record Mirror* 23 July 1970. Ray Davies interviewed by Lon Goddard.
76. Ray Davies's second 1970 interview with Lon Goddard.
77. Critic James Thomas commenting on the television play *The Long Distance Piano Player*.
78. Ray Davies in conversation with Michelle Hush.
79. John Gosling in conversation with the author. Berkhamsted, 29 July 1982.
80. *Melody Maker* 5 December 1970. Ray Davies interviewed by Roy Hollingworth.
81. *Melody Maker* 26 December 1970.

82. Ray Davies in conversation with Keith Altham, early 1970.
83. Ken Glancy's official statement on the signing of the Kinks to R.C.A. Records.
84. *Sounds* 1970. Ray Davies interviewed by Michelle Hush.
85. *Record Mirror* 8 January 1972. Ray Davies interviewed by Lon Goddard.
86. *Melody Maker* 25 December 1971.
87. *Circus* February 1972. Ray Davies interviewed by Janis Schact.
88. *Melody Maker* 17 April 1971. Andrew Oldham interviewed by Michael Watts.
89. Ray Davies commenting on the recruitment of the Mike Cotton Sound.
90. *Disc* 22 April 1972. Ray Davies interviewed by Lisa Robinson.
91. *New Musical Express* 8 July 1972. Dave Davies interviewed by Julie Webb.
92. *New Musical Express* 2 September 1972. Ray Davies interviewed by Tony Norman.
93. *New Musical Express* 20 October 1973. Ray Davies interviewed by Andrew Taylor.
94. *New Musical Express* 3 February 1973. Ray Davies interviewed by Danny Holloway.
95. *New Musical Express* 20 October 1973. Ray Davies interviewed by Andrew Weiner.
96. The Kinks' press secretary, Marion Rainford, commenting on the White City incident.
97. An official press release from Ray Davies explaining the White City incident.
98. *New Musical Express* 11 May 1974. Ray Davies interviewed by James Johnson.
99. *Hit Parader* 1974. Ray Davies interviewed by Lisa Robinson.
100. *Melody Maker* 4 May 1974. Ray Davies interviewed by Karen Hughes.
101. *New Musical Express* 3 August 1974. Extracts from Ian McDonald's review of *Preservation*.
102. *Guardian* 23 December 1974. Robin Denselow's review of the Kinks' 1974 Christmas extravaganza.
103. *Crawdaddy* March 1976. Ray Davies interviewed by Greg Mitchell.
104. *Sounds* 7 June 1975. Ray Davies interviewed by Babara Charone.
105. *Record Mirror And Disc* 7 February 1976. Ray Davies interviewed by Rosalind Russell.
106. An official press release from Ray Davies on signing to Arista Records.
107. An Arista press release by Clive Davis confirming the Kinks signing.
108. Nick Trevisick in conversation with the author. London, July 1982.
109. Ray Davies in conversation with Pauline McLeod.
110. Ray Davies commenting on his camp persona.
111. Andy Pyle in conversation with the author. Tring, August 1982.
112. Ray Davies recalling his attitude towards songwriting, early 1977.
113. *Rolling Stone* 24 March 1977. Ray Davies interviewed by Paul Nelson.
114. Extract from an Arista press release, May 1978.
115. *New Musical Express* 2 April 1977. Extract from Nick Kent's review of the Kinks' Rainbow concert of 24 March 1977.
116. *Melody Maker* 3 December 1977. Ray Davies interviewed by Michael Watts.
117. *New Musical Express* 24 June 1978. Ray Davies interviewed by Tony Stewart.
118. Ray Davies explaining the political emphasis in his songs.
119. *Trouser Press* No. 32. Ray Davies interviewed by Dave Schulps.
120. *Rolling Stone* 2 November 1978. Ray Davies interviewed by Fred Schruers.
121. An Arista memorandum from Andrew Bailey revealing the Mr Misfit promotional campaign.
122. *New Musical Express* 22 July 1978. John Lydon's review of 'Live Life'.
123. Ray Davies's official apology following the 1978 gig cancellations.
124. *The Low Budget Interview* with Ray Davies conducted by Ed Skiaky.
125. *Daily Mail* 7 August 1980. Ray Davies interviewed by Charles Catchpole.
126. *Musicians Only* 15 November 1980. Ray Davies interviewed by Chris Welch.

127. Donnie Burke in conversation with the author. Pimlico, 4 November 1982.
128. *Time Out* 3 April 1981. Barrie Keefe interviewed by Sandy Craig.
129. Chrissie Hynde revealing her love affair with Ray to the national press.
130. *Daily Express* 5 November 1981. Ray Davies interviewed by Anne Nightingale.
131. *Hot Press* 26 December 1981. Ray Davies interviewed by Neil McCormick.
132. *Melody Maker* 9 August 1980. Ray Davies interviewed by Colin Irwin.
133. *Sun* 12 August 1983. Ray Davies interviewed by John Blake.
134. *Daily Mail* 7 September 1983. Ray Davies interviewed by Moira Petty.
135. *Good Times* October 1983.
136. *New Musical Express* 26 November 1983. Chrissie Hynde interviewed by Paul Du Noyer.
137. *Penthouse* 1982. Ray Davies interviewed by Mick Brown.
138. Ray Davies in conversation with Keith Altham, *c.* September 1964.

Discography

SINGLES

		U.K.	*U.S.*
2/64	Long Tall Sally/I Took My Baby Home	Pye 7N 15611	Cameo 345
4/64	You Still Want Me/You Do Something To Me	7N 15636	—
8/64	You Really Got Me/It's Alright	7N 15673	Reprise 0306
10/64	All Day And All Of The Night/I Gotta Move	7N 15714	0334
1/65	Tired Of Waiting For You/Come On Now	7N 15759	0347
3/65	Everybody's Gonna Be Happy/Who'll Be The Next In Line*	7N 15813	0366
5/65	Set Me Free/I Need You	7N 15854	0379
8/65	See My Friend/Never Met A Girl Like You Before	7N 15919	0409
11/65	A Well Respected Man/Such A Shame	—	0420
11/65	Till The End Of The Day/Where Have All The Good Times Gone?	7N 15981	0454
2/66	Dedicated Follower Of Fashion/Sitting On My Sofa	7N 17064	0471
6/66	Sunny Afternoon/I'm Not Like Everybody Else	7N 17125	0497
11/66	Dead End Street/Big Black Smoke	7N 17222	0540
5/67	Mr Pleasant/Harry Rag	—	0587
5/67	Waterloo Sunset/Act Nice And Gentle	7N 17321	0612
10/67	Autumn Almanac/Mr Pleasant	7N 17400	—
10/67	Autumn Almanac/David Watts	—	0647
4/68	Wonderboy/Polly	7N 17468	0691
7/68	Days/She's Got Everything	7N 17573	0762
2/69	Starstruck/Picture Book	—	0806
4/69	Plastic Man/Kink Kong	7N 17724	—
6/69	Drivin'/Mindless Child Of Motherhood	7N 17776	—
8/69	Village Green Preservation Society/Do You Remember Walter?	—	0847
9/69	Shangri-la/This Man He Weeps Tonight	7N 17812	—
12/69	Victoria/Mr Churchill Says	7N 17865	—
6/70	Lola/Berkeley Mews	7N 17961	—
7/70	Lola/Mindless Child Of Motherhood	—	0930
11/70	Apeman/Rats	7N 45016	0979
11/71	God's Children/The Way Love Used To Be†	—	1017
/71	Here Comes Flash/Money Talks	—	R.C.A. 0275
12/71	20th Century Man/Skin And Bone	—	0620
6/72	Supersonic Rocket Ship/You Don't Know My Name	R.C.A. 2211	0807
11/72	Celluloid Heroes/Hot Potatoes	2299	0852

* The U.S. release featured 'Who'll Be The Next In Line' as the A-side.
† See E.P. section for corresponding U.K. release.
†† The U.S. flip side 'Scrapheap City' is a different take to the version on *Preservation II* featuring Ray on lead vocal without accompaniment by the girl chorus.

5/73	One Of The Survivors/Scrapheap City††	—	0940
6/73	Sitting In The Midday Sun/One Of The Survivors	2387	—
8/73	Sitting In The Midday Sun/Sweet Lady Genevieve	—	LPBO 5001
9/73	Sweet Lady Genevieve/Sitting In My Hotel	2418	—
4/74	Mirror Of Love/Cricket	5015	—
5/74	Money Talks/Here Comes Flash	—	APBO 0275
7/74	Mirror Of Love**/He's Evil	5042	PB 10019
10/74	Holiday Romance/Shepherds Of The Nation	2478	—
12/74	Preservation/Salvation Road	—	PB 10121
4/75	Ducks On The Wall/Rush Hour Blues	2546	—
5/75	Starmaker/Ordinary People	—	PB 10251
5/75	You Can't Stop The Music/Have Another Drink	2567	—
12/75	I'm In Disgrace/The Hard Way	—	PB 10551
1/76	No More Looking Back/Jack The Idiot Dunce/The Hard Way	R.C.M. 1	—
3/77	Sleepwalker/Full Moon	ARISTA 97	AS 0240
5/77	Juke Box Music/Life Goes On	—	AS 0247
6/77	Juke Box Music/Sleepless Night	ARISTA 114	—
12/77	Father Christmas/Prince Of The Punks	ARISTA 153	AS 0296
5/78	Rock'n'Roll Fantasy/Artificial Light	ARIST 189	—
6/78	Rock'n'Roll Fantasy/Live Life	—	AS 0342
7/78	Live Life/In A Foreign Land	ARIST 199	—
9/78	Black Messiah/Misfits	ARIST 210	—
10/78	Rock'n'Roll Fantasy/Get Up	—	AS 0342
10/78	Live Life/Black Messiah		AS 0372
1/79	(I Wish I Could Fly Like) Superman*†/Low Budget	ARIST 240	AS 0409
8/79	A Gallon Of Gas/Low Budget	—	AS 0448
9/79	Moving Pictures/In A Space	ARIST 300	—
9/79	Catch Me Now I'm Falling/Low Budget	—	AS 0458
11/79	Pressure/National Health	ARIST 321	—
8/80	Celluloid Heroes†*/Lola†*	—	AS 0541
11/80	You Really Got Me†*/Attitude	—	AS 0577
6/81	Better Things**†/Massive Reductions	ARIST 415	—
10/81	Destroyer/Back To Front	—	AS 0619
10/81	Predictable†††/Back To Front	ARIST 426	—
11/81	Better Things/Yo-Yo	—	AS 0649
11/82	Come Dancing/Noise*††	ARIST 502	AS 1054
6/83	Come Dancing/Noise	—	AS 1 9016
8/83	Don't Forget To Dance/Young Conservatives	—	AS 1 9075
9/83	Don't Forget To Dance/Bernadette††*	ARIST 524	—

** The second release of 'Mirror Of Love' was an alternate take.
*† Also released in the U.K. as a 12″ single – ARIST 12240.
†* These were live versions taken from *One For The Road*.
**† Initial copies of this recording included a free live single – Lola/ David Watts – KINKS 1.
††† Also available as a picture disc – ARIPD 426
*†† Elongated version released in U.K. as 12″ – ARIST 12 502
††* Elongated version released in U.K. as 12″ – ARIST 12 524 'Bernadette' is a different take from the album version.

Over the years several Kinks tracks have been reissued or coupled as back-to-back hits. These include the following:

6/68	Sunny Afternoon/Dead End Street	—	Reprise 0708
6/68	Dedicated Follower Of Fashion/Who'll Be The Next In Line?	—	0712
6/68	Set Me Free/A Well Respected Man	—	0715
6/68	All Day And All Of The Night/Tired Of Waiting For You	—	0719
6/68	You Really Got Me/It's Alright	—	0722
2/72	Lola/Apeman	—	0743
5/72	King Kong/Waterloo Sunset	—	REP 1094
11/73	Where Have All The Good Times Gone?/Lola	7N 45313	—
6/75	Sunny Afternoon/Sitting On My Sofa	7N 45482	—
4/79	You Really Got Me/All Day And All Of The Night	FBS 1	—
2/80	All Day And All Of The Night/Tired Of Waiting For You	—	ERIC 242
2/80	You Really Got Me/All Day And All Of The Night	RK 1027	—
2/80	You Really Got Me/A Well Respected Man	—	ERIC 243
/80	Dedicated Follower Of Fashion/Waterloo Sunset	7N 46102	—
/82	Dedicated Follower Of Fashion/Waterloo Sunset	Old Gold OG 9140	—
2/83	Sunny Afternoon/Tired Of Waiting For You	FBS 15	—

E.P.s

11/64 *Kinksize Session* — Pye NEP 24200
Louie Louie; I've Got That Feeling; I Gotta Go Now; Things Are Getting Better.

2/65 *Kinksize Hits* — Pye NEP 24203
You Really Got Me; It's Alright; All Day And All Of The Night; I Gotta Move.

12/65 *Kwyet Kinks* — Pye NEP 24221
Well Respected Man; Such A Shame; Wait Till The Summer Comes Along; Don't You Fret.

7/66 *Dedicated Kinks* — Pye NEP 24258
Dedicated Follower Of Fashion; Till The End Of The Day; See My Friend; Set Me Free.

4/68 *The Kinks* — Pye NEP 24296
David Watts; Two Sisters; Lazy Old Sun; Situation Vacant.

4/71 *God's Children* — Pye 7NX 8001
God's Children; The Way Love Used To Be; Moments; Dreams.

8/71 *Mini Monster* — Pye PMM 100
You Really Got Me; Set Me Free; Wonderboy; Long Tall Shorty.

5/77 *Big Deal* — Pye BP 105
Lola; Sunny Afternoon; Waterloo Sunset; Dedicated Follower Of Fashion.

11/78 *Yesteryear* — Pye AMEP 1001
Long Tall Sally; I Took My Baby Home; You Still Want Me; You Do Something To Me.

6/80 *Flashbacks* Pye FBEP 104
Waterloo Sunset; David Watts; Well Respected Man; Stop Your Sobbing.

7/80 *Live 4 Track E.P.* Arista ARIST 360
David Watts; Where Have All The Good Times Gone?; Attitude; Victoria.

10/83 *You Really Got Me** P.R.T. KD 1
You Really Got Me; All Day And All Of The Night; Misty Water; Medley: All Day And All Of The Night/You Really Got Me.

*This E.P. is also available as a 12″ (KLD 1) and as a 7″ picture disc (KBD 1).

ALBUMS

The following is a complete list of official Kinks releases in Britain. The serial numbers of identically titled American releases are included except in the case of track discrepancies which are dealt with in the *U.S. Releases* section.

10/64 *Kinks* Pye NPL 18096 (NSPL 83021)
Beautiful Delilah; So Mystifying; Just Can't Go To Sleep; Long Tall Shorty; I Took My Baby Home; I'm A Lover Not A Fighter; You Really Got Me; Cadillac; Bald Headed Woman; Revenge; Too Much Monkey Business; I've Been Driving On Bald Mountain; Stop Your Sobbing; Got Love If You Want It.

2/65 *Kinda Kinks* Pye NPL 18112
Look For Me Baby; Got My Feet On The Ground; Naggin' Woman; Nothin' In This World Can Stop Me Worryin' 'Bout That Girl; Wonder Where My Baby Is; Tired Of Waiting For You; Dancing In The Street; Don't Ever Change; Come On Now; So Long; You Shouldn't Be Sad; Something Better Beginning.

2/66 *The Kinks Kontroversy* Pye NPL 18131/Reprise 6197
Milk Cow Blues; Ring The Bells; Gotta Get The First Plane Home; When I See That Girl Of Mine; I Am Free; Till The End Of The Day; The World Keeps Going Round; I'm On An Island; Where Have All The Good Times Gone?; It's Too Late; What's In Store For Me?; You Can't Win.

11/66 *Face To Face* Pye N(S)PL 18149/Reprise 6228
Party Line; Rosy, Won't You Please Come Home; Dandy; Too Much On My Mind; Session Man; Rainy Day In June; House In The Country; Holiday In Waikiki; Most Exclusive Residence For Sale; Fancy; Little Miss Queen Of Darkness; You're Looking Fine; Sunny Afternoon; I'll Remember.

9/67 *Something Else By The Kinks* Pye N(S)PL 18193/Reprise 6279
David Watts; Death Of A Clown; Two Sisters; No Return; Harry Rag; Tin Soldier Man; Situation Vacant; Love Me Till The Sun Shines; Lazy Old Sun; Afternoon Tea; Funny Face; End Of The Season; Waterloo Sunset.

1/68 *The Kinks Live At Kelvin Hall* Pye N(S)PL 18191/Reprise 6260
Till The End Of The Day; A Well Respected Man; You're Looking Fine; Sunny Afternoon; Dandy; I'm On An Island; Come On Now; You Really Got Me; Medley: Milk Cow Blues, Batman Theme, Tired of Waiting For You.

11/68 *(The Kinks Are) The Village Green Preservation Society* Pye N(S)PL 18233/Reprise 6327
The Village Green Preservation Society; Do You Remember Walter?; Picture Book; Johnny Thunder; Last Of The Steam Powered Trains; Big Sky; Sitting By The Riverside; Animal Farm; Village Green; Starstruck; Phenomenal Cat; All Of My Friends Were There; Wicked Annabella; Monica; People Take Pictures Of Each Other.

10/69 *Arthur Or The Decline And Fall Of The British Empire* Pye NSPL 18317/Reprise 6366
Victoria; Yes Sir, No Sir; Some Mother's Son; Drivin'; Brainwashed; Australia; Shangri-la; Mr Churchill Says; She Bought A Hat Like Princess Marina; Young And Innocent Days; Nothing To Say; Arthur.

11/70 *Kinks Part 1: Lola Vs Powerman And The Money-goround* Pye N(S)PL 18359/Reprise 6423
The Contenders; Strangers; Denmark Street; Get Back In Line; Lola; Top Of The Pops; The Moneygoround; This Time Tomorrow; A Long Way From Home; Rats; Apeman; Powerman; Got To Be Free.

3/71 *Percy* Pye NSPL 18365
God's Children; Lola; The Way Love Used To Be; Completely; Running Round Town; Moments; Animals In The Zoo; Just Friends; Whip Lady; Dreams; Helga; Willesden Green; God's Children – End.

11/71 *Muswell Hillbillies* R.C.A. SF 8243/LPS 4644
20th Century Man; Acute Schizophrenia Paranoia Blues; Holiday; Skin And Bone; Alcohol; Complicated Life; Here Come The People In Grey; Have A Cuppa Tea; Holloway Jail; Oklahoma U.S.A.; Uncle Son; Muswell Hillbilly.

8/72 *Everybody's In Showbiz, Everybody's A Star* R.C.A. DPS 2035/VPS 6065
Here Comes Yet Another Day; Maximum Consumption; Unreal Reality; Hot Potatoes; Sitting In My Hotel; Motorway; You Don't Know My Name; Supersonic Rocket Ship; Look A Little On The Sunny Side; Celluloid Heroes; Top Of The Pops; Brainwashed; Mr Wonderful; Acute Schizophrenia Paranoia Blues; Holiday; Muswell Hillbilly; Alcohol; Banana Boat Song *(Trad.)*; Skin And Bone; Baby Face; Lola.

12/73 *Preservation Act I* R.C.A. SF 8392/LPLI 5002
Morning Song; Daylight; Sweet Lady Genevieve; There's A Change In The Weather; Where Are They Now?; One Of The Survivors; Cricket; Money & Corruption/I Am Your Man; Here Comes Flash; Sitting In The Midday Sun; Demolition.

6/74 *Preservation Act II* R.C.A. LP2 5040/CPL2 5040
Announcement; Introduction To Solution; When A Solution Comes; Money Talks; Announcement; Shepherds Of The Nation; Scum Of The Earth; Second Hand Car Spiv; He's Evil; Mirror Of Love; Announcement; Nobody Gives; Oh Where Oh Where Is Love?; Flash's Dream (The Final Elbow); Flash's Confession; Nothing Lasts Forever; Announcement; Artificial Man; Scrapheap City; Announcement; Salvation Road.

3/75 *Soap Opera* R.C.A. SF 8411/LPLI 5081
Everybody's A Star (Starmaker); Ordinary People; Rush Hour Blues; Nine To Five; When Work Is Over; Have Another Drink; Underneath The Neon Sign; Holiday Romance; You Make It All Worthwhile; Ducks On The Wall; (A) Face In the Crowd; You Can't Stop The Music.

11/75 *Schoolboys In Disgrace* R.C.A. RS 1028/LPLI 5102
Schooldays; Jack The Idiot Dunce; Education; The First Time We Fall In Love; I'm In Disgrace; Headmaster; The Hard Way; The Last Assembly; No More Looking Back; Finale.

2/77 *Sleepwalker* Arista SPARTY 1002/AL 4106
Life On The Road; Mr Big Man; Sleepwalker; Brother; Juke Box Music; Sleepless Night; Stormy Sky; Full Moon; Life Goes On.

5/78 *Misfits* Arista SPART 1055/AB 4167
Misfits; Hay Fever; Live Life; A Rock'n'Roll Fantasy; In A Foreign Land; Permanent Waves; Black Messiah; Out Of The Wardrobe; Trust Your Heart; Get Up.

9/79 *Low Budget* Arista SPART 1099/AB 4240
Attitude; Catch Me Now I'm Falling; Pressure; National Health; (Wish I Could Fly Like) Superman; Low Budget; In A Space; Little Bit Of Emotion; A Gallon Of Gas; Misery; Moving Pictures.

10/80 *One For The Road* Arista DARTY 6/A2L 8401
Opening; Hard Way; Catch Me Now I'm Falling; Where Have All The Good Times Gone?; Intro: Lola; Lola; Pressure; All Day And All Of The Night; 20th Century Man; Misfits; Prince Of The Punks; Stop Your Sobbing; Low Budget; Attitude; Superman; National Health; Till The End Of The Day; Celluloid Heroes; You Really Got Me; Victoria; David Watts.

1/82 *Give The People What They Want* Arista SPART 117/AL 9567
Around The Dial; Give The People What They Want; Killer's Eyes; Predictable; Add It Up; Destroyer; Yo-Yo; Back To Front; Art Lover; A Little Bit Of Abuse; Better Things.

1/82 *Sleepwalker* Fame FA 3048
A Music For Pleasure reduced price reissue.

6/83 *State Of Confusion* Arista 205 275
State of Confusion; Definite Maybe; Labour Of Love; Come Dancing; Property; Don't Forget To Dance; Young Conservatives; Heart Of Gold; Clichés Of The World (B Movie); Bernadette.
Strangely enough, the cassette version of the album includes two additional tracks, 'Noise' and 'Long Distance'. 'Noise' is slightly different from the single B-side, whilst 'Long Distance' is unreleased elsewhere and longer than any track on *State Of Confusion*. Another track, 'Once A Thief', was originally intended for inclusion and appeared on early printings on the cassette insert, though not on the tape.

COMPILATIONS

1/66 *The Kinks* Pye Golden Guinea GGL 0357
(Re-release of *Kinks*)

9/66 *Well Respected Kinks* Marble Arch MAL 612
A Well Respected Man; Where Have All The Good Times Gone?; Till The End Of The

Day; Set Me Free; Tired Of Waiting For You; All Day And All Of The Night; I Gotta Move; Don't You Fret; Wait Till The Summer Comes Along; You Really Got Me.

11/67 *Sunny Afternoon* Marble Arch MAL 716
Sunny Afternoon; I Need You; See My Friends; Big Black Smoke; Louie Louie; Dedicated Follower Of Fashion; Sitting On My Sofa; Such A Shame; I'm Not Like Everybody Else; Dead End Street.

2/69 *Kinda Kinks* Marble Arch MAL 1100
(Re-release of *Kinda Kinks*)

2/70 *The Kinks* Pye NPL 18326
You Really Got Me; Long Tall Shorty; All Day And All Of The Night; Beautiful Delilah; Tired Of Waiting For You; Lover Not A Fighter; A Well Respected Man; Till The End Of The Day; See My Friends; Don't You Fret; Dedicated Follower of Fashion; Sunny Afternoon; Dead End Street; Death Of A Clown; Two Sisters; Big Black Smoke; Susannah's Still Alive; Autumn Almanac; Waterloo Sunset; Last Of The Steam Powered Trains; Wonderboy; Do You Remember Walter?; Dandy; Animal Farm; Days.

10/71 *Lola* Marble Arch HMA 201
Lola; Dedicated Follower Of Fashion; Dancing In The Street; Where Have All The Good Times Gone?; You Really Got Me; A Well Respected Man; Dead End Street; Got My Feet On The Ground; Don't Ever Change; All Day And All Of The Night.

10/71 *Golden Hour Of The Kinks* Pye Golden Hour GH 501
Days; Wonderboy; Autumn Almanac; Waterloo Sunset; Dedicated Follower Of Fashion; Dead End Street; Set Me Free; Sunny Afternoon; Till The End Of The Day; Sitting On My Sofa; Victoria; Well Respected Man; You Really Got Me; All Day And All Of The Night; Tired Of Waiting For You; See My Friends; Louie Louie; Animal Farm; Shangri-la; Where Have All The Good Times Gone?

1/74 *All The Good Times* Pye 11PP 100
A four album presentation boxed set featuring *Kinks Part 1: Lola Vs Powerman And The Moneygoround, Arthur Or The Decline And Fall Of The British Empire* and *The Kinks* double (NPL 18326).

10/73 *Golden House Of The Kinks Volume Two* Pye Golden Hour GH 558
Wonder Where My Baby Is Tonight; Don't Ever Change; Got Love If You Want It; Come On Now; I'm Not Like Everybody Else; Something Better Beginning; Dancing In The Street; Just Can't Go To Sleep; Long Tall Shorty; Got My Feet On The Ground; It's Alright; Don't You Fret; I Need You; Such A Shame; Look For Me Baby; Everybody's Gonna Be Happy; Wait Till The Summer Comes Along; Beautiful Delilah; I Gotta Move; So Long; Nothing In The World; You Shouldn't Be Sad; Stop Your Sobbing.

4/73 *The Kinks* Hallmark HMA 244
Beautiful Delilah; So Mystifying; Just Can't Go To Sleep; Long Tall Shorty; I Took My Baby Home; I'm A Lover Not A Fighter; Cadillac; Bald Headed Woman; Revenge; Too Much Monkey Business; I've Been Driving On Bald Mountain; Stop Your Sobbing.

11/74 *Lola Percy And The Apeman Face To Face With The Village Green Preservation Society . . . Something Else* Pye Golden Hour GHD 50
Lola; The Village Green Preservation Society; Wonderboy; Love Me Till The Sun

Shines; Little Miss Queen Of Darkness; Two Sisters; Sitting By The Riverside; Dandy; Rainy Day In June; Death Of A Clown; Village Green; Johnny Thunder; Party Line; Funny Face; Moments; Do You Remember Walter?; All Of My Friends Were There; Dreams; People Take Pictures Of Each Other; Too Much On My Mind; Picture Book; You're Looking Fine; Apeman; God's Children; Harry Rag; Afternoon Tea; David Watts; Last Of The Steam Powered Trains; Animals In The Zoo; Rosy, Won't You Please Come Home; House In The Country; Situation Vacant; Holiday In Waikiki; Session Man; Phenomenal Cat; Lazy Old Sun; Most Exclusive Residence For Sale; Tin Soldier Man; No Return; End of The Season; Wicked Annabella; Starstruck; Big Sky; The Way Love Used To Be.

6/76 *Celluloid Heroes – The Kinks Greatest* R.C.A. RS 1059
Everybody's A Star (Starmaker); Sitting In My Hotel; Here Comes Yet Another Day; Holiday; Muswell Hillbilly; Celluloid Heroes; 20th Century Man; Sitting In The Midday Sun; One Of The Survivors; Alcohol; Skin And Bone; Face In The Crowd.

10/77 *The Kinks File* Pye FILD 001/1/2
Long Tall Sally; You Still Want Me; You Really Got Me; All Day And All Of The Night; I've Got That Feeling; I Gotta Go Now; Things Are Getting Better; Tired Of Waiting For You; Everybody's Gonna Be Happy; Set Me Free; See My Friends; Well Respected Man; Till The End Of The Day; Dedicated Follower Of Fashion; Sunny Afternoon; Dead End Street; Mr Pleasant; Waterloo Sunset; Death Of A Clown; Autumn Almanac; Susannah's Still Alive; Wonderboy; Lincoln County; Days; Hold My Hand; Plastic Man; Drivin'; Shangri-la; Victoria; Lola; Apeman.

9/78 *20 Golden Greats* Ronco RPL 2031
You Really Got Me; All Day And All Of The Night; Tired Of Waiting For You; Everybody's Gonna Be Happy; Set Me Free; See My Friend; Till The End Of The Day; Dedicated Follower Of Fashion; Sunny Afternoon; Dead End Street; Waterloo Sunset; Death Of A Clown; Autumn Almanac; Susannah's Still Alive; Wonderboy; Days; Plastic Man; Victoria; Lola; Apeman.

4/80 *You Really Got Me* Pye NSPL 18615
You Really Got Me; I Need You; Till The End Of The Day; Come On Now; Long Tall Sally; Cadillac; Beautiful Delilah; Everybody's Gonna Be Happy; Things Are Getting Better; All Day And All Of The Night; Stop Your Sobbing; Don't Ever Change; David Watts; You Still Want Me; Wonder Where My Baby Is Tonight; Don't You Fret; Just Can't Go To Sleep; A Well Respected Man; I'm Not Like Everybody Else; Tired Of Waiting For You.

9/80 *The Kinks Collection* Pickwick PDA 072
Lola; Animal Farm; It's Alright; I Need You; Till The End Of The Day; Stop Your Sobbing; You Really Got Me; I'm Not Like Everybody Else; Victoria; Just Can't Go To Sleep; Tired Of Waiting For You; Well Respected Man; Dedicated Follower Of Fashion; Dead End Street; See My Friend; Louie Louie; I'm A Lover Not A Fighter; Set Me Free; All Day And All Of The Night; Waterloo Sunset; Where Have All The Good Times Gone?; Something Better Beginning; Sunny Afternoon; Come On Now.

3/81 *Spotlight On The Kinks* Pye SPOT 1009
You Really Got Me; Till The End Of The Day; Everybody's Gonna Be Happy; Set Me Free; See My Friends; All Day And All Of The Night; Tired Of Waiting For You;

Dedicated Follower Of Fashion; David Watts; Victoria; Susannah's Still Alive; Mr Pleasant; Sunny Afternoon; Dead End Street; Stop Your Sobbing; Death Of A Clown; Well Respected Man; Waterloo Sunset; Lola; Apeman; Wonderboy; Plastic Man; Autumn Almanac; Days.

9/82 *Spotlight On The Kinks* P.R.T. SPOT 1029
Days; So Mystifying; I'm On An Island; Don't You Fret; Just Can't Go To Sleep; Sitting On My Sofa; Things Are Getting Better; Come On Now; I Need You; Long Tall Shorty; Too Much Monkey Business; Got Love If You Want It; Shangri-la; Australia; Lincoln County; Animal Farm; Holiday In Waikiki; Funny Face; Louie Louie; Look For Me Baby; Wait Till The Summer Comes Along; Where Have All The Good Times Gone?; You Still Want Me; Rats.

4/83 *Shape Of Things To Come* (10″ L.P.) P.R.T. DOW 4
You Really Got Me; All Day And All Of The Night; Till The End Of The Day; Set Me Free; Lola; Tired Of Waiting For You; Sunny Afternoon; Waterloo Sunset.

7/83 *Candy From Mr Dandy* (10″ L.P.) P.R.T. DOW 12
Dedicated Follower Of Fashion; Dead End Street; Death Of A Clown; Everybody's Gonna Be Happy; Well Respected Man; See My Friend; Days; Autumn Almanac.

10/83 *Dead End Street – Greatest Hits* P.R.T. KINKS 1
You Really Got Me; All Day And All Of The Night; Everybody's Gonna Be Happy; Till The End Of The Day; Dead End Street; Sunny Afternoon; Dedicated Follower Of Fashion; Victoria; Set Me Free; Apeman; Tired Of Waiting For You; See My Friend; Death Of A Clown; Days; Lola; Waterloo Sunset; Wonderboy; Plastic Man; Autumn Almanac; Susannah's Still Alive.
An excellent compilation which came complete with a free 10″ album containing six tracks previously unissued in the U.K. – Misty Water; Pictures In The Sand; Spotty Grotty Anna; Groovy Movies; Time Will Tell; Rosemary Rose. However, these have already been deleted and replaced by 'Six Mod Anthems' comprising David Watts; Stop Your Sobbing; Dancing In the Street; Louie Louie; Beautiful Delilah; Long Tall Shorty.

VARIOUS ARTISTS

Apart from the hit compilations in their own right, the Kinks have also appeared on innumerable greatest hits packages by various artists. The following list explains precisely how Pye Records successfully milked the Kinks' back catalogue and made them one of the most over-exposed groups of the 60s.

E.P.s

6/65 *The Hitmakers* Pye NEP 24214
Includes 'You Really Got Me'.

2/66 *The Hitmakers* Pye NEP 24242
Includes 'Tired Of Waiting For You'.

2/66 *The Hitmakers* Pye NEP 24243
Includes 'All Day And All Of The Night'.

L.P.s

12/64 *Hitmakers* Pye NPL 18108
Includes 'You Really Got Me'.

5/65 *Hitmakers Vol. II* Pye NPL 18115
Includes 'All Day And All Of The Night' and 'Tired Of Waiting For You'.

11/65 *Hitmakers Vol. III* Pye NPL 18129
Includes 'See My Friend'.

/66 *Hitmakers Vol. IV* Pye NPL 18144
Includes 'Dedicated Follower Of Fashion' and 'Till The End Of The Day'.

/66 *Golden Hitmakers* Golden Guinea GGL 0362
Includes 'All Day And All Of The Night'.

2/68 *Stars Of '68* Marble Arch MAL(S) 762
Includes 'Waterloo Sunset' and Dave Davies's 'Death Of A Clown'.

9/68 *More Stars Of '68* Marble Arch MAL(S) 794
Includes 'Wonderboy' and Dave Davies's 'Susannah's Still Alive'.

11/68 *More Stars Of '68, Vol. II* Marble Arch MAL(S) 860.
Includes 'Days'.

1/69 *Ten Years Of Golden Hits* Marble Arch MT 10
Includes 'All Day And All Of The Night', 'Sunny Afternoon' and 'Waterloo Sunset'.

/69 *Marble Arch Sampler* Marble Arch MAL(S) 1154
Includes 'Well Respected Man' and 'Dedicated Follower Of Fashion'.

/71 *Golden Hour Of Original Smash Hits* Pye Golden Hour GH505
Includes 'Lola' and 'Victoria'.

4/72 *Golden Hour Of Supergroups Of The 60s* Pye Golden Hour GH525

U.S. RELEASES

The early U.S. album releases often differed in content, usually offering less tracks than their British counterparts. For identical U.S./U.K. track listings refer to previous Albums section for U.S. serial number.

11/64 *You Really Got Me* Reprise R 6143
Beautiful Delilah; So Mystifying; Just Can't Go To Sleep; Long Tall Shorty; You Really Got Me; Cadillac; Bald Headed Woman; Too Much Monkey Business; I've Been Driving On Bald Mountain; Stop Your Sobbing; Got Love If You Want It.

4/65 *Kinks Size* Reprise R 6158
Tired Of Waiting For You; Louie Louie; I've Got That Feeling; Revenge; I Gotta Move; Things Are Getting Better; I Gotta Go Now; I'm A Lover Not A Fighter; Come On Now; All Day And All Of The Night.

8/65 *Kinda Kinks* Reprise R 6173
Look For Me Baby; Got My Feet On The Ground; Nothin' In This World Can Stop Me Worryin' 'Bout That Girl; Wonder Where My Baby Is Tonight; Set Me Free;

Everybody's Gonna Be Happy; Dancing In The Street; Don't Ever Change; So Long; You Shouldn't Be Sad; Something Better Beginning.

11/65 *Kinkdom* Reprise R 6184
A Well Respected Man; Wait Till The Summer Comes Along; Such A Shame; Nagging Woman; See My Friend; Never Met A Girl Like You Before; Who'll Be The Next In Line?; Don't You Fret; I Need You; It's Alright; Louie Louie.

3/66 *The Kinks Kontroversy* Reprise 6197
Identical track listing but a different cover from its U.K. counterpart.

8/67 *Live Kinks* Reprise 6260
Re-titled version of *The Kinks Live At Kelvin Hall* with different artwork.

U.S. COMPILATIONS

8/66 *Greatest Hits* Reprise 6217
You Really Got Me; Tired Of Waiting For You; Set Me Free; Something Better Beginning; Who'll Be The Next In Line; Till The End Of The Day; Dedicated Follower Of Fashion; Well Respected Man; Everybody's Gonna Be Happy; All Day And All Of The Night.

3/71 *The Kinks Kronikles* Reprise 2XS 6454
Victoria; The Village Green Preservation Society; Berkeley Mews; Holiday In Waikiki; Willesden Green; This Is Where I Belong; Waterloo Sunset; David Watts; Dead End Street; Shangri-la; Autumn Almanac; Sunny Afternoon; Get Back In Line; Did You See His Name?; Fancy; Wonderboy; Apeman; King Kong; Mr Pleasant; God's Children; Death Of A Clown; Lola; Mindless Child Of Motherhood; Polly; Big Black Smoke; Susannah's Still Alive; She's Got Everything; Days.
Apart from the rare B-sides, this work included the previously unreleased 'Did You See His Name?' and the Dutch flip-side of 'Mr Pleasant' – 'This Is Where I Belong'.

1/73 *The Great Lost Kinks Album* Reprise MS 2127
Till Death Us Do Part; There's No Life Without Love; Lavender Hill; Groovy Movies; Rosemary Rose; Misty Water; Mr Songbird; When I Turn Off The Living Room Light; The Way Love Used To Be; I'm Not Like Everybody Else; Plastic Man; This Man He Weeps Tonight; Pictures In The Sand; Where Did My Spring Go?
An intriguing collection of mainly unreleased songs several of which were taken from the *Four More Respected Gentlemen/Village Green Preservation Society* sessions.

/75 *History Of British Rock* Sire SAS 3702
Includes 'You Really Got Me'.

/76 *History Of British Rock Vol. II* Sire SASH 3705–2
Includes 'All Day And All Of The Night'.

British Rock Classics Sire R 23 4021
Includes 'All Day And All Of The Night'.

Golden Days Of British Rock Sire 4V 8406
4 L.P. box set includes 'You Really Got Me' and 'Well Respected Man'.

/79 *Songs From the ABKCO Music Catalog* ABKCO MPD 3
A music publisher's disc featuring excerpts from 'Dedicated Follower Of Fashion', 'Sunny Afternoon', 'Death Of A Clown', 'Starstruck' and 'Lola'.

8/80 *Second Time Around* R.C.A. AFL1 3520
The Hard Way; No More Looking Back; Acute Schizophrenia Paranoia Blues; Motorway; Lola; Schooldays; (A) Face In The Crowd; Hot Potatoes; Celluloid Heroes.

2/84 *Compleat Kinks* Compleat
Stop Your Sobbing; Revenge; I'm Not Like Everybody Else; Where Have All The Good Times Gone?; You Really Got Me; I Took My Baby Home; Long Tall Sally; You Still Want Me; You Do Something To Me; Sitting On My Sofa; Till The End Of The Day; Come On Now; Who'll Be The Next In Line?; Dedicated Follower Of Fashion; Something Better Beginning; Tired Of Waiting For You; See My Friend; Set Me Free; I Gotta Move; All Day And All Of The Night.

DAVE DAVIES

Singles

		U.K.	*U.S.*
7/67	Death Of A Clown/Love Me Till The Sun Shines	Pye 7N 17356	Reprise 614
11/67	Susannah's Still Alive/Funny Face	7N 17429	0660
8/68	Lincoln County/There's No Life Without Love	7N 17514	—
1/69	Hold My Hand/Creeping Jean	7N 17678	—
9/80	Imaginations's Real/Wild Man	—	R.C.A. PB 12089
11/80	Doing The Best For You/Nothing More To Lose	—	R.C.A. PB 12147
12/80	Doing The Best For You/Wild Man	PB 9620	—
8/83	Love Gets You/One Night With You	—	Warner Bros 7–29509
11/83	Mean Disposition/Cold Winter	—	Warner Bros 7–29425

E.P.s

4/68 *Dave Davies Hits* Pye NEP 24289
Love Me Till The Sun Shines; Death Of A Clown; Susannah's Still Alive; Funny Face.

L.P.s

7/80 *PL 13603/AFLI 3603* (U.S.) R.C.A. PL 13603/AFLI 3603
Where Do You Come From; Doing The Best For You; Visionary Dreamer; Nothin' More To Lose; The World Is Changing Hands; Move Over; See The Beast; Imagination Real; In You I Believe; Run.

7/81 *Glamour* R.C.A. LP 6005/AFLI 4036
Is This The Only Way?; Glamour; Reveal Yourself; World Of Our Own; Body; Too Serious; Telepathy; 7th Channel; Eastern Eyes.

10/83 *Chosen People* / Warner Bros 23917–1
Tapas (Instrumental); Charity; Mean Disposition; Love Gets You; Danger Zone; True Story; Take One More Chance; Freedom Lies; Matter Of Decision; Is It Any Wonder?; Fire Burning; Chosen People; Cold Winter.

ANOMALIES

Kinky Music (Larry Page Orchestra) Decca LK 4692/Rhino RNLP 058
Tired Of Waiting For You; Come On Now; Something Better Beginning; You Really Got Me; Don't Ever Change; Got My Feet On The Ground; All Day And All Of The Night; One Fine Day; Just Can't Go To Sleep; Revenge; I Took My Baby Home; Everybody's Gonna Be Happy.
An instrumental album including an unreleased Dave Davies number 'One Fine Day'. A vocal version was previously released by another of Page's protégés – Shel Naylor (Decca F11856).

Four More Respected Gentlemen /Reprise RS 6309 (Unreleased)
She's Got Everything; Monica; Mr Songbird; Johnny Thunder; Polly; Days; Animal Farm; Berkeley Mews; Picture Book; Phenomenal Cat; Misty Water.
As discussed in the main text this album was apparently scheduled for release in the States but was finally replaced by *The Kinks Are The Village Green Preservation Society*. All the tracks have since surfaced on flip sides, *The Great Lost Kinks Album* and *The Kinks Kronikles*.

(The Kinks Are) The Village Green Preservation Society Pye N(S)PL 18233
The Village Green Preservation Society; Do You Remember Walter?; Picture Book; Starstruck; Phenomenal Cat; People Take Pictures Of Each Other; Village Green; Mr Songbird; Wicked Annabella; Johnny Thunder; Monica; Days.
This twelve-track version, complete with a different sleeve, was mysteriously withdrawn shortly after its supposed release in late 1968.

PROMOTIONAL RECORDS

/65 *You Really Got Me (E.P.)* Cameo C 256
You Really Got Me; I Gotta Move; Milk Cow Blues.
A specially pressed E.P. for disc jockeys featuring live cuts from the Kinks' U.S. television appearances of 1965.

6/69 *Then, Now And In Between* Reprise PRO 328
Louie Louie; You Really Got Me; I Need You; Till The End Of The Day; Well Respected Man; Dedicated Follower Of Fashion; Dandy; Sunny Afternoon; David Watts; End Of The Season; Sitting By The Riverside; Death Of A Clown; The Village Green Preservation Society; Last Of The Steam Powered Trains; Big Sky; Berkeley Mews; Days; Waterloo Sunset.
This promotional album was issued as part of the 1969 publicity campaign. The work was generally available on a mail order scheme retailing for $2.00.

8/69 *Songbook* Reprise PRO 331
A double album of various Reprise artists including the Kinks' 'Picture Book'.

9/69 *Record Show* Reprise PRO 336
Another double sampler featuring the Kinks' 'Nothing To Say'.

10/69 *October 10, 1969* Reprise PRO 351
Yet another mail order double, released in the States on the same day as *Arthur*. Unfortunately, only 'Shangri-la' is included.

4/70 *Big Ball* Reprise PRO 358
This double sampler featured the rare 'When I Turn Out The Living Room Light'.

11/70 *Looney Tunes* Reprise PRO 423
A treble album sampler featuring 'Apeman'.

12/70 *Kinks Part 1; Lola Vs Powerman And The Moneygoround – Radio Spots* Reprise PRO 440
An advertisement for the album specially pressed for radio stations.

8/71 *Hot Platters* Reprise PRO 474
A double sampler featuring 'Animals In The Zoo'.

1/73 *Dance To The Beat Of Looney Tunes* Reprise PRO 551
A double sampler featuring three cuts from *The Great Lost Kinks Album*.

2/77 *Winter Sampler* Arista SPL 03
Includes 'Sleepwalker' and 'Life Goes On'.

4/77 'Sleepwalker' Arista SP 5
An impressive gold vinyl single. The flip side is a non-Kinks track by the Hollywood Stars.

9/78 *Misfit (E.P.)* Arista SP 22
Rock'n'Roll Fantasy; Black Messiah; Misfits; Permanent Waves.
A square shaped disc in a round picture sleeve!

12/78 *Holiday Classic* Arista SP 34
A seasonal 12″ promo featuring 'Father Christmas' and 'Rock'n'Roll Fantasy'.

10/79 *The Low Budget Interview* Arista SP 69
Low Budget; Interview I; (I Wish I Could Fly Like) Superman; Interview II; Catch Me Now I'm Falling; Interview III; Gallon Of Gas; Interview IV; Attitude.
The interview segments featured Ray Davies talking to Ed Skiaky.

6/80 *Fistful Of Kinks (E.P.)* Arista SP 85
All Day And All Of The Night; Celluloid Heroes; You Really Got Me; Lola.
A one-sided 12″ in-store sampler of tracks from *One For The Road*.

A considerable number of Kinks singles have been issued as advance promotional copies. In the 60s, these were invariably early pressings of officially released singles with white labels. During the last decade, however, U.S. record companies have tended to issue promotional edited cuts or mono-stereo couplings. The following is a list of promotional singles that differ, in any aural respect, from generally released Kinks singles. All songs are full length stereo cuts unless indicated otherwise in parentheses.

7/72	Supersonic Rocket Ship (mono)/Supersonic Rocket Ship	R.C.A. SP 45-380
10/72	Celluloid Heroes (edited)/Celluloid Heroes	SP 45-404
5/74	Money Talks (edited)/Money Talks	DJBO 0275
8/74	Mirror Of Love/Here Comes Flash	JB 10019
12/74	Preservation (edited)/Preservation	JB 10121
5/75	Starmaker (mono)/Starmaker	JH 10251
5/75	Everybody's A Star/Everybody's A Star (mono)	JH 10251
12/75	I'm In Disgrace (mono)/I'm In Disgrace	JH 10551
3/77	Sleepwalker/Sleepwalker (mono)	Arista AS 0240
5/77	Juke Box Music/Juke Box Music (mono)	AS 0247
12/77	Father Christmas/Father Christmas (mono)	AS 0296
6/78	A Rock'n'Roll Fantasy/A Rock'n'Roll Fantasy (mono)	AS 0342
10/78	Live Life/Live Life (mono)	AS 0372
3/79	Superman/Superman (mono)	AS 0409
9/79	Catch Me Now I'm Falling (edited)/Catch Me Now I'm Falling	AS 0458
10/80	You Really Got Me/You Really Got Me (mono)	AS 0577
9/81	Destroyer/Destroyer (mono)	AS 0619
11/81	Better Things/Better Things (mono)	AS 0649

Finally, a five-track E.P. (KINX 4) was issued in 1982 to promote *Give The People What They Want.*

FOREIGN RELEASES

In recent years there has been a growing interest in foreign releases, especially those that differ from their U.K. or U.S. counterparts. The majority of singles issued on the Continent followed standard U.K. couplings but are worth collecting for their often excellent picture sleeves. However, it is the E.P.s and compilation albums that prove most interesting since the Continental record companies invariably followed their own marketing instincts, producing a spate of imaginative and sometimes bizarre releases.

E.P.s

Kinks E.P.s were released sporadically in most Continental countries during the 60s and the main markets were France, Sweden and Spain.

/64 *All Day And All Of The Night* Vogue PNV 24127 (France)
All Day And All Of The Night; I'm A Lover Not A Fighter; I Gotta Move; Long Tall Shorty.

/64 *Kinksize Session* Pye NEP 24200 (Sweden)
I Gotta Go Now; I've Got That Feeling; Things Are Getting Better; Louie Louie.

/64 *You Really Got Me* Pye P2060 (Spain)
You Really Got Me; It's Alright; Long Tall Sally; I Took My Baby Home.

/65 *Got Love If You Want It* Vogue PNV 24131 (France)
Got Love If You Want It; I Took My Baby Home; Cadillac, Beautiful Delilah.

/65 *Kwyet Kinks* Pye NEP 24221 (Sweden)
Wait Till The Summer Comes Along; Such A Shame; Well Respected Man; Don't You Fret.

/65 *Kwyet Kinks* HPY 337–14 (Spain)
Wait Till The Summer Comes Along; Such A Shame; Well Respected Man; Don't You Fret.

/65 *The Kinks* Pye NEP 5036 (Sweden)
All Day And All Of The Night; You Really Got Me; I Gotta Move; It's Alright.

/65 *Tired Of Waiting For You* Vogue PNV 24132 (France)
Tired Of Waiting For You; Things Are Getting Better; Long Tall Sally; Come On Now.

/65 *Tired Of Waiting For You* Pye NEP 5039 (Sweden)
Tired Of Waiting For You; Beautiful Delilah; Come On Now; Too Much Monkey Business.

/65 *Tired Of Waiting For You* Pye P 2071 (Spain)
Tired Of Waiting For You; Come On Now; Everybody's Gonna Be Happy; Who'll Be The Next In Line?

/65 *Set Me Free* Pye P 2083 (Spain)
Set Me Free; I Need You; You Do Something To Me; You Still Want Me.

/65 *Set Me Free* Vogue PNV 24140 (France)
Set Me Free; Dancing In The Street; I Need You; Everybody's Gonna Be Happy.

/65 *You Really Got Me* Pye HPY 337–01 (Spain)
You Really Got Me; Set Me Free; All Day And All Of The Night; Tired Of Waiting For You.

/65 *See My Friend* Pye HPY 337–03 (Spain)
See My Friend; Too Much Monkey Business; Who'll Be The Next In Line?; Everybody's Gonna Be Happy.

/65 *A Well Respected Man* Vogue PNV 24251 (France)
A Well Respected Man; See My Friend; Louie Louie; Never Met A Girl Like You Before.

/66 *Till The End Of The Day* Vogue PNV 24160 (France)
Till The End Of The Day; Where Have All The Good Times Gone?; I'm On An Island; What's In Store For Me?

/66 *The Kinks At The Drop In* Pye NEP 5046 (Sweden)
Wonder Where My Baby Is Tonight; I Need You; Set Me Free; See My Friend.

/66 *The Kinks In Sweden* Pye NEP 5047 (Sweden)
Sunny Afternoon; Milk Cow Blues; I'm Not Like Everybody Else; Gotta Get The First Plane Home.

/66 *Long Tall Sally* Pye NEP 5049 (Sweden)
Long Tall Sally; You Still Want Me; You Do Something To Me; Look For Me Baby.

/66 *Session Con The Kinks* Pye HPY 337–17 (Spain)
Louie Louie; Things Are Getting Better; Dancing In The Street; Come On Now.

/66 *Till The End Of The Day* Pye HPY 337–22 (Spain)
Till The End Of The Day; Where Have All The Good Times Gone?; Milk Cow Blues; When I See That Girl Of Mine.

/66 *Dedicated Follower Of Fashion* Pye HPY 337–24 (Spain)
Dedicated Follower Of Fashion; It's Too Late; Sitting On My Sofa; Gotta Get The First Plane Home.

/66 *Dedicated Follower Of Fashion* Vogue PNV 24167 (France)
Dedicated Follower Of Fashion; Gotta Get The First Plane Home; Sitting On My Sofa; The World Keeps Going Round.

/66 *Sunny Afternoon* Pye HPY 337–31 (Spain)
Sunny Afternoon; I'm Not Like Everybody Else; The World Keeps Going Round; You Can't Win.

/66 *Sunny Afternoon* Vogue PNV 24173 (France)
Sunny Afternoon; You Can't Win; I'm Not Like Everybody Else; When I See That Girl Of Mine.

/66 *Dandy* Vogue PNV 24177 (France)
Dandy; Rosy, Won't You Please Come Home; Party Line; Fancy.

/67 *Dead End Street* Vogue PNV 24184 (France)
Dead End Street; Session Man; Big Black Smoke; House In The Country.

/67 *Dead End Street* Pye HPY 337–34 (Spain)
Dead End Street; Party Line; Dandy; Big Black Smoke.

/67 *Dandy* Pye NEP 5050 (Sweden)
Dandy; Party Line; Mr Pleasant; This Is Where I Belong.

/67 *Mr Pleasant* Vogue PNV 24191 (France)
Mr Pleasant; This Is Where I Belong; Two Sisters; Village Green.

/67 *Death Of A Clown* Vogue 24196 (France)
Death Of A Clown; Love Me Till The Sun Shines; You're Looking Fine; Funny Face.

/67 *Waterloo Sunset* Vogue PNV 24194 (France)
Waterloo Sunset; Act Nice And Gentle; Holiday In Waikiki; Little Miss Queen Of Darkness.

/67 *Waterloo Sunset* Pye HPY 337–38 (Spain)
Waterloo Sunset; Mr Pleasant; This Is Where I Belong; Village Green.

/67 *Waterloo Sunset* Pye EPD 15040 (Germany)
Waterloo Sunset; Act Nice And Gentle; Mr Pleasant; This Is Where I Belong.

L.P.s/COMPILATIONS

The Continental albums are a nightmare for any compiler mainly because of the frequent variance in titles and cover artwork. Obviously, the most interesting albums are those that differ substantially in song content, and it is surprising to learn how independent many of the Continental marketing departments were in compiling works that bore little or no relation to their U.K. or U.S. counterparts.

/64 *The Kinks* Vogue VPV 76018 30 (France)
All Day And All Of The Night; So Mystifying; Stop Your Sobbing; Things Are Getting Better; Cadillac; It's Alright; Beautiful Delilah; You Really Got Me; I Took My Baby Home; I Gotta Move; Got Love If You Want It; Long Tall Shorty; Too Much Monkey Business; I'm A Lover Not A Fighter.

/65 *The Kinks Vol. II* Vogue VPV 76020 30 (France)
Everybody's Gonna Be Happy; Look For Me Baby; You Do Something To Me; Dancing

In The Street; Naggin' Woman; Long Tall Sally; Wonder Where My Baby Is Tonight; Tired Of Waiting For You; You Still Want Me; Come On Now; Who'll Be The Next In Line?; You Shouldn't Be Sad; I Gotta Go Now; Got My Feet On The Ground.

/65 *The Kinks In Germany* Pye 17077 (Germany)
A Well Respected Man; Such A Shame; Wait Till The Summer Comes Along; Don't You Fret; I Need You; Set Me Free; Louie Louie; I Gotta Go Now; I've Got That Feeling; Things Are Getting Better; Never Met A Girl Like You Before; See My Friend.

/65 *The Kinks* Pye SIP 4 (Italy)
You Really Got Me; I Gotta Move; You Still Want Me; Long Tall Shorty; Come On Now; I Need You; Tired Of Waiting For You; It's Alright; Everybody's Gonna Be Happy; All Day And All Of The Night; I Took My Baby Home; Louie Louie.

/65 *Kinks Size* Pye PS 1250 (Japan)
You Really Got Me; Beautiful Delilah; So Mystifying; Just Can't Go To Sleep; Long Tall Shorty; I Took My Baby Home; I'm A Lover Not A Fighter; Too Much Monkey Business; Cadillac; Bald Headed Woman; Revenge; I've Been Driving On Bald Mountain; Stop Your Sobbing; Got Love If You Want It.

/66 *The Kinks* Pye HTSLP 340016 (Germany)
Dandy; Such A Shame; I Gotta Go Now; I Took My Baby Home; Wonder Where My Baby Is Tonight; Naggin' Woman; Sunny Afternoon; Dedicated Follower Of Fashion; Things Are Getting Better; Party Line; I've Got That Feeling; House In The Country; Sitting On My Sofa; A Well Respected Man.

/66 *A Well Respected Man* Vogue VPV 76022 30 (France)
A Well Respected Man; Just Can't Go To Sleep; Such A Shame; I've Been Driving On Bald Mountain; I've Got That Feeling; See My Friend; Louie Louie; Set Me Free; Wait Till The Summer Comes Along; Don't You Fret; Revenge; I Need You.

/68 *The Kinks Are The Village Green Preservation Society* Vogue CLVXPY 18233 (France)
The Village Green Preservation Society; Do You Remember Walter?; Picture Book; Johnny Thunder; Monica; Days; Village Green; Mr Songbird; Wicked Annabella; Starstruck; Phenomenal Cat; People Take Pictures Of Each Other.

/68 *The Kinks Are The Village Green Preservation Society* Pye SLBP 63.003 (Italy)

/68 *The Kinks Are The Village Green Preservation Society* Pye SPL 18233 (Scandinavia)
The Scandinavian copies of the album indicate that they were originally pressed in Britain. Although once generally available, these Continental twelve-track versions are apparently becoming increasingly difficult to unearth.

/70 *The Best Of The Kinks* Pye 66 491 2 (Germany)
Sunny Afternoon; Dandy; Tired Of Waiting For You; Till The End Of The Day; See My Friend; A Well Respected Man; Death Of A Clown; Lola; You Really Got Me; Dedicated Follower Of Fashion; Wonder Where My Baby Is Tonight; Waterloo Sunset; All Day And All Of The Night; Dead End Street; Days; Apeman.

/70 *History Vol. I* Pye LDVS 17184 (Germany)
Beautiful Delilah; So Mystifying; Just Can't Go To Sleep; Long Tall Shorty; I Took My Baby Home; I'm A Lover Not A Fighter; You Really Got Me; Cadillac; Bald Headed

Woman; Revenge; Too Much Monkey Business; I've Been Driving On Bald Mountain; Stop Your Sobbing; Got Love If You Want It; Wonder Where My Baby Is Tonight; Milk Cow Blues; Come On Now; Naggin' Woman; I Need You; It's Too Late; Dancing In The Street; David Watts; Love Me Till The Sun Shines; House In The Country; You're Looking Fine; Sitting On My Sofa.

/70 *History Vol. II* Pye LDVS 17201 (Germany)
You Really Got Me; David Watts; Party Line; Days; Death Of A Clown; Starstruck; Dedicated Follower Of Fashion; Tired Of Waiting For You; Till The End Of The Day; Plastic Man; Everybody's Gonna Be Happy; Shangri-la; Dandy; Sunny Afternoon; Autumn Almanac; Set Me Free; Mr Pleasant; Dead End Street; Victoria; A Well Respected Man; All Day And All Of The Night; Waterloo Sunset; Lincoln County; See My Friend.

/71 *The Kinks* Pye DP 02 (France)
Sunny Afternoon; Sitting On My Sofa; All Day And All Of The Night; Don't You Fret; Look For Me Baby; Set Me Free; You Really Got Me; See My Friend; Where Have All The Good Times Gone?; Naggin' Woman; Such A Shame; Dedicated Follower Of Fashion; A Well Respected Man; Louie Louie; I'm Not Like Everybody Else; Wait Till The Summer Comes Along; Got My Feet On The Ground; I Need You; Dead End Street; Till The End Of The Day; I Gotta Move; Wonder Where My Baby Is Tonight; Tired Of Waiting For You; Dancing In The Street.

/73 *Hit Collection* Pye 86 486 (Germany)
All Day And All Of The Night; A Well Respected Man; Big Black Smoke; Sitting On My Sofa; See My Friend; Tired Of Waiting For You; Don't You Fret; Such A Shame; Louie Louie; I Need You; Till The End Of The Day; I'm Not Like Everybody Else; Wait Till The Summer Comes Along; I Gotta Move; Set Me Free; Where Have All The Good Times Gone?; Dedicated Follower Of Fashion; Sunny Afternoon; You Really Got Me; Dead End Street.

/74 *Pop Chronik* Pye 86962 (Germany)
You Really Got Me; Beautiful Delilah; All Day And All Of The Night; Tired Of Waiting For You; Everybody's Gonna Be Happy; Cadillac; I Took My Baby Home; Naggin' Woman; I'm A Lover Not A Fighter; Such A Shame; Too Much Monkey Business; Wonder Where My Baby Is Tonight; Long Tall Shorty; See My Friend; Till The End Of The Day; Dedicated Follower Of Fashion; Sitting On My Sofa; Sunny Afternoon; Dead End Street, Wonderboy; Waterloo Sunset; Death Of A Clown; Autumn Almanac; Days.

/75 *Encore* Pye DP 30 (France)
Lola; The Village Green Preservation Society; Little Miss Queen Of Darkness; Two Sisters; Sitting By The Riverside; Party Line; Dandy; Funny Face; Village Green; Dreams; People Take Pictures Of Each Other; Picture Book; Death Of A Clown; Apeman; Harry Rag; The Way Love Used to Be; Animals In The Zoo; David Watts; Rosy, Won't You Please Come Home?; No Return; Last Of The Steam Powered Trains; Phenomenal Cat; Starstruck; Afternoon Tea; Big Sky; Tin Soldier Man.

/76 *The Kinks* Vogue VK 32 (Belgium)
Sunny Afternoon; All Day And All Of The Night; Dedicated Follower Of Fashion; You Really Got Me; Dead End Street; Set Me Free; Death Of A Clown; Dandy; A Well Respected Man; I Need You; See My Friend; Where Have All The Good Times Gone?

/77 *The Story Of Pop* Pye 26 471 (Germany)
You Really Got Me; Dead End Street; All Day And All Of The Night; Tired Of Waiting For You; See My Friend; Dandy; Till The End Of The Day; Dedicated Follower Of Fashion; Sunny Afternoon; Wonderboy; Days; Waterloo Sunset.

/77 *Lo Mejor Hora De Kinks* Pye GHL 001 (Spain)
Lola; The Village Green Preservation Society; Love Me Till The Sun Shines; Wonderboy; Little Miss Queen Of Darkness; Two Sisters; Sitting By The Riverside; Dandy; Death Of A Clown; Dreams; Village Green; Johnny Thunder; Party Line; Funny Face; Moments; Do You Remember Walter?; All Of My Friends Were There; People Take Pictures Of Each Other; Too Much On My Mind; Picture Book; You're Looking Fine; Rainy Day In June.

/78 *Lo Mejor De Kinks* R.C.A. NL 42486 (Spain)
He's Evil; Money Talks; The Hard Way; Scrapheap City; Salvation Road, Jack The Idiot Dunce; Flash's Confession; Nothing Lasts Forever; Everybody's A Star (Starmaker); Have Another Drink.

/78 *The Kinks* R.C.A. CL 42 465 (France)
Supersonic Rocket Ship; One Of The Survivors; Sweet Lady Genevieve; Sitting In The Midday Sun; Acute Schizophrenia Paranoia Blues; Maximum Consumption; Celluloid Heroes; Muswell Hillbilly; Baby Face; Alcohol; Holiday; Schooldays; Ducks On The Wall; Lola; Sitting In My Hotel; Daylight; Shepherds Of The Nation; Money And Corruption; Everybody's A Star (Starmaker); Here Comes Yet Another Day; Motorway; You Don't Know My Name; Where Are They Now?; I'm In Disgrace.

/78 *Historia De La Musica Pop Inglesia, Vol. I* Pye BML 011 (Spain)
Days; Set Me Free; You Really Got Me; Shangri-la; All Day And All Of The Night; A Well Respected Man; Sitting On My Sofa; Victoria; Louie Louie; Sunny Afternoon; Till The End Of The Day; Tired Of Waiting For You.

/78 *Historia De La Musica Pop Inglesia, Vol. VII* Pye BML 023 (Spain)
Lola; Everybody's Gonna Be Happy; I Need You; Cadillac; I Gotta Move; It's Alright; Dandy; Waterloo Sunset; Dead End Street; Where Have All The Good Times Gone?; Come On Now; Long Tall Shorty.

/79 *You Really Got Me* Mode MD 9017 (France)
You Really Got Me; Apeman; Dead End Street; Last Of The Steam Powered Trains; Dandy; Sunny Afternoon; I Need You; Lola; Till The End Of The Day; Little Miss Queen Of Darkness; Tin Soldier Man; A Well Respected Man.

/79 *All Day And All Of The Night* Mode MD 9054 (France)
All Day And All Of The Night; See My Friend; Sitting On My Sofa; Village Green Preservation Society; Afternoon Tea; Set Me Free; Louie Louie; Death Of A Clown; Party Line; Animals In The Zoo; Sitting By The Riverside; Tired Of Waiting For You.

/79 *Rock Concert* R.C.A. PL 42992 (Holland)
Top Of The Pops; Brainwashed; Mr Wonderful; Acute Schizophrenia Paranoia Blues; Holiday; Muswell Hillbilly; Alcohol; Banana Boat Song; Skin And Bone; Baby Face; Lola.

/79 *Star Discothek* Pye 200891 241 (Germany)
You Really Got Me; Dead End Street; All Day And All Of The Night; Autumn

Almanac; Mr Pleasant; Apeman; Sunny Afternoon; Dedicated Follower Of Fashion; Days; Waterloo Sunset; Tired Of Waiting For You; Dandy.

/80 *Kinky Gems* P.R.T./MH 13241–1 (Argentina)
Long Tall Sally; You Still Want Me; You Do Something To Me; I've Got That Feeling; Who'll Be The Next In Line?; Never Met A Girl Like You Before; Big Black Smoke; This Is Where I Belong; Act Nice And Gentle; Polly; There Is No Life Without Love; Creeping Jean; King Kong; Berkeley Mews.

/81 *The Kinks* Vogue VK 73 (France)
Lola; Autumn Almanac; Waterloo Sunset; Till The End Of The Day; Sitting On My Sofa; Don't You Fret; Apeman; Tired Of Waiting For You; I Gotta Move; The Village Green Preservation Society; Last Of The Steam Powered Trains; Tin Soldier Man.

/81 *The Kinks* Vogue VMFP 518–19–20 (France)
Lola; Dead End Street; Death Of A Clown; A Well Respected Man; Till The End Of The Day; You Really Got Me; Apeman; Sunny Afternoon; Waterloo Sunset; Dedicated Follower Of Fashion; Dandy; Set Me Free; All Day And All Of The Night; Animals In The Zoo; Starstruck; Shangri-la; The Village Green Preservation Society; People Take Pictures Of Each Other; Sitting On My Sofa; Don't You Fret; Autumn Almanac; Louie Louie; Look For Me Baby; Afternoon Tea; Tired Of Waiting For You; I Need You; Last Of The Steam Powered Trains; Little Miss Queen Of Darkness; Party Line; I Gotta Move; See My Friend; Tin Soldier Man; Mr Pleasant; Plastic Man; Sitting By The Riverside; Phenomenal Cat.

/81 *Hit Station* Marifon/P.R.T. 296029 241 (Germany)
Lola; Tired Of Waiting For You; All Day And All Of The Night; Till The End Of The Day; Waterloo Sunset; Wait Till The Summer Comes Along; You Really Got Me; Dead End Street; Wonderboy; A Well Respected Man; Sunny Afternoon; I Gotta Move.

/81 *Best Of The Kinks* (Club Edition) P.R.T. 015 915132 (Germany)
Lola; Dandy; Apeman; A Well Respected Man; You Really Got Me; All Day And All Of The Night; Tired Of Waiting For You; See My Friend; Waterloo Sunset; Sunny Afternoon; Dedicated Follower Of Fashion; Days; Till The End Of The Day; Victoria; Dead End Street; Set Me Free.

/82 *The Kinks* Amiga 855–888 (East Germany)
You Really Got Me; Dead End Street; Lola; All Day And All Of The Night; Autumn Almanac; Susannah's Still Alive; Mr Pleasant; Apeman; Victoria; Sunny Afternoon; Death Of A Clown; Dedicated Follower Of Fashion; Days; Waterloo Sunset; Tired Of Waiting For You; Dandy.

/83 *More Kinks On Pie* P.R.T./S.M.S. SP20 5042 (Japan)
You Do Something To Me; It's Alright; Louie Louie; I Gotta Go Now; I've Got That Feeling; I Gotta Move; Who'll Be The Next In Line?; Set Me Free; See My Friend; Never Met A Girl Like You Before; Dedicated Follower Of Fashion; Sitting On My Sofa; Wait Till The Summer Comes Along; Such A Shame; Dead End Street; Big Black Smoke; Act Nice and Gentle; Autumn Almanac; Mr Pleasant.

/83 *Kwack Kinks* P.R.T./S.M.S. SP 5043 (Japan)
Susannah's Still Alive; Polly; Wonderboy; Lincoln County; There Is No Life Without

Love; Days; She's Got Everything; This Is Where I Belong; Hold My Hand; Creeping Jean; Plastic Man; King Kong; Mindless Child Of Motherhood; This Man He Weeps Tonight; Berkeley Mews.

/83 *El Disco De Oro De Kinks* P.R.T./Gamma GX 01–1314 (Mexico)
Apeman; Powerman; Monica; Village Green Preservation Society; Set Me Free; Little Miss Queen Of Darkness; Sitting By The Riverside; Sunny Afternoon; Session Man; Louie Louie; I Need You; Lola; Got To Be Free; Milk Cow Blues.

/83 *The Singles 1964–1970* P.R.T./S.M.S. SP 32–5085 (Japan)
Long Tall Sally; You Still Want Me; You Really Got Me; All Day And All Of The Night; Tired Of Waiting For You; Everybody's Gonna Be Happy; Set Me Free; See My Friend; Till The End Of The Day; Dedicated Follower Of Fashion; Sunny Afternoon; Dead End Street; Waterloo Sunset; Death Of A Clown; Autumn Almanac; Susannah's Still Alive; Wonderboy; Lincoln County; Days; Hold My Hand; Plastic Man; Drivin'; Shangri-la; Lola; Victoria; Apeman.

In addition to the above, several albums, including *The Kinks, Kinda Kinks, The Kinks Kontroversy, Face To Face* and *Live At Kelvin Hall* were packaged in different covers in various countries, though the track listings generally remained unaltered.

BOOTLEGS

/71 *Rare Kinks* KINKY WCF 719
Act Nice And Gentle; This Man He Weeps Tonight; Mr Pleasant; King Kong; Creeping Jean; Plastic Man; Lincoln County; Polly; Mindless Child Of Motherhood; She's Got Everything; Berkeley Mews; Hold My Hand; There Is No Life Without Love.
This album is of limited interest since all the tracks have appeared on vinyl in some form.

/73 *It's Kriminal* TMQ (No serial number)
You're Looking Fine; Medley: Little Queenie/Shakin' All Over/Be Bop A Lula; Dedicated Follower Of Fashion; Waterloo Sunset; Sunny Afternoon; Holiday; Victoria; Lola; You Really Got Me; All Day And All Of The Night; Louie Louie; Hang On Sloopy.
A reasonable quality recording taken from a March 1972 performance at the Santa Monica Civic Centre.

/75 *Survivors Kaught Konspicuously in Koncert* TAKRL 1940
Victoria; Here Comes Yet Another Day; Money Talks; Dedicated Follower Of Fashion; Mirror Of Love; Celluloid Heroes; Here Comes Flash; Demolition; He's Evil; Lola.
An excellent quality bootleg recording taken from a B.B.C. broadcast on 27 July 1974.

/75 *Long Tall Sally* TMOQ 71084
Long Tall Sally; I Took My Baby Home; I Gotta Move*; Milk Cow Blues*; I'm A Lover Not A Fighter*; It's Alright*; A Well Respected Man†; Dandy†; Lincoln

* Taped from *Shindig* 1965.
† Taped from *Smothers' Brothers Show* 1965.

County; Hold My Hand; Act Nice And Gentle; Creeping Jean; You Really Got Me**; Money Talks**; Here Comes Yet Another Day††; Skin And Bone††; Celluloid Heroes††.

/75 *Don't Touch That Dial: Soap Opera In Concert* TAKRL 1970
Everybody's A Star (Starmaker); Ordinary People; Rush Hour Blues; Nine To Five; When Work Is Over; Have Another Drink; Underneath The Neon Sign; You Make It All Worthwhile; Ducks On The Wall; A Face In The Crowd; You Can't Stop The Music.
An excellent quality radio recording taped during the 1975 U.S. tour.

/77 *A British Bisquit (Live And Rare)* 'Pye'(!) 0001
Side One (Live): A Well Respected Man; Dedicated Follower Of Fashion; Sunny Afternoon; Ducks On The Wall; (A) Face In The Crowd; You Can't Stop The Music. Side Two (Studio): Long Tall Sally; You Do Something To Me; You Still Want Me; Never Met A Girl Like You Before; Ring The Bells; Gotta Get The First Plane Home; I Am Free; When I See That Girl Of Mine; What's In Store For Me.
The first side is taken from a U.S. broadcast, while side two consists of rare but previously released recordings.

/80 *Misfits Never Die* JUNK (No serial number)
Sleepwalker; Tired Of Waiting For You; Life On The Road; Where Have All The Good Times Gone?; Lola; Misfits; Low Budget; Celluloid Heroes; Medley: A Well Respected Man/Death Of A Clown/Sunny Afternoon; All Day And All Of The Night; Pressure; Twist And Shout; Attitude; Till The End Of The Day.

/80 *Winterland 2/77 Part One* MM 11
One Of The Survivors; Sleepwalker; Medley: Lola/Banana Boat Song/A Well Respected Man/Sunny Afternoon; Waterloo Sunset (Instrumental); The Hard Way; Brother.

/80 *Winterland 2/77 Part Two* MM 12
Stormy Sky; Life Goes On; Full Moon; Lola; Demon Alcohol; You Really Got Me; All Day And All Of The Night.

/81 *The Kinks New Year's Eve 1980/81* SRRS (no serial number)
Introduction: You Really Got Me Blues; Where Have All The Good Times Gone?; Tired Of Waiting For You; Catch Me Now I'm Falling; Bird Dog (Johnny's A Joker); New York City Blues; Lola; Dead End Street; Till The End Of The Day; Low Budget; Imagination Real; Nothing More To Lose; I'm Not Like Everybody Else; Come On Now; You Really Got Me; Preservation; Scrapheap City; Good Golly Miss Molly; You Are My Sunshine; Easy Come, There You Went; Louise; Schooldays; Mirror Of Love; Village Green Preservation Society; Twist And Shout; Life On The Road; Waterloo Sunset.
An interesting, good quality bootleg coupling the Kinks' New Year's Eve concert with a hotch potch of studio outtakes. 'Easy Come, There You Went' and 'Twist And Shout' have been plundered from other bootlegs.

4/83 *Late Late Show* Chamelion (no serial number)
Around The Dial; Where Have All The Good Times Gone?; Catch Me Now I'm Falling;

** Taped from *Midnight Special* 1974.
†† Taped from *In Concert Special* 1973.

Destroyer; Yo-Yo; Dead End Street; Art Lover; Back To Front; Get Back; Till The End Of The Day; Bernadette; All Day And All Of The Night (Reprise).
A high quality bootleg taken from the Rockpalast live broadcast.

/83 *It Is Time* Far Arden MUHU 1004
Medley: Life On The Road/Heartbeat (Paris 1/6/77); Get Back In Line (London 24/12/77); Time (U.S.A. 1973); She's Bought A Hat Like Princess Marina (U.S.A. 1973); Rock'n'Roll Fantasy (Genesco College, New York 1978); A Woman In Love Will Do Anything (sung by Charlotte Cornwall in *Chorus Girls*); Cricket (U.S.A. 1973); Harry Rag (Berkeley Community Theatre 27/2/72); Money (St John's University, Jamaica 23/2/80); Slum Kids (London 24/12/77); Art Lover (Pittsburg 19/1/82).
A hotch potch of tracks from the past decade, totally erratic in quality. Some numbers are excellent stereo recordings while others are barely audible. The album also contains a couple of surprise bootleg singles (*Rare Collection Vols. I–II*) in black and white picture sleeves: 'All Aboard' (studio)/'Milk Cow Blues' (live B.B.C.) and 'Tokio' (live in Tokio 1982)/'Too Serious' (Detroit 16/9/81).

/83 *Kollektable Kinks* Reprieve 6309
Long Tall Sally; I Took My Baby Home; You Still Want Me; You Do Something To Me; Got Love If You Want It; Tell Me Now So I'll Know; A Little Bit Of Sunlight; I Go To Sleep; When I See That Girl Of Mine; There's A New World Just Opening For Me; Sitting On My Sofa; Lincoln County; Act Nice and Gentle; Hold My Hand; People Take Pictures Of Each Other; Creeping Jean; Apeman; Lola; Preservation; Scrapheap City; Mirror Of Love; Slum Kids; Medley: You Really Got Me/All Day And All Of The Night; No More Looking Back; Father Christmas; Prince Of The Punks; Artificial Light; Massive Reductions; Low Budget; (Wish I Could Fly Like) Superman.
An affectionate bootleg compilation consisting of mainly previously released items, but many of them are hard to find mono or stereo mixes, alternate takes and B-sides. Highlights include an alternate take of 'Apeman' only available in Denmark; a live version of 'Slum Kids'; a medley of the group's first two hits and 'No More Looking Back' specially recorded for I.T.V.'s *Supersonic* show titled *Juke Box* in the U.S.; and, most notably, five demo recordings from 1965 – 'Tell Me Now So I'll Know'; 'A Little Bit Of Sunlight'; 'I Go To Sleep'; 'When I See That Girl Of Mine'; and 'There's A New World Opening Up For Me'. The recording quality is remarkable and the compilers have obviously gone to great trouble to provide an aesthetically pleasing bootleg. Note also the serial number which is the same as the unreleased *Four More Respected Gentlemen*! A real labour of love.

/83 *Kinks Attack* Fuji CL 0407
Introduction: Around The Dial; The Hard Way; Medley: Where Have All The Good Times Gone?/Tired Of Waiting For You/Come On Now; Destroyer; Yo-Yo; Woh! Oh Oh Tokio; Lola; Low Budget; Medley: (I Wish I Could Fly Like) Superman/Batman Theme/Shakin' All Over; Celluloid Heroes; Till The End Of The Day; Bernadette; All Day And All Of The Night; Give The People What They Want; Pressure; Stop Your Sobbing; Schooldays; You Really Got Me.
An excellent quality recording though the standard of the pressings leaves a lot to be desired. The rare track 'Woh! Oh Oh Tokio' sounds like an early version of 'Long Distance', which appeared on the cassette version of *State Of Confusion*.

Apart from bootleg albums, there have also been several E.P.s and singles that have appeared in the U.K. and the U.S. during the 70s.

/74 This Strange Effect/(Blank Flipside) S 7431
Approximately 100 copies of this rare recording were pressed by the Kinks' U.S. fan club.

/75 One Night/Good Golly Miss Molly
Another fan club offering this time featuring two solo items by Dave Davies.

/76 You Still Want Me/You Do Something To Me
In one of his fits of exaggeration, Ray once joked to the press that the Kinks' second single sold less than 200 copies. Many people have taken his word as gospel, which no doubt explains the logic of releasing this rare single in bootleg form.

/76 *You Still Want Me* (E.P.) RIST I
You Still Want Me; You Do Something To Me; This Strange Effect; Sitting On My Sofa; Preservation.
A five-track E.P. featuring a demo and rare vinyl recordings.

/78 *Long Tall Sally* (E.P.) 'Cameo'(!) C–315
Long Tall Sally; I Took My Baby Home; You Still Want Me; You Do Something To Me.
An imaginary Cameo E.P. featuring the first two Kinks U.K. singles.

/79 *You Really Got Me* (E.P.) 'Cameo'(!) C–256
You Really Got Me; Gotta Move; Milk Cow Blues.
Another imaginary Cameo E.P. released over a year after its predecessor, in spite of the earlier serial number. The live version of 'You Really Got Me' is taken from U.S. television's *Midnight Special* while 'Milk Cow Blues' was originally featured in *Shindig*.

/83 All Aboard/Too Serious (*Rare Collection Vol. I*) MAHU 1002

/83 Tokyo/Too Serious (*Rare Collection Vol II*) MAHU 1003
The above two singles were freely available with some copies of *It Is Time* (see Bootleg L.P.s) but are also being sold separately.

BOOTLEG TAPES

Since re-establishing their reputation in the States in late 1969, the Kinks have been bootlegged extensively on tape and the following list gives some indication of their changing repertoire over the years. Unfortunately, there is a dearth of pre-1969 taped material, though additional tapes must surely exist and are probably gathering dust on somebody's shelves. The following is a selective catalogue of tapes generally available on the open market.

1965–8
The few tracks generally available from this period are taken from various television and radio programmes rather than concert performances. Several of the cuts are from *Saturday Club*, which specialised in live recordings during the early/mid-60s, but the origins of many of the others remains unclear.

Studio Recordings:
'Milk Cow Blues', 'Dandy', 'Easy Come, There You Went' (instrumental).

Radio/Television Recordings:
'You Really Got Me' (*Beat Room* 1964); 'Wonder Where My Baby Is Tonight' (*Saturday*

Club 1965); 'Set Me Free' (U.S. T.V. *Clay Cole Show* 1965); 'Milk Cow Blues' (U.S. T.V. *Shindig*, 1965); 'I Gotta Move' (U.S. T.V. *Shindig*, 1965); 'I'm A Lover Not A Fighter' (U.S. T.V. *Shindig*, 1965); 'It's Alright' (U.S. T.V. *Shindig*, 1965); 'A Well Respected Man' (U.S. T.V. *Smothers' Brothers Show*, 1965); 'Till The End Of The Day' (German T.V. *Beat Beat Beat*, 1965); 'You Really Got Me' (German T.V. *Beat Beat Beat*, 1965); 'You Really Got Me' (U.S. T.V. *Shindig*, 1965); 'All Day And All Of The Night' (U.S. T.V. *Shindig*, 1965); 'You Really Got Me' (U.S. T.V. *Hullaballoo*, 1965); 'All Day And All Of The Night' (U.S. T.V. *Hullaballoo*, 1965); 'Set Me Free' (Swedish T.V. *Drop In*, 1965); 'Wonder Where My Baby Is Tonight' (Swedish T.V. *Drop In*, 1965); 'See My Friend' (Swedish T.V. *Drop In*, 1965); 'Dandy' (U.S. T.V. *Smothers' Brothers Show c.* 1966, taped from English show); 'Mr Pleasant' (B.B.C. 1967); 'David Watts' (B.B.C. 1967); 'Mr Pleasant' (German T.V. *Beat Club*, 1967); 'Waterloo Sunset' (German T.V. *Beat Club*, 1967); 'Plastic Man' (German T.V. *Beat Club*, 1969).

Source Unknown:
'All Aboard' (unreleased Chuck Berry influenced number, *c.* 1964); 'Milk Cow Blues'; 'Till The End Of The Day'; 'Milk Cow Blues' (elongated version – *Joe Loss Show*?); 'A Well Respected Man' (fast version!); 'You Really Got Me' (Television 1964); 'All Day And All Of The Night' (Television 1964); 'A Well Respected Man' (slower version); 'Money' (Live – Davies substitutes the word 'Beer' for 'Money' throughout the song!); 'Campbelltown Loch' (instrumental). The latter two tracks are reputedly taken from a 1980 concert.

In addition, there are several solo Dave Davies items from B.B.C. radio, *c.* 1967, including 'Love Me Till The Sun Shines'; 'Death Of A Clown'; 'Susannah's Still Alive' and 'Good Luck Charm'. The latter is not the old Elvis Presley hit, but a previously unreleased song, presumably penned by one or both of the Davies brothers.

1969

10/69 *Fillmore East, N.Y.* *Quality: Good (45 mins)*
Till The End Of The Day; Last Of The Steam Powered Trains; Waterloo Sunset; Mindless Child Of Motherhood; Some Mother's Son; You Really Got Me; All Day And All Of The Night; Mr Churchill Says; Milk Cow Blues; See My Friend; Brainwashed.

10/69 *Fillmore East, N.Y. 2nd Performance* *Quality: Good (35 mins)*
Till The End Of The Day; Last Of The Steam Powered Trains; Waterloo Sunset; Mr Churchill Says; Brainwashed; Mindless Child Of Motherhood; Sunny Afternoon; You Really Got Me; All Day And All Of The Night; Victoria; Dedicated Follower Of Fashion; A Well Respected Man; Death Of A Clown; Dandy.

23/10/69 *Boston Tea Party* *Quality: Good (75 mins)*
Last Of The Steam Powered Trains; Mindless Child Of Motherhood; Waterloo Sunset; Mr Churchill Says; Victoria; You Really Got Me/All Day And All Of The Night; Medley: A Well Respected Man/Death Of A Clown/Dandy; Medley: Milk Cow Blues/See My Friend/Party Line/Rip It Up/Brainwashed; Sunny Afternoon; Till The End Of The Day.

25/10/69 *Boston Tea Party* *Quality: Good (75 mins)*
Till The End Of The Day; You're Looking Fine; Waterloo Sunset; Medley: You Really Got Me/All Day And All Of The Night/Mr Churchill Says; Fancy; Last Of The Steam

Powered Trains; Louie Louie; Mindless Child Of Motherhood; Victoria; Mr Churchill Says; Medley: A Well Respected Man/Death Of A Clown/Dandy; Love Me Till The Sun Shines; Sunny Afternoon; Don't You Fret; Medley: Milk Cow Blues/Rip It Up/See My Friend/Brainwashed; The Village Green Preservation Society.

11/69 *Fillmore West, San Francisco, Ca.* *Quality: Fair (35 mins)*
Waterloo Sunset; Mr Churchill Says; Victoria; Big Sky; Don't You Fret; A Well Respected Man; Death Of A Clown; Dandy; Love Me Till The Sun Shines.

1970

6/70 *Pierce College, Northridge, Ca.* *Quality: Very Good (60 mins)*
Till The End Of The Day; Last Of The Steam Powered Trains; Brainwashed; See My Friend; You're Looking Fine; Strangers; Act Nice And Gentle; Waterloo Sunset; Lola; Big Sky; Arthur; Top Of The Pops; You Really Got Me; All Day And All Of The Night; Milk Cow Blues; One Night; Victoria.

6/70 *Philharmonic, N.Y.* *Quality: Good (25 mins)*
Last Of The Steam Powered Trains; Big Sky; Brainwashed; Waterloo Sunset; Top Of The Pops; You're Looking Fine; Milk Cow Blues; One Night.

1971

30/3/71 *Philharmonic, N.Y.* *Quality: Very Good (70 mins)*
Till The End Of The Day; Brainwashed; You're Looking Fine; Apeman; Waterloo Sunset; Sunny Afternoon; Get Back In Line; A Pub With No Beer; Lola; Louise; Big Sky; Milk Cow Blues; See My Friend; Powerman; One Night; You Are My Sunshine; You Really Got Me; All Day And All Of The Night; Top Of The Pops.

3/71 *Queen's College, Flushing, New York* *Quality: Very Good (55 mins)*
Till The End Of The Day; Brainwashed; Apeman; Get Back In Line; Mr Pleasant; Autumn Almanac; Dead End Street; Big Sky; Sunny Afternoon; Lola; Milk Cow Blues; Powerman; Waterloo Sunset; Victoria; Happy Birthday.

4/71 *Civic Center, Santa Monica, Ca.* *Quality: Good (35 mins)*
Victoria; Arthur; Lola, Apeman; Strangers; Get Back In Line; Harry Rag; Days; Big Sky.

4/71 *Civic Hall, Santa Monica, Ca.* *Quality: Excellent (60 Mins)*
Till The End Of The Day; Brainwashed; All Right, O.K., You Win; Apeman; Strangers; Arthur; Get Back In Line; Harry Rag; Sunny Afternoon; Louise; Big Sky; Lola; Top Of The Pops; You Are My Sunshine; You Really Got Me; All Day And All Of The Night; Days; Victoria.

2/12/71 *C.W. Post College, Greenvale, N.Y.* *Quality: Good (60 mins)*
Top Of The Pops; Brainwashed; You're Looking Fine; Lola; Strangers; A Well Respected Man; Complicated Life; Skin And Bone; Acute Schizophrenia Paranoia Blues; Mr Wonderful; Waterloo Sunset; When I Turn Off The Living Room Light; Apeman; Big Sky; You Really Got Me; All Day And All Of The Night; Victoria.

1972

27/2/72 *Live At Berkeley, Ca.* *Quality: Good (75 mins)*
Till The End Of The Day; Brainwashed; Dead End Street; You're Looking Fine; Get Back In Line; Harry Rag; Muswell Hillbilly; Sunny Afternoon; 20th Century Man; Banana Boat Song; Alcohol; Acute Schizophrenia Paranoia Blues; Skin And Bone; Lola; You Really Got Me; All Day And All Of The Night; Victoria; You Are My Sunshine.

5/3/72 *Orpheum Theatre, Boston, Mass.* *Quality: Good (75 mins)*
Top Of The Pops; You're Looking Fine; Get Back In Line; Muswell Hillbilly; Waterloo Sunset; Sunny Afternoon; Banana Boat Song; Brainwashed; Acute Schizophrenia Paranoia Blues; Holiday; Skin And Bone; Alcohol; Complicated Life; Harry Rag; You Are My Sunshine; She's Bought A Hat Like Princess Marina; Baby Face; Lola; You Really Got Me; All Day And All Of The Night; Victoria.

11/3/72 *Emerson Auditorium, Cleveland, Oh.* *Quality: Good (90 mins)*
Top Of The Pops; Brainwashed; Get Back In Line; Waterloo Sunset; Apeman; Sunny Afternoon; Muswell Hillbilly; Acute Schizophrenia Paranoia Blues; Mr Wonderful; You're Looking Fine; Alcohol; Skin And Bone; Lola; Medley: You Really Got Me/All Day And All Of The Night; Till The End Of The Day; Victoria.

12/3/72 *Auditorium, Chicago, Il.* *Quality: Very Good (70 mins)*
Till The End Of The Day; You're Looking Fine; Apeman; Get Back In Line; Acute Schizophrenia Paranoia Blues; Muswell Hillbilly; Sunny Afternoon; Mr Wonderful; Alcohol; Skin And Bone; Lola; Milk Cow Blues; One Night; You Really Got Me; All Day And All Of The Night; Victoria; Louie Louie.

30/8/72 *Central Park, N.Y.* *Quality: Very Good (85 mins)*
Top Of The Pops; Medley: You're Looking Fine/Little Queenie/Be Bop A Lula; Apeman; Dedicated Follower Of Fashion; Waterloo Sunset; Sunny Afternoon; Acute Schizophrenia Paranoia Blues; Here Comes Yet Another Day; Holiday; Alcohol; Skin And Bone; Village Green Preservation Society; You Are My Sunshine; Victoria; Baby Face; Lola; You Really Got Me; All Day And All Of The Night; Louie Louie; Twist And Shout; Hang On Sloopy; Unreal Reality; Milk Cow Blues; One Night.

12/12/72 *Drury Lane Theatre, London* *Quality: Fair (30 mins)*
Village Green Preservation Society; I'm Coming Home; Cricket; Where Are They Now?; Picture Book; People Take Pictures Of Each Other; Time?; Banana Boat Song; Sunny Afternoon; Muswell Hillbilly; Lola; You Really Got Me; All Day And All Of The Night; Hoochie Coochie Man.

15/12/72 *Concertgebouw, Amsterdam* *Quality: Fair (90 mins)*
Top Of The Pops; You're Looking Fine; Little Queenie; Shakin' All Over; Be Bop A Lula; Dedicated Follower Of Fashion; Sunny Afternoon; Lola; Celluloid Heroes; Here Comes Yet Another Day; Brainwashed; Mr Wonderful; Acute Schizophrenia Paranoia Blues; Holiday; Alcohol; Skin And Bone; Baby Face; Good Golly Miss Molly; Victoria; Louie Louie; Hang On Sloopy.

1973

5/4/73 *Live In Toronto* *Quality: Good (65 mins)*
Victoria; Acute Schizophrenia Paranoia Blues; Dedicated Follower Of Fashion;

Waterloo Sunset; Lola; Celluloid Heroes; Here Comes Yet Another Day; Picture Book; Alcohol; Sunny Afternoon; Skin And Bone; Good Golly Miss Molly; You Really Got Me; All Day And All Of The Night.

11/4/73 *Palladium, Hollywood, Ca.* *Quality: Very Good (85 mins)*
Victoria; Brainwashed; Acute Schizophrenia Paranoia Blues; Holiday; Picture Book; People Take Pictures Of Each Other; Mr Wonderful; Till The End Of The Day; Celluloid Heroes; Muswell Hillbilly; Dedicated Follower Of Fashion; Lola; Here Comes Yet Another Day; Harry Rag; Alcohol; Sunny Afternoon; Dead End Street; Skin And Bone; Good Golly Miss Molly; The End Is Near; You Really Got Me; All Day And All Of The Night.

9/73 *Paradiso, Amsterdam* *Quality: Fair (90 mins)*
Victoria; Brainwashed; Sweet Little Sixteen; You're Looking Fine; Little Queenie; Dedicated Follower Of Fashion; Waterloo Sunset; Sunny Afternoon; Celluloid Heroes; Lost John; One Of The Survivors; Lola; Banana Boat Song; Mr Wonderful; Here Comes Yet Another Day; Holiday; Acute Schizophrenia Paranoia Blues; Alcohol; Skin And Bone; Good Golly Miss Molly; You Really Got Me; All Day And All Of The Night.

1974

6/4/74 *Felt Forum, N.Y.* *Quality: Good (70 mins)*
Victoria; One Of The Survivors; Money Talks; Dedicated Follower Of Fashion: Sunny Afternoon; You Really Got Me; All Day And All Of The Night; Mirror Of Love; Celluloid Heroes; Here Comes Yet Another Day; Here Comes Flash; Demolition; Lola; Mr Wonderful; Rock Around The Clock; Alcohol; Skin And Bone; Good Golly Miss Molly.

16/4/74 *Auditorium, Chicago, Il.* *Quality: Very Good (65 mins)*
Victoria; One Of The Survivors; Celluloid Heroes; Money Talks; Waterloo Sunset; Sunny Afternoon; You Really Got Me; All Day And All Of The Night; Here Comes Yet Another Day; Here Comes Flash; Demolition; Lola; Alcohol; Skin And Bone; Good Golly Miss Molly.

20/4/74 *Buffalo, N.Y.* *Quality: Very Good (65 mins)*
Victoria; One Of The Survivors; Celluloid Heroes; Money Talks; You Really Got Me; All Day And All Of The Night; Sunny Afternoon; Lola; Here Comes Yet Another Day; Here Comes Flash; Mr Wonderful; Alcohol; Skin And Bone; Good Golly Miss Molly.

23/9/74 *Tivoli Gardens, Copenhagen* *Quality: Very Good (85 mins)*
Victoria; Here Comes Yet Another Day; Acute Schizophrenia Paranoia Blues; Mr Wonderful; Dedicated Follower Of Fashion; Sunny Afternoon; Get Back In Line; Mirror Of Love; Money Talks; You Really Got Me; Celluloid Heroes; Here Comes Flash; Demolition; He's Evil; Lola; Alcohol; Skin And Bone; Good Golly Miss Molly.

9/74 *Starmaker, Granada Television Broadcast* *Quality: Very Good (35 mins)*
Everybody's A Star (Starmaker); Ordinary People; Rush Hour Blues; Nine To Five; Have Another Drink; You Make It All Worthwhile; A Face In The Crowd; You Can't Stop The Music.

1/12/74 *Music Hall, Mass.* *Quality: Very Good (130 mins)*
Here Comes Yet Another Day; You Really Got Me; All Day And All Of The Night;

Celluloid Heroes; Waterloo Sunset; Sunny Afternoon; Lola; Alcohol; Skin And Bone; Good Golly Miss Molly; Morning Song; Daylight; A Change In The Weather; Money And Corruption; I'm Your Man; Here Comes Flash; Demolition; Money Talks; Shepherds Of The Nation; He's Evil; Scum Of The Earth; Slum Kids; Mirror Of Love; Flash's Dream; Flash's Confession; Nothing Lasts Forever; Artificial Man; Scrapheap City; Preservation.

1975

20/4/75 *Spectrum, Ph.* *Quality: Very Good (110 mins)*
Here Comes Flash; Here Comes Yet Another Day; Demolition; Mirror Of Love; Money Talks; Celluloid Heroes; Banana Boat Song; Lola; Alcohol; Skin And Bone; You Really Got Me; All Day And All Of The Night; Starmaker; Ordinary People; Rush Hour Blues; Nine To Five; Have Another Drink; Underneath The Neon Sign; You Make It All Worthwhile; Ordinary People; A Well Respected Man; Dedicated Follower Of Fashion; Sunny Afternoon; Ducks On The Wall; Face In The Crowd; You Can't Stop The Music.

5/12/75 *Live In Boston, Mass.* *Quality: Very Good (90 mins)*
Everybody's A Star (Starmaker); Ordinary People; Rush Hour Blues; Lola; Sunny Afternoon; Dedicated Follower Of Fashion; Waterloo Sunset; You Really Got Me; All Day And All Of The Night; Alcohol; Schooldays; Jack The Idiot Dunce; Education; The First Time We Fall In Love; I'm In Disgrace; Headmaster; The Last Assembly; No More Looking Back; Education (Reprise); Finale; Money Talks.

1976

20/2/76 *McAllister Audi-Tulane University, New Orleans, La.* *Quality: Very Good/Excellent (100 mins)*
Everybody's A Star (Starmaker); Rush Hour Blues; Waterloo Sunset; You Really Got Me; All Day And All Of The Night; Alcohol; Celluloid Heroes; Schooldays; Schoolboys; Jack The Idiot Dunce; Education; The First Time We Fall In Love; I'm In Disgrace; Headmaster; The Hard Way; The Last Assembly; No More Looking Back; Finale; Money Talks.

31/3/76 *Congress Centre, Hamburg* *Quality: Very Good (100 mins)*
Dave's Blues; Everybody's A Star (Starmaker); Rush Hour Blues; Lola; Dedicated Follower Of Fashion; Waterloo Sunset; You Really Got Me; All Day And All Of The Night; Alcohol; Celluloid Heroes; Schooldays; Jack The Idiot Dunce; Education; The First Time We Fall In Love; I'm In Disgrace; Headmaster; The Hard Way; The Last Assembly; No More Looking Back; Finale; Money Talks.

1977

5/2/77 *Music Hall, Boston, Mass.* *Quality: Very Good (70 mins)*
You Really Got Me; One Of The Survivors; Sleepwalker; Rush Hour Blues; You Make It Worthwhile; Ordinary People; Everybody's A Star (Starmaker); Victoria; A Well Respected Man; Sunny Afternoon; Waterloo Sunset; Supersonic Rocket Ship; Schooldays; The Hard Way; Education; Brother; Stormy Sky; Life Goes On; Celluloid

Heroes; Acute Schizophrenia Paranoia Blues; Banana Boat Song; Lola; Alcohol.

19/2/77 *Winterland, San Franciso, Ca.* *Quality: Excellent (65 mins)*
One Of The Survivors; Sleepwalker; Banana Boat Song; Sunny Afternoon; Waterloo Sunset; Schooldays; Schoolboys; The Hard Way; Education; Brother; Stormy Sky; Life Goes On; Full Moon; Lola; You Really Got Me; All Day And All Of The Night.

3/77 *Civic Auditorium, Santa Monica, Ca.* *Quality: Very Good (58 mins)*
One Of The Survivors; Sleepwalker; Waterloo Sunset; A Well Respected Man; Sunny Afternoon; Celluloid Heroes; Schooldays; Education; Life Goes On; Lola; Alcohol; You Really Got Me; All Day And All Of The Night.

30/4/77 *New Century Theatre, Buffalo, N.Y.* *Quality: Very Good (90 mins)*
One Of The Survivors; Tired Of Waiting For You; Sunny Afternoon; Rush Hour Blues; You Make It All Worthwhile; Ordinary People; Life On The Road; Stormy Sky; Life Goes On; 20th Century Man; Schooldays; Schoolboys; The Hard Way; Education; Full Moon; Sleepwalker; Lola; Alcohol; You Really Got Me; Juke Box Music.

1/6/77 *Pavillion, Paris* *Quality: Very Good (90 mins)*
You Really Got Me; One Of The Survivors; Rush Hour Blues; Tired Of Waiting For You; Sunny Afternoon; A Well Respected Man; Death Of A Clown; Waterloo Sunset; Dedicated Follower Of Fashion; Celluloid Heroes; Medley: Life On The Road/ Heartbeat/Louie Louie/Hang On Sloopy; Stormy Sky; Life Goes On; Schooldays; Schoolboys; The Hard Way; Lola; Alcohol; Skin And Bone; Father Christmas; You Really Got Me.

8/77 *Live In Los Angeles* *Quality: Very Good (60 mins)*
One Of The Survivors; Sleepwalker; Waterloo Sunset; A Well Respected Man; Sunny Afternoon; Celluloid Heroes; Schooldays; Education; Life Goes On; Lola; Alcohol; You Really Got Me; All Day And All Of The Night.

23/11/77 *Brooklyn College, N.Y.* *Quality: Very Good (90 mins)*
Sleepwalker; Life On The Road; Heartbeat; Stormy Sky; Rush Hour Blues; Tired Of Waiting For You; A Well Respected Man; Dedicated Follower Of Fashion; Sunny Afternoon; All Day And All Of The Night; Get Back In Line; Life Goes On; Full Moon; Slum Kids; The Hard Way; Education; See My Friend; Lola; Juke Box Music; Father Christmas; You Really Got Me.

2/12/77 *Le Roy Concert Centre, Pawtucket, Ri.* *Quality: Very Good (55 mins)*
You Really Got Me; Sleepwalker; Life On The Road; Stormy Sky; Rush Hour Blues; Tired Of Waiting For You; Sunny Afternoon; A Well Respected Man; Death Of A Clown; All Day And All Of The Night; Slum Kids; Life Goes On; Skin And Bone; Celluloid Heroes; Schoolboys; Education; Full Moon; Lola; Juke Box Music; Father Christmas; You Really Got Me.

23/12/77 *Rainbow Theatre, London* *Quality: Very Good (110 mins)*
Little Queenie; Beautiful Delilah; Louie Louie; Life On The Road; You Really Got Me; Tired Of Waiting For You; A Well Respected Man; Death Of A Clown; Dedicated Follower Of Fashion; Sunny Afternoon; Dead End Street; Waterloo Sunset; All Day And All Of The Night; Victoria; Rush Hour Blues; Slum Kids; Celluloid Heroes; Get Back In Line; The Hard Way; Education; Alcohol; Skin And Bone; Sleepwalker; Lola; Father Christmas; You Really Got Me; Juke Box Music.

1978

25/6/78 *Universal Amphitheatre, Universal City, L.A., Ca.* *Quality: Excellent (100 mins)*
You Really Got Me; Life On The Road; Sleepwalker; Mr Big Man; Waterloo Sunset; Misfits; Permanent Waves; Hay Fever; Lola; Celluloid Heroes; A Well Respected Man; Death Of A Clown; Sunny Afternoon; Trust Your Heart; You Really Got Me; Slum Kids; Alcohol; Rock'n'Roll Fantasy; All Day And All Of The Night; Live Life; Juke Box Music.

3/8/78 *The Warehouse, New Orleans* *Quality: Very Good (80 mins)*
You Really Got Me; Sleepwalker; Life On The Road; Permanent Waves; Hay Fever; Lola; Misfits; A Well Respected Man; Sunny Afternoon; Trust Your Heart; You Really Got Me; Slum Kids; Alcohol; Rock'n'Roll Fantasy; All Day And All Of The Night; Live Life; Little Queenie; Twist And Shout; Juke Box Music.

8/8/78 *Civic Centre, Springfield, Mass.* *Quality: Very Good (65 mins)*
You Really Got Me; Sleepwalker; Life On The Road; Mr Big Man; Permanent Waves; Hay Fever; Lola; Misfits; A Well Respected Man; Death Of A Clown; Sunny Afternoon; Trust Your Heart; You Really Got Me; Slum Kids; Alcohol.

9/8/78 *Central Park, N.Y.* *Quality: Excellent (90 mins)*
You Really Got Me; Sleepwalker; Life On The Road; Mr Big Man; Permanent Waves; Hay Fever; Lola; Misfits; Celluloid Heroes; Sunny Afternoon; Trust Your Heart; You Really Got Me; Slum Kids; Alcohol; Rock'n'Roll Fantasy; All Day And All Of The Night; Live Life; Twist And Shout; Juke Box Music.

12/8/78 *Festival de Bilzen, Belgium* *Quality: Good (70 mins)*
You Really Got Me; Sleepwalker; Life On The Road; A Well Respected Man; Death Of A Clown; Dedicated Follower Of Fashion; Sunny Afternoon; Misfits; Lola; Permanent Waves; Hay Fever; Trust Your Heart; You Really Got Me; Slum Kids; Alcohol; Rock'n'Roll Fantasy; All Day And All Of The Night; Live Life; Twist And Shout.

20/8/78 *Volkhaus, Zurich* *Quality: Very Good (90 mins)*
You Really Got Me; Sleepwalker; Life On The Road; Lola; Misfits; Hay Fever; A Well Respected Man; Death Of A Clown; Sunny Afternoon; Dedicated Follower Of Fashion; Celluloid Heroes; Trust Your Heart; You Really Got Me; Slum Kids; Alcohol; Rock'n'Roll Fantasy; All Day And All Of The Night; Live Life; Little Queenie; Juke Box Music.

8/10/78 *Genesco College, N.Y.* *Quality: Very Good (75 mins)*
You Really Got Me; Sleepwalker; Life On The Road; Where Have All The Good Times Gone?; Genesco Rock; Hay Fever; Lola; Celluloid Heroes; Low Budget; (Wish I Could Fly Like) Superman; Trust Your Heart; You Really Got Me; Batman Theme; Slum Kids; Rock'n'Roll Fantasy; All Day And All Of The Night; The Hard Way; Ducks On The Wall; Victoria; Twist And Shout.

10/10/78 *Falconer Theatre, Copenhagen* *Quality: Excellent (100 mins)*
You Really Got Me; Sleepwalker; Life On The Road; Mr Big Man; Lola; Dedicated Follower Of Fashion; Misfits; Tired Of Waiting For You; Hay Fever; A Well Respected Man; Death Of A Clown; Sunny Afternoon; Celluloid Heroes; Trust Your Heart; You Really Got Me; Slum Kids; Alcohol; Rock'n'Roll Fantasy; All Day And All Of The Night; Live Life; Little Queenie; Juke Box Music.

17/10/78 *Musikhalle, Hamburg* *Quality: Good (100 mins)*
You Really Got Me; Sleepwalker; Life On The Road; Lola; Misfits; A Well Respected Man; Death Of A Clown; Sunny Afternoon; Dedicated Follower Of Fashion; Hay Fever; Celluloid Heroes; Trust Your Heart; You Really Got Me; Slum Kids; Alcohol; Rock'n'Roll Fantasy; All Day And All Of The Night; Live Life; Little Queenie; Juke Box Music.

22/10/78 *Sofiensaal, Wien, Austria* *Quality: Very Good (85 mins)*
You Really Got Me; Sleepwalker; Life On The Road; Misfits; Celluloid Heroes; Trust Your Heart; Rock'n'Roll Fantasy; Slum Kids; Alcohol; A Well Respected Man; Death Of A Clown; Sunny Afternoon; Dedicated Follower Of Fashion; All Day And All Of The Night; Live Life; Little Queenie; Hay Fever.

29/10/78 *Schowburg, Sittard, Holland* *Quality: Very Good (75 mins)*
You Really Got Me; Sleepwalker; Life On The Road; Lola; Misfits; A Well Respected Man; Death Of A Clown; Sunny Afternoon; Dedicated Follower Of Fashion; Celluloid Heroes; Hay Fever; Trust Your Heart; You Really Got Me; Slum Kids; Alcohol; Rock'n'Roll Fantasy; All Day And All Of The Night; Live Life; Little Queenie.

30/11/78 *Mogador Theatre, Paris* *Quality: Very Good (80 mins)*
You Really Got Me; Sleepwalker; Life On The Road; Lola; Misfits; A Well Respected Man; Death Of A Clown; Sunny Afternoon; Dedicated Follower Of Fashion; Hay Fever; Celluloid Heroes; Trust Your Heart; You Really Got Me; Slum Kids; Alcohol; Rock'n'Roll Fantasy; All Day And All Of The Night; Live Life; Little Queenie; Twist And Shout.

1979

3/2/79 *St Alban's Civic Hall, U.K.* *Quality: Good (90 mins)*
You Really Got Me; Sleepwalker; Life On The Road; Lola; Low Budget; Misfits; (I Wish I Could Fly Like) Superman; Dedicated Follower Of Fashion; A Well Respected Man; Death Of A Clown; Sunny Afternoon; Trust Your Heart; You Really Got Me; Slum Kids; Celluloid Heroes; Waterloo Sunset; All Day And All Of The Night; Live Life; Twist And Shout.

10/8/79 *Cobo Arena, Detroit, Mi.* *Quality: Excellent (90 mins)*
Sleepwalker; Life On The Road; Permanent Waves; Lola; Misfits; Low Budget; (I Wish I Could Fly Like) Superman; Gallon Of Gas; Celluloid Heroes; All Day And All Of The Night; Pressure; Twist And Shout; Victoria.

21/10/79 *Oslo, Norway* *Quality: Excellent (60 mins)*
Sleepwalker; Tired Of Waiting For You; Life On The Road; Lola; Misfits; Low Budget; (I Wish I Could Fly Like) Superman; Gallon Of Gas; Pressure; Twist And Shout; Hey, Hey; Live Life; Little Queenie.

25/10/79 *Audi-Max, Hamburg* *Quality: Very Good (75 mins)*
Sleepwalker; Life On The Road; Lola; Misfits; Low Budget; (I Wish I Could Fly Like) Superman; Gallon Of Gas; You Really Got Me; A Well Respected Man; Sunny Afternoon; Celluloid Heroes; All Day And All Of The Night; Pressure; Catch Me Now I'm Falling.

15/11/79 *Concertgebouw, Amsterdam* *Quality: Very Good (100 mins)*
Sleepwalker; Till The End Of The Day; Where Have All The Good Times Gone?; Lola; Rock'n'Roll Fantasy; Low Budget; (I Wish I Could Fly Like) Superman; Catch Me Now I'm Falling; You Really Got Me; Gallon Of Gas; Celluloid Heroes; A Well Respected Man; Death Of A Clown; Sunny Afternoon; All Day And All Of The Night; Twist And Shout; Pressure; Attitude; Alcohol; Victoria.

19/11/79 *Pavillion, Paris* *Quality: Good (90 mins)*
Sleepwalker; Till The End Of The Day; Where Have All The Good Times Gone?; Lola; Misfits; Low Budget; (I Wish I Could Fly Like) Superman; You Really Got Me; Gallon Of Gas; Celluloid Heroes; A Well Respected Man; Death Of A Clown; Sunny Afternoon; All Day And All Of The Night; Pressure; Twist And Shout; Back In The Line; Rock'n'Roll Fantasy; Victoria, Attitude.

1980

23/2/80 *St John's University, Jamaica, N.Y.* *Quality: Very Good (90 mins)*
You Really Got Me; The Hard Way; Attitude; Catch Me Now I'm Falling; Where Have All The Good Times Gone; Lola; National Health; Low Budget; (I Wish I Could Fly Like) Superman; Celluloid Heroes; You Really Got Me; Gallon of Gas; Stop Your Sobbing; A Well Respected Man; Death Of A Clown; Get Back In The Line; All Day And All Of The Night; Pressure; Twist And Shout; Prince Of The Punks; Money.

24/8/80 *Tampa, Florida* *Quality: Very Good (99 mins)*
You Really Got Me; The Hard Way; Where Have All The Good Times Gone?; Catch Me Now I'm Falling; Bird Dog; Lola; Low Budget; (I Wish I Could Fly Like) Superman; Attitude; Nothing More To Lose; A Well Respected Man; Death Of A Clown; Sunny Afternoon; You Really Got Me; Gallon Of Gas; Celluloid Heroes; All Day And All Of The Night; Louie Louie; Hang On Sloopy; Twist And Shout; Give The People What They Want; David Watts.

6/9/80 *Coba Arena, Detroit* *Quality: Excellent (90 mins)*
You Really Got Me; The Hard Way; Where Have All The Good Times Gone?; Catch Me Now I'm Falling; Bird Dog; Lola; Low Budget; (I Wish I Could Fly Like) Superman; Imagination's Real; Nothing To Lose; You Really Got Me; Gallon Of Gas; Celluloid Heroes; All Day And All Of The Night; Pressure; Twist And Shout; Give The People What They Want.

27/11/80 *Metropol, Berlin* *Quality: Very Good (75 mins)*
You Really Got Me; The Hard Way; Catch Me Now I'm Falling; Bird Dog; Berlin Blues; Lola; Dead End Street; Low Budget; Imagination's Real; Nothing More To Lose; You Really Got Me; Gallon Of Gas; Celluloid Heroes; 20th Century Man; All Day And All Of The Night; Attitude; Pressure; David Watts.

30/11/80 *Philipshalle, Dusseldorf* *Quality: Very Good (90 mins)*
You Really Got Me; The Hard Way; Where Have All The Good Times Gone?; Tired Of Waiting For You; Bird Dog; Catch Me Now I'm Falling; Dusseldorf Blues; Lola; Dead End Street; Low Budget; Imagination's Real; Nothing More To Lose; 20th Century Man; All Day And All Of The Night; Attitude; Pressure; Twist And Shout; Give The People What They Want; David Watts; Land Of 1,000 Dances.

6/12/80 *Theatre de Verdure, Nice, France* *Quality: Excellent (90 mins)*
You Really Got Me; The Hard Way; Where Have All The Good Times Gone?; Tired Of Waiting For You; Bird Dog; Catch Me Now I'm Falling; Nice Blues; Lola; Dead End Street; Low Budget; Imagination's Real; Nothing More To Lose; You Really Got Me; Gallon Of Gas; Till The End Of The Day; Celluloid Heroes; All Day And All Of The Night; Attitude; Pressure; Twist And Shout; Stop Your Sobbing; David Watts; A Well Respected Man; 20th Century Man.

8/12/80 *Pavillion Baltard, Nogent-sur-Marne* *Quality: Very Good (100 mins)*
The Hard Way; Where Have All The Good Times Gone?; Bird Dog; Catch Me Now I'm Falling; Lola; Dead End Street; Low Budget; Imagination's Real; Nothing More To Lose; You Really Got Me; Gallon Of Gas; Celluloid Heroes; Till The End Of The Day; All Day And All Of The Night; What'd I Say; Attitude; Pressure; Twist And Shout; David Watts; Stop Your Sobbing; Give The People What They Want.

30/12/80 *New York*
See bootleg album section for track listing of *New Year's Eve*. A complete recording of the concert is apparently available.

1981

8/5/81 *Chorus Girls: Theatre Royal, London* *Quality: Very Good (50 mins)*
Newham At Work: Privilege; Payback; Reputation; Up In A High Rise Block; Glorious Sight; Let's Have A Dance; A Woman In Love Will Do Anything; Men Are Fools; The Man Of Destiny; England; Everybody's Got A Body.

14/8/81 *Forum, Los Angeles, Ca.* *Quality: Very Good (110 mins)*
Around The Dial; The Hard Way; Bird Dog; Catch Me Now I'm Falling; Yo-Yo; Tired Of Waiting For You; Killer's Eyes; Lola; Back To Front; Too Serious; You Really Got Me; Misfits; You Really Got Me; Gallon Of Gas; Celluloid Heroes; 20th Century Man; All Day And All Of The Night; Give The People What They Want; Pressure; Twist And Shout; Low Budget; David Watts; (I Wish I Could Fly Like) Superman.

16/9/81 *Pine Knob, Detroit, Mi.* *Quality: Very Good (110 mins)*
Around The Dial; The Hard Way; Catch Me Now I'm Falling; Destroyer; Yo-Yo; Better Things; Detroit City Blues; Lola; Too Serious; Stop Your Sobbing; You Really Got Me; Back To Front; Gallon Of Gas; Till The End Of The Day; Celluloid Heroes; 20th Century Man; All Day And All Of The Night; Give The People What They Want; Misfits; Low Budget; Come On Now; Batman Theme; (I Wish I Could Fly Like) Superman; Banana Boat Song.

19/9/81 *Millet Hall, Miami Univ., Oxford, Oh.* *Quality: Very Good (105 mins)*
Around The Dial; The Hard Way; Catch Me Now I'm Falling; Destroyer; Yo-Yo; Lola Blues; Lola; Too Serious; You Really Got Me; Back To Front; Gallon Of Gas; Till The End Of The Day; Celluloid Heroes; 20th Century Man; All Day And All Of The Night; Give The People What They Want; Misfits; Low Budget; Twist And Shout; Batman Theme; (I Wish I Could Fly Like) Superman; Little Queenie; Louie Louie; Hang On Sloopy.

25/9/81 *Maple Leaf Gardens, Toronto* *Quality: Very Good (105 mins)*
Around The Dial; The Hard Way; Destroyer; Yo-Yo; Toronto Blues; Lola; Too Serious;

Art Lover; You Really Got Me; Back To Front; Gallon Of Gas; Till The End Of The Day; Celluloid Heroes; 20th Century Man; All Day And All Of The Night; Give The People What They Want; Misfits; Low Budget; Batman Theme; (I Wish I Could Fly Like) Superman; Shakin' All Over; Little Queenie; Twist And Shout.

3/10/81 *Madison Square Garden, N.Y.* *Quality: Very Good (125 mins)*
Around The Dial; The Hard Way; Destroyer; Yo-Yo; Catch Me Now I'm Falling; Better Things; New York Blues; Lola; Too Serious; Art Lover; Waterloo Sunset; You Really Got Me; Back To Front; Gallon Of Gas; Till The End Of The Day; Celluloid Heroes; 20th Century Man; Killer's Eyes; Give The People What They Want; Misfits; Low Budget; (I Wish I Could Fly Like) Superman; Pressure; Twist And Shout.

6/10/81 *Spectrum, Ph.* *Quality: Very Good (95 mins)*
Around The Dial; The Hard Way; Catch Me Now I'm Falling; Destroyer; Yo-Yo; Better Things; Lola; Too Serious; Art Lover; You Really Got Me; Back To Front; Gallon Of Gas; Till The End Of The Day; Celluloid Heroes; All Day And All Of The Night;Give The People What They Want; Misfits; A Well Respected Man; Low Budget; Add It Up; (I Wish I Could Fly Like) Superman; Shakin' All Over; David Watts; Pressure; Twist And Shout.

1982

19/1/82 *Stanley Theatre, Pittsburgh, Pa.* *Quality: Very Good (90 mins)*
Around The Dial; The Hard Way; Where Have All The Good Times Gone?; Catch Me Now I'm Falling; Bird Dog; Destroyer; Yo-Yo; Pittsburgh Blues; Lola; Gallon Of Gas; Low Budget; Back To Front; Art Lover; Celluloid Heroes; Till The End Of The Day; Bernadette; All Day And All Of The Night; Give The People What They Want; Pressure; Twist And Shout; Misfits; Stop Your Sobbing; David Watts; You Really Got Me.

2/82 *Live In Tokyo* *Quality: Very Good (80 mins)*
Around The Dial; The Hard Way; Where Have All The Good Times Gone?; Tired Of Waiting For You; Comc On Now; Destroyer; Yo-Yo; Tokyo; Lola; Low Budget; Back To Front; Celluloid Heroes; Till The End Of The Day; Bernadette; All Day And All Of The Night; Give The People What They Want; Pressure; Twist And Shout; You Really Got Me.

3/4/82 *Rockpalast, Essen, Germany* *Quality: Excellent (105 mins)*
Around The Dial; The Hard Way; Where Have All The Good Times Gone?; Catch Me Now I'm Falling; Destroyer; Yo-Yo; Lola; Dead End Street; Add It Up; Low Budget; Art Lover; Back To Front; Gallon Of Gas; Celluloid Heroes; Till The End Of The Day; Bernadette; All Day And All Of The Night; Give The People What They Want; Pressure; You Really Got Me; Stop Your Sobbing; David Watts.

22/12/82 *Lyceum Ballroom, London* *Quality: Very Good (85 mins)*
Around The Dial; The Hard Way; Where Have All The Good Times Gone; Tired Of Waiting For You; Come On Now; Destroyer; Yo-Yo; Blues Track; Lola; Come Dancing; David Watts; Dead End Street; Back To Front; Gallon Of Gas; Celluloid Heroes; Till The End Of The Day; Bernadette; All Day And All Of The Night; Pressure; Twist And Shout; A Well Respected Man; Death Of A Clown; Waterloo Sunset; You Really Got Me; Louie Louie.

1983

12/4/83 *Dane County Coliseum, Madison, Wi.* *Quality: Very Good (110 mins)*
Around The Dial; State Of Confusion; The Hard Way; Catch Me Now I'm Falling; Destroyer; Yo-Yo; Come Dancing; Don't Forget To Dance; Madison Blues; Lola; (I Wish I Could Fly Like) Superman; Shakin' All Over; Back To Front; Gallon Of Gas; A Well Respected Man; Art Lover; Till The End Of The Day; Bernadette; All Day And All Of The Night; Pressure; Low Budget; Celluloid Heroes; You Really Got Me.

29/12/83 *Roseland Ballroom, N.Y.* *Quality: Very Good (100 mins)*
Around The Dial; Definite Maybe; State Of Confusion; Where Have All The Good Times Gone?; Destroyer; Yo-Yo; Don't Forget To Dance; Labour Of Love; Clichés Of The World (B-Movie); Come Dancing; Come On Now; The Hard Way; Gallon Of Gas; Till The End Of The Day; All Day And All Of The Night; Celluloid Heroes; Low Budget.

31/12/83 *Roseland Ballroom, N.Y.* *Quality: Very Good (100 mins)*
Around The Dial; Definite Maybe; Catch Me Now I'm Falling; Where Have All The Good Times Gone?; State Of Confusion; Don't Forget To Dance; The Hard Way; Come On Now; 20th Century Man; Come Dancing; Destroyer; Yo-Yo; Batman Theme; (I Wish I Could Fly Like) Superman; Shakin' All Over; Till The End Of The Day; All Day And All Of The Night; Lola; David Watts; Celluloid Heroes; You Really Got Me; Days; Low Budget.

Since completing this book, I have discovered a further wealth of 70s/80s concert material currently circulating on the open market. For approximate track listings readers should refer to the tapes previously mentioned. Although the selection of songs will be slightly different, one can determine the basic set by comparing gig dates in close chronological alignment.

2/72	*Civic Centre, Santa Monica, Ca.*	*Quality: Very Good (45 mins)*
2/72	*Palladium, Hollywood, Ca.*	*Quality: Good (55 mins)*
21/8/72	*Nassau Coliseum, Long Island, N.Y.*	*Quality: Good (60 mins)*
10/72	*Nottingham, England*	*Quality: Fair (70 mins)*
2/4/74	*Spectrum, Philadelphia, Ph.*	*Quality: Good 70 mins)*
10/4/74	*Music Hall, Boston, Mass.*	*Quality: Very Good (70 mins)*
11/74	*Felt Forum, Chester, Pa.*	*Quality: Good (70 mins)*
24/11/74	*Palace Theatre, Albany, N.Y.*	*Quality: Excellent (135 mins)*
29/11/74	*Palace Theatre, Providence, R.I.*	*Quality: Very Good (70 mins)*
21/12/74	*Royalty Theatre, London*	*Quality: Fair (130 mins)*
8/4/75	*Riverside Theatre, Milwaukee, Wi.*	*Quality: Good (100 mins)*
3/5/75	*Bayfront Centre, St Petersburg, Florida*	*Quality: Very Good (115 mins)*
3/6/75	*Colston Hall, Bristol, England*	*Quality: Good (90 mins)*
27/11/75	*Widener College, Chester, Philadelphia, Ph.*	*Quality: Good (90 mins)*
3/12/75	*State University, Brockport, N.Y.*	*Quality: Good (90 mins)*
9/2/76	*Civic Centre, Santa Monica, Ca.*	*Quality: Good (90 mins)*
29/3/76	*Tivoli, Copenhagen, Denmark*	*Quality: Very Good (110 mins)*
6/1/77	*Paris, France*	*Quality: Very Good (80 mins)*
1/2/77	*Palladium, N.Y.*	*Quality: Very Good (90 mins)*
24/4/77	*Rainbow Theatre, London*	*Quality: Excellent (60 mins)*
28/4/77	*Cobo Hall, Detroit, Mi.*	*Quality: Very Good (105 mins)*
29/4/77	*Maple Leaf Gardens, Toronto*	*Quality: Very Good (110 mins)*

4/5/77	*Hofstra University Playhouse, Hempstead, N.Y.*	*Quality: Very Good (110 mins)*
8/12/77	*Palestra Univ., Rochester, N.Y.*	*Quality: Very Good (80 mins)*
11/12/77	*Stockton State College, Pomona, N.J.*	*Quality: Fair (90 mins)*
26/5/78	*Auditorium Theatre, Rochester N.Y.*	*Quality: Very Good (70 mins)*
27/5/78	*New Century Theatre, Buffalo, N.Y.*	*Quality: Very Good (70 mins)*
28/5/78	*Landmark Theatre, Syracuse, N.Y.*	*Quality: Very Good (70 mins)*
2/6/78	*Palladium, New York*	*Quality: Good (90 mins)*
2/6/78	*Palladium, New York (2nd Performance)*	*Quality: Good (100 mins)*
11/6/78	*Uptown Theatre, Chicago, Il.*	*Quality: Very Good (100 mins)*
19/7/78	*San Diego State Univ.*	*Quality: Good (75 mins)*
29/7/78	*McFarlin Auditorium, Dallas, Texas*	*Quality: Very Good (90 mins)*
1/10/78	*Konserthuset, Stockholm, Sweden*	*Quality: Very Good (90 mins)*
16/10/78	*Berlin, West Germany*	*Quality: Good (90 mins)*
18/10/78	*Zurich, Switzerland*	*Quality: Very Good (70 mins)*
23/10/78	*Stadthalle, Offenbach, West Germany*	*Quality: Very Good (70 mins)*
9/2/79	*Memorial Arena, Binghampton, N.Y.*	*Quality: Very Good (100 mins)*
17/2/79	*Penn State Univ., Pa.*	*Quality: Very Good (100 mins)*
22/2/79	*Palace Theatre, Albany, N.Y.*	*Quality: Very Good (80 mins)*
3/3/79	*Rutger's Univ., New Brunswick, N.J.*	*Quality: Very Good (110 mins)*
9/3/79	*Fredonia, N.Y.*	*Quality: Very Good (85 mins)*
10/3/79	*Genesco College, N.Y.*	*Quality: Very Good (80 mins)*
8/7/79	*Kleinhans Music Hall, Buffalo, N.Y.*	*Quality: Good (90 mins)*
17/7/79	*Music Hall, Houston, Texas*	*Quality: Very Good (85 mins)*
28/7/79	*Spectrum, Philadelphia, Pa.*	*Quality: Very Good (95 mins)*
5/8/79	*Lenox, Mass.*	*Quality: Good (90 mins)*
12/8/79	*Auditorium, Milwaukee, Wi.*	*Quality: Excellent (90 mins)*
19/8/79	*Universal Amphitheatre, Universal City, Ca.*	*Quality: Good (105 mins)*
3/9/79	*San Diego, State Univ.*	*Quality: Good (75 mins)*
16/9/79	*Dane County Coliseum, Madison, Wi.*	*Quality: Good (85 mins)*
21/9/79	*Georgetown Univ. Washington D.C.*	*Quality: Good (85 mins)*
9/79	*Civic Centre, Providence, R.I.*	*Quality: Excellent (60 mins)*
20/10/79	*Westfalenhalle, Dortmund, West Germany.*	*Quality: Good (75 mins)*
24/2/80	*Dome Arena, Rochester, N.Y.*	*Quality: Very Good (90 mins)*
27/2/80	*Rutger's Univ., N.J.*	*Quality: Very Good (90 mins)*
22/8/80	*Sunrise Theatre, Fort Lauderdale, Florida*	*Quality: Very Good (80 mins)*
2/9/80	*Auditorium, Milwaukee, Wi.*	*Quality: Very Good (90 mins)*
13/9/80	*Richfield Coliseum, Cleveland, Oh.*	*Quality: Good (90 mins)*
25/9/80	*Sam Houston Coliseum, Houston, Texas*	*Quality: Good (90 mins)*
17/10/80	*War Memorial Auditorium, Buffalo, N.Y.*	*Quality: Fair (90 mins)*
18/10/80	*Civic Centre, Providence, R.I.*	*Quality: Very Good (90 mins)*
27/10/80	*Spectrum, Philadelphia, Pa.*	*Quality: Very Good (100 mins)*
3/12/80	*Zurich, Switzerland*	*Quality: Very Good (95 mins)*
28/12/80	*Capital Centre, Landover, Md.*	*Quality: Very Good (90 mins)*
28/5/81	*Locham, Holland*	*Quality: Fair (65 mins)*
7/8/81	*Summit, Houston, Texas*	*Quality: Good (85 mins)*
21/8/81	*Greek Theatre, Berkeley, Ca.*	*Quality: Excellent (90 mins)*
3/8/81	*Reading Festival, England*	*Quality: Good (95 mins)*
15/9/81	*Rosemont Horizon, Chicago, Il.*	*Quality: Very Good (90 mins)*
17/9/81	*Wings Stadium, Kalamazoo, Mi.*	*Quality: Good (90 mins)*
21/9/81	*Vet's Memorial, Columbus, Oh.*	*Quality: Very Good (95 mins)*
24/9/81	*Memorial Auditorium, Buffalo, N.Y.*	*Quality: Very Good (115 mins)*
3/10/81	*Madison Square Garden, N.Y.*	*Quality: Excellent (125 mins)*

16/10/81	*Civic Centre, Lakeland, Florida*	*Quality: Very Good (100 mins)*
12/1/82	*Memorial Coliseum, New Haven, Ct.*	*Quality: Excellent (105 mins)*
17/1/82	*Coliseum, Charlotte, Nc.*	*Quality: Very Good (100 mins)*
24/1/82	*Civic Centre, Springfield, Mass.*	*Quality: Very Good (70 mins)*
19/6/82	*J.F.K. Stadium, Philadelphia, Pa.*	*Quality: Fair (100 mins)*
31/8/82	*City Coliseum, Austin, Texas*	*Quality: Good (110 mins)*
21/12/82	*The Dome, Brighton, England*	*Quality: Very Good (80 mins)*
9/4/83	*U.C.C. Pavilion, Chicago, Il.*	*Quality: Very Good (60 mins)*
13/4/83	*Auditorium, Milwaukee, Wi.*	*Quality: Very Good (110 mins)*
16/4/83	*Met Center, Minneapolis*	*Quality: Good (105 mins)*
7/5/83	*Irvine Meadows Amphitheatre, Irving, Ca.*	*Quality: Very Good (90 mins)*
13/5/83	*Summit, Houston, Texas*	*Quality: Very Good (100 mins)*
22/5/83	*War Memorial, Rochester, N.Y.*	*Quality: Fair (90 mins)*

Many of the Kinks' television and radio appearances during the 70s and 80s have also been captured on tape. The following is a selective list of some of the more interesting items:

1/73 *In Concert (B.B.C. T.V.)* *Quality: Very Good (30 mins)*
Victoria; Acute Schizophrenia Paranoia Blues; Dedicated Follower Of Fashion; Lola; Holiday; Good Golly Miss Molly; You Really Got Me; All Day And All Of The Night; Waterloo Sunset; Village Green Preservation Society; Village Green (instrumental).

1/73 *In Concert (U.S. T.V.)* *Quality: Very Good (12 mins)*
Here Comes Yet Another Day; Here Comes Flash (censored version!); Skin And Bone.

6/74 *Top Gear (B.B.C. Radio)* *Quality: Excellent (12 mins)*
Demolition; Mirror Of Love; Money Talks.

6/74 *Midnight Special (U.S. T.V.)* *Quality: Very Good (10 mins)*
Money Talks; You Really Got Me; Celluloid Heroes; Here Comes Yet Another Day.

4/76 *Juke Box (U.S. T.V.)* *Quality: Very Good (8 mins)*
You Really Got Me; All Day And All Of The Night; No More Looking Back.
This programme was screened in the U.K. on the show *Supersonic*.

1/77 *Old Grey Whistle Test (B.B.C. T.V.)* *Quality: Very Good (45 mins)*
Sleepwalker; Life Goes On; Stormy Sky; Celluloid Heroes; Muswell Hillbilly; Full Moon; Life On The Road; Juke Box Music; You Really Got Me.

26/2/77 *Saturday Night Live (U.S. T.V.)* *Quality: Very Good (10 mins)*
Medley: You Really Got Me/ All Day And All Of The Night; A Well Respected Man; Lola; Sleepwalker.

8/3/77 *Mike Douglas Show (U.S. T.V.)* *Quality: Very Good (15 mins)*
Sleepwalker; Celluloid Heroes.

4/77 *Supersonic (U.K. T.V.)* *Quality: Very Good (10 mins)*
Sleepwalker; Sweet Little Rock'n'Roller.

10/10/81 *Saturday Night Live (U.S. T.V.)* *Quality: Excellent (10 mins)*
Destroyer; Art Lover; Give The People What They Want (edited version).

COVER VERSIONS

The following is a list of cover versions of songs recorded and released by the Kinks.

'Act Nice And Gentle'	Duster Bennett.
'All Day And All Of The Night'	Beverley Byrd; Jaybirds; Ian and the Zodiacs; Jolt; Kenny and the Kasuals; Larry Page Orchestra; Les Parruques; Gary Lewis and the Playboys; Little Roger and the Goosebumps; Los Rockin' Devils; Preying Mantis; Speed; Bernie Thorme.
'Apeman'	Jimmy Castor Bunch; Serge Lama; James Last; Trinidad Tripoli Steel Band.
'Celluloid Heroes'	Clair Hamill.
'Come On Now'	Larry Page Orchestra.
'Dandy'	Clinton Ford; Nigel Denver Four; David Garrick; Haricots Rouges; Herman's Hermits; James Last; Johnny Lion; Rocking Vicars; Michelle Torr; Osten Warnerbrig.
'David Watts'	Jam.
'Days'	Petula Clark; Flo and Eddie; Hillsiders; Luke Kelly.
'Dead End Street'	Dueslaget; Hit Nuts; Ravers.
'Death Of A Clown'	Geoff Harrison; James Last; Seagulls.
'Dedicated Follower Of Fashion'	Boris; Petula Clark; David Garrick; Joe Loss Orchestra; Ravers.
'Don't Ever Change'	Larry Page Orchestra; Lisa Ryne.
'Don't You Fret'	Bush; Tremours; Johnny Lion.
'End Of The Season'	Lance Percival; Uglys.
'Everybody's Gonna Be Happy'	Larry Page Orchestra.
'Got My Feet On The Ground'	Larry Page Orchestra.
'Have A Cuppa Tea'	Wig Wam.
'House In The Country'	Pretty Things; Uglys.
'I Gotta Move'	Richard Hell; Q65.
'I'm Not Like Everybody Else'	Chocolate Watch Band; Droogs; Sacred Mushrooms; Chris Spedding.
'I'm On An Island'	Roger Dennison; Strangers.
'I Need You'	Count Bishops; Rational Skins; Zackary Thaks.
'I Took My Baby Home'	Larry Page Orchestra.
'It's Too Late'	After Tea; Torson.
'I've Got That Feeling'	Orchids.
'Just Can't Go To Sleep'	Formula One; Larry Page Orchestra; Sneakers.
'Lola'	C.C.S.; Don Fardon; James Last; Nina And Michael; Raincoats; Sweet Power; Nicky Thomas.

'Most Exclusive Residence For Sale'	Los Chincos; Uglys.
'Mr Pleasant'	David Garrick; Nicky Hopkins; James Last.
'Party Line'	Attraction; Viz.
'Permanent Waves'	Zeltinger Band.
'Rainy Day In June'	Stoneground.
'Revenge'	Jay Jays; Larry Page Orchestra; Ray McVay Sound.
'Ring The Bells'	Majority.
'See My Friend'	Records.
'Session Man'	Five's Company.
'Set Me Free'	Jaybirds; Sonny And Cher.
'She's Got Everything'	Krokus; Romantics.
'So Mystifying'	Candidates, Hep Stars; Jay Jays; Petrified Forest; Scorpion.
'So Tired'	Dick Bright and his Sounds of Delight Orchestra; Little Roger and the Goosebumps.
'Something Better Beginning'	Honeycombs; Dick Rivers.
'Stop Your Sobbing'	Pretenders.
'Sunny Afternoon'	Dino, Desi and Billy; Haricots Rouges; Vince Hill; Dave Kelly Blues Band; Standells.
'The Hard Way'	Knack.
'The World Keeps Going Round'	Lancastrians.
'Till Death Us Do Part'	Anthony Booth.
'Till The End Of The Day'	Afrika Korps; Count Bishops; Hounds; Swamp Rats.
'Tired Of Waiting For You'	Frank Alama; Cotton Socks; Flock; Larry Page Orchestra; Suzi Quatro.
'Too Much On My Mind'	Gates Of Eden; Les Crunches.
'Waterloo Sunset'	Peter Convent; Vince Hill; Norman Percival; Soho Gamblers; Caterina Valente.
'Well Respected Man'	Bachelors; Petula Clark; Boudewifu de Graot; Gary Lewis and the Playboys; Los Ovnis; the Phantoms.
'When I See That Girl Of Mine'	Bobby Rydell.
'Where Have All The Good Times Gone?'	David Bowie; Shapes; Van Halen; Zoo.
'Who'll Be The Next In Line?'	Francoise Hardy; Gary Myrick and the Figures; Sir Douglas Quintet.
'Victoria'	Little Roger and the Goosebumps.
'You Really Got Me'	Boss Guitars; Al Caiola; Chatreuse; Dalek I; Eclipse; Girl; Hammersmith Gorillas; Heavy Cruiser; Hot Squirrels; Johnny and the Hurricanes; Steve Marriot's Moments; Buddy Miles; Mott the Hoople; Robert Palmer; Portsmouth

	Sinfonia; Helen Schneider; Johnny Smash; Rosetta Stone; Thundermug; Tight Fit; Van Halen; Wackers; 13th Floor Elevators; 801.
You're Looking Fine'	Hooked; Syndicate Of Sound.

These songs testify to the industry of Eddie Kassner during the mid-60s, and also suggest that Ray Davies is an extraordinarily rich man. Few major artists in the rock field can have seen their songs covered by such a diverse bunch of stars (and nonentities) as listed above.

COVER VERSIONS (PART TWO)

This section lists Ray Davies compositions recorded by other artists but never released in any form by the Kinks. As these recordings are of particular interest to collectors I have included (where possible) serial numbers and release dates.

(*Not officially substantiated)

3/65	'She Just Satisfies'	Jimmy Page	(Fontana TF 533)
4/65	(Baby) I Don't Want To Know'*	Michael Leslie	(Pye 7N 15835)
6/65	'This Strange Effect'	Dave Berry	(Decca F 12188/London 9781)
8/65	'I Go To Sleep'	Applejacks	(Decca F 12216)
9/65	'I Go To Sleep'	Cher	(from the album *All I Really Want To Do* Liberty)
9/65	'I Go To Sleep'	Peggy Lee	(Capitol 15413/Capitol 5488)
9/65	'I Bet You Won't Stay'	Cascades	(Liberty 55822/Liberty 55822)
10/65	'A Little Bit Of Sunlight'	Majority	(Decca 12271)
12/65	'Emptiness'	Honeycombs	(from the album *All Systems Go* Pye NPL 18132)
3/66	'King Of The Whole Wide World'	Leapy Lee	(Decca F 12369)
4/66	'I Go To Sleep'	Truth	(Pye 7N 17095)
4/66	'I Go To Sleep'	Marion	(Page One POF 042)
/66	'I Go To Sleep'	Adrian Pride	(/Warner Bros. WB 5067)
/66	'I Go To Sleep'	Fingers	(Polydor 56 080)
/66	'I Go To Sleep'	Lesley Duncan	(Mercury MF 939)
5/66	'Little Man In A Little Box'	Barry Fantoni	(Fontana 707)
9/66	'All Night Stand'	Thoughts	(Planet PLANET 118)
9/66	'Oh What A Day It's Gonna Be'	Mo And Steve	(Pye 7N 17175)
1/69	'Toymaker'	Wild Silk	(/G.R.T. 3)
2/69	'Toymaker'	Basil	(Columbia DB 8534)
3/69	'Monday, Tuesday, Wednesday'	Wild Silk	(/Kapp 974)
11/69	'Virgin Soldier March'	John Schroeder	(Pye 7N 17861)
11/69	'Son Of A Gun'*	Maple Oak	(Decca F 13308)
/70	'Ballad Of The Virgin Soldiers'	Leon Bibb	(/R.C.A. 74–0322)
3/72	'Nobody's Fool'	Cold Turkey	(Pye 7N 45142)
/81	'I Go To Sleep'	Pretenders	(Real ARE 18)

The majority of these cover versions were the result of combined efforts by publisher Eddie Kassner, manager Larry Page and producer Shel Talmy. Page was determined to transform Davies into a songwriting genius on a par with Lennon/McCartney while Talmy's connections with various record labels provided numerous acts who were more than willing to record Davies's songs.

'She Just Satisfies', the one solo single by Jimmy Page, was a re-write of 'Revenge' with additional lyrics by Barry Mason. Jimmy was a Shel Talmy sessioner during this period and played on a number of Kinks recordings. Although most commentators have assumed that he co-wrote 'Revenge' with Davies (thus prompting the re-recording) the song was actually the work of Larry Page.

Larry Page and Eddie Kassner really went overboard with 'I Go To Sleep' which was recorded by a number of acts, all of whom failed to take it into the charts until Chrissie Hynde popped up fifteen years later with a timely 80s cover. Of all the versions, the most prestigious and financially rewarding for Ray was Peggy Lee's rendition.

The little known English pop group Majority recorded a couple of Davies songs produced by Richard Lloyd at Decca. They even had the audacity to issue 'A Little Bit Of Sunlight' as a flip side, which suggests that it was not one of Ray's more memorable compositions. The same fate reputedly befell '(Baby) I Don't Want To Know' released as the flip of Michael Leslie's 'Momma Don't Know' in April 1965 when Ray's songwriting talent had yet to be fully appreciated. A third non A-side occurred when the Honeycombs relegated 'Emptiness' to their second album, *All Systems Go*, rather than releasing the track as a single. Although Wace attempted to persuade Ray to write some numbers for his latest protégé, David Garrick, no non-Kinks material appeared during this period (1965–6).

While Davies involved himself in a court case with Kassner Music, his new music publishing outlet, Belinda (Carlin), was credited on Leapy Lee's 'King Of The Whole Wide World'. Ray not only wrote, arranged and produced the disc but recruited brother Dave, Peter Quaife and a couple of Goldie's Gingerbreads to play on the session. Leapy Lee played an important part in the life of the Kinks in early 1966 when his humour helped to alleviate their internal problems. Managed by Wace, Leapy was in a perfect position to take advantage of Davies's songwriting talent. At one stage, he was offered a pre-release demo of 'Sunny Afternoon' before Ray decided that the Kinks should issue the song as a single. Leapy suffered a further blow when Ray dangled 'Dandy' (originally titled 'Randy Dandy') before his eyes, only to pass it over to Herman's Hermits at the last minute. It was rough justice for Leapy when the grandiloquent 'King Of The Whole Wide World' ignominiously flopped.

The Barry Fantoni single, originally titled 'Little Man In A Little Box Or Normal Service Will Be Resumed As Soon As Possible', was intended as a pilot for a forthcoming album of Davies compositions. Although an interesting work, the single flopped, Fantoni's television show *Whole Scene Going* was dropped and the much touted collaboration with Davies failed to transpire.

Talmy's Planet label benefitted from a non-Kinks Davies composition in the form of the Thoughts' 'All Night Stand'. During the same month a Manchester duo, Mo and Steve, released 'Oh What A Day It's Gonna Be'. Once more, however, Davies's work was not sufficient to provide the expected hits.

The late 60s releases in this section also disappeared shortly after issue. Wild Silk recorded two Davies compositions, the first of which, 'Toymaker', appeared as the flip side of 'Vision In A Plaster Sky' and was released in the U.S. under the group name Basil. Maple Oak were a Canadian group with whom Peter Quaife became associated following his departure from the Kinks. Although Quaife played bass on their U.K.

released single, 'Son Of A Gun', it is very doubtful whether Ray actually wrote the number as many have assumed. For all Larry Page's early hopes, Davies's extra curricular work failed to establish him as a hit composer. Had he been more successful, the history of the Kinks would have been drastically different. In terms of the group's longevity his commercial failure as a composer may have been a blessing in disguise.

COVER VERSIONS (PART THREE)

This section is a selective list of songs covered by the Kinks in live performance, but never captured on vinyl.

All Right, O.K., You Win
A Pub With No Beer
Bad To Me (performed with Robert Wace)
Be Bop A Lula
Bird Dog
Good Golly Miss Molly
Hang On Sloopy
Heartbeat
Hoochie Coochie Man
If I Had A Hammer (performed with Robert Wace)
I'm Coming Home
Little Queenie
Lost John
Poison Ivy
Rock Around The Clock
Route 66
Sweet Little Sixteen
Twist And Shout
Who's Sorry Now
You Are My Sunshine

UNRELEASED MATERIAL

This section lists the known Ray Davies compositions never released by the Kinks nor covered by any other artist.

A Shoe Without A Lace (co-written by John Dalton)
All Aboard
And I Will Love You
Blasé Blasé
Could Be You're Getting Old
Don't Ever Let Me Go

East West
Easy Come, There You Went
Entertainment
Everybody Wants To Be A Personality
Fallen Idol
Having A Good Time
I Believed You
I Don't Need You Anymore
I Just Want To Be With You
I Respect You
It's You
Lilacs And Daffodils
Listen To Me
Louise
Marathon
Mr Reporter
Once A Thief
Radio
Rocky Mountain
Rosie Rooke
Restless
Schoolboys
Slum Kids
Stage Fright
Television
Tell Me Now So I'll Know
That's All I Want
The Poseur (possibly the original title of 'Dedicated Follower Of Fashion')
There's A New World That's Opening For Me
This I Know
Tokyo
We All Understand
When I'm Walking
You Ain't What You Used To Be

In addition to these songs, the sessions for the first unreleased Dave Davies solo album also spawned several tracks that have yet to appear on any official single or album release. These include: 'Are You Ready Girl?'; 'Crying'; 'Do You Wish To Be A Man?'; and 'The Shoemaker's Daughter'. Whether these four songs were written by Ray, in collaboration with Dave, remains unclear. Needless to say, the above list is merely a small selection of the many songs that Ray Davies has composed over the years. Inevitably, there are many additional songs that remain in fragmentary form plus others that were abandoned along with numerous projects over the years. Shel Talmy has little doubt that some of Davies's greatest work lies buried in the vaults:

Ray is one of the most prolific writers I've ever run into. He might go home and come back the next day with forty songs . . . With the amount of stuff he wrote there was no way we could record everything. What's left is probably an undiscovered mine. If somebody got in and went through the stuff they'd probably find a dozen hits there.